Engi-Shiki

PROCEDURES OF THE ENGI ERA
BOOKS I–V

A *Monumenta Nipponica*
Monograph

from

The Japan Foundation

Twelve-layered Ceremonial Court Dress *(jūnihitoe)* of the Heian period. Photo courtesy of Izutsu Gafū 井筒雅風.

Engi-Shiki

PROCEDURES
OF THE ENGI ERA

BOOKS I–V

TRANSLATED WITH INTRODUCTION
AND NOTES BY
FELICIA GRESSITT BOCK

PUBLISHED BY
SOPHIA UNIVERSITY, TOKYO

PUBLISHED BY

SOPHIA UNIVERSITY

7 KIOI-CHŌ, CHIYODA-KU

TOKYO, 102

PRINTED IN JAPAN

PETER BROGREN, THE VOYAGERS' PRESS, TOKYO

Preface

THE *Engi-shiki*, or Procedures of the Engi era (A.D. 901–22), are a great body of regulations designed to supplement the administrative codes which were drawn up in the early eighth century. Because of their wide scope and the minute details included, they are an invaluable source of information about Japan in the Nara and early Heian periods—eighth, ninth and early tenth centuries.

The compiling of these procedures during the Engi era (and the Enchō era which followed it) was brought about by the fact that the laws codified at the beginning of the Nara period were of such a concise nature that amplification and clarifications as to how to implement those laws were absolutely necessary. At first glance the *Engi-shiki* appear to be a huge aggregate of lists, enumerations, specifications, registers and statistics. Such they are, but in relation to the department of government under which these fall, they provide many essential regulations for carrying out the day-to-day details of civil and religious administration and requirements of office.

What were these laws? A brief account of the evolution of law in Japanese society is given in Chapter One of this study. Starting with the tribal customs of the proto-historic age (third to sixth centuries A.D.), there is a gradual change as Chinese influences came into the island country in the process of the formation of a unified Japanese state. In the early seventh century Prince Regent Shōtoku adopted a number of Chinese forms and is credited with the issuing of Seventeen Articles of Good Government, a set of rules for the successful administration of the country. In the mid-seventh century the Reforms of Taika were decreed to bring into being a new system of provincial and district administration, new laws of land tenure and distribution, and the strengthening of the central government.

Increased reliance on Chinese forms came about in the late seventh century with the composition of law codes modeled after those of Sui and T'ang. The process of writing laws came to its climax with the issuance of the Taihō Code and Yōrō Code in the early years of the eighth century, the Nara period. It was for the purpose of interpreting and implementing those codes—civil and penal—that the procedures *(shiki)* and penalties *(kyaku)* were written.

There are 50 books *(kan)* in the *Engi-shiki*. The portion which is most readable and has most relevance today is the first ten books of procedures *(shiki)* for carrying out the *jingi-ryō*, the laws concerning the native religion. In order to understand the administrative structure which supervised this native—or *kami*—religion, Chapter Two of this study is devoted to the *Jingi-kan*, the department of *kami* affairs, its staff and its functions.

Part of this official religion was concerned with the festivals held on the premises of the *Jingi-kan* in the precinct of the Imperial Palace; and its authority also extended to *kami* worship within the palace, to the celebration of national festivals at the official shrines throughout the whole country and more particularly the large and family-connected shrines in and near the Capital. The procedures for these annual and occasional festivals of the Palace, the *Jingi-kan* and the shrines are the subject-matter of Books I, II and III of the *Engi-shiki*.

Besides the great shrines connected with noble families, there is the Shrine of the Great Deity in Ise Province, the Sun Goddess who was considered to be an-cestress of the Imperial line. Book IV of the *Engi-shiki* contains the procedures for worship of the Great Deity and auxiliary *kami* and for architectural ornamenta-tion and treasures of the Shrine. Book V is devoted to procedures for the Bureau of the Consecrated Imperial Princess, who was the Sovereign's personal represent-ative to the Great Deity, the Sun Goddess. The history and significance of this cult are discussed in Chapter Three of this study.

To appreciate the *Engi-shiki* as a text we must take into account the dual nature of its background: namely, the history of the development of that system of law of which this is an essential part, and secondly, the growth of the official *kami* cult. These two streams converge in the compilation of procedures *(shiki)* over a span of nearly two centuries, culminating in the first ten books of religious pro-cedures. The present study presents five of these books in translation. It cannot be a legal study nor even an analysis of the native religion, but is an approach to the *Engi-shiki* through interpretation of its language. For, as Prof. Hulsewé so fittingly put it in the Preface to his *Remnants of Han Law,* one could use only the philologist's approach to such an unexplored field as the Chinese law of 2000 years ago. So with the Japanese law of 1250 years ago, we must examine the evidence as it comes—whether religious, social, legal or historical, to discover the workings of that unique system in which religious ceremonial as well as civil ceremonial was of such great importance to the ruling class, and was written into a lasting document.

To put the myriad regulations of those five books into English presents a con-siderable challenge. The *Engi-shiki* form a handbook for the officials of that long ago time, written in an altogether dry, terse, hybrid language called Chinese writing *(kambun)*. It is not easy from such a medium to reconstruct the vivid actualities of the Nara and Heian culture—the majesty of the sovereign and the court, the awesome reverence accorded the Deities of Heaven and Earth, and the glorious pageantry of the many public ceremonies and festivals participated in by civil and religious officials, not to mention the gay drinking and feasting on the part of all after the solemn ceremonies are over.

It is not possible to recapture the language spoken by court and clergy in that age, for we are bound here by the iron-clad form of the *kambun* style. In this text a process has already taken place—whereby native religious terms, names of social and occupational groups, titles of nobility, and the terminology of sacramental robes and utensils have all been couched in Chinese writing. Some of the terms for personnel and for ceremonial articles in the *kami* religion have therefore been left untranslated in order to avoid giving an erroneous impression. Wherever possible an English equivalent has been found. Instead of trying to duplicate an archaistic or formalistic style, the whole is presented in the simplest, most readable English possible. A further discussion of the language of the *Engi-shiki* is given in Chapter Four.

To aid the reader in finding the meanings of untranslated words or in finding explanations and information on topics of interest to him, an index is provided with references to page numbers in the text and to explanatory notes. To give an idea of the total scope of the *Engi-shiki*, the table of contents of the entire fifty books is given in Appendix I. As the individual books do not have tables of contents, a partial listing for each of the first five books is found in the appendices; the listings give some of the important subjects of each book, according to Miyagi Eishō's 'items', which are numbered and documented. His extensive research on the text of the *Engi-shiki* has been heavily relied upon for this study. Another appendix gives the whole list of pharmacopoeia required for the Bureau of the Consecrated Imperial Princess; this list serves as an interesting source to compare with the list of medicinals in the Shōsōin Imperial Repository.

CONTENTS

延喜武

Chapter One

DEVELOPMENT OF LAW IN JAPAN

To appreciate the significance of the *Engi-shiki*, or Ceremonial Procedures of the Engi era, we need to look into the background of the system of law which came about during the seventh, eighth and early ninth centuries in Japan, and investigate its two main streams of supply. The spread of T'ang law throughout East Asia in the seventh and eighth centuries has been compared to the spread of Roman law throughout the continent of Europe. There is this difference, however, that while Roman law was inherited by those countries as a result of the conquests of Rome's legions and the ensuing occupations, the T'ang system of law and administration was voluntarily imported into the tributary nations beyond the borders of the great T'ang empire. The 'Western Peripheral Lands' beyond the west frontier, Pohai in the northeast, the three kingdoms of Korea farther east and, finally, Japan in the Eastern Sea, all took unto themselves portions of the Chinese administrative and legal institutions as met their particular interests or needs—over a period of centuries which began much earlier than T'ang (618–960) but continued through Sui and T'ang.[1]

The Japanese commenced to raise their level of culture by importing material innovations and Chinese learning from Koguryŏ and Paekche at least by A.D. 400, and for a long time following that used the Korean states as go-betweens for the importation of arts, letters, and notably Buddhism, from China. By about 600, however, direct communication between Japan and the Sui Empire commenced. And from that time forth the pace of cultural development accelerated in unprecedented fashion. Probably the Japanese, of all peoples who adopted the T'ang legal system, were the ones who imported Chinese institutions the most enthusiastically and rapidly, and adapted and assimilated them the most studiously. This was partly because the culture of Japan was materially and intellectually less developed than that of the Korean kingdoms due to geographical isolation, and also because Japan strongly felt the need to strengthen and unify the nation under a centralized authority during the seventh century.

---

[1] The old kingdom of Silla is said to have imported *lü* and *ling* from China in A.D. 520. There were subsequent importations by the kingdoms of Koguryŏ, Paekche and Silla. Although Japan in the sixth century imported Chinese learning, both Confucian and Buddhist, she did not adopt the law system. Cf. Y. Ishio, *Nihon kodaihō no kenkyū*, pp. 71–2. Japan imported the administrative structure and codes piecemeal during the seventh century and first part of the eighth. During the reign of Hsüan-tsung of the T'ang (713–55), the 'Western Countries' and unified Silla imported new forms of legislation from T'ang. Cf. M. Takikawa, *Shina hōsei-shi kenkyū*, p. 2.

The purpose of this review of Japan's development in respect to legal institutions is not so much to analyze the degree to which the Japanese applied and assimilated the Chinese system of law as simply to outline various conditions of Japanese society before the introduction of Chinese institutions (pre-*ritsu-ryō* period) and describe the circumstances of the adoption of codes based on Chinese models (*ritsu-ryō* period), culminating in the long process of drafting supplemental legislation: namely, the *kyaku* and *shiki* (to A.D. 927). But first let us look at that which existed in Japan prior to the introduction of foreign ideas of administration and law.

First of all, there are those few intriguing comments in the Chinese dynastic histories about the denizens of the Land of Wo, generally agreed by scholars to be descriptions of early life in Kyushu of about the first two centuries of our era. In the *Wei chih* account of the Wo people, we read that 'There is no stealing and there is very little dispute or litigation. In case someone breaks the law—for a light offense his wife and children are confiscated; for a heavy offense the whole family, including relatives, is extirpated.' A little further on we read that 'they collect land tax and poll tax . . .'[2] We may wonder what the Chinese observer meant by such sophisticated terms as 'litigation', 'break the law', and 'poll tax'. That there were any written laws or punishments or such a thing as a lawsuit is of course unthinkable at that early time. The nature of the taxes and the method by which the upper-class people were supported by the lower (at least two classes are alluded to in the text), remains a puzzle. We can conclude only that there were strict tribal regulations to which all persons were bound, and that penalties for infringements were extremely severe.

A custom briefly described in the *Wei chih* account is that of the *ch'ih-shuai*, or 'fortune-keeper', a man surrounded by such a host of taboos that he reminds us of the *flamen dialis,* the priest of Jove in Roman religion. On the piety and conformity of the *ch'ih-shuai* rested the fate of the whole community. He was required to abstain from a variety of things: he was a 'man who does not comb his hair, nor rid himself of fleas, has clothing soiled and dirty, eats no meat and has no contact with women.' If we compare these taboos to the ceremonial taboos of the later Japanese there are indeed contradictions. Abstention from meat and from sexual intercourse are among the requirements for total abstinence in the *kami* religion, but lack of bodily cleanliness would be the first and most obvious defilement for which purification *(harae)* or lustration *(misogi)* would be mandatory. It would therefore be difficult to relate the unkempt, louse- or flea-ridden, scapegoat-type individual described above to anything—particularly to the group of hereditary abstainers *(imbe* or *imibe)*—in the *kami* religion of the Yamato people.

The nature of the early Japanese religious taboos and tribal restrictions can be revealed only in part, as our evidence from pre-literate times is so scanty. However, upon such evidence as can be found here and there in the *Kojiki* and *Nihongi*—chronicles which appeared in the early eighth century—in the ancient rituals *(norito)* which are recorded in the *Engi-shiki,* decrees of the sovereigns *(semmyō)*

---

[2] From the *San kuo chih, Wei chih,* Bk. 30, *Wo jen chüan.*

and some of the ancient poems in the *Man'yōshū,* the earliest of Japanese anthologies, we can reconstruct a partial outline.

The customs of the Yamato people will be treated under the following headings:

1 *tsumi*—offenses (and their expiation);
2 *mikotonori*—words of the sovereign;
3 *kukadachi*—trial by ordeal;
4 shamans—as interpreters of the will of the *kami* or deities.

First, as to the *tsumi,* the offenses of which a person might be found guilty: an ancient list is set down in the chronicles and repeated in the ritual of the Great Purification *(ō-harae no norito).*[3] They are divided into two classes, the first of which are clearly infringements against tribal laws of an agricultural community whose livelihood depended on the success of the crops. These were labeled 'heavenly offenses' *(ama-tsu-tsumi),* and included:

> breaking down the ridges [between rice paddies], covering the irrigation ditches, opening the sluices [causing flood], double planting [sowing other seeds between the rows of rice], setting up stakes [denoting false ownership], skinning alive, flaying [an animal] backwards, and defecation in the wrong place.

All these acts of mischief were ascribed to the great deity Susano-o-no-mikoto, 'brother' of the Sun Goddess (Amaterasu-ō-mikami) in the myths, and perhaps that is why the word 'heavenly' is used. We may interpret it as simply 'pristine'. The references to skinning and flaying of animals may be indicative of some surviving practices whose origin was in the animal-breeding peoples of northeast Asia from whom the Yamato may have been descended.

The second classification of *tsumi* was so-called 'earthly offenses' *(kuni-tsu-tsumi),* which subdivide into two types: the infringements of tribal taboos and the defilements caused by natural events. They were:

> the cutting of live flesh, cutting of dead flesh, white leprosy, skin excrescences, offense of violating one's own mother, offense of violating one's child, cohabitation with animals, affliction from crawling things, affliction from the deities on high, affliction from birds above, the killing of animals, defilements caused by witchcraft.

We might add to this incest between children of the same mother, though marriage of children of different mothers but one father was not taboo. We see by the foregoing that deliberate breaking of the rule constituted defilement, but so did visitation of calamity, curse, deformity and disease from divine or natural causes.

Against these offenses there were prescribed certain rites which must be performed in order for the defiled person *(tsumi-bito)* to be purged of his defilement. There were various forms of purgation: purification *(harae),* some form of exorcism or 'driving out' to remove pollution of any sort; ablution or lustration

---

[3] The ritual of great purification, *ōharae no norito,* is translated by Dr. Karl Florenz, *TASJ,* XXVII (1900), pp. 1–112, and also by Donald Philippi in his *Norito* (1960), pp. 45–9. The most helpful information is in the introductory portion of Florenz, 'Ancient Japanese Rituals'.

(misogi), using pure water to wash away impurities—physical and spiritual—from the body of the defiled one; abstinence *(imi),* divided into partial abstinence *(ara-imi)* and total abstinence *(ma-imi)*; in addition, the repetition of expiatory formulae (the *norito* are the ones for public or national use) and the making of expiatory offerings *(harae-tsu-mono),* which are varied in nature and make their appearance at every festival and service listed in the *Engi-shiki*; and lastly fines, which were imposed to absolve a person of some social crime like stealing another man's wife.

The national purification was held on occasion to remove defilement from the people as a whole. Apparently it was not a regular thing in ancient times, but was held after a natural disaster had occurred, or the death of a sovereign, or when public offenses became especially numerous. After Chinese influence came into the Japanese administrative pattern, however, the holding of national purification was regularized. The Yōrō codes of the eighth century specified that it must be held on the last day of the sixth month and last day of the twelfth month, with the whole nation participating.

Secondly, the old tribal law was in the hands of the sovereign, who handed down his rulings in the form of *mikotonori.* In the early days he held the dual role of chief priest and chief administrator and no particular distinction was made between civil and religious. (It is to be noted that the laws called *ryō* did not distinguish between these, either.) If we analyze *mikotonori,* we find that *mi* means august or divine—for the sovereign was the descendant of and the spokesman for the *kami*; *koto* (like *rês* in Latin) meant a thing which was intangible or abstract (thus it came to mean *word,* the first kind of abstraction); and *nori,* from the verb *noru,* to announce or tell, meant enjoinder or command. *Nori* came to be the indigenous word for 'law' and its origin may lie in the idea of the *kami* taking possession of a person and making the divine will known thus. At any rate, the sovereign was the one who made known the divine commands of the *kami* to the people.[4] As we enter the semihistorical period we find that there was great abuse of privilege by the sovereigns. There were arbitrary acts of personal revenge, wanton harming of subjects, slayings ordered for any offender. To Yūryaku Tennō, for instance, are attributed such sadistic acts that he won for himself the title 'the greatly wicked emperor'.

Thirdly, the practice of *kukadachi (kugatachi),* trial by boiling water, is mentioned several times in the *Nihongi,* and trial by fire is also implied. Scholars differ as to the origin of the term and the custom. It has been claimed that *kuka* is a corruption of *kega,* 'defilement', and that *tatsu (tachi)* means 'to judge or decide' (i.e. on one's guilt). More weight, however, is given to the theory that this custom came from Korea and the word itself is derived from Korean *kuk,* 'hot soup' and *chat,* 'to grope' or 'seek out'. The notion behind the testing of guilt in the trial by boiling water seems to be that justice is dealt out by the *kami.*[5] The persons suspected of committing a wrong against the community were made to immerse their hands (arms) in boiling water or mud. In the episode 'Ordeal at Amagashi' related in the

4 H. Ono, *Ritsuryō-zen Nihon kodaihō,* p. 46.

5 *Ibid.* p. 7. There is a question of whether   priests were present, because of this being a form of 'divine judgment'.

Nihongi, during the reign of sovereign Ingyō Tennō in the fifth century non-noble persons were accused of trying to claim noble lineage and surnames. The claimants were submitted to the ordeal. Those who were not harmed by the boiling water would be declared innocent. However, the text says that those who were making false claims were so frightened that most of them ran away rather than face trial.[6]

The ordeal by fire was also probably practiced in prehistoric times, an example of it being found in the story of the birth of the child of the Heavenly Grandson of the Sun Goddess. His wife, Ka-ashi-tsu-hime, when about to give birth to her child, insists that it is the child of the Heavenly Grandson, but he doubts her, since they had spent only one night together. To prove that she has been faithful and that this is his child, she sets fire to the parturition hut, vowing that if it is not his child it will be devoured by fire. As the fire burns, three children are born from the smoke. The fire fails to harm the children or the mother.[7] Thus are born ancestors of the line of Yamato sovereigns.

The existence of trial by fire and trial by boiling-water methods may also be corroborated by the persistence to this day of the *chinka-shiki,* or fire-subduing ritual held in Shimmachi, Komazawa-chō in Tokyo, twice a year, at which the participants walk over glowing coals. And also the *kugatachi-shiki,* or hot-water ritual, similarly enacted.[8]

Fourthly, as for the shamans, they must have flourished in the early Japanese religion and still do flourish in the folk religion of today. If we go back to the Chinese dynastic annals for evidence, the Han and Wei accounts of the land of Wo tell of a great chieftainess who ruled the 'Queen Country' (probably a part of Kyushu) and was 'well versed in the way of spirits' and successfully deluded her people. The remarks seem to indicate a powerful shamaness who ruled her subjects through her skill in interpreting the will of the deities. Later, in the Japanese myths we have the story of the many deities trying to lure the Sun Goddess Amaterasu-ō-mikami out of her seclusion in the Heavenly Rock Cave (whither she betook herself after the offenses committed against her by Susano-o-no-mikoto). The goddess Ame-no-uzume-no-mikoto performed an inspired dance to entice the Great Deity out of the cave; this dance appears to have been a deity-possession ritual, perhaps the first shamanic performance we have on record. This very dance is believed to be the origin of the *Mitama-shizume* festival for 'Quieting the Divine Spirit' (or *Chinkon-sai*).[9] It is possible that Ame-no-uzume was the ancestress of the female shamans attached to shrines. However, to call all the Shrine Maidens (*mikannagi* or *mikanko*) shamans would be stretching the point much too far. We

[6] W. Aston, *Nihongi,* I, pp. 316–17. Another episode in the *Nihongi* tells of Takeuchi no Sukune who was accused of a crime by Umashi no Sukune. To settle the matter of guilt, both of them underwent ordeal by boiling water, and Takeuchi came out victorious. *Ibid.* I, p. 258. And another mention of *kukadachi, ibid.* II, p. 22 (A.D. 530).

[7] Aston, I, pp. 72–3, 85–6, 89.

[8] D. C. Holtom, *The National Faith of Japan,* p. 238. *Kugatachi* equals *kukadachi.*

[9] Haguenauer believes that the descendants of Ame-no-uzume formed an hereditary clan of sorceresses or shamans at the Imperial Court. This, however, does not account for the many groups of sacred maidens and of dancers attached to the *Jingi-kan* and the shrines, great and small. Cf. C. Haguenauer, 'La Danse rituelle dans la cérémonie du Chinkonsai', *JA,* 216, 2 (April-June 1930), p. 303.

are on safer ground if we conclude the Sarume dancers in the *Jingi-kan* (*v*. Chapter II) were hereditary shamans. But again, their functions are not sufficiently fully described to give proof of this. Tradition seems to point to a line of male shamans who in historical times had lost that function, but continued to be mediators between the deities and the people: namely, the Nakatomi (liturgists), who claimed their descent from Ame-no-koyane-no-mikoto, and the Imbe (abstainers), who performed purifications and abstinence and claimed their descent from the deity Futotama-no-mikoto.[10] Both of these ancestor gods are in the group of deities enshrined in Ise, as we see in Book IV of the *Engi-shiki*.

THE BEGINNINGS OF WRITTEN LAW

THE early tribal law, then, seems to have consisted of interpreting the will of the *kami*, preserving ceremonial purity in the presence of the *kami*, using means for determining the judgment of the *kami* and dispensing justice—the latter usually in the hands of the sovereign. An anomaly appears in the text of the *Nihongi* under the reign of Buretsu Tennō (r. 504–10), where it says: 'He was fond of criminal law and well versed in the statutes.' So far as we know, there was no written law in Japan at that time. But the passage does indicate that there was a knowledge that such things existed elsewhere; and as a matter of fact, the phraseology is taken right out of a story about the emperor Ming-ti of the Later Han.[11] The *Nihongi* stories also tell of severe penalties, notably punishment by death, in the reigns of Buretsu and Yūryaku. As a matter of fact, there is very little that seems just or wise in the reigns of either of them, and we can surmise that there was a deterioration of the strict tribal custom of the prehistoric and semi-historic times, with an increase in tyrannous practices by the ruler.

By the beginning of the seventh century a new dimension came into the administrative control of the country. In the Suiko period, under the regency of Prince Shōtoku, we see a new era dawning with the introduction of forms and institutions from China which were thought beneficial to the building and strengthening of a centralized bureaucracy in Japan. It was not until this centralized bureaucracy—as opposed to control fragmented in the hands of a number of landed powerful clans—became established that the government could make the further step of adopting formal codes of law. There is no question but that Prince Shōtoku was determined to strengthen the country in every way to face the formidable growing power of Silla. In seeking to do this he began with a study of the very foundations of Chinese legal theory.

In the regency of Prince Shōtoku the system of Cap Ranks was taken over from Sui China. Twelve ranks were established then; later the number of ranks was increased and made to correspond with official position in the administrative hierarchy. Prince Shōtoku was a scholar in Buddhist studies and gave official Court support to the building of temples and monasteries. To him is ascribed the

---

[10] Ono, p. 51. However, he points out that descent of the *kami* to mediums was more often to women than to men.

[11] *Hou Han Shu*, II, (本紀), end of p ssage on Ming Ti.

adoption of the Chinese calendrical system, the commencement of the recording of history, and other progressive measures. Most significant in the legal history of Japan was the formulation of the Seventeen Articles of Good Government, the so-called Constitution of Prince Shōtoku. Some scholars doubt that this document actually appeared during the Prince's lifetime. But whether it was his own creation or the later result of his researches, it matters not; the fact is that it represents an earnest answer to the gaping need for written law as a guide to the conduct of administration and justice. The 'Seventeen Article Constitution' exhibits a great familiarity with Chinese classical sources, for its phraseology is taken from the *Book of Odes,* the *Shang-shu* (Book of the legalist Shang Yang, d. 338 B.C.), the *Filial Piety Classic,* the *Lun-yü* (so-called Analects of Confucius), the *Tso-chüan,* the *Li-chi,* Kuan-tzu, Mencius, Micius, Chuang-tzu, Han-fei-tzu, the *Shih-chi,* the *Han-shu* and classical Chinese anthologies.[12] This showed a real effort to sort out the best and most useful principles of effective and benevolent government discernible in the 'Confucian' classical texts and Han Confucianists. The next step, had the Prince Regent been able to devote more years to it, might have been the study of Han written law, and then the Sui codes.[13] Indeed, Shōtoku showed his enlightenment in understanding that the coming of the bureaucratic state meant the systematic development of law.

After the death of Prince Shōtoku there was a scramble for power as the effort increased to remove the almighty Soga family from its proximity to the throne. The *coup d'état* of 645 had as its alleged objective the strengthening of the sovereign's position,[14] but the actual result was the strengthening of the central bureaucracy by means of more regulations patterned along lines used in China: land redistribution commenced in order to break up the acquisition by powerful families of too much land, the taking of census was introduced, collection of revenues for the central government was systematized, control over waterways and barriers between the provinces was put under the central government as opposed to control by provincial landholders, and so on. These and other changes were spelled out in the edict known as the *Kaishin no chō* ('Edict of Reform') promulgated in 646, the second year of 'Great Change' (Taika).

A party was formed to continue the process of governmental reform begun by Prince Shōtoku. The anti-Soga nobleman, Nakatomi no Kamatari (later given the surname Fujiwara) espoused the cause of the young prince, Naka no Ooe, and eventually helped him to be enthroned as the sovereign Tenchi. This alliance brought about the weakening of the powers of the provincial magnates and the strengthening of the throne by the further introduction of Chinese-style institutions, the latter fortified by the return of monks and scholars from long periods of study in T'ang China.

Tenchi Tennō (r. 662–71) is credited with the attempt to secure the govern-

---

12 T. Sakamoto, *Taika kaishin no kenkyū,* p. 176. He quotes from Masayuki Okada: *Oomi Nara chō no kambungaku.*

13 A drawback to Japan's progress in administrative development was the overthrow of the Sui Dynasty and the subsequent abolishing of the Ta-yeh *lü* and *ling* by the founder of the T'ang Dynasty. See M. Takikawa, p. 4.

14 Cf. R. Ishii, *Taika kaishin to Kamakura bakufu no seiritsu,* p. 8.

ment upon a foundation of written laws. This sovereign is said to have sponsored the compilation of twenty-two books *(kan)* of civil statutes known as the *Oomi-ryō,* the civil code of Oomi, named after his palace in Oomi Province at Ootsu on Lake Biwa. The text is not extant, but references to its one time existence indicate a crucial need for the ruling house to establish a system of laws for governing the land.

The next compilation was the *Asuka-Kiyomibara-ryō,* named for the palace of Temmu Tennō (successor to Tenchi) at Asuka, Yamato Province. Temmu in 681 expressed the desire to revise the laws,[15] and his son Prince Kusakabe must already have been at the task, for a set of *ritsu* and *ryō* were completed under his direction by 683, the same year he was designated Heir Apparent.[16] There is no evidence that the Oomi code of Tenchi Tennō was ever enacted. But according to the *Nihongi,* in the third year of Empress Jitō (689) the *Kiyomibara-ryō* was promulgated, for it says: 'A book of legal enactments in twenty-two volumes was distributed to all the Governors.'[17] Very likely the scope was approximately that of the earlier *Oomi-ryō,* as the number of books is the same. Whether either of these codes contained a penal section is not known for sure, but the title *ryō* does not indicate that they did.

Why neither of these early *ryō* are any longer extant remains a problem. It is conceivable that they were in a sense failures. It may be that they attempted to do what was at the time too difficult: to compile a set of laws following the format of the Sui and T'ang laws which would be uniquely Japanese in character. The attempt was probably made to preserve ancient Japanese notions of interpreting the divine will of the *kami* and to keep the traditional methods of 'justice' known only in Japan, yet couching all in the legal language of the Han, Sui and T'ang. It was a case of foreign man-made legislation coming into conflict with the 'divine law' of a primitive society.

The next development was outright adoption of forms based on the Chinese models. The Taihō Penal and Civil Codes *(Taihō-ritsu-ryō)* drafted in 701 (Taihō 1) and promulgated in 702, were described as the 'first' of such laws of the land. The models used chiefly were the Yung-hui laws of 651, which contained twelve books of penal law, thirteen of civil law, forty books of *shih*[4] and eighteen of *ko*[2].[18] Considerable doubts beset us in regard to details of the contents of the Taihō codes, for only a few fragments of them survive, and the rest, like Sallust's *Historia,* can only be outlined in part by piecing together references to them in other works, as the commentaries on them: the *Ryō no gige* (833) and the *Ryō no shūge* (920), and by assuming that they bore general similarity to the T'ang codes and that the subsequent Yōrō Codes were similar to the Taihō in structure, language and content.

Next came the Yōrō Penal and Civil Codes *(Yōrō-ritsu-ryō)* which were drafted

15 Aston, II, p. 350. What Aston translates as 'laws' is *ritsu-ryō* 律令 in the original.

16 R. Ishii, p. 31.

17 The title *Kiyomibara-ryō* does not appear in the history of national laws contained in the introduction to the Kōnin Detailed Legislation, *Kōnin kyaku shiki jō,* of the 9th century. Cf. Y. Ishio, p. 68.

18 M. Takikawa, p. 5.

in the year 718. Although often referred to as a 'revision' of the Taihō Codes, we may question the validity of such a label. The fact that the Taihō are no longer extant should caution any scholar against the use of the term 'revision'. In the *Shoku-nihongi* it is recorded that Fujiwara no Fubito (son of the aforementioned Fujiwara no Kamatari and greatest statesman of his time) was given the sovereign's command to revise and amend the Taihō Codes.[19] That statement, however, does not prove that he did revise and amend. What Fubito and his large staff of scholars did accomplish was a monumental labor of compilation of a new set of penal and civil statutes. Careful scrutiny of the texts of the *Yōrō-ritsu-ryō* and comparison of these with the fragments of the *Taihō-ritsu-ryō* as well as with the contemporary T'ang codes brings to light the fact that the Yōrō Codes bear much greater resemblance to the first set of K'ai-yüan Codes (there were three compilations of *lü*[4] and *ling*[4] during the K'ai-yüan era in 715, 719 and 737) than they do to what we know of the Taihō.[20]

Curiously enough, this set of laws, the Yōrō Codes, which were compiled and edited so laboriously, were not enacted until thirty-nine years after they were drafted—in the year 757. Here is another baffling occurrence in the history of written law: if the legal foundation for government was so sorely needed, why was the expressly ordered 'new law' not enacted forthwith? It is thought by some that after Fubito's death his titanic labors of compilation were brought to the forefront by his descendant, Fujiwara no Nakamaro, to gain recognition for himself and enhance the Fujiwara name, whatever other reasons there may have been.[21] There must be reasons why the new codes were left sleeping for a generation, not the least of which may be the great preoccupation of the Court with developments in the Buddhist sphere, not to mention the complicated political intrigues around the daughter of Shōmu Tennō, who came to the throne twice.

By this time in the Nara period the whole administrative structure had been set up along the lines of that of T'ang China—with eight ministries, their respective bureaus and offices, presided over by a host of officials, commencing with the Great Minister of State *(dajō-daijin)* on down through Great Ministers of Left and Right, Counselors of the Left, Middle and Right, Imperial Advisers, Chiefs of Ministries and Bureaus, assistants, petty officials, *ad infinitum*.

A particular difference between the administrative structure of T'ang and that

---

19 *Shoku-Nihongi*, Book VII.

20 Y. Ishio, p. 106. The Yōrō 養老 differs from the Taihō 大寶 code in the titles of sections of the law: for example, *government posts* in the Taihō is called *kan'in-ryō* 官員令 and in the Yōrō is called *shokuin-ryō*, 職員令 in conformance with the K'ai-yüan *ling*. Furthermore, the Taika Reform Edict had set up a new land-holding law which called for redistribution of the land on the Chinese system of every six years. The Taihō section on paddy-fields (田令) changed this to call for redistribution after 18 years. However, the Yōrō Code changes it from 18 to 10 years, marking a compromise between the earlier and later legisla-

tion. In the same section, the Taihō describes lands allotted to absentee officials abroad as *kuge-den* (公廨田), whereas the Yōrō uses the more familiar *shikibun-den* (職分田). As for taxation laws, the Taihō has a section on public imposts labeled *kōshi-ryō* (考仕令) while the Yōrō entitles the section *kōka-ryō* (考課令), the term found in the *T'ang hui-yao* (唐會要), vol. 81. Whole passages of the Yōrō, when compared with the Taihō fragments, show great divergence from the latter and a closer resemblance to the T'ang laws of the K'ai-yüan period. See Y. Ishio, pp. 112 ff.

21 *Nihon bunka-shi taikei*, III, p. 59.

of Nara was that instead of having a Bureau of Sacrifices and a Bureau of Rites within the civil government as in China, the Japanese administration was divided into a civil branch, the *Dajō-kan*, and a religious branch, the *Jingi-kan*. The *Jingi-kan*, according to the Yōrō Codes, was ranked above the civil branch in position because of its prestige and antiquity. The *Jingi-kan* was the branch which organized and managed the *kami* cult with all its hereditary religious functionaries and traditional observances. One enigma in this set-up is the fact that despite its sanctity and higher prestige, the *Jingi-kan* was headed by an official called the Chief *(jingi-haku)* who was no higher than fourth rank in the system of Court Ranks, while the *dajō-daijin*, the Great Minister of State, was of first Court Rank.

Let us now look into the content of the codes of law. The law in China was compiled in five categories: *lü*[4], *ling*[4], *ko*[2], *shih*[4], *ch'ih*[4], with a sixth if one includes the *li*[3], or 'rites' which were ceremonial regulations. These are explained as follows:

律 *lü*: punishments and penalties, as accumulated from Han times and added to during Sui and T'ang.

令 *ling*: the statutes and civil regulations, which defined the administrative structure and all its functions under these 27 headings:

Offices and Ranks; the Three Imperial Tutors; the Censorate; Officials of the Ministries; Officials of the Courts; Palace Guards; the Palaces of the Heir Apparent and the Princes; Administration of the Provinces; Circuits; Garrisons and Militia; Ladies-in-Waiting; Sacrifices to Ancestors; Laws of Households; Civil Service and Examinations therefor; Costume; Ceremonial; Land Division, Allotment and Tenure; Documents; Taxes and Forced Labor; Granaries and Storehouses; Animal Husbandry; Customs Barriers and Markets; Sanitation; Prison-keepers; Public Works; Mourning and Burial; and miscellaneous.

In addition to this main body of the law there were:

格 *ko*: decrees issued by the Emperor as single regulations which have permanent significance;

式 *shih*: detailed regulations and ordinances, mainly executive rulings and examples or precedents for administrative acts. During T'ang 33 sections of these were written.

勅 *ch'ih*: Imperial Edicts.[22]

Turning to Japan, the Yōrō Code *(Yōrō-ryō)* was compiled in ten books *(kan)* in twelve sections *(hen)*, and its subject headings closely resemble those of the T'ang codes: Offices and Ranks; Official Personnel; Personnel of the Women's Palace; Personnel of the Palace of the Heir Apparent; Stewards; Deities *(jingi)*; Monks and Nuns [Buddhists]; Households; Rice Fields; Forced Labor; Learning; Civil Examinations; Succession and Inheritance; Taxes; Stipends; Palace Guards; Military Defenses; Court Ceremonial; Costume; Building and Repairs; Public Documents; Storehouses and Granaries; Animal Husbandry; Medicine; Leaves

---

22 Based on K. Bünger, *Quellen zur Rechtsgeschichte der T'ang-Zeit*, pp. 23–4.

of Absence; Mourning and Burial; Barriers and Markets; Arrests; Prisons; and miscellaneous.[23]

While the T'ang arrangement was probably utterly realistic for the administration of the great Chinese empire, we cannot be sure to what degree the Yōrō provisions met the needs of the island people. Some differences in the subject headings indicate that adjustments had been made to the special conditions of Japanese society: the kingship, the *kami* cult, the private ownership of land, the traditions concerning inheritance, the marriage laws or absence of them. Furthermore, it is significant that these *ryō* were based not only on the *ling*[4] of the T'ang law, but upon consultation of the *ko*[2] and *shih*[4] as well. More than that, they represented some assimilation of the principles of the T'ang system of administration—by this time— and of the commentaries which had been written in Chinese upon the earlier *ling*[4] and *lü*[4].[24] Thus the Yōrō Code was the culmination of a conscious effort to study and make a selective use of the T'ang legislation in the process of devising an integrated legal basis for government which would utilize foreign models without obliterating native custom and precedent. Although the central government, the economy and the culture as a whole were affected by the enactment of the codes, nevertheless, a study of public documents of the eighth and ninth centuries will show appreciable distance between the law and the actual practice.[25]

KYAKU AND SHIKI

THE process of adapting legislation based on the foreign model to the Japanese administration of government was a long process. For the better part of two centuries, after the compilation and subsequent enactment of the Yōrō Codes, supplementary legislation was written, largely in the form of *kyaku* and *shiki*. The *kyaku* were individual regulations set up for interpretation and implementation of the *ritsu*, or penal provisions of the Yōrō, most of which are lost. The *shiki*, on the other hand, were made to supplement and amplify the *ryō*, or civil and religious provisions, and they mushroomed into a great bulk of minute regulations which certainly attest to the difficulty of the struggle to adapt the Chinese pattern of law to the Japanese setting without sacrificing any of their existing traditions.

During the Kōnin era (810–24) under Saga Tennō, a number of *kyaku* and *shiki* were drawn up. The process was resumed during the Jōgan era (859–74) by the command of the Sovereign Seiwa Tennō. During Kōnin 40 and in Jōgan 20, books *(kan)* of *shiki* were compiled to give officialdom the specific details of procedure for carrying out the civil and religious provisions of the Yōrō Codes. Even this amount of supplementation was not sufficient to explain the application of the *ryō*, however.

Responding to the command of the sovereign Daigo Tennō (893–931) the Great Minister of the Left Fujiwara no Tokihira[26] and staff completed and presented to the throne ten books of *kyaku*. It was 904, fourth year of the Engi era,

---

23 Based on *Nihon bunkashi taikei*, III, p. 60.
24 M. Takikawa, pp. 123–4.
25 J. Murao, *Ritsuryō-sei no kichō*, p. 9.

26 The same who had presented the *Nihon sandai jitsuroku* 日本三代實錄, last of the *Rikkokushi* 六國史 (Six National Histories), in 887.

and they were called 'Engi Detailed Supplementary Penal Code'.[27] These were
promulgated in the year 909. Then in 905 (Engi 5), the same sovereign bade the
same Great Minister Tokihira to take up the task of continuing the compilation of
shiki which had been begun and discontinued twice during the preceding century.
Tokihira and a large staff of scholars set to work on this project of making a com-
pendium of all-inclusive *shiki*. As the work of compilation was so diverse and
complicated, there were obstacles and delays and setbacks, not the least of which
was the death of Tokihira in 909. His mantle fell upon a kinsman, Fujiwara no
Tadahira, then Great Counselor *(dainagon)*, who was urged by the throne to
complete the undertaking. Ultimately, fifty books *(kan)* of *shiki* were completed
and presented to the throne in 927 (Enchō 5) with the name *Engi-shiki*, or 'Engi
Detailed Supplementary Civil Code'.[28] But the enactment of the *Engi-shiki* did not
take place until forty years later, in 967!

In the structure of the *Yōrō-ryō* it could be noted that the laws concerning
kami worship, *jingi-ryō*, come after the provisions for the Palace, the Court and high
officialdom, while they precede the provisions for Buddhist monks and nuns, and
on down through all lesser departments of the government.[29] But, as pointed out
earlier, the *Jingi-kan*, or *kami* worship branch of the government took precedence
over the *Dajō-kan* or civil branch. Here is one of the inconsistencies that resulted
from following the T'ang *ling* as a model. But in the case of the *shiki,* the precedence
of *kami* worship and ceremonies over the civil affairs is strictly observed. The first
ten books deal with *jingi,* or shall we say, detailed supplementary legislation pertaining to affairs under the *Jingi-kan ;* while the other forty books prescribe details of
procedure under the *ryō* for all departments and bureaus under the *Dajō-kan.*
This is not to say, however, that secular affairs of government were separate from
religious. There was, in fact, a great deal of overlapping both in the law and in
practice.

TEXT OF THE ENGI-SHIKI

As was customary in official documents of the Nara and Heian periods, the *Engi-
shiki* are composed in Chinese. However, like the codes themselves, they contain a
composite of Chinese language and indigenous traditions and native nomenclature.
We can see in the details about early indigenous institutions, customs, ceremonial
articles, foodstuffs, and so forth, a certain regimentation and standardization
imposed by the stiff style of the *kambun*. As a consequence of adopting Chinese
writing, the names of most of the government departments as well as of religious
ceremonies have both a Chinese pronunciation and a Japanese reading. Names

[27] This is the rendition given by Robert
Reischauer in his *Early Japanese History*. A satis-
factory translation of *kyaku* 格 has yet to be given.
Perhaps 'penal procedures' is the closest we can
get.

[28] This again is Reischauer's rendition. 'Procedures' is the word I have chosen for *shiki* 式, but
I have added 'ceremonial' because the *shiki*

presented in this study are all related to religious
and civil ceremonial.

[29] In the Yōrō Code Buddhism is covered in
the section 'Monks and Nuns'. In the *E-S* the
regulations concerning Buddhism are found in
Book XXI under the Bureau for Aliens and Buddhists *(gemba-ryō* 玄蕃寮), a bureau in the Ministry
of Civil Administration *(jibu-shō* 治部省).

of ceremonial articles of dress, food, vessels and offerings appear in Chinese characters. There is occasionally a gloss given in characters used phonetically or for their meaning, but more frequently, modern scholarship has provided Japanese syllabary *(kana)* alongside for pronunciation of terms which are rare or ambiguous. In the difficult matter of pronunciation of names of shrines, many of which no longer exist, the careful researches of Matsushita Kenrin in the Tokugawa period recovered long-lost readings.

Gradually the task of formalizing and regularizing the forms of age-old festivals was achieved and their details were put down in writing. Not only would this benefit posterity, but it helped to put the native *kami* religion on a high footing, increase its prestige, and make it better able to compete with the imported faith— Buddhism—with its rich traditions, abundant literature, great temples adorned with images, paintings and fragrance of incense.

The *Engi-shiki* are cited as the only source of the whole body of sacred rituals— the 26 *norito*—which make up Book VIII. However, in the first ten books we are given the setting in which these rituals were used: not only the total list of festivals and the requirements for carrying them out, but the locations of shrines, the deities enshrined in them, and the lists of civil and religious officials who participate in ceremonies and who recite the ritual.

As to the problem of whether these procedures were enforced, let us look for a moment into the reasons why the compilation of these *shiki* was so persistently urged. Toward the end of the ninth century, in response to a request by the throne (Daigo Tennō) for comments on the conduct of public affairs, a statesman by the name of Miyoshi Kiyoyuki, who was an Imperial Adviser *(sangi)*, wrote an unusual work, a 'Memorial in Twelve Opinions', which was presented in 914. In it he reviews a number of different things, including a section on the annual celebrations of the *Toshigoi* and *Tsukinami* festivals (see below) by the officials of the *Jingi-kan*. From the remarks of Kiyoyuki we can see that things had come to a sorry pass. In the first of twelve articles, written in Chinese, Kiyoyuki speaks of the necessity of crop production and the need for averting disasters of flood and drought, then goes on:

> . . . for these reasons, the Court of the Sovereign holds in each year on the 4th day of the 2nd month the *Toshigoi* Festival and on the 11th days of the 6th month and the 12th month the *Tsukinami* Festival in the *Jingi-kan*. For these, strict ceremonial purification and fasting are held and prayers are everywhere made to the Deities of Heaven and Earth, in order to ensure abundant crops. The procedure is that the Court Nobles, at the head of the Secretaries and the civil officials, come to worship in the *Jingi-kan*. For every individual shrine the *Jingi-kan* [officials] set up offerings: the symbolic ones, one bottle of clear sake, one iron spear, displayed upon the offering tables. If shrines are accorded horses (one horse for the *Toshigoi* and two for the *Tsukinami* festival) then the Left and Right Mount Bureaus lead the procession of sacred horses. Then [the liturgist of] the *Jingi-kan* recites the prayer for the festival. When that is done, the said festival offerings are

distributed to the various representatives to present them at their own shrines. The priests should have performed purification and fasting and then reverently bear them to present them each at his own shrine. But, in the very presence of the high nobility, they proceed to take the offerings of silk and tuck them into their bosoms, they throw away the handle of the spear and take only the head, they tip up the bottles of sake and drain them in a single draught. Indeed, not one person has gone out of the gates of the *Jingi-kan* bearing the offerings intact! How much more so with the sacred horses! Straightway traders outside the Ikuhōmon[30] buy them all and take them and depart. In this situation can the festival deities rejoice in the sacrifices? If they do not rejoice in the sacrifices how can we expect abundance and prosperity? I humbly entreat [your Majesty] to depute one person of the rank of scribe[31] or above, to each of the provinces to take charge of the priests and cause them to receive and take home these festival offerings, and in sincerity to deposit them properly at the home shrine as if they were in the presence of the deities. . . .[32]

If Kiyoyuki's preoccupation with the graft and abuses at these national ceremonies was great to the point of indignation, so also did it bring results. We find his name among the list of scholars on the staff of Tokihira engaged in compiling the *shiki*, which, if followed conscientiously, would certainly put an end to the abuses he describes. That there was strong motivation not only to codify, but to rectify and bring into line many loosely defined ceremonial procedures seems evident from the succession of events in the compilation.

About twenty-five different texts of the *Engi-shiki* survive, though some are not at all complete. The earliest date from the end of the Heian period. The early edition of *Kokushi-taikei* bases its modern text of the *Engi-shiki* on the *rufu-bon* or printed edition used in Tokugawa times. The old manuscripts upon which that edition was based include those of the Unshū-ke (Matsudaira family) and of Inoue Yorikuni. The newest *Kokushi-taikei* edition of 1955 uses the *hampon* printed text of 1723 (Kyōhō 8) as its main text but also makes use of the old manuscripts of the Kongōji temple, of the (Marquis) Ichijō family, of the (Marquis) Kujō family, the (Count) Sanjōnishi family, and others—all carefully compared in addition to the aforementioned texts used for the earlier (1904) edition. Although five available editions of the *Engi-shiki* have been consulted for this study, the new *Kokushi-taikei* (1955) edition, being the most up-to-date and scientifically edited, is the principal one used. The editors have utilized the twenty-five available manuscripts, as well as consulted the source books of the age in which the *shiki* were written: the *Shoku-nihongi*, the *Nihon-kōki*, the *Shoku-Nihon-kōki*, *(Nihon) Montoku-tennō-jitsuroku*, *(Nihon) Sandai-jitsuroku*, *Kuji-hongi*, the *Shinsen-*

---

30 The gate of the sovereign's palace nearest to which the *Jingi-kan* was situated. This is further discussed in Chapter II, p. 21.

31 A *shishō* 史生.

32 From the *Iken jūnikajō* (意見十二箇條) of Miyoshi Kiyoyuki 三好清行, found in *Gunsho ruijū*, XVII, pp. 105–28. A translation of this text into German is found in *Miyoshi Kiyoyuki* by Inge-Lore Kluge, pp. 40 ff. This was an *iken-fūji* 意見封事, an 'opinion offered to to the Throne'.

shōjiroku, Ruijū-sandai-kyaku, Seiji-yōryaku, Wamyō-ruijūshō, Jingi-shiryō and commentaries on the *norito*.[33]

The foregoing indicates that the 1955 edition is the most reliable and most meticulously edited as far as the exegetical sources and methods employed can be evaluated. However, for a broader kind of reference work, the fine edition of the *Kōgaku-sōshō* contains a great number of headnotes which provide the translator with explanations and background material not available in any other edition. For instance, in Book I a character is introduced which is a *kokuji* not found even in Ueda's *Daijiten*. The *Kōgaku-sōsho* edition is the only one which defines this character, although it is identified in the *Daijingū gishiki-kai*, a commentary on the Book of Ceremonial of the Great Shrine (*Kōtai-jingū gishiki-chō*), which was written in 804 and serves as a valuable complement to the regulations of the *Engi-shiki*.

The titles of the first ten books of the *Engi-shiki*, namely, the portion which deals with all matters under the *Jingi-kan*, are as follows:

Book I   —   Festivals of Four Seasons (A)
Book II   —   Festivals of Four Seasons (B)
Book III   —   Extraordinary Festivals
Book IV   —   The Shrine of the Great Deity in Ise
Book V   —   The Bureau of the Consecrated Princess
                    [of the Great Shrine]
Book VI   —   The Office of the Consecrated Princess
                    [of the Kamo Shrines]
Book VII   —   Great New Food Festival for the Enthronement
                    (*Daijō-sai*)
Book VIII —   The Rituals (*norito*)
Book IX   —   Register of Deities (A)
Book X   —   Register of Deities (B)

The first five books have been rendered into English by this translator, and are herewith presented, together with some discussion of their significance in the development of the Japanese native religion. The *norito* of Book VIII were in part translated by Mr. Satow and Dr. Florenz, and a new translation which is complete has been done by Donald Philippi. The most useful book from the standpoint of describing the earliest practices in Japanese religion that are recorded is Book VII. Some of its material is incorporated in D. C. Holtom's *The Japanese Enthronement Ceremonies*. The last two books (IX and X) dealing with the *kami* religion are geographically arranged and give us a complete list of deities and the shrines where

---

[33] The National Learning (*kokugaku* 國學) scholars of the Tokugawa period made significant researches on parts of the *E-S*. Whereas Kada Azumamaro 荷田春滿 (1668–1736) commenced the study of *ritsu-ryō*, his pupil, Kamo Mabuchi 賀茂眞淵 (1697–1769), undertook the study of specific *shiki*. His work includes studies of the *norito* (rituals) in the *E-S* and a commentary on the Great Purification Ritual, *ōharae no norito* 大祓の祝詞. Later, Motoori Norinaga 本居宣長 (1730–1801) made a further study called *Ooharae no kotoba no kōshaku* 大祓詞後釋. After him, Hirata Atsutane 平田篤胤 wrote *Ooharae no kotoba no saishaku* 大祓詞再釋. It was Matsushita Kenrin 松下見林 (1637–1703) who labored over establishing correct readings for the names of shrines in Books IX and X of the *E-S*. Cf. E. Miyagi, *Engishiki no kenkyū*, II, pp. 62–3.

they were worshipped throughout the country as a whole in the Heian period.[34]

The remaining forty books of the *Engi-shiki,* dealing with regulations under the *Dajō-kan,* are not wholly unrelated to the first ten. There are many references back and forth; for instance, regulations concerning the Great Shrines of Ise and the Itsuki-no-miya are found in the sections on the Needlework Bureau (Book XIV), The Bureau of Housekeeping (Book XXXVIII), The Mount Bureau (Book XLVIII), Bureau of Carpentry (Book XXXIV), and others. The cross-referencing is indicative of the interrelationship between the worship of the deities and the conduct of the state.

[34] The *Jimmyō-chō* 神名帳 or Register of Deities, which comprises Books IX and X of the *E-S,* uses obsolete names of districts (*kōri* 郡) in some instances and in so doing does not agree with the district names used in Book XXII containing *shiki* for the Ministry of Peoples' Affairs (*mimbu-shō* 民部省). Cf. S. Kida, 'Engi-shiki no zusan', *Rekishi-chiri,* 33, 3 (1919), p. 246.

Chapter Two

THE JINGI-KAN

W E have spoken of the need which was urgent in the centralization process in seventh-century Japan to make secure the position and influence of the throne. The attempt was made to accomplish this by various steps: by reducing the autonomous powers of the provincial landholding families, by establishing governorships of the provinces appointed by the throne, and by removing the chief threat to the power of the throne, namely, the arbitrary control by the Soga Clan. Following the Taika Reform there was the gradual growth of a bureaucracy modelled on the pattern of the governmental hierarchy of China. An additional buttress to the prestige of the throne was the formalizing of the *Jingi-kan* in order to organize and systematize the traditional *kami* worship of the Court and of the people. While the establishment of this organ of government may be regarded as partly a reaction against the phenomenal prosperity of Buddhism, it was first and foremost motivated by the desire to make the traditions of the ruling family, observed in the palace, and the clan deities of this family, the apex of the national cult.

It is important in this connection to grasp the seriousness of the juxtaposition of Buddhism with the worship of the native deities. From the time of its introduction (*c*. A.D. 552) into Japan, Buddhism had great appeal as something exotic and splendid, associated with kings and nobles. But the reception given to it was at first stormy and fraught with great controversy. The hereditary groups of priests, the Nakatomi and Imbe, believed the foreign religion to be an offense against the native gods. It was half a century before Buddhism gained as secure a position in Japan as it had in Korea. By the beginning of the seventh century the belief in the efficacy of images and icons was demonstrated in the creation of splendid sculptures and paintings in the temples and monasteries which were built in rapid succession during the reign of Empress Suiko. More important than the outward splendor perhaps was the fact that Prince Regent Shōtoku proved to be a scholar not only of Chinese classics but also of Buddhist texts, for he performed the difficult task of writing commentaries on three principal sutras then known in Japan. This unlocked the door of the meaning of the Buddhist scriptures for those of the nobility who were literate. With the increased interest in and support of Buddhism the danger began to loom that this new faith might eclipse the *kami* cult.

The earliest religion of the Japanese was very likely pure nature worship, which Genchi Katō has called 'animatism'. This was followed by the development of 'animism' which supposes a spirit and power inherent in the visible objects of

B

nature.[35] In the first stage there was worship of the heavenly bodies, trees, mountains, and so on. In the second stage we find the Goddess of the Sun, the Moon God, the Storm God, God of Thunder, God of Fire, and innumerable other gods—'800 myriad', as the chronicles put it. In the proto-historic period the term *matsuri-goto* may have referred to the ruler's combined function of governing the people and officiating at the rites to the *kami*. However, another term was used which meant the worship phase alone: *kami-goto*; 'kami affairs' referred specifically to the celebrations and supplications made to the deities.[36]

Let us look into the origin of the name *Jingi-kan* which was given to the organ of government which supervised all *kami* affairs after the establishment of an administrative system on the Chinese patterns during the seventh century. Various translations have been made for *Jingi-kan*: Ernest Satow called it the 'office for worship of the Shintau gods'; in the translation of the *Kogoshūi*, Katō and Hoshino call it the 'Shinto Bureau'; Robert Reischauer says 'Department of Shinto'; and G. B. Sansom uses the ambiguous term 'Department of Religion'. The latter is to be avoided in view of the importance of Buddhism as a national religion, though of course it was not included in this department. The other translations seem inappropriate because they use the foreign adaptation Shinto, which meant 'Way of the Gods' comparable to 'Way of the Buddha' and 'Way of Confucianism'—a term of literary value, but not actually used in practice in the language of the Heian period as shown in the *Engi-shiki*. I therefore leave '*Jingi-kan*' untranslated.

We cannot escape the fact that *Jingi-kan* is a foreign adaptation, however. The term *jingi* appears to be a contraction of the Chinese double binomial, *tien-shên ti-ch'i* 天神地祇 'deities of heaven and gods of earth'. It comes from ancient Chinese folk religion. In the *Chou Li* ('Rites of Chou', composed in the early Han but describing customs far more ancient), it says that the Grand Master of Ceremonies conducted the worship of *shên* 神, *kuei* 鬼 and *ch'i* 祇, of 'deities of heaven, spirits of the dead, and gods of the earth'.[37] If these were the classifications of deities in ancient China, there is no need to assume that they are paralleled exactly in Japanese religion. However, the parallelistic phrase seems to have appealed to the poetic sense of the Japanese. In the earliest writings we find Japanese paraphrases: *amatsu-kami kunitsu-kami*, 'deities of heaven and earth'. The Japanese paraphrase does not differentiate between celestial deities and the gods of the earth as does the original Chinese, but uses *kami* for both. Of course, it would not be hard at all for a Japanese to think in terms of upper and lower gods: deities of the upper atmosphere as contrasted to deities of the mountains *(yama no kami)* and moors *(no no kami)*. But other than localizing of this sort, there is no evidence of any particular classifications of *kami*.[38] The expression *amatsu-kami kunitsu-kami* occurs in the *Nihongi*, the *Kojiki* and in poems of the *Man'yōshū* collection (A.D. 759), while in a *semmyō* (Imperial edict) of 708 are the words: 'the *kami* that dwell in heaven and the *kami* that dwell in the land', and in two *semmyō* of 745

35 G. Katō, *Shinto*, pp. 2, 7, 8.
36 T. Muraoka, *Zoku Nihon shisō-shi no kenkyū*, p. 420.
37 Cf. G. B. Sansom, *Early Japanese Law and* *Administration*, pp. 122–3.
38 S. Tsuda, *Jōdai Nihon no shakai oyobi shisō*, p. 39.

and 749, respectively, the expression is used: 'the *kami* who dwell in heaven and the *kami* who dwell on the earth.'[39] The *kan* of *Jingi-kan* was also a Chinese borrowing and was the term used exclusively for the two highest departments, or councils, of the government.

The role of the *Jingi-kan* was an integrating one. This department had the function of supporting the ancestral deities of the ruling family as supreme for the land as well as the function of providing an over-all organization to bring together local gods of the small rural communities as well as the *ujigami* (*v.* Chap. III) of the influential families. The *Jingi-kan* supervised all the officially sponsored shrines: in the Capital, in the five Inner Provinces, and throughout the other provinces of the Seven Circuits.[40] Its duty was to oversee the registers of the entire priesthood *(hafuribe)* and of the religious corporations *(kambe* or *kamutomo)*, and the personnel of the *Jingi-kan* itself and the staffing of principal shrines.

As we have pointed out, in ancient times the administration of the country and the rites to the deities were an inseparable function of the ruler. As the Yamato state grew and political duties increased, however, there came the development of civil organs of government as distinct from the religious ceremonies. But the sovereign continued to perform his role in the traditional ceremonies pertaining to the *kami*: the enthronement ceremonies culminating in the Great Food Festival *(Daijō-sai)*, also the Tasting of the First Fruits *(Niiname-sai)*, the Great Purification ceremony, the festivals at the Shrine of the Great Deity in Ise and ceremonies to the deities worshiped in the sovereign's palace. If the sovereign did not personally participate in all these ceremonies, his official delegate was sent to represent him. In the case of the festivals at the Shrine of the Great Deity in Ise, this was the Consecrated Royal Princess (Itsuki-no-miya).

As *kami* worship came to be separated from secular matters, it was necessary to establish a separate office for the deity affairs under the charge of a chief priest other than the sovereign. It is possible that this institution came about because of influence from abroad. At any rate, by the reign of Keitai Tennō (r. 510–27) and during subsequent reigns of Kimmei and Kōgyoku, the presence of a chief of deity affairs is indicated although use of the term *jingi-haku* may be an anachronism in the *Nihongi* text. After the Taika Reform but before the reign of Tenchi Tennō, the term *kanzukasa*, 'office of the *kami*', was in use. Incidentally, this is the pure Japanese reading for *Jingi-kan* (神祇官). In the reign of Kōtoku (r. 645–54), the head of the Imbe Uji, Imbe no Obito, was appointed Chief of the *kanzukasa* (主神司). In the reign of Mommu, with the compilation and enactment of the *Taihō-ryō*, this office was put on an equal footing with the *Dajō-kan* and thenceforth called *Jingi-kan*. It is important to note, however, that an office called *kanzukasa* forms a part of the structure of the Bureau of the Consecrated Princess *(saigū-ryō)* and we find it mentioned in the text of Book V of the *Engi-shiki*. At the time of the

---

[39] *Ibid.* pp. 73–4.

[40] The Inner Provinces (*kinai* 畿內) were: Yamashiro 山城, Yamato 大和, Kawachi 河內, Izumi 和泉 and Settsu 攝津. The Seven Circuits or regions (*shichidō* 七道) were: the Tōkaidō 東海 道 (in which Ise Province was located), Tōzandō 東山道, Hokurikudō 北陸道, San'indō 山陰道, Nankaidō 南海道, San'yōdō 山陽道, and Saikaidō 西海道.

compilation of the *Engi-shiki*, we note that the chief of the *Jingi-kan* was of the Oonakatomi Uji, as the signature indicates. (That would have been just prior to A.D. 927.)

The *Jingi-kan* was staffed by the chief, *jingi-haku* (神祇伯, also pronounced *jingi-no-kami*), who according to the law *(ryō)* must be of Junior 4th Rank, Lower Grade; under him a senior assistant chief, a *taiyū* (大副), who must be of Junior 5th Rank, Lower Grade; then a junior assistant, a *shōyū* (少副), who must be of Junior 6th Rank, Upper Grade; a secretary, *taijō* (大祐), and an assistant secretary, *shōjō* (少祐), of 7th Rank; as recorders or scribes: a *taishi* (大史) and a *shōshi* (少史), both of 8th Rank. Under these officers came the hereditary religious corporations *(kambe)* numbering thirty persons from the Nakatomi (liturgists) and Imbe (abstainers) clans, besides twenty-eight Urabe clansmen as diviners. In addition there were the chief diviners *(miyaji* 宮主), the master diviners *(urabe chōjō)*, the masters and players of the sacred *koto* and sacred flute *(fue)*, the shrine maidens *(mikannagi* 御巫), the *sarume* dancers, the *heza* (戸座), young boy assistants to the diviners, and also the children who kindled the fire for the diviners to heat the bones or the tortoise shell.[41]

In ancient times the Imbe and Nakatomi had equal authority in the religious rites, but under Fujiwara dominance (let us say, after the formation of the *Jingi-kan*) the power of the Imbe clan declined and the Nakatomi were the most influential group. The Nakatomi functioned as liturgists and were present at the place of celebration on all festival days to recite the ritual for the occasion. The Imbe were next in importance, however, and as hereditary abstainers supervised the *kambe* who assisted them in the preparation of sacred offerings and articles for the presentations to the *kami* at the festivals. The diviners group *(urabe)* included officials of traditional divination[42] who were reckoned subordinate to the tortoise diviners *(kiboku)* who employed arts imported from China. The *urabe* were enlisted from the three provinces of Izu, Iki and Tsushima. Those who were most skilled in divining arts were called masters or superiors *(chōjō)*, while the 'chief diviners' *(miyaji)* were those who performed the auguries for the Court: he who divined for the sovereign was the *ō-miyaji*, for the empress palace was *chūgū-miyaji* and for the palace of the heir apparent *tōgū-miyaji*. The masters and players of sacred *koto* and flute performed the music for sacred dancing at festivals: the *kagura* (神樂). The Sacred Maidens *(mikannagi)* were young women who served the deities in presenting offerings and other functions. In the *Jingi-kan* they performed the services to twenty-three deities, including the eight deities of the *hasshin-den*, or 'Eight Deities Hall', and lesser gods worshiped within the confines of the *Jingi-kan*. The *sarume* were daughters of the Sarume Uji said to be the descendants of Ame-no-uzume-no-mikoto, who was the deity performing the god-possession dance in front of the Heavenly Rock Cave to lure out the Sun-Goddess and restore

41 *Kojiruien*, XIV, pp. 267–8; and *Shintō daijiten*, II, p. 209.

42 'All important matters were settled only after the Clan Chieftain had consulted the Clan Deity. This was often done by roasting the shoulder blade of a deer and studying the resulting cracks. This method of Divination was called *futomani* 太占.' R. K. Reischauer, A, p. 9. In the *E-S*, IV and V, however, 'reading the cracks in the tortoise shell' is the usual method.

light to the earth.[43] The *sarume* are more likely shamans than are the *mikannagi*, as stated in Chapter One.

The corporations of *kamutomo (kambe)* were all engaged in *kami* affairs. They are mentioned in the *Nihongi* in the reigns of Sujin and Suinin Tennō. The *Kogoshūi* says that in former times the *kambe* officials came from a large group of families enjoying hereditary positions in religious functions: the Nakatomi, the Imbe, the Sarume, the Kagami-tsukuri (the mirror-makers), the Tama-tsukuri (jewelmakers), the Tatenui, the Shizuori, Hatori and Kanhatori, the Omi and Kan'omi, and others.[44] We will meet Kanhatori, Kan'omi and Kasanui in connection with the weaving of 'deity raiment' for presentation at the Shrine of the Great Deity. After the Taika Reform and during the *ritsu-ryō* period, these groups of hereditary religious workers were set up with incomes from *fuko* (封戸) or sustenance households. Their support was specifically from deity sustenance households, *kami-fuko* (神封戸), which meant that because of their position in sacred affairs these groups were given support from the income from, but were not afforded the right to ownership of, certain allotted lands. They had the power to collect all, or a portion of, the land tax (*so* 租), the commuted tax (*yō* 庸) and regular tribute-in-kind (*chō* 調) from the said allotted lands.[45] We shall see in the regulations of the *Engi-shiki* the specific amounts of offerings to shrines, emoluments to the various deity groups and to civil officials who participate in festivals—often specifying whether *yō, chō* or special deity tax (神税) category.

The physical location of the *Jingi-kan* was within the gates of the sovereign's palace. It was a double compound surrounded by a double fence and situated inside and just south of the Ikuhōmon (郁芳門), one of the twelve gates of the palace. Its area was divided into a large West or Sacred Compound (Sai-in 齋院 or 西院) and a slightly smaller East Compound. In the West or Sacred Compound there were a number of buildings, including the main office building of the *Jingi-kan* and the Eight Deities Hall. Concerning the tradition here, the *Kogoshūi* says that:

> A holy site with sacred trees and stones was erected in the Imperial Court and in consequence the following divinities were worshipped there: Taka-mi-musubi or the Divine Male Producer; Kamu-mi-musubi, or the Divine Female Producer, Tamatsume-musubi or the Soul-detaining Producer, Iku-musubi or the Vivifying Producer, Taru-musubi or the Producer of Perfect Bodily Health and Strength, Oomiya-no-me-no-kami, Kotoshiro-nushi-no-kami, Miketsu-kami (homage is now paid to these Eight Gods by the Court Priestesses of Shinto). . . .[46]

These producing *(musubi)* deities are important in the creation myths and evidently are associated with the founding of the race and perhaps of the ruling clan. More will be said about some of them later in relation to specific festivals. These deities are not to be interpreted as ethereal deities, nor deities of any special sort.

---

43 *Kojiruien*, XIV, pp. 267–8.
44 Katō and Hoshino, *Kogoshūi*, p. 36. The last four families mentioned are various weavers of textiles.

45 *Shintō daijiten*, II, p. 204. Also Reischauer, *Early Japanese History*, B, p. 149 (*jikifu* 食封).
46 Katō and Hoshino, p. 34.

The absence of the Sun Goddess is conspicuous, but there is the remote possibility that her identity has merged with that of Takami-musubi-no-kami.[47]

Besides the Eight Deities Hall and the main office of the *Jingi-kan,* there were in the West Compound the South Building, the East Building, the Hall of the Abstainers (Imbe), the Hall for Symbolic Offerings *(mitegura),* and the treasury. The main building was where the dignitaries assembled and officials of the *Jingi-kan* presided over ceremonies for the *Toshigoi, Tsukinami* and other national festivals. Lesser officials carried out further duties connected with the festivals in the South Building, and the so-called West Office is where the deity food for sacred offerings was prepared. On the other hand, in the East Compound there were also a North, an East and a South Building, the kitchens, the sacred well, clumps of sacred trees *(sakaki)* and a bamboo grove. The total area occupied by the compounds of the *Jingi-kan* was equivalent to the areas of the *daizen-shiki* or Office of the Palace Table, the *ōi-ryō* or Bureau of the Palace Kitchen and the *gagaku-ryō* or Bureau of Court Music.[48] Measurements are lacking, but it evidently was not very extensive. The diagram of the *Jingi-kan* (Pl. I) illustrates its ground plan.

While Chinese overlay in the *Jingi-kan* is apparent in its nomenclature and organizational structure, the forms of worship remained very much the same as they had been in earlier times.[49] It is true that festivals were regularized and the participation of the high civil officials called for a cooperation between *Jingi-kan* and *Dajō-kan.* We must bear in mind, in this connection, that the higher the official, the greater his proximity to the throne, and the more likely that he had a role in the conduct of national festivals under the aegis of the *Jingi-kan.* We will observe the details of this in the translation of Books IV and V of the *Engi-shiki.*

The establishment of the *Jingi-kan* did not in any way imply a separation of the religion from civil government. Far from it. The Yōrō Code set down the administrative structure of the *Jingi-kan:* then in the section *jingi-ryō,* or laws concerning religion (lit., 'the deities'), prescribes the observances, celebrations and festivals to be conducted throughout the year, both in the *Jingi-kan* and at the major shrines in the Capital and in the provinces. The Great New Food Festival for the Enthronement *(Daijō-sai)* is specified as well as the Great Purification *(ōharae)* to be participated in by all officialdom as a national ceremony twice a year. The kind of overlapping of civil and religious subjects that is present both in the laws *(ryō),* and the *shiki* as the extension of the law, can be seen in the laws for the Ministry of Civil Affairs *(jibu-shō)* in the Yōrō Code. This section covers: ceremonial for this ministry, genealogies, religious festivals, House names, succession, marriage, omens, funeral rites, Imperial mausolea, as well as the Bureau of Buddhists and Aliens *(gemba-ryō).*

In like manner the *Engi-shiki,* the supplementary procedures for carrying out the

---

47 S. Tsuda, *Jōdai Nihon no shakai oyobi shisō,* pp. 70-1 and 93.

48 See *Kojiruien,* XIV, pp. 192-3 for diagram of the ground plan of all departments of the Imperial Palace.

49 The *saishi* (祭祀), or festivals under the *Jingi-kan,* were entirely different from the cere-

monies of that name under the Court of T'ang China. The 'national' festivals supervised by the *Jingi-kan* had their origin in local folk festivals, while the ceremonies carried on at the sovereign's Court were not directly under the *Jingi-kan.* Cf. S. Tsuda, *Jōdai Nihon no shakai oyobi shisō,* p. 559.

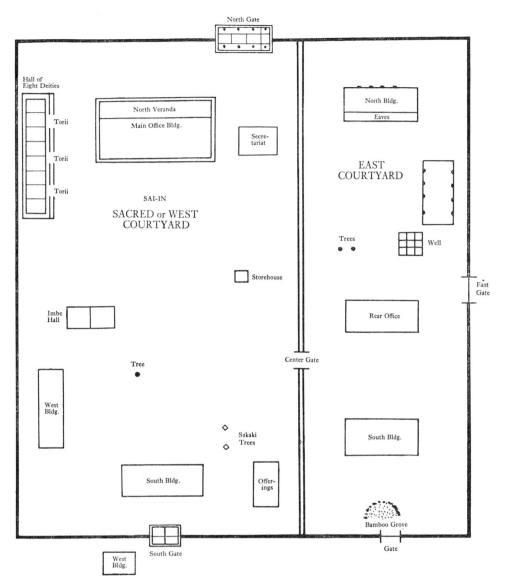

North Gate

Hall of
Eight Deities

Torii

Torii

Torii

SAI-IN

SACRED or WEST
COURTYARD

North Veranda

Main Office Bldg.

Secre-
tariat

North Bldg.

Eaves

EAST
COURTYARD

Trees

Well

Storehouse

East
Gate

Imbe
Hall

Rear Office

Tree

Center Gate

West
Bldg.

Sakaki
Trees

South Bldg.

South Bldg.

Offer-
ings

Bamboo Grove

West
Bldg.

South Gate

Gate

Plate I Ground plan of the *Jingi-kan* adapted from *Kojirui-en*, XIV, 286.

law, clearly show the interrelation of the civil administration and the *kami* religion, demonstrated by the corroboration between functions under the *Jingi-kan* and the *Dajō-kan*. For instance, the *shiki* in Book XI on the *Dajō-kan* include regulations for the Deity Food Ritual *(jinkonjiki)*, a part of the *Tsukinami* festival which is treated in Book I of *Engi-shiki*. Also in Book XI procedures are given for the Great Purification, sending of Messengers to the Ise Shrines, the *Mitama-shizume* festival *(Chinkon-sai)* and others in which officials of the *Dajō-kan* were obliged to participate. Then in Book XII on the Ministry of Central Affairs *(nakatsukasa-shō)* are *shiki* for regulating presentation of offerings at the Great Shrines of Ise by officials of that ministry. Thus we find items pertaining to festivals and ceremonies of the *Jingi-kan* appearing also in other parts of the *Engi-shiki* because they concern civil officials in various ministries under the *Dajō-kan*.

Chapter Three

THE CULT OF THE SUN GODDESS

The sinking sun tinges huge streamers
of clouds above the sea,
Foretelling a moonlit night
of pure lucidity.

—Prince Naka no Ooe

SUN, moon and storm—the three mightiest powers of nature—were the chief objects of worship of the Yamato people. Of all the myriad deities in their pantheon, these gods of light and darkness were of supreme importance to the early agricultural society, whose clock was alternate night and day and whose calendar the solar year from vernal to autumnal equinox and from solstice to solstice.

These three principal deities—the *kami* of light and darkness—were symbolized in myth and legend by the mirror, the crescent-shaped precious stones and the cloud-cluster sword.[51] This last, the *ama-no-murakumo no tsurugi*, was perhaps the symbol of the lightning's flash. These almighty *kami* controlled the seasons, telling the farmer when to plough, when to put in the seed rice, when to transplant the rice, and when the harvest was due. Nothing was more sacred in the life of the Yamato people than the producing of rice, the staff of life. There was a divine link between the sun as giver of light, life and fertility and the yield of rice from the luxuriant earth. Tradition tells us that after the Sun Goddess was enshrined in the Great Shrine of Ise it was the Food Goddess who was brought from elsewhere and enshrined in the Watarai Shrine nearby to be worshipped as second in importance only to the Sun Goddess herself.

The deities of sun, moon and storm were worshiped in many places, as everyone who tilled the soil needed the divine help of these gods of the seasons and the weather. Particularly at times when good weather was crucially needed for the crops there were special festivals to propitiate these deities—notably at the beginning of the new year after the crisis of the winter solstice was past, and again

---

50 This poem by Prince Naka no Ooe 中大兄 皇子, who became Tenchi Tennō 天智天皇, is No. 15 in the anthology of 759, the *Man'yōshū*:

> *Watatsumi no*
> *toyohata kumo ni*
> *Irihi sashi*
> *koyoi no tsukuyo*

akirakeku koso.

51 These are the traditional symbols of sovereignty, called the *sanshu no jingi* 三種の神器, or *mikusa no kandakara* 三種の神寶, 'Three Kinds of Divine Treasures', and were transmitted from one sovereign to the next as imperial regalia. Cf. Holtom, *Enthronement Ceremonies*, pp. 2 ff.

when the first ripened grain was ready for harvest. The first is preserved in the festival of the 2nd month, the *Toshigoi-matsuri* or 'Festival of Prayers for the Year', and the latter is perpetuated in the succession of harvest festivals: the *Niiname-sai* or 'Tasting of the First Fruits' and the *Kanname-sai,* or 'Festival of First Fruits to the Deities', and also the *Daijō-sai* or 'Great New Food Ceremony'[52] which was part of the enthronement ceremonies of a new sovereign. The field dances connected with the planting, transplanting and harvesting of rice which were called *ta-mai* constituted the origin of dances performed at the Court of the Yamato Sovereign. Later the repertoire became greatly developed and enlarged with additions of dances from Korea and China.

We know that the worship of the Sun Goddess came to be established in the Province of Ise, but how and when and why are difficult to discover. In the beginning there was no shrine. In the early Yamato way of worship a sacred grove, a hallowed piece of ground, a particular tree or a rock was designated as sacred. A spot where the presence of deity was felt was perhaps marked by branches of the sacred *sakaki* tree stuck into the ground and hung with streamers of hemp or bark-cloth. Or, a central *sakaki* branch so festooned would be set about by a low, rectangular fence also hung with strands of hemp and bark-cloth. This was known as *himorogi*. In later times the *himorogi* was placed on top of an eight-legged table and used for offerings within a shrine.[53]

The earliest mention of the practice of worshiping the Sun Goddess occurs in the chronicles in the reign of Sujin Tennō (*c.* 230–58?) and indicates that Amaterasu-ō-mikami, the Heaven-illuminating Great August Deity, and other deities were prayed to in the house of the Sovereign. Sujin is said to have feared the concentration of so much divine power under his roof so thereupon sent his daughter, Toyosuki-iri-hime, away from home with the sacred sword and mirror, therewith to conduct the worship of the Great Goddess at a sacred site in another village.[54] The time, place and persons are not so important here as is the fact that we see the Sun Goddess as a household god in the residence of the leading family of the Yamato people. Also significant is the fact that it was not the sovereign himself but a female member of his immediate family who was in charge of rites to the chief deity, and furthermore, that she underwent a sort of temporary banishment in order to serve this deity.

The temporary banishment is repeated, according to the chronicles, in the next reign, that of Suinin Tennō (*c.* 259–90), when the location beside the Isuzu River in Watarai District in the Province of Ise is first mentioned.[55] Though the district and provincial lines may have been drawn later, the setting of the

---

52 Today the *Niiname-sai* 新嘗祭 is celebrated November 23–4 when the emperor offers the first-fruits of the year's grain harvest and partakes thereof himself. *Kanname-sai* 神嘗祭 is a festival of the Grand Shrine of Ise when first-fruits are offered to the goddess. It is celebrated in the Outer Shrine (*gekū* 外宮) on Oct. 15–16, and in the Inner Shrine (*naikū* 內宮) on Oct. 16–17. From Jinja Honchō 神社本廳, *Basic Terms of Shintō,* p. 1.

53 Holtom, *Enthronement Ceremonies,* p. 99; and T. Tanaka, *Nihon jōdai shakai,* p. 299.

54 For the story in Sujin's 崇神 reign, see W.G. Aston, *Nihongi,* I, pp. 151–2, or Katō and Hoshino, *Kogoshūi,* pp. 36–7.

55 For the story in Suinin's reign, see Aston, *Nihongi,* I, p. 176, or Chamberlain, *Kojiki,* p. 210.

crystal-clear stream along whose banks grow majestic, giant cryptomeria, and whose background rises in the densely forested heights of Kamijiyama ('Deity Path Mountains') was unquestionably the habitation of divinity. The selection of the site began a tradition which is now certainly more than 1200 years old. But the origin of the shrines in this part of Ise is lost in the mists of legend. It is said that when the Imperial Princess Yamato-hime came to the Isuzu River to set up the worship of Amaterasu-ō-mikami there the area was already consecrated to a sun deity, called simply *hi-no-kami*. There is no evidence to support the idea that a shrine was built for the worship of Amaterasu-ō-mikami as far back as the reign of Suinin. The story says that Yamato-hime put up an abstinence hut on the bank of the Isuzu which had the name *iso-no-miya*—the 'seashore palace', indicating nothing more than its proximity to Ise Bay.[56]

In the reign of the next sovereign, Keikō (*c*. 291–323), there is recorded a curious anachronism. Keikō is said to have sent his daughter, Princess Ionu, to conduct worship of Amaterasu-ō-mikami in Ise—in the 20th year of his reign. Later on (40th year) it is written that the Imperial Prince, Yamato-takeru-no-mikoto, passed through Ise on his way to conduct a campaign in the East against the 'barbarian Emishi', or Ainu. Before sailing from Ise he received at the hand of 'his aunt', Yamato-hime, the divine sword, variously known as *ame-no-murakumo* (heavenly cloud-cluster) and *kusanagi* (herb-queller). Also, as he sailed to the eastern provinces it is said a large mirror was hung on the prow of the Prince's ship to protect him from harm. The cult sword and the cult mirror both appear as protectors of the Yamato sovereign's House. That Yamato-hime appears again so many years after her appointment to serve the Great Goddess leads us to surmise that either Yamato-hime was a title given to Imperial princesses sent away for the purpose of conducting that worship, or else that the story is allegorical for some major move of the Yamato Court to enlarge its dominion and establish a stronghold in Ise.[57]

We have noted that some form of sun deity worship was already in existence in the Watarai District. But were there other reasons for making this location the center of worship of the ancestral deity of the Imperial House? Amaterasu-ō-mikami, the Heaven-illuminating Great August Deity, is in the myths clearly identified as the progenitrix of the line of Yamato sovereigns. If we regard her as the deified ancestress of the Imperial House, we may also go so far as to take the euhemeristic view

---

[56] K. Naoki, *Amaterasu-ō-mikami*, pp. 33–4. As Naoki points out, the *Jimmyō-chō* or Register of Deities comprising Books IX and X of the *Engishiki* lists seven different shrines to *Amaterasu-ō-mikami*. (They are distributed among the provinces of Yamato, Kawachi, Settsu, Tamba 丹波, Chikugo 筑後 and Harima 播磨.) Besides these are listed four Himuka (日向) shrines, seven Hioki, or Heki, (日置) shrines, a *hinomatsuri* and a *hinode* —all of them survivals of some primeval sun worship.

[57] For the story in Keikō's 景行 reign, see Aston, *Nihongi*, I, pp. 205–11, or Florenz, *Die historischen Quellen*, p. 441. Prof. Tsuda Sōkichi 津田左右吉

does not believe Yamato-hime 倭姫 to have been an actual person. For one thing, the names of provinces (Oomi 近江, Mino 美濃, Ise 伊勢) through which she is supposed to have traveled are those of the province and district system set up much later after the Taika Reforms. Cf. Naoki, *Amaterasu-ō-mikami*, p. 21. A greatly embellished account of the wanderings of this princess forms the fifth portion of the *Shintō gobusho* 神道五部書, a tendentious work of the late Heian or early Kamakura, and is entitled 'Yamato-hime no mikoto seiki'. This has been translated into German by Horst Hammitzsch.

that she was an actual flesh and blood female ancestor who had some connection with this part of Ise. Perhaps she led an expedition from Kyushu, or elsewhere, into Ise Bay and thence to the Yamato Plain. Or, another possibility is that the tomb of this ancestress was in what became the Watarai District and a princess of the family of the Sovereign was sent thither to worship the spirit of the ancestress. Either of these theories would tie in with the belief of a modern scholar that women were chiefly the directors of religious rites among the Yamato people and that graveside services and the worship of ancestral spirits were carried on by women.[58] Whether the matrilineal genealogy of the Imperial House is one explanation of why that house had no surname is problematical. It is well to observe that the male ancestors of the Imperial House, while deified, had no major shrines specifically dedicated to their spirits—this is true of Ninigi-no-mikoto, the 'Heavenly Grandson' of the Sun Goddess, and his descendant, Jimmu Tennō, the first of the line of human sovereigns.

Since writing was not used in Japan before about 400, when Chinese characters were introduced by Korean scholars, it is impossible to rely on chronicle accounts of events until those of the late fifth century. According to history scholars of today, the reign of Yūryaku (457–80) marks the beginning of evidence of positive concern on the part of the Imperial House for the shrine to their ancestress in Ise. At this time the Yamato Court had consolidated its position and its eastward expansion was well under way.[59] The Dynastic History of the Liu Sung quotes a communique from this Yamato Sovereign to the Chinese Court which said '. . . our forbears . . . in the east conquered fifty-five countries of hairy men; and in the west, they brought to their knees sixty-six countries of the various barbarians. Crossing the sea to the north, they subjugated ninety-five countries.'[60] This testifies to the campaigns against Emishi (Ainu) in East Japan, the Kumaso in Kyushu and the wars against the Korean kingdoms across the Japan Sea.

As a matter of fact, by this time the Province of Ise, particularly south Ise and the Watarai plain where the Great Shrines were later built, became of vital economic and political importance to the Yamato state. The strategic importance of south Ise with its large protected bay was older than history. The Watarai District controlled the mouth of Ise Bay (latterly known as Owari Bay, at the head of which is Nagoya), thus controlling the sea route to the east, as well as the sea route to the Inland Sea and the port of Naniwa. After the campaigns against south Korea were over and the subjugation of tribes in Kyushu completed, these maritime routes up and down the coast from Ise Bay were of paramount importance.[61]

---

[58] Nakayama, *Nihon fujo-shi*, pp. 259 ff., advances the belief that graveside services preceded shrine services to deities, and that religious festivals had their origins in the ceremonies of offering flowers, singing and dancing for the soul of the deceased. As for burial mounds from the late 4th and early 5th century—they are found in Ise and even farther east, although the centers of Court influence in those times were Naniwa 難波 and Kawachi. Cf. Fujitani and Naoki, *Ise jingū*, p. 15.

[59] The power of the Yamato Court becomes securely established by the time of Yūryaku 雄略. Tanaka, *Jingū no sōki to hatten*, p. 52.

[60] From Tsunoda *et al.*, *Sources of the Japanese Tradition*, I, p. 10.

[61] The land route to the eastern provinces went from the capital through Yamato Province, Iga 伊賀 Province, north Ise and on to Owari 尾張. The sea route was reached by going through Yamato and south Ise to Anotsu 安濃津 or Oo-⋆

The centralization of government which took on strength in the seventh century depended on revenues from the outlying provinces. Rice, silks, hemp, skins, many marine products and horses were collected as tribute and taxes from the eastern maritime provinces of Ise, Shima, Owari, Mikawa, Tōtoumi, Suruga and Sagami, and could all be moved by ship, then by land through Ise and Oomi to the Capital. Of course the Great Shrines collected tribute and taxes direct from their deity households in the aforementioned provinces.

In order to develop new agricultural lands farther to the east and north, it was necessary to combat the Emishi—absorb them, kill them or drive them farther to the north to colder, less productive regions. By the Nara period the Yamato state had pressed the frontier northward into Mutsu and Dewa (the Tōhoku region of today), as we know from the biography of Sakanoue no Tamuramaro, who was sent thither as the barbarian-subduing generalissimo of the East.[62]

To go back to the reign of Yūryaku, it is said that he sent an Imperial Princess, called either Watarashi-hime or Takuhata-hime, to take charge of the worship of Amaterasu-ō-mikami at Watarai in Ise. She was accused of an illicit affair (this is the first indication of the existence of a rule that the princess must be a virgin) while in service, so she took the sacred mirror, went to a secluded spot on the Isuzu, buried the mirror there and hung herself.[63] We are now in a period when the chronicles can be given some credibility, so this sad tale tells us that there probably was no 'Shrine of the Great Deity' as yet, and also that the princess held a very insecure position in those days. She was not heavily backed up by the Court and officialdom—a very great contrast to the splendor and wealth of her position during Nara and Heian times.[64]

We can conclude then that by the end of the fifth century the interest of the Imperial House in the Ise region was very high for (1) political reasons of expansion and extension of its power, (2) economic reasons in the collecting of revenues, and (3) the spiritual identification. It seems safe to conclude that the worship of Amaterasu-ō-mikami was moved to this spot from elsewhere, and that the Watarai Plain was already the seat of an established worship to a deity of Ise who was very likely a sun god and protector god of the locality.[65] The worship of the ancestress of the Imperial House may have been superimposed upon the existing worship and some of the latter's features retained. We read in the *Engi-shiki*, IV, of the *hinomi uchindo*, who were a sacerdotal group whose function was to make prayers and offerings to the sun and the wind to ensure good weather. One interpretation of the amalgamation is that the native deity, a sun god and protector god and therefore a god important to the crops, was enshrined in the Watarai Shrine—'outer' of the two Great Shrines, as they later came to be. By the time the *Engi-shiki* were compiled this older native deity appears to be overshadowed by the worship of the Food Goddess, Toyouke-no-kami, in the Watarai or Toyouke Shrine.[66]

*minato 大湊 on Ise Bay then by boat to the ports of Owari and other eastern provinces. Cf. Fujitani and Naoki, *Ise jingū*, p. 21.

62 Sakanoue no Tamuramaro's 坂上田村麻呂 tour of Mutsu 陸奥 and Dewa 出羽 was made in 804. Cf. H. Bohner, 'Tamuramaro denki', *Monu-*

menta Nipponica, II, 2 (1939), pp. 241–53.

63 Aston, *Nihongi*, I, p. 341.

64 Fujitani and Naoki, *Ise jingū*, p. 20.

65 Naoki, *Amaterasu-ō-mikami*, p. 33.

66 The tradition according to the *Gishiki-chō* 儀式帳 of 804 is that during Yūryaku's reign the*

We must not overlook the mention in the legendary time of Sujin of the Eastern Provinces. The story says that the aforementioned Toyosuki-iri-hime was Sujin's daughter by his first wife, and that he later married the Great Princess of Ama, ancestress of the chiefs of Owari, and begot twelve more children—seven kings and five queens. *Ama,* which means fisherman, was a place name in Owari.[67] This account at least shows that Owari, which was farther east than Ise, had close ties with the Imperial House at a very early time, if there is any truth in the chronicles. Later, however, we find that in the sixth century in the reign of Keitai (510–27) kinship ties between the Imperial House and local magnates of the Eastern Provinces were such that Ise acquired greater importance than ever before as the gateway to the east. Incidentally, Keitai himself was not of the direct lineage—he was brought from Echizen Province when a crisis had failed to produce an Imperial successor to the throne. His Imperial Consort was Princess Meko, the daughter of a powerful landed family of Owari Province. Their two sons both succeeded to the throne after Keitai.[68]

Keitai is said to have sent his daughter, Princess Sasage, to serve the Great Deity of Ise. However, there is no record of a princess being sent to Ise again until the 29th sovereign, Kimmei (r. 540–72), appointed a daughter, Princess Iwakuma. It is believed that a sister of Kimmei may have been sent to Ise to serve during a part of his long reign.[69]

The increase of travel and transport through south Ise in the process of developing production in the Eastern Provinces and bringing in more tax goods from there had the effect of increasing the importance of the spiritual center in Ise. However, we have no indication that shrine buildings were yet erected, nor is there evidence of participation in rites to Amaterasu-ō-mikami by anyone other than the daughter of the sovereign. The next sovereigns after Kimmei, namely Bitatsu and Yōmei, did appoint princesses. But Princess Sugate-hime, who was appointed by Yōmei, according to the records served during the reign of her father and also during those of Sushun and Empress Suiko (regency of Shōtoku Taishi)—a total of 37 years! This seeming departure from custom was followed by an interval of fifty years in which no record of a princess sent to serve the Great Goddess in Ise appears.[70]

The absence for so long an interval of mention of worship being accorded Amaterasu-ō-mikami at Watarai in Ise is something of a puzzle. The economic importance of Ise must have continued apace during the seventh century. But the

---

*worship of Toyouke-no-ōkami 豐受大神, or Mike-tsu-no-kami 御饌津神 (august food deity) of Hiji-no-manai in Tangō Province was moved to the Watarai Shrine. This is not mentioned in the chronicles. The probability is that the Watarai 度會 Shrine already existed as the seat of the native deity, whereas Toyouke-no-ōkami was enshrined there at a later time. Fujitani and Naoki, *Ise jingū,* pp. 27–8.

67 Chamberlain, *Kojiki,* pp. 208–9.
68 Fujitani and Naoki, *Ise jingū,* pp. 22–3.
69 *Ibid.* p. 23.
70 This does not mean there is no mention at

all of the Great Goddess of Ise; for after Shōtoku Taishi 聖德太子 came out ahead in the struggle with the Chieftain Mononobe no Moriya 物部 守屋, he sent the Chieftain Nakatomi no Kuniko 中臣國子 as Imperial Messenger to Ise. Also, offerings were sent by the Court to the Great Goddess of Ise both before and after the defeat of Soga no Iruka 蘇我入鹿 (645)—which may have been because of Nakatomi no Kamatari's devotion to the *kami* worship and the Imperial line, which he was supporting. Cf. Tanaka, *Jingū no sōki to hatten,* p. 85. See also Aston, *Nihongi,* II, pp. 184, 190.

spiritual significance of the ancestral cult may for a while have been overshadowed by two things: first the great surge of enthusiasm for Buddhist teachings and temple building on the part of the Court; second, the great governmental reorganization culminating in the Taika Reforms (645–6) and the political uncertainties and disorders of the three decades which followed. The promoting of the Buddhist faith demanded much time, wealth and attention from Empress Suiko and the Prince Regent, and may briefly have threatened the continuity of the ancestral cult. The Taika Reforms brought about unprecedented administrative changes effective among nobility close to the throne and throughout the provinces as well.

The Taika Reforms brought about reorganization of the whole country: the autonomy of local magnates was reduced, while governors of the provinces were appointed from the capital. The land ownership, tenure and land taxes were all put on a new basis. Registers of population, books of account and a system of the receipt and regranting of farm lands for distribution were put into effect. The old tax levies and the forced labor were ordered abolished, and a system of commuted taxes *(yō)* set up to replace them.

During the reorganization, in the reign of Kōtoku (645–54) Imperial granaries were established in ten hamlets which made up Take Village and Yamada in Watarai, Ise Province. (According to the Taika Reforms a hamlet consisted of 50 households.) The foregoing hamlets were the nuclei of the Take and Watarai Districts, two of the three Deity Districts *(shingun)* belonging to the Ise Shrines.[71] Now at last we see that the shrine complex had grown into something which was being provided with a solid economic base of support. Not only so, but an office was established to manage the business of the shrines under the direction of a member of the Nakatomi Uji, who were nobility close to the throne. From this it can be readily seen that although the records tell of no Imperial princess serving the Great Goddess in Ise at this time, the worship was being carried on by the priestly clan of Nakatomi and their support was being guaranteed.

Although the Sun Goddess may have suffered partial eclipse during the years of bloody turmoil and of political overhauling in the middle and latter part of the seventh century, a change was in store. A crisis of succession occurred at the death of Tenchi Tennō (d. 671), and a severe struggle ensued which turned into a civil war between the forces of Prince Ooama, younger brother of Tenchi, and Prince Ootomo, a son of Tenchi by the *uneme* Yakako. Some historians take the position that Prince Ootomo did accede to the throne as Kōbun Tennō, but he did not live to be enthroned.[72] This conflict, the Jinshin War, ended in the victory of Ooama over Ootomo, and Ooama was enthroned as Temmu Tennō. His success in battle came about, it is said, when Prince Ooama was encamped on the To-o River and made distant obeisance to the Great Deity of Ise. The incident is immortalized in poetry by Kakinomoto Hitomaro in the *Man'yōshū*, where he writes of 'the divine wind from the Itsuki-no-miya of Watarai' which aided the prince in overcoming his adversary.[73] It is just a story perhaps, but after his enthronement Temmu

[71] Fujitani and Naoki, *Ise jingū*, p. 32.
[72] Naoki, *Jinshin no ran*, p. 7, and imperial genealogy, p. 24.
[73] *Ibid.* pp. 190–1; also his *Amaterasu-ō-mikami*, p. 25.

demonstrated his gratitude to the Great Deity. After what seems to have been a fifty-year lapse, in 673 Temmu sent a daughter, Princess O-oku, to serve the Great Goddess in Ise. Subsequently, other princesses served during his reign. Support to the Ise Shrines now was on the increase and the position of the shrines became more secure, especially with the regularizing of the custom of having a princess in residence in Watarai, and hence more prominence was given to the celebration of festivals at the Great Shrines.

Another development in the time of Temmu was a more general revival of worship of native deities which took the form of nobles erecting shrines to the deities of their own Houses—the *ujigami*. The *uji* was a name-group which for convenience we may call House. Although some scholars contest the notion that an *uji* was a kinship group, the evidence is strong that the *uji* was made up of blood relatives to a defined limit and these all had the same name. The founder of the *uji* was the one who had established the name.[74] The *ujigami* were the founder's gods or the tutelary deities of that House. These *ujigami* were usually nature gods and were worshiped in the locality where the House had its origin. Thus, they were not ancestor-gods.[75]

The Imperial House may have taken the lead in combining the worship of the ancestor-god with that of the *ujigami* or tutelary divinity of the Imperial House. For in Temmu's reign the Shrine of the Great Deity in Ise took on a new dimension as the seat of the *ujigami* of the Imperial House, who was simultaneously the Great Ancestress, Amaterasu-ō-mikami. Other *uji* which appear to have done this were the Imbe branch family, who established the Imbe Jinja of Awa, and the Nakatomi, who enshrined their deities in the Hiraoka Shrine. These two shrines, it is apparent, were among the few in which the *ujigami* and the ancestor-*kami* were identical.[76]

One cannot say with certainty just when the noble Houses established shrines to their *ujigami*. The latter expression does not appear in the *Kojiki* or *Nihongi* chronicles; '*ujigami*' first appears in the *Man'yōshū* in a poem in which Ootomo no Sakanoue refers to the deities of his *uji*.[77] During the last of the seventh and the early eighth century quite a number of shrines come into prominence which were erected to enshrine the *ujigami* of the then powerful Houses. The enshrinement of the *ujigami* of the Mononobe Chieftains *(muraji)* was the Isonokami Jingū; that of the *ujigami* of the Yamato Chieftains *(atae)* was the Ooyamato Jinja; that of the Tsumori Chieftains *(muraji)* was the great Sumiyoshi Jinja in Settsu; and the *ujigami* shrine of the Hata no Kimi, who were the head family of the House of Hata, was the Fushimi Inari Jinja in Yamashiro.[78] Another Hata branch family were hereditary priests of the Matsuno-o Jinja where their *ujigami* were enshrined.[79] Another important shrine complex was that of the Upper and Lower Kamo Shrines

---

74 A. Oota, *Nihon jōdai shakai soshiki*, p. 294.

75 T. Wakamori, *Nihon minzoku-shi*, p. 51. Also, S. Shimode, *Sosenjin seiritsu no shakaiteki kiban*, p. 52.

76 Oota, *Nihon jōdai shakai*, p. 303.

77 Wakamori, *Nihon minzoku-shi*, p. 57.

78 Oota, *op. cit.*, p. 302. The '*muraji*' (連) and '*atae*' (直) were among the titles (*kabane* 姓)

denoting the rank of the heads of Houses in the old *uji* 氏 and *kabane* system. These titles continued to be used for a long time after the Chinese system of Court Ranks was adopted (first under Shōtoku Taishi, and added to later).

79 B. Lewin, *Aya und Hata*, pp. 72 ff. Matsuno-o Jinja 松尾神社 was founded in the 8th century by a branch of the Hata 秦 Uji.

in the capital, founded by the Hata. The upper shrine was the seat of the Lightning God, Wake-ikazuchi no Kami, and the lower shrine was that of the grandparents of that deity and was called Kamo no Mioya Jinja (Kamo Shrine of the August Parents).[80]

This affinity of the Kamo Shrines with the House of Hata raises the problem for us of why an Imperial princess was sent to represent the Imperial House at those shrines in procedures parallel to those concerning the appointment of the Consecrated Imperial Princess to the Shrine of the Great Deity in Ise. The Imperial princess consecrated to the Kamo Shrines was called Saiō or Itsuki-no-miko, and the regulations for her office are the substance of Book VI of the *Engi-shiki* (not discussed here). The institution of Saiō was presumably founded as a means of enhancing the prestige and power of the Imperial House, but it did not endure beyond the early Heian period. The connection between the Imperial House and the Kamo Shrines remains unclear.

After the turbulent events of the mid-seventh century, a luminary rose up to become a power behind the throne—Nakatomi no Kamatari schooled himself for statesmanship and supported Prince Naka no Ooe and helped him to become enthroned as the Sovereign Tenchi. Kamatari established a new House and was awarded a new name—Fujiwara. After Nara became the capital, the House of Fujiwara moved the worship of its *ujigami* to the new Kasuga Jinja by the capital. These deities of the House were Take-mikazuchi and Futsunushi, and to them was also added Ame-no-koyane-no-mikoto, ancestor-god of the Nakatomi.[81]

We read that a member of the Nakatomi, Nakatomi no Ooshima by name, was in charge of all matters relating to worship of the deities in the reign of Empress Jitō (r. 681–91), in other words he held the position which later was called Chief (*haku*) of the *Jingi-kan* when that department was formally established a short while later. Also during Jitō's reign (sixth year) it says Masters (*daibu*) were sent to deliver tribute from envoys from Silla as offerings to the Great Deities of Ise, Ooyamato, Sumiyoshi, Kii and Unatari. In this Ise seems to be on a par with four other principal shrines. But in the same year, on a journey through the provinces just east of the capital, the Empress conferred Court Rank on local chieftains (*miyatsuko*) of Iga, Ise and Shima Provinces and of the Deity Districts belonging to the Great Shrines of Ise—showing the growing importance of the shrines. Subsequently, it is written, the Great Deity of Ise sent to the Empress asking that Ise Province be exempted from payment of taxes and forced labor (*corvée*) for that year![82]

A change had been taking place in the administration of the Great Shrines during the late 7th century. We saw that a shrine office existed in Ise during Kōtoku's reign. Also, the trend of the central government was to concentrate power and wealth in the capital at the expense of the territorial magnates. The old, well-

[80] *Ibid.* p. 173.

[81] Oota, *op. cit.*, p. 304.

[82] Aston, *Nihongi*, II, pp. 406–8, and Florenz, *Die historischen Quellen*, pp. 405–6. Also noteworthy is the statement that commuted taxes and forced labor for the year were remitted to those households which had provided horsemen for the service of the empress in the provinces of Oomi, Mino, Owari, Mikawa and Tōtoumi 遠江, *loc. cit.*

C

entrenched Watarai family of the Watarai District were left in control of the 'outer'
or Watarai Shrine as its hereditary priests. But greater prestige was given to the
Shrine of the Great Deity, Amaterasu-ō-mikami, and the chief priests of this
shrine were appointed from the Arakida family, a branch of the Nakatomi.[83] This
connection to the Court via the Nakatomi, who were hereditary liturgists of the
Office of Deities (subsequently *Jingi-kan*), put the Shrine of the Great Deity—both
ancestress and *ujigami* of the Imperial House—on an elevated plane, and had the
effect of reducing the influence of the Watarai House. The whole trend at this time
was to invest the Court and the members of the central bureaucracy with control
and power while removing the influence of the local landed families.[84]

The economic base of the Great Shrines of Ise appears to have grown steadily.
We noted that during Kōtoku's time Imperial granaries were increased in Take
and Watarai Districts, which became the first two Deity Districts supporting the
shrines. In Tenchi's reign the third of these districts was set up (in 664), but it did
not actually constitute the addition of lands, for four hamlets were taken away
from the ten hamlets of Take District to form the new Iino District.[85] Later, of
course, all three of these districts gave their tax yield to the Great Shrines.

The direct income to the shrines came from the rice yield of the *shinden*, sacred
paddies or 'deity paddies', and from *fuko*, 'sustenance households' which one can
think of as individual farms. There are no records to tell us exactly how many
paddies and how many sustenance households supported the shrines in the seventh
century. But certainly with the significant recognition given to the Ise Shrines during the reigns of Temmu and Jitō, the support was increased. By the early eighth
century the Ise Shrines rank highest among national official shrines. They are
mentioned in Imperial edicts in the eighth century and the practice of Emperor,
Empress and Crown Prince sending offerings to the Ise Shrines became a regular
official function.[86] In the latter eighth century there begin to appear figures on the
economic holdings of the shrines. In an official record of 780 (Hōki 11) the number
of sustenance households belonging to the Ise Shrines is given as 1,023. In a record
of 806 (Taidō 1), in which the total number of households is given as 1,130, the
breakdown is as follows: 101 households in Yamato Province, 20 in Iga, 944 in
Ise, 65 in Shima, 40 in Owari, 20 in Mikawa and 40 in Tōtoumi. Of course these
figures add up to 1,230 households, which is no doubt the correct figure.[87] These
particular households who supported the shrines were called *kambe* or *shinko*,
'deity households', because they gave one-half of their tax rice *(denso)* to the Great
Shrines.[88] The annual tax was reckoned at 40 *soku* of rice-in-ear per household.[89]
In addition to the rice tax, these households supplied both adult and young workers

83 Fujitani and Naoki, *Ise jingū*, p. 29. As to origin of the Watarai name, see Naoki, *Amaterasu-
ō-mikami*, 30.

84 Fujitani and Naoki, *Ise jingū*, p. 45.

85 *Ibid*. p. 33. This was the so-called 'public
district' (*kōgun* 公郡). But later all three, Take,
Watarai and Iino were called the 'deity districts'
(*shingun* 神郡) and were made up of the 'deity
households' whose taxes were collected by the

Great Shrines.

86 Temmu is said to have been the first
sovereign who went in person to present offerings
at the Great Shrines. Cf. Imaki, *et al.*, *Nihon
bunka-shi*, p. 67.

87 Tanaka, *Jingū no sōki to hatten*, p. 178.

88 E. Miyagi, *Engi-shiki no kenkyū*, II, p. 316.

89 Tanaka, *op. cit.* p. 180.

to the shrines. Services of workers might be substituted for by payment of further taxes in kind. All of the taxes in kind *(chō)* and commuted taxes *(yō)* were collected from these households by the Great Shrines.[90]

There may have been some increase in the number of households supporting the Great Shrines during the ninth century. According to an order of the *Dajō-kan (dajōkampu)* of 821, the annual required income for the Ise Shrines was 41,000 *soku* of rice-in-ear. Reckoning at 40 *soku* per household that would be about 1,375 sustenance households. The same order indicated that the income in tax rice *(denso)* that year amounted to no more than 36,500 *soku*, leaving a deficit of some 4,600 *soku* which had to be made up out of regular tax rice from the granaries of the central government.[91]

A century later in the *Engi-shiki,* IV, we find the number of supporting households substantially the same. There is an increase of one household in Shima Province, a decrease of 15 in Yamato, but an increase within Ise. We find a total of 353 outside of Ise Province, and presumably there were around 900 within Ise, a number which later on, after completion of the *Engi-shiki,* was increased.[92]

Another clue to the establishment of the Great Shrines of Ise as a national and official cult was the issuance of an Imperial Order to rebuild the shrines every twenty years. We do not know when the shrine buildings first were built, but very evidently they were in existence by the reign of Temmu. Apparently the re-building order was issued in the reign of Empress Jitō but the text thereof is not extant, and it is necessary to arrive at this conclusion by working backward from the recorded rebuildings of the shrines. The first appears to have been completed in 690, the second 20 years later in 709, the third 21 years later in 729, the fourth 19 years after that in 747, and so forth.[93] This reconstruction of the shrines, or 'removal' *(sengū)* as it is called, required a tremendous outlay over and above what was needed for the regular annual cost of maintaining the shrines. Book IV does not tell us from which forest the timbers were to be taken, nor how much timber was required, but the metal fittings which are specified required, according to the text, some 173 lbs. of finished copper, 225 lbs. of semi-finished copper and about 11 lbs. of gold and a small amount of silver.

The Superintendent of the Great Shrines was, in fact, not only the spiritual head but also a business manager, tax collector, general administrator and the holder of police power over the personnel attached to the shrines.[94] It is plain to see that his functions and responsibilities were on a par with the governors of provinces, and his title, salary, prestige and method of appointment by the Court were all parallel to those of a governor. This is borne out by the regulations in Book IV.

Thus we see that after the Taika Reforms went into effect and the central bureau-

[90] Miyagi, *Engi-shiki no kenkyū*; Fujitani and Naoki, *Ise jingū,* p. 54.

[91] *Ibid.* p. 53.

[92] Miyagi, *Engi-shiki no kenkyū,* II, p. 366, n. 1.

[93] Fujitani and Naoki, *Ise jingū,* p. 38. The *Yōrō-ryō* says nothing about the rebuilding of Ise Shrines, but the *Kōtai-jingū gishiki-chō* 皇大神宮儀式帳 of 804 does state the regulation that the

shrines must be rebuilt every twenty years. So does the *Engi-shiki,* which furthermore gives architectural specifications and details of contents of the shrines. The twenty-year period counts both the initial and terminal year, so that here nineteen years is twenty by Japanese count.

[94] Fujitani and Naoki, *op. cit.* p. 38.

cracy came to hold all the governmental powers in the capital, not only did the Imperial succession become more secure and regular, but the institutions surrounding the throne became systematized and formalized. First, the *Jingi-kan,* as the religious hierarchy which supervised the officially registered shrines throughout the country, came into prominence; then the Ise Shrines, as the official enshrinement of the ancestor-*kami* and patron deity of the Imperial House, rose to highest rank and became the apex of the national system of shrines. Along with this development, the appointing of a virgin daughter of the reigning sovereign to represent him in ceremonies at the Ise Shrines became a regular practice. This princess and her bureaucratic entourage were not provided for in the laws of the Oomi, Taihō or Yōrō codes. (Naturally, there was no Chinese precedent to inspire such a provision.) However, the nationalization and formalization of the worship of the Great Goddess, Amaterasu-ō-mikami, resulted in a multiplicity of regulations which are set down in the *Engi-shiki*—in Book IV on the Shrine of the Great Deity, and in Book V on the Consecrated Princess.

We have been speaking of the 'Great Shrines' of Ise, but actually, the adjective 'great' or 'grand' (太) was not used until during the Nara period. This is another indication that the rank of the shrines was raised after Temmu's reign. The expression which occurs before that time is simply the 'Great God' *(ōkami* or *daijin)* of Ise.

After mid-Nara the ancestor *kami* of the Imperial House was recognized as a national deity. Testimony to this is the well-known story of Shōmu Tennō sending the monk Gyōgi to Ise to obtain an oracle from the Great Goddess which would approve the casting of the mighty sculpture of Roshana Buddha for the Tōdaiji, the Great East Temple. During this period too the office of a *saishu,* or Master of Ceremonies, became regularized and the office filled by a member of the Nakatomi appointed by the Court to officiate at festivals at the Great Shrines. The *saishu*—like the Superintendent of the Shrines and the Consecrated Princess and staff of her Bureau—were officials outside the provisions of the law codes *(ryō)* but were recognized formally as organs of government and were strictly provided for in the *shiki* drafted in late Nara and early Heian periods.[95]

The Great Shrines reached their highest development in early Heian and the ceremonial procedures *(shiki)* of Books IV and V of the *Engi-shiki* (as well as Book VI on the Princess sent to the Kamo Shrines) establish the rules for the Superintendent, the *saishū,* and the Imperial Princesses and remained the authority for the procedures for festivals at the Great Shrines for all time. Thus, the *Engi-shiki* give us what no other legal document gives (they are indeed the consummation of the whole *ritsu-ryō* system which developed over a period of centuries) and represent the practical and usable extension of the law *(ryō)* which was but an administrative framework.

95　The development of the Bureau of the Consecrated Imperial Princess, the *saigū-ryō* 齋宮寮, was continuous at least from the time of Temmu Tennō 天武天皇. In 728 an Imperial Edict established the ten departments (*tsukasa* 司) of this Bureau. Three more were added by the end of the 8th century. Cf. Fujitani and Naoki, pp. 46–7.

Chapter Four

INTRODUCTION TO THE TRANSLATION

A THE LANGUAGE OF THE ENGI-SHIKI

THE *Engi-shiki* is a government handbook of ceremonial procedures for the use of officials. It is written in *kambun*—that is, in Chinese form—as was the practice in official documents in Nara and Heian times.

Although the text is in general composed in *kambun,* it is not uniform throughout. We have noted that a great many compilers worked over a long period of time to put together the fifty books of *shiki* of the Engi era. However, they used as a framework the *shiki* which had been compiled during the Kōnin and Jōgan eras and added to them materials which had appeared earlier and later, as well. Books IX and X, for example, containing the *Jimmyō-chō* or Register of Deities, list all national shrines in geographical order, and in this compilation names of certain districts *(kōri)* are according to old designations and divisions used before the Taika Reforms. In other words, the compilers of the *Engi-shiki* did not take the trouble to bring up to date the names of districts in these two books.

Book VIII also has material which antedates most of the rest of the *Engi-shiki.* The literary value of the *Engi-shiki* lies primarily in this book, which contains in their entirety the twenty-seven extant *norito,* or rituals. These are believed to be the oldest existing Japanese literature. They are in a language similar to that of the *semmyō,* the Imperial edicts in Japanese. The language of the *norito* is definitely Japanese but is written with a mixture of Chinese characters used semantically and having Japanese readings along with characters used purely phonetically.

Other portions of the *Engi-shiki* text illustrate the lack of a uniform style throughout. The two initial sections—the Memorial and the Preface—are written in a typically Chinese style adopted for memorials to the Throne in the *ritsu-ryō* period. They are full of phrases in balance, poetic imagery, allusions to Chinese legend and expressions borrowed out of Chinese classical texts. They give the highlights of the compilation story as well as show the erudition of the compilers.[96]

In almost every book of the *Engi-shiki* there are statistical passages which are not in sentence form. Books IX and X referred to above consist entirely of such passages, as these books list the numbers, names and classifications of the (important) deities enshrined in all the official shrines of the country, by province

---

[96] An analysis of the text of the memorial is found in J. Satō, 'Jō-Engi-kyaku-shiki-hyō yak-kai' in *Kokugakuin zasshi,* IX, 10, supp., pp. 1–8 and x, 11, supp., pp. 9–10. And an analysis of the preface to the *Engi-shiki* by Satō in his 'Engi-shiki-jo yakkai', *ibid.* IX, 11, supp., pp. 1–6 (1903).

and district. Also, in the first seven books we find interspersed passages which are nothing but lists—of food offerings, goods offerings and others, to be presented at specific festivals. Besides these there are lists of shrines. Book III, for example, gives a list of 285 shrines at which offerings are to be made to the deity of Nibu-kawakami; and in Book IV there will be seen endless lists of the articles and materials required for the ornamentation and furnishing of the Great Shrines of Ise. In Book XXV on the Bureau of Census *(kazue-ryō)*, for instance, are listed categories of households and of persons to be taxed, and in Book XXVII on the Bureau of Taxation *(chikara-ryō)* are lists of tax rates.

As an example of the style which prevails through most of the *Engi-shiki,* however, let us look at the stately opening lines of Book V on the Bureau of the Consecrated Imperial Princess *(saigū-ryō)*. The translation will be found below on p. 151. First I present the original, then two different possible transcriptions into Japanese sentences:

凡天皇即位者。定伊勢太神宮齋王。仍
簡內親王未嫁者卜之。（若無內親王者。
依世次。簡定女王卜之。）訖卽遣勅使於彼家。
告示事由。神祇祐已上一人率僚下。隨
勅使共向。卜部解除。神部以木綿著賢木。
立殿四面及內外門。（賢木。木綿所司儲之。
解除料散米酒肴等本家儲之。）其後擇
日時。百官爲大祓。（同尋常二季儀。）

One transcription is:

> Oyoso sumera-mikoto mi-kurai ni tsukitamawaba, Ise no ōmikami-no-miya no itsuki-no-miko o sadamete, sunawachi imada totsugazaru hime-miko o erabite, kore o uranau. (Moshi itsuki-no-hime-miko nakereba, yotsugi ni yorite nyo-ō o erabi-sadamete, kore o uranau.) Owarite sunawachi chokushi o ka no ie ni tsukawashite koto no yoshi o kokuji-su. Jingi-no-jō ijō ichinin ryōka o hikiite, chokushi ni shitagaite tomo ni mukau. Urabe haraeshi, kambe yuu o motte sakaki ni tsukete, tono no shimen oyobi uchito no mon ni tateru. (Sakaki, yuu wa shoshi kore o mōkeru; harae no ryō no uchimaki, sake, sakana nado wa honke kore o mōkeru.) Sono-go, hi-toki o erabite, hyakkan ō-harae o nasu. (Jinjō no niki no gi ni onajiku.)

In the above transcription the verbs are in the positive form, whereas, another possibility is to put them into the imperative. The following transcription, taken from the *Shinten* edition of the *Engi-shiki* (1936), interprets the main verbs as imperatives:

> Oyoso tennō mi-kurai ni tsukitamawaba, Ise no Oomikami-no-miya no itsuki-no-miko o sadameyo. Yorite hime-miko no imada totsugazaru mono o erabite boku-seyo. (Moshi hime-miko nakuba, yotsuide ni yorite nyo-ō o erabi-sadamete kore o boku-seyo.) Owarite sunawachi chokushi o ka no ie ni tsukawashite koto no yoshi o tsuge-shimese. Jingi no jō ijō ichi-nin ryōka o hikiite chokushi ni shitagaite tomo ni mukae. Urabe wa haraeshi, kambe

wa yuu o mote sakaki ni tsuke, tono no shimen oyobi uchito no mon ni tateyo. (Sakaki, yuu wa shoshi kore o mōke; harae no ryō no uchimaki, sake, sakana nado wa honke kore o mōkeyo.) Sono nochi, nichiji o erabite, hyakkan ō-harae o nase. (Tsune no niki no gi ni onajiku seyo.)

Since this passage is a legal regulation introduced by the formal Chinese opening *fan* 凡, *oyoso* in Japanese, meaning 'at all times', I have rendered the main verbs into the positive or declarative mood, not the imperative. It is conceivable that they were intended as imperatives, but this particular passage argues against it. The subject of the first sentence is the sovereign—*tennō* or *sumera-mikoto*—whom one would hardly expect to address with an imperative. Another interpretation, of course, is to read into the sentence an additional subject, 'they', for the verbs *sadamete, erabite* and *uranau*. However, historical sources such as the *Nihongi* and *Shoku-nihongi* tell us that the sovereign did the appointing of the princess, while the diviners did the divining, which undoubtedly preceded the appointing.

Typical of the language of the text are the alternate readings possible—Japanese or Sino-Japanese—for sets of characters. Just as we have the two possible words for sovereign above, so also there are alternate readings for Consecrated Imperial Princess, namely, *itsuki-naishinnō* and *itsuki-no-hime-miko*. Many times in Books IV and V, however, the shorter term, omitting the 'inner' for Imperial, is used and the reading may be either *itsuki-no-miko* or *saigū* 齋宮, 'Consecrated Princess'. In the passage quoted above we notice that an Imperial Princess is contrasted with other princesses of the blood, *nyo-ō*, who were not of the immediate family of the sovereign. Generally in the text the term *itsuki-no-miya* refers to the palace or dwelling of the Princess in Ise, while the same characters pronounced *saigū* meant the princess herself.

The foregoing shows that it was the practice in Heian times to use either Sino-Japanese or native Japanese pronunciations of certain compounds. On the other hand, we find that not always was more than one reading of a term available. During the *ritsu-ryō* period, that is from the Taika Reforms onward, Chinese titles and Chinese legal terms were in ever wider use, but the Japanese language was at the time much poorer in vocabulary than the contemporary language of the Great T'ang. For example, under the *ritsu-ryō* system the ministries of the government were divided into bureaus, *ryō* 寮, and these in turn were subdivided into offices, *shi* 司, but Japanese lacked the words to distinguish between these. We noted in Chapter II that the *Jingi-kan*—usually called by that name—also had the native Japanese name of *kanzukasa* (a syncope for *kami-tsukasa*) which was written with the same characters as was *Jingi-kan* (both meaning Office of Deities). Thus, *tsukasa* is a possible reading for *kan* 官, which in this case has to be translated 'Council' to parallel the 'Great Council of State' which is used to translate *Dajō-kan*. After the Taika Reforms the governors of provinces were known as *kuni-no-tsukasa* 國司, or *kokushi*. Of the same standing was *miya-no-tsukasa* 宮司, or *gūji*, the high priest or 'superintendent' of a great shrine—such as the Great Shrines of Ise and the Katori Jingū. Furthermore, the Bureau of the Consecrated Princess, *saigū-ryō* 齋宮寮, is also called *itsuki-no-miya no tsukasa*. Under this bureau (*ryō* or *tsukasa*)

we find a department called *kanzukasa* ('office of deities'), having the same pronunciation but written differently from the word equivalent to *Jingi-kan*. Thus we
find four different levels of government departments all known as *tsukasa* in Japanese, but written with the respective Chinese characters 官, 寮, 司, and again,
on a lower level, 司. This last was used for the position of governor as well as for
the office under a bureau.

The titles *kuni-no-tsukasa (kokushi)* and *miya-no-tsukasa (gūji)* refer equally
to the office and to the official himself. It is not always easy to tell which is meant.
In Book IV, the *ōmikami-no-miya no tsukasa* or *daijingūji,* 太神宮司, which I have
translated the 'superintendent of the Great Shrines', poses problems. When the
title appears we do not know whether the official himself is meant or the office
which administers the Shrine of the Great Deity or both the Great Shrines. It
could refer to one person, or two, or a whole staff. Near the end of Book IV appears
a regulation concerning salary for the *daijingūji* which throws some light on the
problem. It reads thus:

> 凡太神宮司二員。大宮司一員正六位上官。少宮司一員正七位上官。其季祿以神
> 税給之。

Transcribed, this is:

> Oyoso ōmikami-no-miya no tsukasa ni-in; dai-gūji ichi-in shō-roku-i-jō
> no kan; shō-gūji ichi-in, shō-shichi-i-no-jō no kan. Sono kiroku wa shinzei
> o motte kore o kyū-su.

And the translation is:

> At all times [there are] two officials of the Shrine of the Great Deity: one
> Chief Priest of the Shrine, an official of Senior 6th Rank Upper Grade; one
> Assistant Priest, an official of Senior 7th Rank Upper Grade. Their yearly
> salary is provided from deity taxes.

In the translation of Book IV, I have adhered to 'superintendent' as a translation
instead of 'official', 'governor', 'chief priest' or 'assistant priest'—any of which
are translations of *tsukasa* (in the case of the last two, *miya-no-tsukasa,* great and
small, respectively). As the assistant superintendent *(shōgūji)* is not specifically
mentioned elsewhere in Book IV, it seems safe to conclude that *daijingūji* can be
either singular or collective, referring to both the superintendent and the assistant.
The translation 'priest' is to be avoided, since the priestly families attached to the
Shrine of the Great Deity and the Watarai Shrine were from the Arakida and
Watarai families, respectively, whereas the superintendent of the Shrines and
the assistant were nobles appointed by the Court to serve in those capacities, and
the superintendent, at least, was customarily a member of the Nakatomi family.

The translation 'deity' for the Japanese *kami* used herein is not an ideal translation and has as its justification that the idea of *kami* is diverse: it may mean god,
goddess, divinity or the divine spirit inhabiting a tree, rock or mountain. The use
of deity seems appropriately vague and inclusive. It is used wherever the character
kami (shin) occurs.

Another feature of the translation is that in the interests of saving space the many numerals that occur in the text are transliterated as arabic numerals rather than spelled out as proper literary form would require.

B ENGI-SHIKI, BOOK I

PURSUANT to the provisions of the *jingi-ryō* (laws concerning *kami* worship) of the Taihō and Yōrō Codes, the first ten books of the *Engi-shiki* deal with procedures for all matters handled by the *Jingi-kan*. Book I covers the 'Festivals of the Four Seasons', the annual festivals to deities celebrated under the auspices of the *Jingi-kan* at all the official shrines. The text tells us there are three categories of festival—great, middle and small. Only one festival occupies the top category of great: namely, the *Daijō-sai* or Great New Food Festival of the Enthronement which takes place once in the reign of each sovereign. This is mentioned at the beginning of Book I but the procedures for it are contained in Book VII.

In the second, or middle, category there are five national festivals: *Toshigoi, Tsukinami* (in 6th and 12th months), *Kanname, Niiname* and *Kamo*. These important occasions are participated in by the host of civil officials as well as those of the *Jingi-kan*. The procedures include the lists of shrines throughout the country which hold the celebration and to which the office of the *Jingi-kan* sent symbolic offerings.

There are thirteen festivals in the 'small' category, the first two, *Oomi* and *Kaze-no-kami,* involved both civil and religious officialdom, while the other eleven required the participation of *Jingi-kan* officials but not those of the *Dajō-kan*.

A dramatic passage early in Book I prescribes the procedures for holding the *Toshigoi* festival within the compound of the *Jingi-kan* in the Capital. The same order of service applied to the holding of the *Tsukinami* festival. The latter originally was a monthly, but later a twice-yearly celebration. The procedures give us a picture of the protocol and pageantry displayed as representatives of all officialdom from the sovereign down to the least functionary took part in the ceremonies. The *Toshigoi* was of vital importance to the nation based on agriculture, for it was the time of praying for successful planting and good crops in the spring season. A part of this festival was the worship of the many water-dividing *(mikomari)* deities whose help was needed for irrigating the paddy fields of the inner provinces to ensure an abundant rice crop.

After the *Toshigoi* and *Tsukinami* festivals, others on the national religious calendar were to honor the deities of Kasuga and also Hiraoka Shrine—*ujigami* of the Fujiwara Uji, and festivals to the deities of Ooharano, of Sono and Kara in the Imperial Palace, the *Hanashizume* festival to ward off epidemic diseases and the festival to the Kaze-no-kami, the 'Wind Gods of Tatsuta' so often mentioned in the *Nihongi*. These are followed by requirements for Thank Offerings *(miagamono),* the Great Purification held twice yearly to rid the whole nation of defilement and offenses to the deities, the festivals of fire propitiation (i.e. prevention), and the Banquet to the Deities of the Roads to ward off illness and evil spirits.

What then were the requirements for these festivals? A long list of very precise offering materials greets us with almost every festival. While the lists may seem endless and repetitive, it is well to see what kinds of things they comprise.

First, there are the symbolic offerings *(mitegura)* consisting of the sacred expiatory wand *(nusa)* or a branch of *sakaki* tree, adorned with silk or bark-cloth or else lengths or streamers of silk, or five colors of pongee or similar material. Then come bark-cloth, which is soft, and hemp, which is rough, to symbolize 'soft and coarse offerings', followed by other kinds of cloth.

Secondly, a great variety of foods in small amounts are offered to the deities— usually commencing with abalone *(awabi)* and bonito *(katsuo)* and other kinds of fish or meat, sometimes beans or grains, and always rice and sake made from rice, and also salt.

Thirdly come the ceremonial implements—the mattocks which are used for preparing the ground for rice planting and for tilling, then sometimes other farm implements and spears, swords, bows, arrows or mirrors. Then the many ceremonial dishes and vessels, followed by those which are used to serve food to participants.

Sacramental foods for the deities are presumably afterward consumed by the staff of the shrine or *Jingi-kan*. But we also find long lists of foodstuffs which are to be consumed by the participants after the offerings to the *kami* have been made. There are also lists of exact quantities of food supplies to be given as emoluments to the various officials, musicians, diviners and other participants in the festival ceremonies. Thus, after the religious rites have been performed, there is frequently the performance of instrumental music, singing and dancing together with the drinking and feasting.

It may be surprising to find that these annual festivals commence not with the first month but with the *Toshigoi* festival in the second month, which was the beginning of the agricultural year. What then of New Year's? We find no reference to the first month in Book I. But in Book IV there is a regulation that says on the first day of every year the *negi, uchindo,* and others make presentations of sacred sake steeped in spices and herbs to the deities enshrined in the Great Shrines of Ise and all their auxiliary shrines. This concoction was believed to promote health and longevity and became part of popular New Year's celebrations. At the shrines, however, special obeisances made in the direction of the Imperial Court, followed by a great feast for the staffs of the shrines, and on the third day with obeisance to the Consecrated Princess (if she was in residence), appear to be the extent of New Year's festivities.

The last seven items of Book I have to do with festivals held within the Imperial Palace for the special protection of this sanctified area against defilement, disease, fire and evil spirits. The *Ootono-hogai,* which has been called the Blessing or Luck Wishing of the Great Hall (or Palace), it must be noted, was a ceremony not confined to the Imperial Palace, but held to bring blessing and good fortune upon the Middle Palace (of the Imperial Consort) and East Palace (of the Heir Apparent) and also, as prescribed in Book V, for the temporary places occupied by the Consecrated Imperial Princess when she was away from the Court for the purpose of serving the Great Deity, the Sun Goddess.

The succession of events on the religious calendar covered in Book I takes us through the first half of the year.

C ENGI-SHIKI, BOOK II

THE second book of the *Engi-shiki* is a continuation of the procedures for the annual national festivals. It commences with the festivals held in the 9th month. These are the all-important harvest festivals to give thanks to the deities for the new crop of rice. The first of them is the *Kanname-matsuri* held at the Shrine of the Great Deity in Ise in order to present newly harvested grain to the ancestral deity of the Imperial House. Then in the 11th month a similar banquet was held in the Capital, the *Ainame* (or *Aimube*) *matsuri,* the 'Together Tasting' of sacred food in which the sovereign partook together with the deities of rice and sake made from the new crop. A grand sum of 71 deities received special offerings of food at this occasion. The next festival is one associated with the winter solstice, the *Mitamashizume-no-matsuri (Chinkon-sai),* the Pacification or Propitiation of the August Spirits of the Sovereign. It was held in the Palace and included in the ceremonies was the ritual dance by the Sarume dancers, supposedly a traditional dance handed down from the provocative dance performed on top of a tub by the goddess Ame-no-uzume to lure the Sun Goddess out of her retreat in the Heavenly Rock Cave.

Another harvest festival was the so-called Festival of First Fruits, the *Niiname-matsuri,* a nation-wide ceremony of offering new grain to a total of 304 deities. In addition, there are regular propitiatory ceremonies for maintaining ceremonial purity in the Palace as well as for the fires for cooking and lighting in the Palace. Finally, there are monthly purifications and regular thank offerings to be made to complete the very full calendar of religious events.

D ENGI-SHIKI, BOOK III

THE third book of the *Engi-shiki* contains the procedures for the occasional or 'Extraordinary Festivals'. These are unscheduled events, but of course may occur frequently as in the case of the ground-hallowing for constructing a new building, and particularly the *Amagoi* or Praying-for-Rain Festival, held for 85 major deities when dry conditions prevail. Its counterpart, the *Amadome* or rain-stopping ceremony, is only mentioned in passing. The list of deities throughout the whole country which are to be prayed to comes to 285. Starting with deities worshiped in the Palace, the list is arranged according to provinces. They are called *myōjin,* 'name deities', and are local deities capable of sending rain. The requirements for services to these deities are identical, but there is the stipulation that if 'Great Prayers' are to be held, the cloth offerings are to be increased—presumably if drought is prolonged.

Next comes the religious festival for the despatching of an ambassador to a foreign country. That the foreign land is T'ang China is quite clear from the title of the next festival, which is that held for the Tree Spirits and Mountain Deity whence come the wood for the ship which will carry the embassy to T'ang. Then there is, in connection with the Sumiyoshi Shrine in Naniwa, the festival for dedicating the wharf whence the ship will sail. Besides the festival for sending off an embassy to China, there were celebrations to worship the deities of the boundaries and roadsides when a foreign envoy was received at the Capital.

Following those, there comes the unusual occasional festival for the Izumo-no-kuni-no-miyatsuko, or Local Chieftain of Izumo Province. A great deal of description is included here and we can only conclude that this was both because this festival was infrequently held and because the Izumo Chieftain had a singular function and some special relation to the Yamato Court which conferred Court Rank upon him. After conferral, the Chieftain is required to recite a very long ritual *(norito)* which alludes to a combination of ancestral deities—some associated with the Imperial House, and some not. But included are the Musubi Gods, Izanagi, and other deities of the creation myths, as well as 'Ame-no-ho-hi-no-mikoto', the distant ancestor of the 'omi of Idumo' and also Futsunushi-no-mikoto, who was one of the ancestral deities of the Fujiwara Uji.[97] This laudatory ritual therefore appears to be a synthesis of praises to deities of both the Izumo and Yamato traditions and may have been of political significance for its unifying sentiment.

The final portion of Book III is a diverse collection of 57 regulations each commencing with *oyoso* 凡, which are such a miscellany that they can only be treated as a kind of appendix to the first four books. There are, for instance, some which deal with the extraordinary festivals which are the subject of Book III, but there are some dealing specifically with the Great Shrines of Ise and therefore should be at the end of Book IV. There are many which deal with matters relating to annual festivals and therefore should be at the end of either Book I or Book II. It appears to be some kind of oversight or lack of diligence on the part of the compilers of the *Engi-shiki*. The probability is that these regulations were added later and instead of being assigned to the respective book where they belonged were simply put at the end of Book III for convenience.

Of course the '*oyoso*' which introduces so many regulations cannot be translated by 'at all times' in every instance. Sometimes logic compels us to use 'every time that', or 'whenever', or in the case of a negative regulation, 'at no time'.

E ENGI-SHIKI, BOOK IV

THE fourth and fifth books of the *Engi-shiki* relate to the conduct of ceremonies at the Great Shrines of Ise and both books contain more descriptive passages than do the bulk of the regulations in the other books. These two books bear out the assertion that there was a restoration of importance to the Ise Shrines and the cult of the ancestral deities of the Imperial House following upon the triumphs of Buddhism in the Nara period. At the close of that period, the sovereign Kammu moved the capital away from Nara (first to Nagaoka, then to another site) establishing an all-new capital, Heian-kyō, on the site of present Kyoto. This was in order to make a fresh start and extricate governmental processes from the feuding of the aristocracy and political machinations of ambitious Buddhist priests, not to mention

---

[97] For a translation of the whole ritual, see D. Philippi, *Norito,* pp. 72–5.

the vast outlay of government funds for Buddhist enterprises and the rise of excessive allowances to noblemen for their official expenses.

Moreover, Kammu Tennō was interested in Confucian studies and in native traditions and institutions. In particular, he wished to revivify the weakened and abused system of law which had been so admirably developed in the Yōrō Codes of a century before him.[98] He wished to restore the power and influence of the Imperial House along with the old kinship principle *(miuchi)* by which relatives of the Sovereign and the Imperial House had in former times taken leadership in the government.[99]

The law codes of the seventh and early eighth centuries had been set down on Chinese models and were in effect an ideal pattern to be followed. They seemed somehow abstract, theoretical and even didactic. The codes needed means for specific adaptation to Japanese society, which with its aristocratic class holding all the wealth and power, was by its nature antagonistic to the Chinese notions of publicly owned land and a public citizenry that had been introduced and attempted with the Taika Reforms of 645–6.

Significant in the study of the procedures *(shiki)* for implementing the codes is that individual *shiki* had been promulgated from time to time to regulate official conduct, but the systematic drafting and compiling of *shiki* began at the instigation of Kammu in the Enryaku era. In 804 (Enryaku 23) appeared the regulations for conduct of ceremonies and other matters relating to the Great Shrines of Ise known as the *Gishiki-chō*. This 'Handbook of Ceremonial for the Imperial Great Shrine' and its second part, 'Handbook of Ceremonial for the Toyouke Shrine', are indispensable for the study of Book IV of *Engi-shiki*.[100] After that, compilation of *shiki* (and *kyaku*) continued in order to provide a means for adapting the laws to the actual practices in religious ceremonies as well as governmental processes.

Kammu's vision of reconstructing a well-ordered society governed by law could not be brought into reality in his time but came to fruition with the presentation to the throne of the 40 books of the *Kōnin-shiki* and 10 books of *Kōnin-kyaku* in the year 820. In his preface to the *Kōnin-kyaku* and *shiki*, Fujiwara Fuyutsugu lauds the 'previous sovereign', in reference to Kammu, whose inspiration brought about this great compilation.[101] The three sovereigns mentioned were motivated

---

98 Miyagi, II, p. 91.

99 T. Wakamori, *Nihon minzoku-shi*, pp. 116 ff. The *miuchi* 身內 or kinship principle, was at the heart of the *uji* and *kabane* social system of pre-Taika 大化 Japan. The close kinship ties between the Fujiwara and the Imperial Family prompted Kammu Tennō 桓武天皇 to work very hard to strengthen both houses to enhance Imperial prestige.

100 The *Kōtaijingū-gishiki-chō* and *Toyouke-no-miya-gishiki-chō* 豐受宮儀式帳, to use the full title of each part, were written in response to Court Order by the staff of the Shrines under the Superintendent (*daijingūji* 太神宮司) Oonakatomi Sanetsugu. The first part is signed by the Chief

Priest (*kannushi* 神主) of the Shrine of the Great Deity, Arakida Tadanari, and by the *ō-uchindo* 大內人, Isobe Shōyō. At the end of the second part, as well as the signatures there is the stamp of approval of a board of seven officials of the *Jingi-kan*. The text is found in H. Hanawa, *Gunshoruijū*, I, pp. 1–83. In the Tokugawa period a descendant of the line, Arakida Tsunetada 荒木田經雅 (1743–1805) wrote a commentary on the *Gishiki-chō*, now available in published form in two volumes, hereafter referred to as *Daijingū-gishikikai*.

101 Fortunately, the text of this preface survives and under the title *Kōnin-kyaku-shiki-jō* 弘仁格式, may be read in *Zoku-zoku gunsho-ruijū*, VI, pp. 482–3.

by the desire to see Imperial dignity restored, the Imperial House and the nobility maintaining harmonious relationship in the conduct of government, with traditional worship under the *Jingi-kan* reverently supported and, on the other hand, the Buddhist clergy strictly controlled. If the mid-seventh to mid-eighth century was the age of drafting and promulgation of administrative laws, it was the early ninth to early tenth century that brought forth the detailed regulations which reflect the actual practices of officialdom.

While *kōtai-shiki*[102] and *gi-shiki*[103] continued to be issued at intervals, the next great step in compilation of *kyaku* and *shiki* was the *Jōgan-kyaku-shiki* in 871 (Jōgan 13). Of the 40 books *(kan)* of the previously issued *Kōnin-shiki* the first ten dealt with regulations for worship under the *jingi-kan*—a pattern which the *Engi-shiki* of 927 follows. The *Jōgan-shiki*, however, is believed to have had a much more conndesed format consisting of 20 books *(kan)* of which only five were devoted to *Jingi-kan* procedures.[104] Of the five, the first two dealt with festivals and all matters concerning shrines, including the Ise Shrines, while three books were devoted to registers of deities *(Jimmyō-chō)*. As the full texts of neither *Kōnin-shiki* nor *Jōgan-shiki* are extant, we have to rely upon subsequent textual references, but mainly on the text of the *Engi-shiki* itself, in order to reconstruct the outline of these works.

For the purpose of identifying the sources of Book IV of the *Engi-shiki* dealing with the Ise Shrines, some reconstructed fragments of *Kōnin-shiki* are available for comparison.[105] These have been inserted in the table below to illustrate the *Kōnin-shiki* as the intermediate stage between the *Gishiki-chō* text of 804 and the sections of *Engi-shiki* dealing with the two Great Shrines.

There are 38 items (條) in Book IV (see App. v), of which about two-thirds are based upon prior information contained in the *Gishiki-chō*. In Book IV the two Great Shrines are treated in a unified fashion—as regards architecture, buildings, sacred precincts, personnel and the procedures for the festivals throughout the religious calendar. The *Gishiki-chō*, on the other hand, first treats the Shrine of the Great Deity (the Inner Shrine) in a collection of 23 items, and following these treats the Watarai Shrine (Toyouke-no-miya or Outer Shrine) in nine items, a total of 32. These items are developed and greatly expanded in both Books IV and V of the *Engi-shiki*. In Book IV additional material—not previously dealt with in the *Gishiki-chō*—includes architectural ornamentation of the Shrines, items on the Superintendent of the Shrines, the envoys who present offerings from the Imperial Court, emoluments to participants in festivals, tribute and taxes, Deity Households and Sustenance Households. As for Book V, although it is founded

---

102 *Kōtai-shiki* 交替式, lit., 'exchange procedures', had appeared sporadically during the 7th and 8th centuries to regulate official appointments and changes of office. Originally decrees, they were later incorporated in Enryaku 延暦, Jōgan 貞觀 and Engi *kōtai-shiki*. Cf. Miyagi, II, p. 107. Texts are found in *Kokushi taikei*, (1904) XIII, pp. 1–84. *(v. n. 597, infra)*.

103 *Gishiki*, lit., 'ceremonial procedures,' had

been issued sporadically and were designed to regulate ceremonial in Court affairs. *Gishiki* compilations from Kōnin, Jōgan and Engi are no longer extant as separate texts. Miyagi, II, p. 124.

104 The reconstructed plan of the *Jōgan-shiki* is given in Miyagi, II, p. 115.

105 The fragment on the Great Shrines of Ise of Book III of the *Kōnin-shiki* is seen in *Zoku-zoku-gunsho-ruijū*, VI, p. 492.

TABLE I

*Comparison of Item on Shrine of the Great Deity
in Three Different Texts*

Gishiki-chō (804)	*Kōnin-shiki*, III (820)	*Engi-shiki*, IV (927)
Kōtaijingū 19 buildings [enshrined:]	Ise daijingū	Ise daijingū
Amaterasu-ō-mikami (or, Oohirume-no- Mikoto), 2 others (on left, Ame-no- tajikara; on right, Yorozuhata-hime) [location:]	Three deities: Amaterasu-ō-mikami and two others.	Three deities: Amaterasu-ō-mika- mi and two others.
in Watarai-no-kōri, Uji-no-sato, Isuzu- kawakami. . . . . [staff:]	same	same
1 *negi* 1 Uji *uchindo* 3 *mono-imi*	1 *negi* 3 *ō-uchindo* 5 *mono-imi*	1 *negi* 4 *ō-uchindo* 9 *ko-uchindo* 9 *mono-imi* 9 fathers (of above)
[separate shrines:] Aramatsuri Tsukiyomi Takihara Takihara-no-nami Izawa	————	Aramatsuri Izanagi Tsukiyomi Takihara Takihara-no-nami Izawa

upon old traditions concerning the Consecrated Imperial Princess, there is very little in the text that links it to that of the *Gishiki-chō,* save for item 13, on procedures for the festivals of three seasons.

Item 1 of *Engi-shiki* Book IV lists the Shrine of the Great Deity and its six separate shrines *(bekkū)* and the personnel attached to each. The *Gishiki-chō* a century before had listed only five separate shrines (all called *miya*) for at that time there was no shrine to Izanagi, the male creator-god. The Izanagi-no-miya apparently became established as a separate shrine during the ninth century and thus is listed in the *Engi-shiki.*[106]

In item 2 of *Engi-shiki* Book IV, the Watarai Shrine (dedicated to Toyouke-no-

---

[106] The establishing of a separate shrine for Izanagi 伊弉諾 and Izanami 伊弉冉, the creator gods, dates from 867 (Jōgan 9), when the worship of these two of the four deities enshrined in the Tsukiyomi-no-miya was moved to the Izanagi-no-miya. Cf. Miyagi, I, pp. 74, n. 2.

ōkami) is treated. Both this text and the *Gishiki-chō* assign one separate shrine to the Watarai-no-miya, namely, the Taka-miya, which enshrined the turbulent spirit *(ara-mitama)* of Toyouke-no-ōkami. It is the counterpart of the Aramatsuri-no-miya, a separate shrine of the Shrine of the Great Deity which enshrined the turbulent spirit of Amaterasu-ō-mikami. There is close agreement in the two texts as to the forty auxiliary enshrinements: the 24 minor shrines which were auxiliaries to the Shrine of the Great Deity and the 16 minor shrines affiliated with the Watarai (Toyouke) Shrine. There are some differences in the readings of the names of individual shrines, but these are insignificant. A great discrepancy exists, however, between the list of shrines in Book IV and the list in the *Jimmyō-chō* (Register of Deities) in Book IX of the *Engi-shiki*. The latter lists 58 shrines, major and minor, in Watarai District of Ise Province. Thus Book IX and Book X appear to represent an earlier grouping of shrines dating from the latter seventh century and not altered with the compiling of the *Engi-shiki*.[107]

On the preceding page is given a comparative list of details in item 1 of Book IV and the corresponding item in the earlier texts. It may be seen by comparing these few details that there is an increase in the staff complement of the Shrine of the Great Deity, and likewise of the Watarai Shrine, in the interval between compilation of the *Gishiki-chō* and that of the *Engi-shiki*. In listing staff, the *Gishiki-chō* gives the names and ranks (if any) of the actual persons who served the deities of the Great Shrines in their respective capacities at the time of the writing of this document.

Furthermore, the *Gishiki-chō* records briefly the traditions concerning the founding of the Shrine of the Great Deity[108] and of the Toyouke Shrine.[109] Here we find evidences of the nature of the hereditary priesthood of the two Great Shrines. It is specified in the *Gishiki-chō* that the chief priest *(kannushi)* of the Shrine of the Great Deity is a *negi* who is a member of the House of Arakida and is of the Court Rank known as Upper Grade *Daiso*.[110] The *Gishiki-chō*, unlike the *Engi-shiki* which is designed to be a permanent guide to officials, tells the names of the consecrated children *(mono-imi)* and sacerdotal participants *(uchindo)*. For example, the child dedicated to caretaking of the shrine *(miyamori no mono-imi)* at the time of writing of the *Gishiki-chō* is named as Isobe no Agemaro, son of Isobe no Yoitsumaro.[111]

In the treatment of festivals annually observed at the two Great Shrines, the *Engi-shiki* treats the two shrines together, from which the impression is gained that their status was very nearly identical in the Engi era. On the other hand, the *Gishiki-chō* text treats them separately, giving precedence to the Shrine of the

---

107 The arrangement of shrines by district and province in *Engi-shiki* IX and X definitely belongs to an earlier period than the divisions of districts found in other books, as can readily be seen by comparing with *Engi-shiki* XXII on the Ministry of Peoples' Affairs *(mimbu-shō)*. The *Jimmyō-chō* (n. 34) districts are closer to what are found in the *fudoki* 風土記 of the early 8th century. Cf. S. Kida, 'Engi-shiki no zusan' ('Inconsistencies in

the *Engi-shiki*'), *Rekishi-chiri*, 33, 3, pp. 258–60.

108 *Gunsho-ruijū*, I, p. 3.

109 *Ibid.* I, p. 53.

110 This was one of the ranks in the system introduced in the Suiko 推古 period under Shōtoku Taishi 聖徳太子. It was below the 12 pairs of ranks, and may be called 'Beginning Rank'. Cf. n. 378.

111 *Gunsho-ruijū*, I, pp. 23–4.

Great Deity. However, it covers the religious calendar of events for each of the shrines month by month, with particular emphasis on the 'festivals of three seasons' *(miori no matsuri)*, which were the old agricultural feasts of the 6th, 9th and 12th months of the lunar calendar. Apart from the fact that the *Engi-shiki* compilers avoided duplication and repetition of what the *Gishiki-chō* had already stated—its information being largely supplemental and additional—its emphasis shifts to the great national festivals, the *Toshigoi, Kammiso* and *Tsukinami* festivals and the Great Purification on the last day of the 6th month.

In comparing the lists of offerings made to the Great Shrines, we find that item 12 in *Engi-shiki* IV on the yearly requirements (furnishings) for presentation of sacred food offerings to the deities lists only the silks, cloth and mats to be provided by the superintendent of the Shrines. In this regard the *Gishiki-chō* had earlier presented details of the preparation of food offerings. It gives a list of the vessels and utensils which are used to prepare and serve the daily morning and evening food offerings at the Shrine of the Great Deity, the Aramatsuri, Tsukiyomi, Takihara and Izawa Shrines. The list includes such things as: 42 august cook-stoves, 42 rice kettles, 42 basins, 42 bottles, 42 spouted vessels, 42 pairs of chopsticks, 42 mortars, 42 pestles, 42 winnowing baskets and an additional list of 12 water buckets, 300 water bowls, 240 pedestaled dishes, 360 coverless dishes and 450 sake cups.[112] This is a list which is not duplicated in the *Engi-shiki.*

Book IV states requirements for purification in its item 8 and item 11 as to when purification is to be performed and as to what materials and articles are needed; but the actual procedure for purification ceremony is not stated. The *Gishiki-chō* in its first item spells out the ancient formula of 'Heavenly Offenses' and 'Earthly Offenses' as recounted in the ritual *(norito)* for the Great Purification, text of which is given in Chap. I above.[113] It goes on to specify that persons guilty of an offense must put forth various expiatory offerings *(harae-tsu-mono)* in accordance with the seriousness of the offense.[114] Again, these are fundamentals given in the *Gishiki-chō* but not repeated in *Engi-shiki.*

When we come to items 15 and 16 of *Engi-shiki* IV dealing with the rebuilding of the shrines we find a staggering array of detailed regulations. It seems patent that all these details are intended to supplement the architectural specifications which were given in the *Gishiki-chō.* The latter tells us the exact number of buildings in each shrine compound, their names, dimensions and the type and perimeter of fence around them. For instance, the Shrine of the Great Deity consists of one compound *(in* 院), containing a main hall *(shōden)* 3 *jō* 6 *shaku* long, 1 *jō* 8 *shaku* wide and 1 *jō* 1 *shaku* high, with a stairway 6 *shaku* long and 5 *shaku* wide and a balcony 3 *shaku* high and 2½ *shaku* wide around the four sides of the building. Gold ornamentation in floral motif is mentioned but no detail of it given. The lock and key of gold are stipulated, as well as the four gable boards *(higi* or *chigi)*, 2 *jō* 8 *shaku* long, 8 *sun* wide and 4 *sun* thick, the 10 ornamental crossbeams *(katsuogi)*

---

112 *Ibid.* I, pp. 25–6.
113 The list of offenses is given above in Chap. I, p. 3. The text of the 'Great Exorcism of the

Last Day of the Sixth Month' is translated by Philippi, *Norito,* pp. 45 ff.
114 Jingū Shichō, *Daijingū-gishikikai,* I, p. 139.

each 7 *shaku* long and 1 *shaku* 7 *sun* in diameter, their ends to be decorated in gold.[115] Other buildings of this compound were: two treasure-houses *(takaradono)*, wait-ing-hall for the Consecrated Princess, one for her girl attendants, an offerings hall, storehouse, four guard-houses, a carriage house (for the palanquin of the Princess), a stable, a feasting hall and its outbuildings, including a compound for brewing sake and a group of buildings for the Consecrated Princess (see next section of this chapter).[116]

In the foregoing it is important to note that the *Gishiki-chō* gives specifics for dimensions of buildings and their components, architectural features and the fences and gates to the compounds. The *Engi-shiki* text does not duplicate these specifica-tions but adds to it voluminous supplemental specifications for adornment and fur-nishing of the buildings. By the Engi era, however, the compound of the Con-secrated Princess was not located adjacent to the Great Shrine as was the case in the Enryaku era of the *Gishiki-chō*.

The metal ornamentation of the plain wood of the two Great Shrines is believed to have been added during the Nara period (eighth century), but if so, it was not described in technical detail until Book IV of the *Engi-shiki* was written. In this book items 24 and 35 having to do with repairs to the buildings of the Great Shrines and the *saigū-ryō* (Bureau of the Consecrated Princess) respectively, are also material not found in any previous text. Item 15 refers to the regular rebuilding of the Great Shrines every twenty years in keeping with the supposed edict of Empress Jitō in 689.[117] The *Gishiki-chō* also gives directions for the rebuilding.[118]

Item 17 on the sacred articles for the shrines and item 18 on the sacred treasures have some precedent in the *Gishiki-chō*, but both items indicate a greater variety and luxury in the articles to be dedicated to the shrines. The list of sacred treasures in the *Gishiki-chō* totals 19, while the *Engi-shiki* text lists the same in much more detail and adds two more (the forked-head arrows and the 'kite-tail *koto*'), making 21 in all, not including mirrors.[119]

Over the period between composition of the *Gishiki-chō* and compilation of the *Engi-shiki* there is some increase in the staffs of the shrines. Numbers and functions of the *negi, uchindo, mono-imi,* and such, do not show much change during the period in question. However, the notable change is in the overall administration of the Great Shrines. Although the superintendent *(daijingūji)* appointed to the shrines at the time of the *Gishiki-chō* is named as being Nakatomi no Katsumi no Murajisuke, the function of this official is mainly as a figurehead and representative of the Imperial Court.[120] But clearly we can see in items 28, 29 and 34 of *Engi-shiki* IV that the status of this court appointee had risen greatly and he ranked the same as the Provincial Governor. These items reveal his annual stipend of rice,

---

115 See table of measurements, p. 187. The reference to 'gold' is no doubt to gilded bronze.

116 *Gunsho-ruijū*, I, pp. 5–6. *Daijingū-gishikikai,* I, pp. 161 ff.

117 Discussed in Ch. Three above. The edict is not given in the *Nihongi* in so many words, but there is a reference to it under the year 689 in the *Daijingū-shōzatsu-jiki* 太神宮諸雑事記, a record

of the Great Shrine purporting to commence with its founding in Suinin's reign and ending in the year 1069 (Enkyū 延久 1). Cf. Miyagi, I, p. 90, item 15.

118 *Gunsho-ruijū*, I, p. 8; *Daijingū-gishikikai,* I, pp. 241 ff.

119 Miyagi, I, p. 98.

120 *Daijingū-gishikikai,* II, pp. 31, 33.

the conditions for his receiving a document of honorable dismissal at the end of his term of office, and other responsibilities. In addition, item 28 tells us he has a full-time assistant superintendent. None of this material is contained in the *Gishiki-chō*.

Another item in the *Engi-shiki* IV not found in the *Gishiki-chō* is that pertaining to the messenger who presents offerings from the Imperial Court (item 27). In the *jingi-ryō* (of the Yōrō Codes) it stipulates that those who present offerings must be of 5th Rank or higher, selected by divination; the same for festivals at the Ise Shrines.[121] But the procedures to be followed by these envoys who present offerings, as well as those who supervise the making of sacred treasures for the shrines (item 17) are spelled out only in the *Engi-shiki*.

The increase in lands taxed for the benefit of the Ise Shrines over a century of time becomes apparent when comparing the *Engi-shiki* IV with the *Gishiki-chō*. The latter speaks of 6 *chō* 9 *tan* of deity paddies *(shinden* or *mitoshiro)* in Watarai District, from which the rice yield went to the Great Shrines.[122] In item 27 of *Engi-shiki* IV the deity paddies total 36 *chō* 1 *tan*, are distributed in Yamato and Iga Provinces as well as in districts of Ise Province. It is difficult to compare allotments of rice for the *negi*, *uchindo*, *mono-imi* and others because the *Gishiki-chō* gives amounts per diem per person in number of *wa* of rice-in-ear (out of a total of 4,585 *soku*).[123] However, in the *Engi-shiki* amounts are given on a per annum basis— indicating a year-round salary system for members of the shrines staff. Amounts are given in *shō* and *gō* of winnowed rice—further evidence of augmented rice production under the Provincial Governor of Ise and the prefects of the three Deity Districts (Watarai, Iino and Take).

As to the sacred horses sent by the Court to the two Great Shrines, the *Gishiki-chō* says: 1 *chō* 1 *tan* of land for grazing the two horses is allotted. But the *Engi-shiki* IV, item 22 indicates two horses for *each* of the two Great Shrines.[124]

F ENGI-SHIKI, BOOK V
Some time again
the sacred Princess will resume,
and dust will vanish from this
her hallowed room.

Saigyō[125]

THE *Engi-shiki* Book V presents almost exclusively new material which had not been assembled in one document before. This Book contains the *shiki* for the Bureau

---

121 Miyagi, I, p. 106.

122 *Gunsho-ruijū*, I, pp. 31–2. Yield from deity paddies was apportioned for the festivals, regular sacred food offerings, deity sake, for shrine staff and for sacred horses, as well.

123 *Ibid.* I, pp. 33–4; *Daijingū-gishikikai*, I, p. 87.

124 *Daijingū-gishikikai*, I, p. 796. The horses were sent by the Court from the Left and Right Mount Bureaus *(samaryō* 左馬寮, *umaryō* 右馬寮)

for the use of the Shrines. *Ibid.* II, p. 365.

125 Saigyō 西行 composed this poem after seeing the deserted Itsuki-no-miya in Ise about the year 1188 when no princess was in residence, about 10 years after the death of Princess Atsuko, daughter of Go-Shirakawa 後白河. The embankment had crumbled and the buildings were dilapidated. Cf. Oyama, *Saigyō hōshi meika hyōshaku*, p. 285.

of the Consecrated Princess, the *saigū-ryō*. This princess of the blood represented the Imperial House at the festival ceremonies at the Shrine of the Great Deity, Amaterasu-ō-mikami, and the Watarai Shrine to Toyouke-no-ōkami, goddess of food. As this is the longest and most descriptive book of the *Engi-shiki*, it affords us a unique glimpse into the actual practices and procedures in religious festivals under the *Jingi-kan*, in particular the festivals celebrated at the Ise Shrines. These celebrations, it must be remembered, were not public and popular, but like the celebrations in the *Jingi-kan* enclosure of the palace, were the prerogative of aristocratic officialdom. They were conducted and participated in by only the persons who held the position and rank designated in these *shiki*.

As previously mentioned, the *jingi-ryō* (of the Yōrō Codes) did not include the Bureau of the Consecrated Princess. Traditions concerning the origin of the custom of appointing a princess to worship the Sun Goddess go back to the semi-legendary sovereigns Sujin and Suinin and are recorded in the chronicles, *Kojiki* and *Nihongi*, and in the *Kogoshūi*. Following the *Nihongi* text, we find that the daughters of these sovereigns were appointed to serve at the Shrine of the Great Deity in Ise: Keikō, Chūai, Yūryaku, Keitai, Kimmei, Bitatsu, Yōmei; and after a half-century interval, of Tenchi and Temmu. By this time the procedure for appointing was more regularized and the shrines had risen to greater significance in the administrative scheme. The national histories continued to record appointment of Imperial Princesses throughout the Nara period despite the fervor for Buddhism—for two of Shōmu's daughters served the Sun Goddess at Ise, as also two granddaughters, who were daughters of Empress Kōken (Shōtoku), one in each of her reigns. By the beginning of the Heian period the procedures were well established for the selection of a Princess, her preparation for service, and her role at the Ise Shrines. In the *Gishiki-chō* (804) there are numbers of references to the Itsuki-hime-miko (Consecrated Imperial Princess). The Itsuki-no-miya, or Saigū as it came to be pronounced, appears to be the subject of Book IV of the *Kōnin-shiki* (no longer extant).[126] Whatever regulations concerning the Saigū there may have been in the *Jōgan-shiki* are believed to have been contained within the first two books on *jingi* (deities).[127]

The *Gishiki-chō* retells the traditions about Toyosuki-iri-hime (daughter of Sujin) and Yamato-hime (daughter of Suinin), founders of the line, so to speak.[128] In keeping with the story of the 'abstinence palace' (Itsuki-no-miya) set up for Yamato-hime next to the place of worship to Amaterasu, in the time of the *Gishiki-chō* there was a compound of buildings for the use of the Consecrated Princess adjacent to each of the Great Shrines, the Watarai (Toyouke) Shrine as well as the Shrine of the Great Deity. The full list is given for each of these, and we may cite the list of those buildings attached to the Shrine of the Great Deity as example:[129]

> One compound of the 'riverside dwelling' of the Consecrated Princess;

---

126 See plan of the *Kōnin-shiki* as reconstructed in Miyagi, II, p. 102.

127 I conclude this from Miyagi's remark that procedures concerning the Sai-in 齋院 (princess consecrated to the Kamo 賀茂 Shrines) must have been included in the *jingi* 神祇 section of the *Jōgan-shiki* 貞觀式. Miyagi, II, pp. 116–17.

128 *Gunsho-ruijū*, I, p. 3.

129 *Ibid.* I, p. 6.

One Main Hall (Shōden), length 4 *jō*, width 1 *jō* 7 *shaku*, height 1 *jō*;

One building for Ceremonial Articles (including dress);

One carriage-house for the palanquin (length 2 *jō*, width 1 *jō*, height 8 *shaku*);

One privy (length 1 *jō*, width 8 *shaku*, height 7 *shaku*);

One August Dining Compound: two halls (each 2 *jō* long, 1 *jō* wide, 8 *shaku* high; one fence (15 *jō* perimeter);

One Feasting Compound, surrounded by fence 64 *jō* long.

Similar specifications are given for the buildings of the compound of the Consecrated Princess at the Toyouke Shrine where in addition to an August Dining Hall an August Kitchen is included, both surrounded by a board fence 8 *shaku* high.[130]

We can see from the presence of these compounds of buildings that the Princess and her entourage were lodged within the sacred precincts of the Great Shrines at least through the Nara period. However, by the time of the *Engi-shiki*, the staff of the Bureau of the Consecrated Princess had grown and the residence of the Princess as well as the offices of the bureau *(saigū-ryō)* and quarters for attendants and servants were located in a compound away from the shrines somewhere in the Take District.

The term *itsuki-no-miya*, or *saigū*, has been rendered into English in various ways, such as 'high priestess', 'the Vestal at Ise', 'Vestal Virgin', and so on. The characters signify 'taboo august dwelling', or 'palace of abstinence', and were used for the princess herself or for her dwelling. In the *Engi-shiki* text the practice appears to have been to read *itsuki-no-miya* for her dwelling and *saigū* for the princess herself.[131] But also in the text appear the full title, *itsuki-no-hime-miko*, 'princess august child of abstinence' or 'Imperial Princess of abstinence', and simply *itsuki-miko*, 'Princess of abstinence'. Therefore, 'Consecrated (Imperial) Princess' is the translation, 'Imperial' to be used if *hime* is included.

Book V opens with the impressive statement of the rule that whenever a new sovereign accedes to the throne he appoints, with the aid of divination, a princess of the blood to represent the Imperial House in the worship of the Great Deity of Ise. Usually a daughter was selected, but sometimes a niece or granddaughter of the reigning sovereign was chosen. Commencing with the legendary Toyosuki-iri-hime and her successor as priestess to the Sun Goddess, Yamato-hime, records were kept of successive royal princesses appointed to serve at the Ise Shrines over a span of about 75 reigns.[132]

After the selection of a princess was made, a messenger was sent by the Court to make formal announcement of the fact to the Deity at the Great Shrine of Ise. Thereupon, the princess entered her first sacred residence, the Shosai-in.[133] From the moment of her appointment certain taboos had to be kept in order to protect

---

130 *Ibid.* I, p. 53.

131 T. Torao, *Engi-shiki,* p. 98.

132 The entire list is found as the first item in *Saigū-ki* in *Gunsho-ruijū* II, and in *Shintō daijiten*.

133 Cf. *Kojiruien*, IX, p. 682. In Empress Gen-

shō's 元正 reign (715–24) a new building was erected for the purpose; in Kōkō's 光孝 reign (885–9) the building of the *gagaku-ryō* 雅樂寮 (Bureau of Court Music) was used.

her and her entourage from ceremonial defilement. A list of 16 substitutions for words which must not be used is given in the *Engi-shiki* Book V. This is two more than the older list of 14 appearing in the *Gishiki-chō*[134]—the additional ones being *me-kaminaga* instead of *ama* for a Buddhist nun, and *koritaki* instead of *tō* (堂) for a Buddhist hall. The tabooed words and their substitutes are not listed in a classified order in the *Gishiki-chō,* but the *Engi-shiki* text lists seven having to do with Buddhism first, followed by another seven having to do with other kinds of pollution, ending with two more Buddhist terms.

While the princess was in temporary residence in the Shosai-in, a location was determined by divination for putting up the No-no-miya, the so-called 'Palace-in-the-fields'. When this palace was built the princess moved into it in the eighth month of the year in which she was appointed (or of the next year, if appointed in the last three months of a given year). Before entering either of these temporary palaces the princess went through purification rites, including lustration in the pure, running water of one of the rivers of the capital.[135] While in the No-no-miya, the princess on the first of each month donned the sacred bark-cloth headdress *(yū-kazura)* and made distant obeisance to the Shrine of the Great Deity in Ise. The *shiki* of Book V also tell the procedures for propitiatory festivals to be carried out for the various deities of the temporary residences, as well as the procedures for offerings to be made for the national festivals—such as the *Toshigoi* (Prayers for the Year) festival held annually under the direction of the Bureau of the Princess.

In the third year of her preparation, in the ninth month, the Princess was at length ready to proceed from the No-no-miya to Ise Province and the Shrine of the Great Deity. This occasion was a great event for the entire Court and Capital, and also for the villages along the procession route through Yamashiro, Oomi and Ise Provinces. On the auspicious day the Princess was received in audience by the sovereign in the Imperial Audience Hall of the Palace (Daigoku-den). An Imperial mandate was read confirming her consecration to the worship of the Great Deity in Ise. Special offerings were made in the Palace and announcement thereof was sent by Imperial Envoy to the Great Shrine of Ise. Although the *Engi-shiki* text does not refer to it, an intimate ceremony then took place in which the sovereign personally bestowed upon the Princess a comb, placing it in her hair. The origin of the custom has long since been forgotten, but this 'comb of separation' *(wakare-no-mikushi)* must have symbolized some imparting of magic power from the sovereign to the Princess who would be his representative to the Great Deity. With the passage of time no doubt the comb came to be regarded as a talisman to protect the Princess during her term away from court.[136] From earliest times in Japan combs were believed to be endowed with magical potency and much lore exists about them.[137]

134 *Gunsho-ruijū,* I, p. 3.

135 The Kamo and Katsurano Rivers are recorded as having been used during the Heian period. Cf. *Kojiruien,* IX, p. 682.

136 *Ibid.* IX, p. 681.

137 Through the ages combs played an important role in Japanese myth and literature. In the creation myth of Izanagi and Izanami, the male god threw a comb from the right bun of his hair and as it fell to the ground it sprouted into a thicket of bamboo. Cf. Aston, *Nihongi,* I, p. 24. In the Izumo 出雲 myth cycle, the Storm God Susano-o 素戔嗚尊 wooed the princess Kushinada-hime 櫛名田姫, and while so doing turned her into a fine-toothed comb, and later consummated his marriage with her. This is an etiological myth in*

The progress to Ise was an affair of solemn pageantry in Heian times. The entire 9th month was declared a month of abstinence in the Capital, which meant that no mourning or funerals could be held and all pollution must be avoided. The seven great streets were ceremonially cleansed and the route to be taken by the procession of the princess through the provinces was ceremonially purified by sending ahead two members each of *Jingi-kan* officials *(kambe)* and diviners *(urabe)*. The procession of the princess consisted of officials of both *Dajō-kan* and *Jingi-kan,* the princess, her ladies-in-waiting, girl attendants, male attendants, *toneri* and other high-ranking nobles on horseback, all followed by stewards, outriders, cooks, brewers, porters and servants.

The term of service of the Consecrated Princess was to coincide with the reign of the sovereign who appointed her, but there were from time to time irregularities owing to special circumstances. As her title indicated, this princess must at all times remain ritually pure and undefiled. She was under strict taboos as to food, vocabulary and exposure to any defilement, deliberate or accidental. As noted in Chapter I above, ceremonial defilement occurred if one had any association with illness, death, mourning, sexual intercourse, birth, blood or filth of any sort. Thus, as regards the Consecrated Princess, if she suffered defilement, or if the reigning sovereign abdicated, her term of service in Ise ended. Defilement occurred if either of her parents became ill or died while she was in office, or if her virginity was violated. In the long line of princesses who served only two were said to have been recalled because of an illicit affair.[138]

With exceptions, such as the long term of Princess Sugate-hime (who appears to have held the office during the successive reigns of Yōmei, Sushun and Suiko) and the 50-year lapse after her time until the next appointee, the institution of Consecrated Princess endured as long as the Imperial House could afford the outlay necessary to send an Imperial representative with appropriate retinue to the Ise Shrines. Her clothing, the enormous staff of her bureau, the various palaces and buildings built for her, the elaborate furnishings and provisions required for all these were calculated to reflect the Imperial glory and prestige. But they were costly. The long list of pharmacopoeia stipulated in the *shiki* for her highness' use even outdoes the impressive list of medicinals dedicated in the Shōsōin by Empress

---

*which *kushi* means both 'wondrous' and 'comb'. Aston, I, p. 52. In the enthronement ceremonies for the Japanese sovereign a comb is included in the paraphernalia on a shelf standing to the east of the traditional couch-throne provided in the sacred food ritual. Of this Dr. Holtom writes: 'But for whom is the throne prepared? The living Emperor does not mount it, no historical documents explain why it is there. The presence of the comb has suggested to some interpreters that a female personage is expected—perhaps the Great Amaterasu-ō-mikami herself. But other provision is made for the worship of Amaterasu-ō-mikami in the ritual; no historical records say explicitly that the throne is hers, and, finally, combs were worn

in early Japan by men and women alike.' D. C. Holtom, *Enthronement Ceremonies,* pp. 122–4. Prehistoric combs have been unearthed that were made of wood painted red, of bone, bamboo and of iron. In historic times cedar and boxwood were commonly used. In Nara period carved ivory was imported. It says in the *E-S,* Book XI, that noble ladies of Third Rank and above were permitted to wear ivory combs, while those of Fourth Rank and below only wood. In *E-S,* XV, ceremonial requirements include a year's supply of 366 combs for the palaces of the Emperor, Imperial Consort and Heir Apparent.

138 *Kojiruien,* IX, p. 682.

Kōmyō after the death of Emperor Shōmu in 756 at the height of the Nara age of splendor.[139]

Only with the decline of the Imperial House and Fujiwara House and the rise of a new government by shoguns in Kamakura did the custom of sending an Imperial princess to the Ise Shrines fade away. The last princesses to be selected were daughters of Emperor Godaigo. One was appointed in 1330 (Gentoku 2) and is recorded as having entered her No-no-miya. Then, during the exile of Godaigo, a second princess was chosen in 1333 (Genkō 3) but did not even enter a Shosai-in.[140] Thus the Itsuki-no-miya disappears from Ise and the Saigū from the pages of history.

Although *Engi-shiki*'s Book V became obsolete with the disappearance of the practice of keeping an Imperial princess at the Ise Shrines, one cannot say the same of Book IV about the shrines themselves. The survival through the ages of a great many of the regulations for celebration of festivals at the Great Shrines of Ise is apparent today. Great festivals—*Toshigoi, Tsukinami, Kanname, Niiname, Kammiso, Sengū* and Special Presentations of Offerings *(rinji hōhei)*—are observed now as they were in Heian times with the difference that the shrines are the mecca of multitudes of believers rather than being restricted to Imperial Household and Court.

G CONCLUSIONS

WE may now ask what was the net significance of the completion of the monumental task of compiling *kyaku* and *shiki* which culminated in the issuance and subsequent enactment of the *Engi-shiki*. Did the vision and hope of the sovereign Kammu result in the realization of a workable instrument of the law? Did the issuance of the *Engi-shiki* aid in perpetuating the existence of a society based on the *ritsu-ryō* system? What proportion of the *Engi-shiki* is of permanent usefulness?

The cornerstone of evaluation resides in the premise that, were there no *kyaku* and *shiki,* the *ritsu* and *ryō* would have perished altogether at an early date. Since there were no *kyaku* or *shiki* in the very beginning of written law in Japan, the earliest codes probably perished for lack of implementation and enforcement. The *Oomi-ryō* and *Kiyomihara-ryō* were bodies of law without any appendages. The supplementary legislation came from occasional Imperial decrees which established rules to be followed, and eventually from Orders of the Great Council of State *(dajōkampu).* After the compilation of the *Taihō-ryō,* the body of law at last commenced to have arms and legs attached which gave meaning and applicability to the code. From the Kōnin era onward *kyaku* and *shiki* were the vital extension of the code.

---

[139] In Appendix III below I have tabulated the 71 medicinal items in order of number of strokes and have given a Western name wherever possible. It must be noted that the species names are mostly for Japanese species, whereas it is perfectly possible that these pharmacopoeia were imported and represent continental rather than native species or varieties.

[140] The *Saigū-ki* in *Gunsho ruijū,* III, does not include these two princesses at all but names the daughter of Go-Uda 後宇多 the last of the line as she was the last one to serve in Ise.

Those who call the *Engi-shiki* a document commemorative of an earlier age may have some merit—for some parts of it were out of date by the time the task of compilation was completed.[141] However, the bulk of the regulations in its fifty books were an indispensable handbook and guide for all officialdom. Whereas the *Yōrō-ryō* was primarily an administrative code on the T'ang model and served to prescribe the structure of all administrative departments of the government, the *shiki* not only provided the supplementary regulations for the management of those departments, but also spelled out what was required of the governed themselves, as well as of the ruling class. This is particularly apparent in the procedures of Book IV for 'The Shrine of the Great Deity' which reveal the sources of income to the Great Shrines and the numbers of sustenance households under shrines administration and the types and amounts of tax goods and tribute goods to be collected from the provinces for shrine support. After they were set down, the *kyaku,* and more especially the *shiki,* came to be the true mirror of the actual practices during Nara and Heian periods, as far as adaptation and application of the written law of Yōrō was concerned.

But we note that the *ritsu-ryō* system did not long endure. By the time the *Engi-shiki* was completed, the seeds of destruction had already sprouted. Perhaps the greatest detriment to the continuance of the system and the society founded upon it was the lack of enforcement mechanism to cause the nobles of the court and governors of provinces—as well as their underlings—to comply with the form of the codes and the letter of the *shiki.*

It was the aforementioned Fujiwara Fuyutsugu himself, despite the lofty aims expressed by his directing of the compilation of Kōnin *kyaku* and *shiki,* who assumed extraordinary powers for his own House. In his effort to secure a monopoly of political power for the Fujiwara, he by-passed the three-man '*chūnagon* rule' which was intended to maintain a balance of power in the government. He became first chief of the newly created Sovereign's Private Office *(kurōdodokoro)*. He made that office and the Police Headquarters *(kebiishichō)* the principal tools of administration and justice, thus causing the established organs of the government to lose their proper function and eventually become empty forms.[142]

But it would be erroneous to infer that the House of Fujiwara was invested with supreme power—as distinct from the Imperial House. There were times when the two houses were virtually one and the same. The fantastic wealth inherited by Empress Kōmyō from her father, Fujiwara no Fubito, under whom the *Yōrō-ryō* was compiled, greatly exceeded the amount to which her rank entitled her according to the law.[143] Thus we see that already a century before Kammu there were abuses of the system on the part of those in the highest ranks, and acquisition of property had reached extremes which threatened the life of the *ritsu-ryō* aristocracy. When we read of the personal income of Empress Kōmyō we can appreciate how

---

141 The expression 'document commemorating an earlier age' is applied to the *E-S* in the article treating of it in *Nihon rekishi daijiten.*

142 Growth of the power of the Fujiwara Uji resulted in their becoming the top influential family in the society, with complete and direct access to the Throne (to whom they were of course related) without any intermediary. Miyagi, II, p. 110.

143 K. Inoue, *Nihon kodai no seiji to shūkyō,* pp. 34-5.

she was able to dedicate the magnificent collection of treasures of the Shōsōin repository commemorating the reign of Shōmu Tennō. The support given to individual Buddhist temples during this period by members of the Imperial House
and Fujiwara House, moreover, staggers the imagination and bespeaks possession
of income-producing estates of enormous scale.[144]

Politically speaking, the undermining of the *ritsu-ryō* system meant ultimately
the destruction of the very class which had created the system and whose existence
depended on its perpetuation. But as abuses grew and regulations were ignored
the system began to crumble. The late Heian period marks the decline of *ritsu-ryō*
and the failure to implement and enforce the detailed, specific rules of the *kyaku*
and *shiki*. The regulations for the *Dajō-kan* and its many bureaus and offices gradually fell into disuse. In other words, the content of much of the latter 40 books
of the *Engi-shiki* proceeded to become a 'relic of an earlier age'. But regulations
for worship of the deities—that is, the first 10 books on the *Jingi-kan*—had a
greater vitality and something close to immortality. One reason they have survived
to the present (in part, at least) is that deities, rituals and festivals were known
long before the *ritsu-ryō* system was devised. The systemization of the *Jingi-kan*
took place simultaneously with that of other parts of the government, but the
ancient agricultural rites and celebrations endured the ravages of political rivalry,
competition of Buddhism and even the lack of support during the later age when
the Imperial House suffered impoverishment and obscurity.

It was the National Learning scholars of the Tokugawa period who revived the
study of Shinto texts and institutions. They not only analyzed the myths and legends
of the old chronicles but they studied the *Engi-shiki* for its historical meaning
and valid content. Although Book V is now no longer used, the general plan of Books
IX and X, the Register of Deities *(Jimmyō-chō)*, with its listing of all government
shrines, has importance today. Some festivals of the Great Shrines of Ise, as outlined in Book IV, are still held, and the rituals *(norito)* are in present use, as is
much of Book VII which contains the procedures for the enthronement ceremonies of the sovereign. The rebuilding of the Ise Shrines at twenty-year intervals throughout the centuries to the exact specifications contained in *Gishiki-chō*
and *Engi-shiki* IV, is living testimony to the eternal value of these texts.

---

144 R. Takeuchi, *Ritsuryō-sei to kizoku seiken*, II, p. 519.

ENGI-SHIKI, BOOK ONE

FESTIVALS OF THE FOUR SEASONS[145] (PART I)

WHENEVER the Great New Food Festival of the Accession[146] takes place it is a Great Festival. The festivals of *Toshigoi, Tsukinami, Kanname, Niiname* and *Kamo* are Middle Festivals, while those of *Oomi, Kaze-no-kami, Hanashizume, Saigusa, Ainame, Mitamashizume, Hoshizume, Michiae,* the Sono and Kara Deities, *Matsuno-o, Hirano, Kasuga* and *Ooharano* are Small Festivals. (Those up to and including *Kaze-no-kami* are celebrated by all the civil officials, while those from *Hanashizume* on are celebrated by the festival officials only;[147] moreover, since Small Festivals are celebrated by festival officials only, they are not celebrated at the Imperial Palace, but an Imperial Messenger is sent to the celebration.)

The *Toshigoi* festival is always held on the 4th day of the 2nd month.[148] The *Oomi* and *Kaze-no-kami* festivals are both held on the 4th day of the 4th and 7th months. The *Tsukinami* festival is held on the 11th day of the 6th and the 12th months. The *Kanname* festival is held on the 11th day of the 9th month. Festivals held on days of the rat, horse, hare and cock are given in this text. The rest of the festivals are not fixed as to date; to suit the occasion a day is selected and the festival is held.

FESTIVALS OF THE SECOND MONTH

Toshigoi Festival,[149] 3,132 deities:

145 The *shijisai* 四時祭, or 'festivals of the four seasons', are the annually held national festivals based on the *Jingi-ryō* 神祇令 of the law codes, treated here in Books I and II.

146 The *Senso-ōmube* (or *ōnie* or *ōname*) *no matsuri* 践祚大嘗祭, also called *Senso daijō-sai,* takes place when a new emperor worships the ancestral deities and the deities of heaven and earth in a solemn, traditional feast of new grain. This of course is not an annual celebration, but is mentioned here in order to define what a 'great' celebration is. The entire set of procedures for the *Senso-ōmube no matsuri* are contained in *E-S,* Bk. VII.

147 This shows the extent to which the whole bureaucracy of civils officials under both *Dajō-kan* and *Jingi-kan* took part in these national festivals.

After those first seven, the somewhat lesser festivals, the latter eleven, are conducted by *saikan* 祭官, officials of the *Jingi-kan* in charge of festival ceremonies.

148 There were twelve lunar months with an intercalary month every third year. The days of the month were designated by the twelve calendrical signs of: rat, ox, tiger, hare, dragon, snake, horse, sheep, monkey, bird, dog, hog, as well as by the consecutive numbering. The new year commenced 15 days after the winter solstice and the first season was 'spring'. Therefore the period corresponding to January to mid-March was spring, and so on.

149 Both the *jingi-ryō* and *Ryō no shūge* 令集解 state that the *Toshigoi* festival is celebrated in the *Jingi-kan* and that the host of officials *(hyakkan★*

Major [deities] 492 (of which 304 are worshiped by the central government with offerings on top of offering-tables,[150] and 188 are worshiped by the provincial governments).

Minor [deities] 2,640 (of which 433 are worshiped by the central government with offerings below the offering-tables, and 2,207 are worshiped by the provincial governments).

There are 737 deities worshiped by the *Jingi-kan*:

304 deities are presented with offerings on top of the tables (30 in the Palace; 3 within the Capital; in the Inner Provinces,[151] 53 in Yamashiro, 128 in Yamato, 23 in Kawachi, one in Izumi, 26 in Settsu; in the Tōkaidō Region, 14 in Ise Prov., 1 in Izu, 1 in Musashi, 1 in Awa, 1 in Shimōsa, 1 in Hitachi; the Tōzan-dō Region, 5 in Oomi; the Hokurikudō, 1 in Wakasa; the San'indō Region, 1 in Tango; the San'yōdō Region, 3 in Harima, 1 in Aki; the Nankaidō Region, 8 in Kii and 2 in Awa).

At 198 Shrines:[152]

for each presentation [are required] 5 *shaku* of pongee, 1 *shaku* each of five colors of thin pongee,[153] 1 *shaku* of colored hemp-cloth,[154] 2 *ryō* of bark-cloth,[155] 5 *ryō* of hemp, 1 *jō* 4 *shaku* of tax cloth,[156] a sword case of colored hemp-cloth (3 *sun* of cloth), a sword case of pongee (3 *sun* of pongee), a sword case of common cloth (3 *sun* of cloth), one *yokura-oki* and one *yakura-oki*,[157]

---

*百官) gather there to celebrate it. This 'Prayers for the Year Festival' was held to pray for freedom from calamity and for a year of abundant crops.

150　The respective ranks of *kami* are evident from whether they are presented offerings on top of the offering tables or upon mats at the level of the worshiper: *anjō* 案上 and *ange* 案下, respectively.

151　The five *kinai* provinces around the capital. The rest of the country was divided into seven circuits or regions, of which six are included here. See n. 40.

152　The term 'shrines' is used as equivalent of *yashiro* 社, although in the *Jimmyō-chō* of the *E-S*, these are all designated as *jinja* 神社, i.e. *kami no yashiro*.

153　First in the list here are the components of the *mitegura* 幣, also called *o-nusa,* the symbolic offerings. These had a variety of forms, as: an expiatory wand adorned with streamers of bark-cloth, hemp, or silk, or a branch of the sacred *sakaki* 榊 tree *(Cleyera japonica)* with cloth or paper hung on it, and so on. The five colors of coarse silk or pongee and the bark-cloth and hemp were symbolic. While *goshiki* 五色 may simply mean 'five kinds', it here signifies strips or streamers of pongee in blue, red, yellow, white and black. These colors are derived from the natural dyes: blue from the wild indigo plant, red from a fine red-yellow earth, yellow from either safflower or the seeds of gardenia, white is bleached

white, and black is made from the acorn-like nut of *tsurubami* 橡 *(Corylus heterophylla)*. Cf. *Kokushi jiten,* IV, p. 90.

154　*Shizu* or *shidori* 倭文, a cloth woven from fibers, usually hemp but paper-mulberry and ramie were also used, in which the woof threads were dyed blue, red, and so forth, to make a mottled pattern.

155　Hemp and bark-cloth represent the primeval clothing materials, and in the period under discussion were used for the clothing of common people and also in religious offerings. Bark-cloth, *yū* 木綿, was made by stripping, soaking and pounding the inner bark of the paper-mulberry, of which two varieties were used: *kaji* 構 *(Broussonetia kazinoki)* and *kōzo* 楮 *(Broussonetia papyrifera)*. The product resembles the kapa or tapa of the Polynesians. This and other types of bark-cloth are still made in some parts of Japan today. Cf. S. Gotō, *Nihon fukusō-shi,* p. 37.

156　Strictly speaking *yōfu* 庸布 is read *chikara-shiro-nuno,* cloth in lieu of labor, or 'corvée cloth'. In the Heian period, however, commutation of forced labor had given way to simple collection of taxes of which this was one. The cloth was primarily of hemp.

157　*Yokura-oki* and *yakura-oki* were types of offering-tables made of four or of eight pieces of wood, respectively. The former stood 1 *shaku* 2 *sun* high, the latter 2 *shaku* 4 *sun*. They came into being for the purpose of placing expiatory offerings*

1 shield, 1 spearhead, 1 bow, 1 quiver, a pair of deer antlers, one mattock,[158] 4 *shō* of sake, 5 *ryō* each of abalone and bonito,[159] 2 *shō* of dried meat,[160] 6 *ryō* each of *wakame, arame*[161] and assorted seaweeds, 1 *shō* of salt, 1 wine-jar of sake, 5 *shaku* of leaf-matting for wrapping.

106 presentations:

For each, 5 *shaku* of pongee, 1 *shaku* each of five colors of thin pongee, 2 *ryō* of bark-cloth, 5 *ryō* of hemp; one each: sword case of colored hemp-cloth, sword case of pongee and sword case of ordinary cloth; one *yokura-oki* and one *yakura-oki*, 1 shield, 1 spearhead, 5 *shaku* of leaf-matting for wrapping.

For the 433 presentations for the *Toshigoi* which are not offered up on top of the tables: all are 'small' rank—six in the Palace; in the Inner Provinces, in Yamashiro 69, in Yamato 158, in Kawachi 90, in Izumi 61 and in Settsu 49.

At 375 Shrines:

for each presentation, 3 *shaku* of pongee, 2 *ryō* of bark-cloth, 5 *ryō* of hemp, one *yokura-oki*, one *yakura-oki*, 1 shield, 1 spearhead, 1 *jō* 4 *shaku* of tax cloth, 3 *shaku* of leaf-matting for wrapping; for 65 of the presentations, one mattock and 1 quiver each and for 28 of them, an additional mattock, and for three a quiver each. (See the *Jimmyō-chō*).[162]

For 58 presentations:

for each, 3 *shaku* of pongee, 2 *ryō* of bark-cloth, 5 *ryō* of hemp, one *yokura-oki,* one *yakura-oki*, 1 shield, 1 spearhead, 3 *shaku* of leaf-matting for wrapping. The foregoing are celebrated by the *Jingi-kan*, the symbolic offerings are prepared as prescribed above and the same reported to the *Jingi-kan*. The deities to be worshiped by the Three Royal Persons,[163] the Heir Apparent and the Sacred Maidens[164] receive 8 presentations each with

---

*(harae-tsu-mono 祓つ物) before the deities to atone for a defilement. Later they were customarily used in the purification (harae 祓).

158 The character is 鍬, which may be read *suki*, a spade or digging tool, or *kuwa,* a mattock or hoe. Whichever interpretation is used, the tool symbolizes the commencing of tilling to plant the rice which is the source of nourishment for the people.

159 *Awabi* 鮑 (abalone or sea-ear) and *katsuo* 鰹 (bonito) were obtained from particularly designated waters of the sea for use in offerings to the deities. The small-size abalone were ceremonially cut with a purified knife and sprinkled with salt and the dried strips tied in special fashion for presentation.

160 *Kitai* 腊, jerky or dried strips of meat from deer or other animals. The frequent appearance of this item and the large amounts of it indicate that meat was commonly eaten and was apparently forbidden (in the *kami* religion) only at times of fasting for purification purposes *(ara-imi and ma-imi*, cf. n. 174).

161 *Wakame* (or me) 海藻 *(Undaria pinnatifida Sur.* or *Alaria pinnatifida)* and *arame* (or *manaka-*

shi) 滑海藻 *(Ecklonia bicyclis* or *Eisenia bicyclis)* are common, edible seaweeds which most frequently appear in the lists of food offerings. It may be that these two are chosen for the symbolism in their names: *wakame* is also called *nikime* 和布, so that together with *arame* it would constitute 'soft and coarse' offerings from the sea.

162 Cf. n. 34. It is a complete list of the government sponsored shrines (*kansha* 官社) throughout the country, arranged by region (circuit), province and district. Names of deities are given only for the most important shrines, in and around the Capital and inner provinces.

163 The 'Three Great Ones' or Three Royal Persons, after Chinese tradition, are the mother of the Sovereign, the Empress Dowager and the Empress Consort.

164 *Mikanko* or *mikannagi* 御巫 is here translated 'Sacred Maidens', as they are the young women in charge of sacred duties in the Imperial Palace, the *Jingi-kan* and the large shrines. The etymology of the term is disputed, one theory being that it comes from *kamu-nagi* 神和, to propitiate or calm the deities. Their pristine function is thought to be that of mediums.

offerings placed on top of the tables. But on occasion there may be increase or decrease, so a fixed number is not stated. At the Shrine of the Great Deity and the Watarai Shrine[165] a horse is added for each (1 *tan* of tax cloth for headstalls of their bridles). To the Mitoshi Shrine[166] are added: a white horse, a white boar and a white cock. One horse is added for each of these: Takami-musubi-no-kami and Oomiyanome-no-kami[167] and to each of these 19: the *yamanokuchi* shrines of Amakashi, Asuka, Iware, Osaka, Hase, Yoshino, Kose, Kamo, Taima, Oosaka, Ikoma, Tsuke, Yagyū, as well as the *mikomari* shrines of Yoshino, Uda, Katsuragi and Chikkei.[168] For the ceremonial headdresses for members of the *Jingi-kan* and others who wear them, 1 *kin* of Aki bark-cloth; for the Nakatomi who recites the ritual[169] are required 5 *tan* of tax cloth and one short mat. (For the *Tsukinami* festival and Great New Food Festival the requirements for headdresses and ritual recitation are the same as this.) Fifteen days before the festival day 8 members of the Imbe[170] and a Palace Woodworker are ordered to make the ceremonial articles for offerings to deities. (But the quivers are made by the quiver-weavers, and spearhandles are sent up by the Province of Sanuki to be received by the Bureau of Carpentry 5 days before the festival.) An official of the Imbe inspects the making of them.

But if there is no one of official rank in the Imbe and there are not enough for the complement of nine Imbe in the *kambe*,[171] one of the civil officials is made to serve in dual capacity. Required for their pure robes:[172] 2 *jō* 7 *shaku* of ordinary cloth per person (1 *tan* fine-weave for officials of rank). Allotments per day for a person: 2 *shō* of rice, 6 *gō* of sake (1 *shō* for 5th Rank), 3 *ryō* of sushi[173] (5 *ryō* for 5th Rank as well as 2 *ryō* each of Azuma abalone, squid and boiled bonito), 2 *shaku* of salt (5 *shaku* for 5th Rank), 2 *ryō* of *wakame*. But material for pure robes and the foregoing foodstuffs are not furnished to the woodworkers. On the day of total abstinence,[174] at daybreak the various symbolic offerings are consecrated both on top and below the

---

165 That is, the Shrine of the Great Deity (Sun Goddess) and the Watarai Shrine, treated in Bk. IV, below.

166 Mitoshi (or Mitoshiro) 御歳, shrine to an agricultural deity.

167 Two of the eight deities enshrined in the *Jingi-kan*, in the *hasshinden*.

168 These are the deities controlling water supply and distribution enshrined in the *yamanokuchi* ('opening of the mountain') and *mikomari* ('water-dividing') shrines. Some of the locations listed have more than one shrine, hence the total of 19. Cf. the list of shrines for the *Amagoi* festival in Yamato Prov. given in Bk. III.

169 *Norito (notto* or *notokoto)* 祝詞.

170 Imbe (Imube, Imibe) 忌部 were hereditary 'abstainers' or avoiders of pollution. From prehistoric days they 'performed or supervised rites of abstention, the observance of taboos, on behalf of the whole community, so as to ensure the ceremonial purity of worship.' G. B. Sansom,

A History of Japan to 1334, p. 36.

171 *Kambe* or *kamutomo* 神部 were officials of the *Jingi-kan* appointed from the Nakatomi or Imbe Uji. The Taihō Code specified their number as 30.

172 Pure robes, *kiyomawari* 潔衣, were a type of sacred robe (*saifuku*) which was made of hemp-cloth ceremonially cleansed and worn only for *kami* affairs. The *hosonuno* 細布 or 'fine-weave' was a finely spun and woven hemp resembling linen, as it is sometimes translated.

173 Sushi 鮨: fish or meat, pickled and eaten with rice.

174 Preceding the *Toshigoi-matsuri* and other festivals of its rank, officials who were to participate practiced partial abstinence, *ara-imi* 散齋, for 3 days, and complete abstinence, *ma-imi* 致齋, for one day prior to the commencement of festival ceremonies. Collectively these fast days are called *saibi* 齋日, days of avoidance.

offering tables in the Sai-in[175] of the *Jingi-kan* (the officials in charge having previously spread the offering mats beneath the ceremonial tables). The Bureau of Housekeeping[176] sets up the seats within and without. (The setting up of seats is the same for the other festivals.) The officials of the *Jingi-kan* lead the procession of Sacred Maidens and others and enter through the Center Gate and take their places by the West Building. They face east with rank ascending to the north.[177] The Great Ministers and below enter through the North Gate and take seats by the North Building. (The Great Ministers face south, Imperial Advisers[178] and above take seats to the east of the building and face west; princes and masters[179] take seats to the west of the building and face east.)

The Sacred Maidens go to seats at the foot of the building. The higher officials[180] enter through the South Gate and go to seats in the South Building. They face north with rank ascending to the east. The *kambe* leading the *hafuribe*[181] and others, enter and stand in the court south of the West Building. Officials of the *Jingi-kan* already have come down to their seats in front of the building. The Great Ministers and below and all the host of officials come down to their seats in front of the building. The Nakatomi come forward to their seats and recite the ritual.[182] At the end of each stanza the *hafuribe*

[175] The Sai-in 齋院, the taboo or sacred court-yard of the *Jingi-kan,* was also written 西院 'west courtyard'. Here in a large rectangular area, south of the Main or North Building of the *Jingi-kan,* we must picture the four sides set up with temporary shelters and seats (i.e. seat-mats) especially for the festival. This description of the arrangement of positions for the *Toshigoi* celebration serves as a guide for subsequent festival procedures within the compound of the *Jingi-kan.*

[176] The *kamon-ryō* 掃部寮, a bureau under the Ministry of the Imperial Household (*kunai-shō* 宮內省) is treated in *E-S,* Bk. XXXVII.

[177] The Center Gate connects the East with the West (or Sacred) Courtyard, so that these officials enter and file across the court by the West Building, and are facing eastward. Since the north, according to Chinese tradition, was the place of highest honor, the highest officials (of the *Dajō-kan*) are located there, and all other officials are arranged in descending order of rank from north towards south, or as the text says, their rank 'ascends to the north'.

[178] *Sangi* 参議 (Imperial Advisers), of which the full complement was eight, in the *Dajō-kan.*

[179] *Daibu (taifu)* 大夫 was the title of the highest official of the Palace Table Office (*daizen-shiki* 大膳職), the Office of the Imperial Consort's Palace (*chūgū-shiki* 中宮職) and other offices under ministries of the government.

[180] That is, the *gunkan* 群官, generic for the high officials of *Dajō-kan* and *Jingi-kan,* as opposed

to the *moromoro-no-tsukasa* 諸司 *(shoshi),* officials of all descriptions of lesser ranks.

[181] *Hafuri* or *hafuri-be* 祝部 is used not only for lesser priests at the shrines but also as a generic term for the three grades of shrine priests: *kannushi, negi* and *hafuri.* Since the upper grades of *kannushi* (chief of the shrine) and *negi* (petitioner) are not mentioned in this passage, the term *hafuri* appears to refer collectively to the three levels of priests.

[182] Text of the *norito* for the *Toshigoi-matsuri* is given in *E-S,* bk. VIII. In his translation, Philippi calls it the 'Grain-Petitioning Festival' *(norito)* addressed to the Sovereign Deities of the Grain, a small portion of which goes:
Then the first fruits will be presented
    In a thousand stalks, eight hundred stalks;
Raising high the soaring necks
    Of the countless wine vessels, filled to the
        brim;
Both in liquor and in stalks I will fulfill your
    praises.
From that which grows in the vast fields and
    plains—
    The sweet herbs and the bitter herbs—
To that which lives in the blue ocean—
    The wide-finned and the narrow-finned
        fishes
    The seaweeds of the deep and the seaweeds
        of the shore—
As well as garments
    Of colored cloth, radiant cloth,★

make the verbal response.[183] When the recitation is over the Nakatomi withdraw and the Great Ministers and below and the host of officials clap hands twice. They do not make the verbal response. But after this all return to their original seats. The chief of the *Jingi-kan* gives the order for the symbolic offerings to be distributed and presented. The chief ritualist[184] makes the verbal response and two Imbe come forward and stand on either side of the offering-tables. The chief ritualist as his official duty calls to the Sacred Maidens and the *hafuri* of the shrines. The *hafuri* make the verbal response and come forward. The Imbe complete distribution of the symbolic offerings (the symbolic offering for the Shrine of the Great Deity[185] is placed on a separate offering-table and a messenger is sent to present it). The chief ritualist returns to his seat and announces that distribution of the symbolic offerings is done; the host of officials withdraw. (Ceremonial for the *Tsukinami* festival is the same as this.)

The presentations to 2,395 *Toshigoi* deities by the Provincial Governments: 188 are Great (33 in the Tōkaidō Region, 38 in the Tōzandō, 13 in the Hokurikudō, 36 in the San'indō, 12 in the San'yōdō, 19 in the Nankaidō, and 38 in the Saikaidō). For each presentation 3 *ryō* of silk thread and 3 *ryō* of floss silk are required.

Presentations to 2,207 Minor Deities (680 in the Tōkaidō, 340 in the Tōzandō, 338 in the Hokurikudō, 523 in the San'indō, 124 in the San'yōdō, 134 in the Nankaidō and 69 in the Saikaidō). For each presentation 2 ryō of silk thread and 2 *ryō* of floss silk are required.

For the foregoing the Governor of the Province and those under him follow precedent. They perform partial abstinence for 3 days and total abstinence for one day, then they celebrate the festival. (The day of the festival and ceremony of dividing the symbolic offerings conforms to those celebrated by the *Jingi-kan*.)

One presentation for the Naru-ikazuchi-no-kami[186] (repeated in the 11th month; enshrined in Sōnokami District, Yamato Prov.):

2 *hiki* of pongee, 2 skeins of silk thread, 2 *mochi* of floss silk, 6 *shaku* each of five colors of thin pongee, 4 *shaku* of colored hemp-cloth, 2 *tan* of tribute cloth,[187] 2 *tan* of tax cloth, 1 *kin* each of bark-cloth and hemp, 4 mattocks, 5 *to* of white rice, 2 *to* of glutinous rice, 1 *to* each of soybeans and red beans, 2 *to* of sake, 4 *soku* of rice-in-ear, 2 *kin* each of abalone, bonito and assorted

---

*Plain cloth and coarse cloth—
In these I will fulfill your praises.
Before the Sovereign Deities of the Grain
   I will provide a white horse, a white boar,
  a white cock,
   And various types of offerings. . . .
(quoted from D. L. Philippi, *Norito,* pp. 17–18)

183 The verbal response, *ishō* 稱唯, sounded like 'Oh!', and was the expression of assent or approval. Since it is written this way and not phonetically represented one cannot give the exact sound of it; but 'Aye!' in English would be equivalent in meaning.

184 *Sokan* 史, the chief ritualist of the *Jingi-kan.*

185 *Oomikami-no-miya* 大御神宮, the shrine of the Great Deity (the Sun Goddess) in the province of Ise.

186 Naru-ikazuchi or Koikazuchi-no-kami 鳴 雷神, the Thunder God.

187 *Chōfu* 調布 or *tsukinuno*, was cloth, mainly of hemp, exacted as tribute from the provinces and constituting a type of tax additional to tax or *corvée* cloth.

dried meat, 5 salmon, 2 *to* assorted sushi, 2 *kin* of *wakame*, 2 *kin* assorted seaweeds, 2 *to* of salt, money for purchase of fruit (amount according to season), two white-wood boxes,[188] 4 cypress-wood boxes, one high table, 2 earthenware jugs, 4 cooking-pots, 20 uncovered dishes, 4 gourds,[189] 1 bale of oak wood, 4 straw-mats, 6 food-mats, one palanquin[190] (foregoing are required for the festival); 2 *tan* of tax cloth, 1 *kin* each of bark-cloth and hemp, 4 mattocks, 1 *to* of rice, 1 *to* of sake, 2 *soku* of rice-in-ear, 4 *kin* each of abalone and bonito, 1 *to* of dried meat, 6 *kin* of *wakame*, 6 *kin* assorted seaweeds, 4 *shō* of salt, 2 earthenware bottles, 5 saucers, 2 seat-mats, one palanquin (foregoing are required for the Purification). For the ritual, a tunic of the color assigned to the rank,[191] 3 *jō* 7 *shaku* of dark-blue pongee, 3 *jō* 5 *shaku* of green silk for the lining. For the above one member of the Nakatomi is sent to make the festival offerings.

Festival to the Four Kasuga Deities.[192]

Required for the festival deities:

1 great *kin* of Aki bark-cloth, 7 *shaku* of pongee, 2 *jō* 3 *shaku* of tribute cloth (foregoing are government goods, requested from the *Jingi-kan*), 1 *tan* 8 *shaku* bleached cloth, 12 *tan* of commercial cloth,[193] 8 round boxes[194] (foregoing are sustenance goods[195] requested from the Imperial Table Office); 6 *soku* of rice-in-ear (to be sent by the *Jingi-kan*), 3 *to* each of rice and glutinous rice, 5 *shō* each of soybeans and red beans (foregoing to be sent by the Palace

---

[188] *Akabitsu* 明櫃, lit., 'radiant box', was a type of box made of white unfinished wood in which ceremonial articles were kept.

[189] Two different characters are used which can be translated 'gourd'. The first is *hisago* or *shaku* 勺, 杓, a gourd used as a dipper measure and holding 1/10 of a *gō*. The second is *narihisago* 匏 (used here), which Thunberg says Kaempfer identified as *Cucurbita lagenaria,* one of at least nine varieties of gourds, and used commonly as a utensil. For convenience I use 'dipper' for the first and 'gourd' for the second in translating.

[190] Palanquins of various styles were used for members of the Imperial House or highest nobility. The type given here is *koshiko* 輦籠 or *koshikago.* Other names include *koshi* 輿, *tagoshi* 腰輿, *gayo* 賀輿, and so on. They not only served to transport the august personage but to shield him or her from public view as well.

[191] *Tōjiki* 當色, 'appropriate color', refers to Court robes of Rank dyed in colors prescribed by law for that Rank. According to regulations issued under Kōtoku Tennō in Taika 3 (A.D. 647) part of the scheme for seven colors and 13 ranks and six hats or caps was:

Great and Small Woven Cap
  Dress Color: Deep Violet
Great and Small Embroidered Cap
  Dress Color: Same
Great and Small Violet Cap

  Dress Color: Light Violet
Great and Small Brocade Cap
  Dress Color: True scarlet
Great and Small Blue Cap
  Dress Color: Dark blue
Great and Small Black Cap
  Dress Color: Green

(Based on N. Nagashima, *Nihon ifuku-shi.*) The system was called *tōjiki kinjiki no sei*, 'system of prescribed and prohibited colors'. The regulations were modified after Taika with the inclusion of additional Court Ranks. In this particular passage, the *nakatomi* official who recites the ritual is to receive articles of clothing and silk for his robes.

[192] The Kasuga festival, still held today, venerated the four deities enshrined in the Kasuga Shrine in Nara. These were the *ujigami* 氏神 of the Fujiwara Uji who were moved to this shrine when it was founded.

[193] *Tan'i* 商布, or *shōfu*, was cloth used for exchange purposes, as opposed to tribute cloth (*tsukinuno, chōfu*) and cloth in lieu of forced labor (*chikarashiro-nuno, yōfu* 庸布).

[194] Round boxes, *hako* 筥, to contain cooked rice.

[195] *Fumotsu* 封物 was the paddy tax (*denso* 田租) and other goods collected from sustenance households (*fuko* 封戸), in this case to support the Imperial House.

Kitchen Bureau), 1 *koku* 5 *to* of sake (use sake brewed at the shrine), 5 *shō* of salt, 6 *kin* each of abalone, bonito, squid, sea-bream and *wakame*, 12 *kin* of dried meat, 2 *to* of assorted fruit, 1 *to* of citrus fruit, 4 Kara stoves,[196] 2 large jars, 2 chopping-bowls, 6 jugs, 10 cooking-pots, 6 washing vessels, 40 each of uncovered dishes and saucers, 20 deep bowls, 30 cups, 8 sake cups (add stands), 2 water-buckets, 4 split-wood boxes, 4 gourds, 2 dippers, 1 winnowing-basket, 1 large basket, 2 bales of oak wood, 4 reed mats, 10 food-mats (foregoing are sent by the Palace Table Office).

Requirements for the Scattering Ceremony:[197]

20 sheets of white paper, 40 sheets of colored paper, 1 *tan* of bleached cloth (foregoing are sustenance goods), 6 *to* of sake (use sake brewed at the shrine) 2 *jō* each of five colors of thin pongee, 2 *kin* of bark-cloth, 1 *kin* of hemp, 100 strips of bark-cloth in five colors, 200 beads in five colors, 1 *hiki* of pongee, 1 skein of silk thread, 1 *mochi* of floss silk (foregoing are government goods, requested from the *Jingi-kan*), 1 *to* 5 *shō* each of rice and glutinous rice, 5 *shō* each of soybeans and red beans (foregoing to be sent from the Palace Kitchen Bureau), 6 *kin* each of abalone, bonito and seabream, 2 salmon, 6 *kin* of *wakame*, 5 *shō* of salt, 3 *to* of assorted fruit, 1 bale of oak wood, 4 splitwood boxes, 2 food-mats (foregoing to be sent by the Palace Table Office).

Requirements for the purification:[198]

2 *shaku* each of five colors of thin pongee, 3 *kin* of bark-cloth, 2 *kin* of hemp, 4 mattocks (foregoing are government goods, requested from the *Jingi-kan*), 7 *shō* of sake (use sake brewed at the shrine), 2 basketfuls of abalone, bonito and dried meat, 6 *kin* of *wakame*, 1 *shō* of salt, 1 jug (foregoing are sent by the Palace Table Office), 5 *shō* of rice (sent by the Palace Kitchen Bureau), 2 *soku* of rice-in-ear (sent by the *Jingi-kan*), 1 *tan* of tax cloth and 2 *tan* of commercial cloth. (The foregoing are sustenance goods.)

Required for adorning the sanctuaries:[199]

2 *jō* 4 *shaku* each of five colors of thin pongee, 4 *shaku* of pongee, 1 *mochi* of floss silk, 8 *kin* of bark-cloth, 1 *kin* of hemp (foregoing are government goods requested from the *Jingi-kan*), 10 *kin* of rattan, 1 log of cypress (foregoing are sent by the Bureau of Carpentry), 6 *ryō* of silk thread for stringing the *koto* (sent by the *Jingi-kan*).

Required for brewing the deity sake and for food for brewers (order these before the festival):

4 *koku* of unpolished rice, 5 *shaku* of tribute cloth, 2 gourds, 1 dipper, 1

---

[196] *Kara* was an old term for the Empire of China. Here, the character 韓, which meant the Korean states. The connotation of '*kara*' is exotic or foreign-style and it is used for articles of Chinese or Korean design: *karakama*, the cook-stove here, *karagushi* (n. 206), *karabitsu* (n. 329) and *karakagi* (n. 373).

[197] Festival or ceremony of scattering, in which paper was cut in small bits (*kiri-nusa* 切幣)

and scattered in order to cleanse and purify an area.

[198] In this case *harae* is written *kaijo* 解除 (instead of 祓) but the meaning is the same: lit. 'driving out', a process of removing defilement from the shrine area.

[199] That is, the *shinden* 神殿, or *miaraka*, in which the deities are enshrined.

winnowing basket, 1 Kara stove, 10 bundles of oak (foregoing are sustenance goods used for brewing the sake), 14 sake jugs, 2 great jars for sake (to collect the sake on the festival day), 1 *tan* of tax-cloth (to cover 4 large jars and 14 jugs), 3 *to* 6 *shō* of white rice, 3 *shō* of sushi, 30 bundles of *wakame*, 9 *gō* of salt (foregoing are for food for one brew mistress and 2 brewers for 15 days).

Required for purification of the brewing of deity sake:[200]

4 *shaku* each of five colors of silk, 4 *jō* of pongee, 4 skeins of silk thread, 4 *mochi* of floss silk, 2 *kin* each of bark-cloth and hemp, 1 *to* of white rice, 2 *to* of sake, 6 *kin* each of abalone, bonito, dried meat and *wakame*, 4 *shō* of salt, 4 *soku* of rice-in-ear, 8 sheets of yellow-bark,[201] 4 each of mattocks, bottles and earthenware jugs, 6 saucers, 2 food-mats, 1 gourd, 20 bundles of oak, 4 *tan* of tax cloth, 1 *tan* of ordinary cloth[202] for reciting the ritual.

Required for Festival to the Stove for Brewing Deity Sake (to be requested before the festival):

2 *shaku* each of five colors of silk, 1 *shaku* colored hemp-cloth, 8 *ryō* each of bark-cloth and hemp, 2 mattocks, 4 *shō* each of rice and sake, 2 *kin* each of abalone and bonito, 8 *ryō* of dried meat, 2 *kin* of *wakame*, 2 *shō* of salt, 1 *tan* of ordinary cloth for reciting the ritual.

Required for sacred robes:[203]

for one *mono-imi*,[204] 3 *jō* 5 *shaku* of stencil-dyed silk,[205] one silk-gauze sash, 4 *ryō* of violet silk thread, 1 pair of brocade shoes (foregoing are sustenance goods), 2 lengths of brocade (one 3 *shaku* 5 *sun*, the other 6 *shaku* long, both 4 *sun* wide), 3 *hiki* 2 *jō* 9 *shaku* of pongee, 1 *hiki* of green pongee, 7 *shaku* of thin silk, 2 Kara combs,[206] 1 *kin* 2 *ryō* of safflower,[207] 3 *shaku* 5 *sun* of Azuma

---

200 *Miwa* 神酒, the sake brewed for offering to the deities.

201 Yellow-bark, *kihada* 黄蘗, refers to the inner bark of a species of oak, *Pterocarpus flavus*, which was used as a medicine and as dyestuff. It produced the color 'chrome lemon' *(kihada-iro)*. *Shikimei daijiten.*

202 *Nuno* 布 *(fu)* meant plain, or ordinary cloth, usually made from hemp, although ramie, *kudzu* and other fibres were used. When finely woven, hemp-cloth resembled linen.

203 Sacred robes, *saifuku* 齋服 were usually white, and worn over court dress *(sōzoku* 装束*)* by officials participating in ceremonies and festivals to the deities. If a color design was worn it was *aozuri* 青摺 (see n. 308, below). The sash worn with such robes was red-violet in color, 1 *jō* 4 *shaku* in length, and was dyed by pounding on *suō* 蘇芳 (Judas-tree) dye. Other types of *saifuku* include pure robes, *kiyomawari* (n. 172) and lustrous robes, *akawa (myōe)* (n. 220). N. Nagashima, *Nihon ifuku-shi*, pp. 334–5.

204 *Mono-imi* 物忌, lit. 'abstainers from things', were children who served the shrine and

were entrusted with celebrating festivals. To distinguish them, boys were called *miyamori* 宮守 or *ōmonoimi*, and girls were called *kora* 子良. Their abstinence consisted of observing prohibitions concerning food and drink and avoiding contact with defilement of any sort. Adult abstainers were *imbe. Kōgaku sōsho*, III, p. 6.

205 *Kyōkechi* 夾纈 was a method of dyeing silks which reached its height of development in the Nara period but the technical details of which have since been lost. The material to be dyed was folded double and clamped between two thin boards having perforated design, then the dye was applied. Some fine examples survive in the Shōsōin 正倉院 collection, including a piece of stencil-dyed silk gauze and a screen of silk on which the bisymmetric design is softly executed. L. Katoh, *Textiles*, p. 4; and K. Morita, *Nihon no senshoku*, pl. 28.

206 *Karagushi* 韓櫛, 'Chinese combs', were more elaborately decorated than the plain white-wood domestic ones.

207 *Kurenai* or *benibana* 紅花, used to produce a pinkish-red dye.

pongee,[208] 3½ *mochi* of floss silk, 5 *shō* of gardenias.[209] For robes of color prescribed for their rank—for one chief priest[210] and for one member of the *Jingi-kan* (these to be furnished by the Bureau of Palace Storehouses), 2 *hiki* of pongee, 2 *mochi* of floss silk (foregoing are government goods), 2 *tan* of fine-weave cloth, 2 *tan* of tribute cloth (sustenance goods), 2 *hiki* of pongee for kneeling cushions for the chief priest, 3 skeins of silk thread and 2 *tan* of tribute cloth. For each of two players of the sacred *koto*,[211] 1 *hiki* 3 *jō* of pongee, 3 *mochi* of floss silk. For each of 8 cooks and 2 diviners, 2 *jō* 7 *shaku* of tribute cloth from Sado, 2 *ryō* of safflower (foregoing are government goods). For each of two guards for the sanctuary, 2 *tan* of commercial cloth (foregoing are sustenance goods).

The requirements for the festival are as stated above and it is celebrated on the first monkey day, in spring the 2nd month and winter the 11th month. The sustenance goods come out of 500 *tan* of tribute cloth from deity sustenance of Katori[212] and Kashima[213] Great Shrines of Shimōsa and Hitachi, respectively (200 *tan* of deity sustenance from Katori and 300 from Kashima); 300 *tan* of tax cloth, 600 *tan* of commercial cloth, 600 *kin* of hemp (foregoing is deity sustenance from Kashima) and 600 sheets of paper (deity sustenance from Katori) are collected and sent to the *Jingi-kan,* then are stored in its storehouse. They are apportioned and used according to the text above, the officials in charge preparing and allotting as required.

For one *mono-imi* the food for one day is: 1 *shō* 2 *gō* of white rice, 1 *shaku* 2 *satsu* of salt; for two members of the *kambe* who are in charge, per day: 1 *shō* 6 *gō* of white rice, 1 *shaku* 6 *satsu* of salt; for two manservants (manservants from deity sustenance of Kashima Shrine in Hitachi Prov.) each per day: 2 *shō* unpolished rice, 2 *shaku* of salt. For clothing for each *kambe*: in summer, 4 *jō* 5 *shaku* of pongee, in winter, 1 *hiki* 2 *jō* of pongee and 4 *mochi* of floss silk (deity sustenance goods used for both).

Festival to the Four Deities of Ooharano[214]

Requirements for this festival are the same as for the Kasuga festival. It is

---

208 *Azuma* 東, 'the East', was a general term for the eastern seaboard provinces.

209 *Kuchinashi* 支子, or *Gardenia florida, L.,* the dried seeds of which were used to produce a yellow dye for silks, and were also used in medicine.

210 *Kannushi* 神主 *(kamunushi)* was the chief of a shrine who held his position by imperial appointment. The title *kanzukasa* 神司 *(kamutsukasa)* was equivalent to this. (*Shintō daijiten*) Here it is the chief priest of Kasuga Shrine.

211 *Koto* 琴, the horizontal harp or zithern.

212 Katori Jingū 香取神宮 in Shimōsa 下總 Province was one seat of the *ujigami* (clan deities) of the Fujiwara Uji, and though the worship of these (Iwainushi-no-mikoto 伊波比主命 at least) was added to the Kasuga Jinja in the Capital in the Nara period, at the same time the deities of Katori were raised to 'Senior Fourth Rank, Lower

Grade' of Court Rank. The close relation between Katori and Kasuga shrines can be seen in this item which specifies deity sustenance support from one to the other. Miyagi, II, p. 483.

213 Kashima Jingū 鹿島神宮, in Hitachi 常陸 Province, was another seat of some *ujigami* of the Fujiwara. In the Nara period these deities were accorded 'Senior Third Rank' in the scale. It enshrined Takemikazuchi-no-mikoto 建御雷命 and Futsunushi-no-mikoto 經津主命, who became enshrined in the Kasuga Jinja in Nara after its founding. Miyagi, II, pp. 482–3.

214 The Festival of Ooharano to the four deities enshrined in Ooharano. This shrine and its festival are closely connected to the Kasuga and Hiraoka festivals and the Fujiwara family. Miyagi, I, 29; II, 432.

celebrated on the first hare day of the 2nd month in spring and on the middle rat day of the 11th month in winter.

Festival for the Three Deities of Sono and Kara[215] (one Sono and two Kara deities) [Required:]

8 *shaku* each of five colors of silk, 4 *shaku* each of stencil-dyed silk, violet tie-dyed silk,[216] scarlet silk, pale-green silk and glossy red silk, 2 *jō* of undyed silk, 2 *ryō* of glossy silk thread, 4 *jō* of fine-weave cloth, 2 *tan* of commercial cloth, 1 *kin* of Aki bark-cloth, 8 *kin* of common bark-cloth, 1 *kan* of coins, 4 round bells, 100 beads in five colors, 30 sheets of paper, 2 *to* of rice, 2 *to* of glutinous rice, 5 *shō* each of soybeans and red beans, 2 *to* 2 *shō* of sake, 2 *shō* of oil, 180 pieces of citrus fruit, 2 round boxes, 8 coarse boxes, 4 food-mats, 10 each of jugs and cooking-pots, 4 metal bowls, 6 jars, 40 saucers, 6 sake stands, 4 dishes, 4 cucurbits, 90 bundles of oak, 4 baskets of charcoal, 2½ burdens of kindling wood, 4 reed-mats (foregoing are for the festival to the deities); 3 *shaku* each of five colors of silk (for the *kagura*[217] in the morning).

1 *jō* 2 *shaku* of five colors of silk, 1 *hiki* of pongee, 4 *shaku* of blue silk, 2 skeins 8 *ryō* of silk thread, 2 *mochi* of floss silk, 2 *jō* each of five colors of thin pongee, 1 *tan* of tribute cloth, 2 *jō* of washed cloth, 4 *tan* of commercial cloth, 4 *kin* of common bark-cloth, 2 *kin* of hemp, 30 sheets of paper, 30 sheets of colored paper, 800 *mon* in coin, 4 mattocks, 8 *soku* of rice-in-ear (supplied by the *Jingi-kan*), 1 *to* of rice, 1 *to* 2 *shō* of sake, 1 *to* of soy dregs, 2 *tsubu* of salt, 10 saucers, 2 jars, 4 baskets of assorted dried meats, 30 sheets of yellow-bark, 20 bundles of oak (foregoing are for the Purification); 1 *koku* unpolished rice, 5 *to* of white rice, 1 *hiki* of pongee, 512 *mon* in coin (foregoing for brewing deity sake); 5 *to* 6 *shō* of cooked rice, 1 *to* 8 *shō* of sake (for 8 cooks, 2 diviners, and 10 persons of the Deity Mountain[218]).

Required for sacred robes:

for each of two *mono-imi*, 3 *jō* each of stencil-dyed silk and light green silk, 1 *hiki* 2 *jō* 5 *shaku* of pongee, 1 *hiki* 5 *jō* 6 *shaku* 5 *sun* of silk, one overskirt, one sash, 2 *jō* 4 *shaku* of blue silk, 1 *jō* 5 *shaku* of scarlet silk, 2 *ryō* of violet silk thread, 4 *mochi* of floss silk, 3 *shaku* 5 *sun* of Azuma pongee, 1 pair of shoes, 5 *ryō* of safflower, 5 *shō* of gardenias. For one Sacred Maiden, 1 *hiki* of pongee, 1 *hiki* of light green silk, 2 *mochi* of floss silk, one overskirt. For *mono-imi* and Sacred Maiden, 1 *hiki* of green pongee apiece. For one young girl who offers up the sacred articles, 1 *hiki* of pongee, 2 *mochi* of floss silk, 1 *tan* of tribute cloth, one overskirt. For two maidservants, 2 *jō* 1 *shaku* of tribute cloth, 2 *jō* 1 *shaku* of dark-blue cloth and 5 *shaku* of fine-weave cloth apiece. For the member of the *Jingi-kan*, one robe of color prescribed for his rank. For two

215 The Sono and Kara deities 園韓神 were worshiped within the Imperial Wine Office in the Palace.

216 *Yuhata* 纈 (a contraction of *yuihata*), also read *kukurizome,* corresponds to modern *shibori-zome* 絞染 or *shibori,* for tie-dyed silk. The *Wamyō-*

shō 和名抄 gives 由波太.

217 *Kagura* 神樂, lit. 'deity pleasure', is sacred music and dance performed for the entertainment of the deities as a part of the festival ceremonies.

218 *Kamiyamabito* 神山人.

koto players, 3 *jō* 6 *shaku* of yellow silk, 3 *jō* 6 *shaku* of silk and 3 *mochi* of floss silk apiece. For two diviners, 2 *jō* 7 *shaku* of tribute cloth apiece. For each of eight cooks, 2 *jō* 7 *shaku* of tribute cloth, 2 *ryō* of safflower. And for one watchman of the shrine, 1 *tan* of commercial cloth.

The above is celebrated on ox days in spring in the 2nd month, and in winter in the 11th month (in spring an ox day following the Kasuga festival is used, in winter an ox day preceding the New Food Festival). A person of Imperial Adviser's rank or higher comes to the place of the festival to attend the event; the arrival of his lady-in-waiting signals the beginning of celebration. But the officials in charge prepare the various requirements for offering. (See the *Gishiki* for this matter.)

Festival to the Four Oomiyanome Deities[219] (enshrined in the Imperial Wine Office):
2 *jō* 6 *shaku* each of five colors of pongee and of plain pongee, 4 *mochi* of floss silk, 2 *jō* 4 *shaku* of 6 large *kin* each of bark-cloth and hemp, 4 skeins of silk thread (all these for the symbolic offerings); 1 *jō* 8 *shaku* each of violet and of scarlet pongee (these are for deity garments and silk umbrellas); 2 *tan* 2 *shaku* plain cloth (for spreading, for coverings and for wrapping the symbolic offerings); 5 sheets of yellow-bark, 50 sheets of paper, 1 *koku* 2 *to* of white rice, 2 *to* 5 *shō* of glutinous rice, 6 *shō* each of soybeans and red beans, 9 *to* of sake, 20 *kin* each of abalone and bonito, 48 *kin* of dried meat, 2 *to* 5 *shō* of *sushi*, 8 salmon, 1 *to* 5 *shō* of salt, 500 *mon* in coin (for cost of fresh seafood, fresh fruits and unglazed pots), 4 *shō* of oil, 1 *mochi* of floss silk (for hanging the lamps), 4 bottles, 4 sake jars, 8 sake stands, 8 saucers, 8 each of jugs and cooking-pots, 4 white wood boxes, 6 split-wood boxes, 4 tables (each 4 *shaku* high and 2 *shaku* wide), 2 short tables, 8 food-mats, 8 gourds, 2 bales of oak, 9½ burdens of kindling wood (cost); 4 *soku* of rice-in-ear (sent by the *Jingi-kan*), one robe of color prescribed for rank (for the official who is chief priest and Imbe), 3 *hiki* of stiff silk, 3 skeins of silk thread (all for his kneeling cushions), 2 *tan* 2 *jō* 8 *shaku* of plain cloth (for lustrous robes[220] and divided skirts for four cooks).

The above required articles to be requested and received from the *Jingi-kan* in advance of the festival, which is celebrated on the first horse day in the 2nd month in spring and the 11th month in winter, and the chief of ceremonies makes them ready.

Festival to the Four Deities of Hiraoka :[221]
Required for the festival deities:
2 *jō* 4 *shaku* each of five colors of pongee, 4 skeins of silk thread, 4 *tan* of

---

[219] Oomiyanome-no-mikoto 大宮賣命 was one of the eight deities enshrined in the *Jingi-kan*. Here four deities including this one are worshiped in the Imperial Wine Office. Oomiyanome is traditionally another name for Ame-no-uzume-no-mikoto 天鈿女命. *Jingi-jiten*, p. 138.

[220] *Akawa* 明衣 or *myōe*, a kind of sacred robe (*saifuku*, n. 203) worn to maintain purity in festi-

vals. They were usually white, lustrous robes made of raw silk (生絹) worn over the customary clothing. *Kōgaku sōsho*, III, p. 62; *Shintō daijiten*, III, p. 325.

[221] Hiraoka Jinja 枚岡神社 in Kawachi 河內 Province (at present a *kampei taisha* 官幣大社 in Osaka pref.). This also was a shrine of the Fujiwara Uji, whose *ujigami*, namely: Ameno-koyane-no-*

bleached cloth, 8 *kin* of Aki bark–cloth, 8 *kin* of hemp, 1 *tan* 1 *jō* 7 *shaku* of commercial cloth for wrapping the symbolic offerings, 2 white-wood boxes, one box carrier and one carrying-pole (foregoing for the symbolic offerings are government goods, requested from the *Jingi-kan*), 4 *tan* of plain cloth (sustenance goods), 6 *to* 4 *shō* of white rice, 7 *to* of sake, 4 *shō* each of soybeans and red beans, 1 *to* of sushi, 4 *kin* of dried meat, 4 *kin* each of squid and bonito, 1 basket of assorted foods, 4 *kin* of *wakame*, 2 *kin* of *arame*, one fresh salmon, 4 *shō* of salt, 1 *to* 5 *shō* of fruit, 4 *soku* of rice-in-ear, 2 each of Kara stoves and large ceremonial jars, 1 winnowing basket, 4 water-bowls, 2 chopping bowls, 4 jugs, 5 cooking-pots, 2 sake jars, 4 each of washing vessels and coverless vessels, 20 covered dishes, 8 sake cups, 40 saucers, 2 dippers, 2 water-buckets, 4 gourds, 4 reed-mats, 12 food-mats, 1 large basket, 3 bales of oak, 5 burdens of kindling-wood. (For the foregoing use regular taxes[222] from Kawachi Prov.)

Required for the Purification:

2 *shaku* each of 5 colors of pongee, 3 *kin* of common bark-cloth, 2 *kin* of hemp, 4 mattocks, 2 *tan* of commercial exchange cloth, 1 *tan* of tax cloth (foregoing are government goods to be requested from the *Jingi-kan*); 1 *to* of sake, 3 *shō* of sushi, 2 *shō* of dried meat, 4 *kin* each of squid and bonito, 4 *kin* of *wakame*, 2 *shō* of salt, 2 *soku* of rice-in-ear, 3 jugs, 3 cooking-pots, 4 bottles, 6 saucers, 2 dippers, 2 water-buckets, 2 gourds, 2 food mats, 1 large basket, 12 sheets of yellow-bark. (For the foregoing use regular taxes from Kawachi Prov.)

Required for the Scattering Ceremony:

2 *jō* each of 5 colors of pongee, 1 *hiki* of pongee, 1 skein 4 *ryō* of silk thread, 2 *kin* of common bark-cloth, 2 *kin* of hemp, 20 sheets of paper, 1 *tan* of bleached cloth, 30 sheets of colored paper, 200 colored beads, 100 sheets of five colors of bark-cloth. (Foregoing are requested from the *Jingi-kan*.)

Required for Court dress[223] at the sanctuary:

2 *jō* 4 *shaku* of each of five colors of pongee, 4 *shaku* of pongee, 2 *kin* of hemp, 1 *mochi* of floss, 10 *kin* of rattan, 1 load of cypress wood. (Foregoing are government goods, to be requested from the *Jingi-kan*.)

Required for Festival to the Deity of the Stove for Brewing the Deity Sake (request these before the festival):

2 *shaku* each of five colors of pongee, 1 *shaku* of colored hemp-cloth, 8 *ryō* of bark-cloth, 2 mattocks. (Foregoing are government goods to be requested from the *Jingi-kan*.)

---

*mikoto, Himegami 比賣神, Takemikazuchi-no-mikoto (see n. 273) and Iwainushi-no-mikoto, were said to be added to the Kasuga Shrine at the Nara capital in the reign of Empress Gemmyō 元明 (A.D. 708–14).

222 *Shōzei* 正税 *ōchikara*, was the regular tax on land, paid to the government in rice. It was stored in government granaries and used to meet general expenses. R.K. Reischauer, A, p. 222. G.

Sansom calls it 'tax proper'; *TASJ*, ser. I, XI, p. 127.

223 Court dress, *shōzoku (sōzoku)* 装束, is the ceremonial dress and accessories required to be worn by officials of all ranks when on duty. Both male and female officials were bound by the rules of costume and color thereof by the regulations prescribed in the *tōjiki no sei* (see n. 191).

Required for purification in the brewing of deity sake (request these before the festival):

4 *shaku* each of five colors of pongee, 4 *jō* of pongee, 4 skeins of silk thread, 2 *kin* each of bark-cloth and hemp, 4 *tan* of tax cloth, 4 mattocks, 8 sheets of yellow-bark, 1 *tan* of cloth for cushions for reciting the ritual (foregoing are government goods to be requested from the *Jingi-kan*); 5 *to* of white rice (use regular taxes from Kawachi Prov.), 1 *tan* of tax cloth for various uses in storing the sake, 5 *shaku* of cloth for covering the mouths of the brewing jars (government goods, requested from the *Jingi-kan*), 1 Kara stove (for brewing the sake; from regular taxes of Kawachi Prov.).

Food required for the various attendants:[224]

1 *koku* 3 *shō* 2 *gō* of white rice, 1 *to* 8 *shō* of sushi, 11 *kin* 4 *ryō* of dried meat, 11 *kin* 4 *ryō* of wakame, 1 *shō* 8 *gō* of salt, 3 *to* 5 *shō* of sake (for all use regular taxes of Kawachi Prov.).

Required for sacred robes:

for Court dress for one *mono-imi*, 4 *hiki* 9 *shaku* of stiff silk, 3 *jō* 5 *shaku* of stencil-dyed pongee, 3 *mochi* 6 *ryō* of floss silk, 9 *shaku* 5 *sun* of brocade, 7 *shaku* of thin silk, 1 *kin* 3 *ryō* of safflower, 5 *shō* of gardenias, 1 pair of brocade shoes, 4 *ryō* of violet silk thread, two Kara combs; for the chief priest of the shrine, 1 garment of color prescribed for his rank; for one Court dress, 2 *hiki* of stiff silk, 2 *tan* of fine-weave cloth, 2 *mochi* of floss silk, 2 *tan* of plain cloth (same as this for one member of the *Jingi-kan*); for cushions, 2 *hiki* of stiff silk, 3 skeins of silk thread, 2 *tan* of plain cloth; for Court dress for one *koto* player, 1 *hiki* 3 *jō* of stiff silk, 3 *mochi* of floss silk, 2 *tan* of tax cloth; for 8 cooks, 6 *tan* 2 *jō* 8 *shaku* of plain cloth (3 *jō* 5 *shaku* apiece); 1 *kin* 4 *ryō* of safflower; for two diviners, 2 *tan* of commercial exchange cloth (1 *tan* apiece; all government goods requested from the *Jingi-kan*); for one *hafuri* and one *negi*,[225] each 12 *tan* of ordinary cloth (from sustenance goods).

Required for emoluments[226] for the same festival:

38 *tan* of tribute cloth (8 *tan* each for the messenger who bears the symbolic offerings and the chief priest, 2 *tan* for the *mono-imi*, 8 *tan* each for the *negi* and *hafuri*, 1 *tan* each for *koto* player and flute player, 1 *tan* each for two *urabe*), 16 *tan* of tax cloth (2 apiece for each of 8 cooks).

The above is celebrated on the first monkey day of the 2nd month in spring and the 11th month in winter. The official of the *Jingi-kan* leads the various attendants in participating in the matters of the festival.

---

224 *Zōshiki* 雑色, lit. 'of various colors'. Properly this term was used for members of the *kurōdodokoro* 藏人所, the Sovereign's Private Office. But in the *E-S* it is used to mean various functionaries of low rank.

225 *Negi* 禰宜, sometimes called high priests, were the class of priests below the *kannushi* (see n. 181) and above the *hafuri*. Prof. Kitagawa of Chicago Univ. uses the translation 'petitioner' on the basis that *negi* comes from *negau* 願う, to beseech, and the *negi* petitions the *kami* in behalf

of the worshiper. H. Zachert calls the *negi* 'der Beter' (*Semmyō* 宣命, 142). But Prof. K. Sakurai, *negi* of the Grand Shrine of Ise, believes the etymology to be based on the component *ne* being the same as that found in Oo-yamato-no-neko, an archaic title for the Sovereign, and *gi* being the masculine honorific ending, as found in *Izanagi-Izanami*, and *himorogi-himoromi*, and so on.

226 Emoluments, *roku* 祿, amounted to salary for the officials, functionaries and attendants who participated in the festival ceremonies.

FESTIVALS OF THE THIRD MONTH

Festival to the Two Hanashizume Deities[227]

One at the Oomiwa Shrine:[228]

    1 *hiki* of pongee, 1 skein 3 *ryō* of silk thread, 1 *mochi* of floss silk, 3 *shaku* each of five colors of thin pongee 6 *shaku* of colored hemp-cloth, 1 *tan* 1 *jō* of ordinary cloth, 3 *kin* 6 *ryō* each of bark-cloth and hemp, 6 *ryō* of nettle hemp,[229] 7 bows, 2 rounds of arrows, 10 deerskins (the 3 foregoing are supplied by the *Jingi-kan*), 2 feathers, 3 sets of deer antlers, 3 *kin* 5 *ryō* of iron, 1 *shō* of lacquer, 3 *kin* 5 *ryō* of yellow-bark, 10 *ryō* of madder-root,[230] 20 *kin* of rattan,[231] 5 *shō* of clear sake, 6 *to* 5 *shō* of turbid sake, 2 *kin* 6 *ryō* of abalone, 5 *kin* 5 *ryō* of bonito, 8 *shō* of dried meat, 5 *shō* 5 *ryō* of *wakame*, 2 *shō* of salt, 1 jug, 1 each: ritual clay urn,[232] spouted vessel, short-stemmed dish and sake cup, 2 leaf-mats for wrapping.

One at the Sai Shrine:[233]

    2 *hiki* of pongee, 3 skeins of silk thread, 1 *mochi* 4 *ryō* of floss silk, 3 *shaku* each of five colors of thin pongee, 6 *shaku* of colored hemp-cloth, 1 *tan* 1 *jō* of plain cloth, 6 *kin* 10 *ryō* each of bark-cloth and hemp, 8 *ryō* of nettle hemp, 7 bows, 2 rounds of arrows, 10 deerskins (*Jingi-kan* supplies the last three), 2 feathers, 4 pairs of deer antlers, 3 *kin* 5 *ryō* of iron, 1 *shō* of lacquer, 3 *kin* 5 *ryō* of yellow-bark, 1 *kin* of madder-root, 20 *kin* of rattan, 5 *shō* of clear sake, 6 *to* 5 *shō* of turbid sake, 3 *kin* of abalone, 5 *kin* 5 *ryō* of bonito, 8 *shō* of dried meat, 5 *kin* 5 *ryō* of *wakame*, 2 *shō* of salt, 1 each: ritual clay urn, spouted vessel, short-stemmed dish and sake cup, 2 leaf-mats for wrapping.

FESTIVALS OF THE FOURTH MONTH

To Three Deities of the Saigusa Festival[234] (at Izakawa Shrines):

[227] *Hanashizume* or *Chinka-sai* 鎮花祭, lit. the 'Festival of Pacifying the Flowers', was held at the end of the third month to give prayers for freedom from sickness. It was held to the two deities of Oomiwa 大神 and Sai 狭井, who were supposed to be the enshrined spirits of Oomono-nushi-no-kami 大物主神. The festival is said to have originated with the outbreak of an epidemic in the reign of Sujin Tennō 崇神天皇 (230–258?). *Jingi-jiten*, p. 612.

[228] In the *Jimmyo-chō* of *E-S* Bk. IX, this shrine is registered as the Oomiwa-ōmononushi (大神大物主) no Jinja in Shikinokami 城上 District, Yamato Prov., dedicated to the *nikimitama* 和御魂 (august benign spirit) of the god Oomono-nushi. A modern account says that 32 villages surround Mt. Miwa and the 30,000 people who are adherents (*ujiko* 氏子) of the Oomiwa Shrine do not go onto the sacred mountain or cut its trees. There is no worship hall because the mountain itself is the hall which enshrines the deity. H. Kishimoto, 'The Worship of Mt. Miwa', in *Guide to the Kansai Area*, pp. 35–6.

[229] Namely, *kemushi* 枲.

[230] *Akane* 茜, madder-root, used to make a bright scarlet dye. L. Katoh, *Textiles*, p. 66.

[231] *Tsuzura* 黒葛, a vine used for making baskets.

[232] *Tsubaha* 都婆波.

[233] The Sai-no-yashiro 狭井社, in the same district as Oomiwa Shrine, is recorded in the *Jimmyō-chō* (*E-S*, Bk. IX) as the shrine in which resides the *aramitama* 荒御魂 (august turbulent spirit) of Oomiwa.

[234] *Saigusa-matsuri* 三枝祭 was the festival of Izakawa-no-yashiro 率川社 in Yamato Prov., Isonokami 石上 District. It gets its name from the fact that the flowers of *saigusa* 三枝 (*saegusa*) are used to decorate sake casks for the celebration. H. Aida, *Chūkai yōrōryō*, p. 343.

1 *hiki* of pongee, 1 skein 3 *ryō* of silk thread, 5 *ryō* of floss silk, 1 *jō* 2 *shaku* each of five colors of thin pongee, 3 *shaku* of colored hemp-cloth, 2 *tan* 2 *shaku* of tribute cloth, 5 *tan* of tax cloth, 10 *kin* each of bark-cloth and hemp, 6 *ryō* of nettle hemp, 3 bows, 1 round of arrows, 1 feather, one pair of deer antlers, 3 *kin* 5 *ryō* of iron, 100 *soku* of rice-in-ear for sake (from deity taxes[235]), 2 *kin* of abalone, 4 *kin* of bonito, 6 *shō* of dried meat, 4 *kin* of *wakame*, 1 *shō* 5 *gō* of salt, 3 each of shallow jars, water basins, ritual clay urns, spouted vessels, short-stemmed dishes and sake cups, 15 saucers.

The symbolic offerings for the above 3 shrines as given in the foregoing text are assigned to the *hafuribe* to be offered at the festival.

For One Deity of the Oomi Festival[236] (Hirose Shrine; repeated in the 7th month):
1 *hiki* 8 *shaku* of pongee, 2 skeins of silk thread, 5 *ryō* of floss silk, 1 *jō* 5 *shaku* each of five colors of thin pongee, 1 *jō* 3 *shaku* of colored hemp-cloth, 1 *tan* 1 *jō* of tribute cloth, 1 *tan* 1 *jō* 4 *shaku* of tax cloth, 2 *ryō* of bark-cloth, 2 *kin* 5 *ryō* of hemp (5 *ryō* for the festival, 2 *kin* for the purification), one each *yokura-oki* and *yakura-oki*, 1 shield, 3 *kin* 5 *ryō* of iron, 1 saddle, 3 *koku* of rice, 2 *koku* 5 *to* of sake, 10 *soku* of rice-in-ear, 8 *kin* each of abalone, bonito and squid, 8 salmon, 8 *to* of dried meat, 1 *to* 5 *shō* of small dried fish,[237] 12 *kin* of *wakame*, 10 *kin* of *arame*, 16 *kin* of assorted seaweeds, 2 *to* of salt, 2 leaf-mats for wrapping, 1 horse, 2 *tan* of tax cloth for the *hafuri*. On the appointed day six presentations are made in the august districts[238] and 14 at *yamanokuchi* shrines. For each of those symbolic offerings: 1 *shaku* of each of five colors of thin pongee, 5 *sun* of colored hemp cloth, 2 *ryō* of bark-cloth, 5 *ryō* of hemp, 1 spearhead (use iron from the shrine's portion for this), one each *yokura-oki* and *yakura-oki*, 1 shield, 1 *jō* 4 *shaku* of tax cloth, 2 *shaku* of leaf-mat for wrapping. For sake and food shrine provisions are used. But for each of the six presentations in the august districts 3 *shaku* of pongee is added.

For Two Deities of the Kaze-no-kami Festival[239] (at Tatsuta Shrines; repeated in the 7th month):
2 *hiki* of pongee, 4 skeins of silk thread, 1 *mochi* 4 *ryō* of floss silk, 2 *jō* each of five colors of thin pongee, 1 *jō* 3 *shaku* of colored hemp-cloth, 1 *tan* 1 *jō* of

---

235 *Kamijikara* 神税, or *shinzei*, a tax in rice collected by official shrines. It was also called *kakejikara* 懸税 when the first ears of ripened rice were hung on the shrine fence as offering to the deities. See Aston, *Nihongi*, II, p. 336. After Taidō 大同 4 (A.D. 809) the amount of deity tax was regulated so as to increase the levy for support and maintenance of official shrines. Miyagi, *Engi-shiki no kenkyū*, II, p. 536.

236 *Oomi-matsuri*, according to the *Ryō no gige* 令義解, was held both at Hirose 廣瀬 and Tatsuta 龍田 Shrines to ensure pure water for the submerging of the rice seedlings and ensure their growth. Aida, *Chūkai yōrōryō*, p. 344.

237 The second time this term *hisame* 比佐魚

appears, an interlinear gloss explains that the word is 'small fish' and that in the *Nihongi* it is written 小雨.

238 The *mi-agata* 御縣 were districts (*kōri* 郡) the yield from which was collected to support the Imperial House.

239 The *Kasakamu* or *Kaze-no-kami matsuri* was held for the pair of 'wind gods', Shinatsuhiko-no-mikoto, and Shinatobe-no-mikoto, at Tatsuta in Heguri District, Yamato Prov. H. Aida, *op. cit.*, p. 344. The festival was regularized as far back as Temmu's reign, when it is mentioned in the 4th and 5th years (*Nihongi*), as well as in Empress Jitō's reign. The text here refers to 'two shrines' (*yashiro*).

plain cloth, 5 *tan* of tax cloth, 6 *kin* 9 *ryō* of hemp (5 *kin* 2 *ryō* for the festival, 1 *kin* 7 *ryō* for the purification), 8 *ryō* of nettle hemp, 4 bows, 1 round of arrows, 2 feathers (the two foregoing are sent by Yamato Prov.), 2 sets of deer antlers, 4 deerskins, 6 *kin* 10 *ryō* of iron, 2 saddles, 1 spindle, 1 shuttle and 1 reel (the last three items painted in gold),[240] 1 *shō* of lacquer, 1 *shō* of gold paint, 3 *kin* 5 *ryō* of yellow-bark, 16 *kin* 9 *ryō* of nettle hemp, 20 *kin* of rattan, 1 *koku* 5 *to* each of rice and sake, 5 *soku* of rice-in-ear, 7 *kin* each of abalone, bonito and squid, 7 salmon, 7 *to* of dried meat, 1 *to* 5 *shō* of small dried fish, 8 *kin* of *wakame*, 10 *kin* of *arame*, 14 *kin* of assorted seaweeds, 1 *to* of salt, 3 leaf-mats for wrapping, 2 horses, 2 *tan* of tax cloth for the *hafuri*.

To the above two shrines one prince of 5th rank or above is sent to each and a member of the *Jingi-kan* of 6th rank or above to each, as [Court] representatives (accompanying them: one *urabe* to each and two *kambe* to each), one official at least as deputy governor of the province, a chief steward has charge of matters, and by means of exchange, each district is caused to furnish 2 loads of foodstuffs. For the cost of foodstuffs and for rice-in-ear for the rice and sake, use the regular taxes of the province. The remainder is requested and supplied by the officials in charge, except for the saddles which are replaced whenever they give out.

Matsuno-o Festival:[241]

1 *jō* each of five colors of pongee, 1 *jō* of stiff silk, 1 *jō* of colored hemp-cloth, 2 skeins of silk thread, 2 *mochi* of floss silk, 4 large *ryō* of bark-cloth, 10 *ryō* of hemp, 1 mat for wrapping, 200 *mon* in coin (for cost of foodstuffs), 2 *tan* of tribute cloth (for cushions), 2 *tan* of *sayomi* cloth[242] (for robe of prescribed color), 1 carrying-pole and one porter.

The above is celebrated on the first monkey day of the 4th month in summer. One recorder and one secretary go to the shrine area and are in charge of matters.

Festival to the Four Deities of Hirano (Imaki-no-kami, Kudo-no-kami, Furuseki-no-kami jointly with Hime-no-kami):[243]

3 *jō* 2 *shaku* each of five colors of silk, 3 *jō* 2 *shaku* of stiff silk, 1 *jō* 6 *shaku* of colored hemp-cloth, 4 skeins of silk thread, 4 *mochi* of floss silk, 16 *kin* each of bark-cloth and hemp, 3 *jō* 2 *shaku* of plain cloth for wrapping the symbolic offerings (foregoing are all for the symbolic offerings), 4 *to* of rice, 4 *to* of glutinous rice, 1 *to* each of soybeans and red beans, 1 *to* 3 *shō* of oil (for various uses), 24 *kin* each of abalone, bonito and *wakame*, 4 *to* of dried meat, 1 *to* 6

---

240 The listing of spindle or thread-holder (*tatari* 多多利), shuttle (*oke* 麻笥), and reel (*kasehi* 加世比) suggests that weaving also was important to Tatsuta and was perhaps associated with the female deity of the pair, Shinatobe-no-mikoto.

241 The Matsuno-o *matsuri* is not one of the festivals listed in the Yōrō Code and therefore is an addition in the *E-S*.

242 *Sayomi no nuno* 貲布, a coarse cloth made from the bark of the *shina-no-ki* 科の木, a kind of linden *(Tilia cordata)*. This was a type of tax cloth.

243 The festival of Hirano 平野 Shrine likewise does not appear in the Yōrō Code as it was founded in the Heian period, in the Enryaku or Kōnin era. It does figure in the *Jōgan-shiki* and in the *Jōgan-gishiki* where first monkey days of the 4th and 11th months are stipulated for it. The *Sandai jitsuroku* mentions it for the year Ten'an 2 (858). Miyagi, *op. cit.*, I, p. 32.

shō of salt, 16 split-wood boxes, 24 each of jars and sake cups (furnished with stands), 16 each of jugs and cooking-pots, 4 each of large jars and bottles, 8 Kara cook-stoves, 16 gourds, 20 food mats, 160 bundles of oak, four 8-legged tables, 8 cypress logs, 9 burdens of kindling, 3 palanquins, 5 *tan* 2 *shaku* of bleached cloth for covering and spreading, 3 *mochi* of floss silk for hanging up the lamps, 5 *to* 3 *shō* 3 *gō* of sake, 2 *tan* of tribute cloth (foregoing are for the festival deities), 1 *jō* 1 *shaku* of stiff silk, 1 *jō* 2 *shaku* each of five colors of pongee, 1 *jō* 2 *shaku* of colored hemp-cloth, 4 *kin* each of bark-cloth and hemp (for the Scattering Ceremony).

8 *shaku* each of five colors of silk, 4 *jō* of stiff silk, 4 *shaku* of colored hemp-cloth, 4 *kin* each of bark-cloth and hemp, 8 mattocks, 8 *soku* of rice-in-ear (furnished by the *Jingi-kan*), 8 *to* of rice, 2 *to* 7 *shō* of sake, 2 *to* of glutinous rice, 8 *shō* each of soybeans and red beans, 8 *kin* each of abalone, bonito and *wakame*, 4 *to* of dried meat, 8 *shō* of salt, 8 each of jars and chopping bowls, 40 saucers, 4 cucurbits, 8 bundles of oak, 3 palanquins, 8 food-mats, 5 burdens of kindling, 4 *tan* of tribute cloth for cost of various articles, 6 *tan* of tax cloth for reciting the ritual (foregoing are for the purification and the festival for the august stove and well), 4 *kin* of bark-cloth, 4 *to* each of rice and glutinous rice, 8 *shō* of soybeans, 1 *to* 2 *shō* of red beans, 3 *to* of sake, 4 *kin* each of abalone, bonito and *wakame*, 4 *to* of dried meat (foregoing are for the Festival to the Deity of the Mountain).

2 *koku* of rice, 3 large jars, 3 large tables, 3 mortars, 3 sake kegs, 6 pestles, 3 winnowing baskets, 3 gourds (foregoing 6 items to be replaced whenever they give out), 3 *tan* plain cloth (for the brewing of deity sake), 3 *koku* 9 *to* of cooked rice, 16 *kin* of *wakame*, 6 *to* of dried meat, 8 *shō* of salt (for the food allowance for two days for 16 cooks and 30 guards).

For sacred robes:

for *mono-imi* and princes, 5 *hiki* of stiff silk for a summer garment (1 *hiki* additional for winter), 10 *mochi* of floss silk, 6 short *kin* of safflower, 1 *kan* 630 *mon* in coin (same in winter); for [members of the] Yamato Uji and Ooe Uji, 2 *hiki* of stiff silk apiece for a summer garment (in winter an additional *hiki*), 3 *mochi* of floss silk, 3 short *kin* of safflower, 630 *mon* in coin (same in winter); for two *koto* players, for summer garments 3 *jō* of stiff silk and 2 *jō* 8 *shaku* of plain cloth apiece, for winter 3 *jō* of yellow silk, 1 *hiki* of stiff silk, 3 *mochi* of floss silk apiece; for 16 cooks, for summer garments, 3 *jō* of stiff silk, 3 *jō* 2 *shaku* of plain cloth and 1 *ryō* 1 *bu* of safflower apiece, for winter 3 *jō* yellow silk, 1 *jō* 2 *shaku* of plain cloth apiece; for four female cooks,[244] for summer 4 *jō* 5 *shaku* of stiff silk, 1 *jō* of plain cloth apiece, for winter 1 *hiki* 3 *jō* of stiff silk, 2 *mochi* of floss silk and 1 *jō* of plain cloth apiece; for two chief priests,[245] in summer 3 *hiki* of stiff silk for cushions and 3 skeins of silk thread apiece; for four diviners, for summer 1 *hiki* of stiff silk and 1 skein of silk thread, 2 *jō* 8 *shaku* of ordinary cloth apiece, for winter the same again;

---

244 Female cooks are *kashikime* 炊女.   245 That is, *kannushi* 神主.

robes of color prescribed for their rank are furnished to the two chiefs of ceremonies and two members of the *Jingi-kan* (the same for the Imbe and the *hafuri*).

At the winter festival emoluments are given to 18 persons: 2 chief priests, 2 officials of the *Jingi-kan*, 2 *koto* players, 2 chief diviners, 2 scribes, 5 of the *kambe*, 3 diviners, according to the method of emoluments.

The above is celebrated on the first monkey day in the 4th month in summer and the 11th month in winter. Government goods are used throughout and the sacred articles to be offered are requested and received by the *Jingi-kan* which prepares them; while as for various necessary supplies the respective officials in charge furnish these. At dawn on the festival day, the officials in charge put up the light curtains for [the passage of] the Heir Apparent and the drapes for the host of officials in the festival courtyard. The Great Ministers and those under them take their several places. That done, the inspector of ceremonies[246] comes forward and addresses the Imperial Advisers and those higher who participate in the affair, and causes the civil administrators[247] to start up the music; [officials of] the Treasury present the bark-cloth for headdresses; then the Nakatomi who is chief of the shrine comes forward and recites the ritual. That done, the singing and dancing commence. (First come the mountain people, then an official of the *Jingi-kan*, then the Nakatomi who is chief of the shrine, then two chamberlains, then two *udoneri* and two *ōdoneri*.[248]) By this time the sake and food have been served to the host of officials. When they are finished they all retire.

Festival of the Gates on Four Sides[249] (repeat in the 12th month):

4 *jō* each of five colors of silk, 4 *jō* of pongee, 8 skeins of silk thread, 8 *kin* each of bark-cloth and hemp, 8 *mochi* of floss silk, 200 sheets of paper, 4 *jō* of colored hemp-cloth, 8 *tan* of ordinary cloth, 100 *mon* in coin, 16 mattocks, 50 sheets of yellow-bark, 8 *to* of glutinous rice, 4 *to* each of soybeans and red beans, 8 *to* of rice, 5 *to* of sake, 8 *to* of soy dregs, 16 *soku* of rice-in-ear, 16 grains of salt, 16 salmon, 4 *kin* each of abalone, bonito, dried meat and *wakame*, 4 each of straw-mats and rush-mats, 16 food-mats, 8 each of white-wood boxes and split-wood boxes, 80 saucers, 4 palanquins, 5 gourds, 2 bales of oak.

Festival of Waters of the Sacred River (repeated in the 12th month; the same is held in the Middle Palace):

2 *jō* 5 *shaku* of each of five colors of silk, 2 *jō* 5 *shaku* of pongee, 5 *mochi* of

---

246 The *kanshi no kan* 監祀官.

247 *Jibu* 治部 officials of the *jibu-shō*, the Ministry of Civil Administration which had charge of marriages, inheritance, genealogies, burial mounds, mausolea, and so forth, and performance of music.

248 The *toneri* 舍人 system was made up of youths of the nobility who automatically attained Court Rank at age 21. They were selected from about 100 noble families of 4th and 5th Court Rank. They served as personal palace attendants to guard and accompany the imperial party or members of the sovereign's family. The system included *toneri*, and also: 'great *toneri*', *ōdoneri* 大舍人; 'inner *toneri*', *udoneri* 內舍人, as here. Those attached to a shrine were *miya-no-toneri* 宮舍人, and those attached to the Bureau of the Consecrated Princess, *ryō-no-toneri* 寮舍人, as will be seen in Book v, below.

249 To protect the gates in the fence around the perimeter of the Imperial Palace.

floss silk, 2 *shaku* of colored hemp-cloth, 5 skeins of silk thread, 5 *kin* each of bark-cloth and hemp, 100 sheets of paper, 5 *tan* of plain cloth, 80 *mon* in coin, 5 mattocks, 2 *to* of sake, 5 *to* each of rice and soy dregs, 1 *to* each of soybeans and red beans, 3 *to* of glutinous rice, 5 *soku* of rice-in-ear, 5 salmon, 2 *kin* each of abalone, bonito, dried meat and *wakame,* 5 grains of salt, 2 white-wood boxes, 50 saucers, 5 food-mats, 2 each of straw-mats and rush-mats, 5 split-wood boxes, 1 palanquin, 1 bale of oak, 5 gourds.

For the above, the Festival of the Four Sides is conducted by the Sacred Maidens of the Palace and the Festival of the Waters of the Sacred River is conducted by the Igazuri Maidens.

Festival to the Three Kantoki Deities[250] (residing northwest of Kaguraoka, Atagi District, Yamashiro Prov.):

6 *shaku* each of five colors of pongee, 1 *hiki* 3 *jō* of stiff silk, 1 skein 8 *ryō* of silk thread, 1 *mochi* of floss silk, 6 *shaku* of colored hemp-cloth, 1 *tan* 2 *jō* of tribute cloth, 3 *tan* of tax cloth, 3 *kin* each of bark-cloth and hemp, 6 mattocks, 1 garment of color prescribed for rank, 6 *tan* of plain cloth for cost of raw foods and various fruits, 3 *to* of sake, 4 *to* 5 *shō* of white rice, 1 *to* 5 *shō* of glutinous rice, 7 *shō* 5 *gō* each of soybeans and red beans, 3 salmon, 1 *to* 5 *shō* of sushi, 3 *kin* each of abalone, bonito and dried meat, 7 *shō* 5 *gō* of salt, 3 *kin* each of *wakame* and assorted seaweeds, 15 saucers, 3 bottles, 3 cooking-pots, 2 white-wood boxes, 3 split-wood boxes, 3 gourds, 3 each of straw-mats and rush-mats, 4 food-mats, 60 bundles of oak, 1 palanquin, 3 *soku* of rice-in-ear.

For the above, the officials arrive in advance of the festival and ask the secretaries[251] to request and prepare the articles. One diviner is made to select an auspicious day and the festival is held then (the same is done in the 11th month).

FESTIVALS OF THE SIXTH MONTH
(repeated in the 12th Month)

Miagamono[252] *Festival* (repeated in the Middle Palace):

4 *jō* each of five colors of silk, 4 *jō* of pongee, 8 skeins of silk thread, 8 *mochi* of floss silk, 8 *tan* of plain cloth, 100 *mon* in coin, 8 mattocks, 100 sheets of paper, 8 large *kin* each of bark-cloth and hemp, 8 *to* each of rice, sake and dregs, 8 salmon, 8 baskets of mixed foodstuffs (such as assorted seaweeds, dried meats, abalone and bonito), 8 grains of salt, 8 each of straw-mats, rush-mats and foodmats, 40 sheets of yellow-bark, 8 *soku* of rice-in-ear, 8 white-wood boxes, 2 bales of oak, 8 dippers, 23 shallow bowls, 4 palanquins.

(The above commences on the 1st and lasts to the 8th day of the 6th month;

---

250 Or, Kamutoki or Hyakuraku—deities of thunder worshiped regularly to avert calamity. But see n. 322.

251 *Benkan* 辨官 were secretaries of the *Dajō-kan* of which there were two each: Great, Middle and Small.

252 *Miagamono* 御贖物, thank offerings. These particular ceremonies were held in the Imperial Palace and duplicated in the Middle or Consort's Palace.

the Sacred Maidens conduct the events each day; for the Palace of the Heir Apparent the duration and the amounts of goods are all reduced by half.)

Divining the August Person[253]—*Two Presentations to the Deities of the Divining Area* (celebrated on the first and last days of the divining):

> 2 *tan* of plain cloth, 2 *tan* of tax cloth, 8 *ryō* of bark-cloth, 1 *kin* of hemp, 2 mattocks, 1 *to* of sake, 4 *kin* each of abalone, bonito and *wakame*, 2 *shō* of salt, 1 shallow bowl, 2 saucers, 1 gourd, 4 bundles of oak, 2 food-mats, 1 straw-mat (foregoing are for the festival), 1 tortoise shell, 20 stalks of bamboo, 4 bowls of *sue* ware,[254] 2 hatchets, 4 augers, 4 knives (foregoing are for the divination).

For the above, the officials in charge having already informed the *Jingi-kan*, the host of officials are notified. If there should be a violation of the ground, a move must be made with the utmost care. There are 2 Nakatomi, one chief diviner, and 8 other diviners, all fitted out in lustrous robes (the Nakatomi in fine-weave cloth, the diviners in tribute cloth). It begins on the first of the month and the divination is completed before the 10th, and results presented to his Majesty. At dawn on that day the text of the previously prepared announcement is presented (it is put in a lacquer box and placed on the offering-table). The vice-ministers[255] and above waiting outside the Ensei Gate, take the offering-table and proceed to the Great Minister.[256] The Great Minister ascends to the Palace, and entering the Imperial Household Ministry[257] makes the announcement. Having done so, he summons the *Jingi-kan* [officials], they reply in assent, and the chief, the assistant chief or deputy, together raise the table, enter and place it in the divination courtyard. The Imperial Messenger[258] calls out: 'Come ye!' The chief of the *Jingi-kan* responds and joins in lifting the table to place it in the Palace on a split-bamboo mat which is spread there. One Nakatomi goes to the board on which ranks are posted; the others withdraw. A lady-in-waiting[259] takes the report and offers it to His Majesty. After he has looked at it, the messenger calls out: 'Come ye!' The Nakatomi responds with assent and ascends to take a seat in the Palace. Opening up the report, he reads it in a hushed voice. The messenger states that the content is to be carried out. The Great Ministers give the verbal assent. Then the Nakatomi give the verbal assent and withdraw. The officer of the August Gates[260] then ascends into the Palace, removes the offering table and places it in the courtyard. The *Jingi-kan* officials carry it and depart.

---

253 The interlinear gloss says that *gyotai* 御體 is pronounced *Omima*. It refers to the august body of the sovereign on which divination was performed.

254 *Sue* 陶 ware *(sueki)* was a dark-grey fired clay ware, of which many examples survive. In this instance, the ceremonial vessel made of this clay is a bowl, *moi* 椀.

255 The *suke* 副, or deputy chiefs of ministries.

256 As the term *daijin* 大臣 is used it could include the *dajō-daijin,* Great Minister of State,

as well as the *sadaijin* and *udaijin,* Great Ministers of Left and Right, or any of the chiefs of the Eight Ministries of government.

257 The *kunai-shō* 宮內省 or *miyanouchi-no-tsukasa,* one of the Eight Ministries.

258 The *choku* 勅 (elsewhere *chokushi* 勅使).

259 *Naishi* 內侍: ladies of noble rank who were personal attendants upon the sovereign and his family.

260 The *mikado-no-tsukasa* 閽司.

Tsukinami Festival—to 304 Deities worshiped with the Symbolic Offering on top of the Tables (all Great) :[261]

At 198 shrines:

> for each presentation, 5 *shaku* of pongee, 1 *shaku* each of five colors of thin pongee, 1 *shaku* of colored hemp-cloth, 2 *ryō* of bark-cloth, 5 *ryō* of hemp, one each of colored hemp-cloth sword case, pongee sword case and plain-cloth sword case, one each of *yokura-oki* and *yakura-oki*, 1 bow, 1 quiver, 1 shield, 1 spearhead, 1 pair of deer antlers, 1 mattock, 1 *jō* 4 *shaku* of tax cloth, 4 *shō* of sake, 5 *ryō* each of abalone and bonito, 2 *shō* of dried meat, 6 *ryō* each of *wakame, arame* and assorted seaweeds, 1 *shō* of salt, 1 sake jar, 5 *shaku* of leaf-mat for wrapping, one short *tatami* for reciting the ritual.

For 106 presentations to deities:

> for each, 5 *shaku* of pongee, 1 *shaku* each of five colors of thin pongee, 1 *shaku* of colored hemp-cloth, 2 *ryō* of bark-cloth, 5 *ryō* of hemp, one each of *yokura-oki* and *yakura-oki*, 1 shield, 1 spearhead, 5 *shaku* of leaf-mat for wrapping.

The deities worshiped in the above are all the same as for the *Toshigoi* festival: out of them the Shrine of the Great Deity, the Watarai Shrine, Takami-musubi-no-kami and Oomiyanome-no-kami each receive one horse in addition. (But for the first two, 1 *tan* of tax cloth for the headstalls of the bridles is also added.) Five days before the festival 9 Imbe and 1 woodworker are assigned to build the ceremonial articles for offerings to the deities. (The supervision of this and the requirements for purified robes and foods is the same as for the *Toshigoi*.) When the festival is over, one Nakatomi leads the Chief Diviner and other diviners to the Imperial Household Ministry where they determine by divination who will be *omibito*[262] to serve the *Jinkonjiki*.

Requirements for the Jinkonjiki :[263]

> 1 *jō* 2 *shaku* of ramie cloth[264] (for august headbands), 2 *jō* 2 *shaku* of stiff silk (for the sieves), 4 *ryō* silk thread (to sew sieves, etc.), 3 *tan* 1 *jō* of plain cloth (for headbands for the cooks), 1 *jō* 2 *shaku* of bleached cloth (to cover the water jars), 3 *jō* 2 *shaku* of fine-weave cloth (for tunics and sleeve-ties for the diviner's assistants), 1 *kin* 5 *ryō* of bark-cloth (to wrap the august food), 2 swords with carved handles, 10 long-swords, 10 short-swords, 6 round boxes, 2 coarse boxes, 3 white-wood boxes; for august food and gruel, 2 *to* of white rice for

---

261 The *Tsukinami-matsuri* 月次祭 ('successive months festival') began as a monthly service of thanksgiving. By the time the *jingi-ryō* of the codes were formulated it appears to have become a twice-yearly agricultural feast the purposes of which were the same as those of the *Toshigoi-matsuri* (n. 149 above). The shrines and deities to be worshiped duplicated those of the *Toshigoi*. Aida, *op. cit.,* p. 354.

262 *Omibito* 小齋人, lit. those under small taboo, were persons who served in deity affairs having to do with divination and at the time of **great** festivals. They don *omigoromo* 小忌衣

(abstinence garments) and perform partial abstinence (*araimi* 散齋) during their service.

263 The *Jinkonjiki* 神今食 (*kamu-ima-ke*), was a sacred food ritual in which the sovereign was to partake of specially prepared and cooked rice in the company of the divine Imperial Ancestress, Amaterasu-ō-mikami. It is said to have been founded in Reiki 靈龜 2 (A.D. 716) though the first historical mention in the *Shoku-nihongi* is in Enryaku 9 (790). Aida, p. 345.

264 The *kana* gloss here reads *tezukuri* 紵 indicating hand-woven cloth from *karamushi* 苧, ramie; or, *karamushi-no-nuno*, ramie cloth.

each, 2 *to* of millet, 5 each of shallow dishes of *sue* ware[265] and of jars, 4 each of ewers, basins, sake pitchers, 6 each of washing bowls and small saucers, 20 pedestalled dishes, 4 ritual water pitchers,[266] 8 *sue* ware bowls, 4 chopping bowls, 2 mortars, 20 coverless clay bowls, 8 water bowls, 8 trays for the boxes, 2 handbasins, 8 platters, 2 clay hot-water basins, 4 bottles, 10 cooking-pots, 2 braziers, 10 offering-tables, 2 low tables, 2 mallets, 2 chopping blocks, 4 bales of oak, 20 gourds, 2 ritual elongated basins,[267] 3 *shō* of oil, 3 *jō* of gray silk[268] (for garments for the diviner's assistants, in winter 1 *hiki* of pongee, 6 *mochi* of floss silk, 1 pair of shoes).

The above articles to be offered are assigned respectively to the Office of the Imperial Table and the Water Office. Officials of the *Jingi-kan* lead the *kambe* and others up to the palace twice: evening and morning to participate in this affair. When the festival is over the various articles which were offered are bestowed on the Nakatomi, Imbe, Chief Diviner, and so on, the same as is done at the time of the Great New Food Festival.

The Ootono-hogai[269] (repeated in the Middle Palace):

4 *ryō* of silk thread, 1 *kin* of Aki bark-cloth, 4 round boxes (each 1 *shaku* 5 *sun* in diam.), 4 *shō* of rice, 2 *shō* of sake, 1 jar, 2 sake cups, 2 offering-tables.

For the above, early on the morning after the *Jinkonjiki*, they place 4 round boxes (one is filled with beads, one with cut up bark-cloth, one with rice and the other with jars of sake) upon eight-legged tables. Four *kambe* take these up. They are wearing bark-cloth headdresses and sleeve-ties.[270] Officials of the Nakatomi and Imbe with the Chief Diviner, scribes and various *kambe* all form a guard on left and right. The Sacred Maidens form a line behind the offering-tables and go to the Ensei Gate. They place the tables in front of the gate; the *ōdoneri* knock on the the gate. Officials of the Imperial Household Ministry go out and summon the Nakatomi. They make the verbal assent. Both officials are wearing bark-cloth headdresses (the Imbe in addition have bark-cloth sleeve-ties), they stand before the offering-tables and then proceed directly to the Great Hall. In the meantime the Sacred Maidens have entered through the

---

265 The vessel indicated here is a *sarake* 㼠. The character is a *kokuji* 國字, or native Japanese character, and the sound probably an aphetic form of *asarake,* which meant a shallow vessel. The interlinear gloss says it is made of clay and resembles a *suzurigame* 硯瓶 (the container for water which is poured on an inkstone).

266 *Tashiraka* 多志良加 is described as a vessel used to pour water over the emperor's hands in ritual washing. D.C. Holtom, *Enthronement Ceremonies,* pp. 134, 138.

267 *Ebi-no-hatabune* 蚧鯖槽, lit., 'shrimp-fin boat', the basin used for the emperor's hand washing. The gloss says: 'together with august hand-washing place'. See n. 522.

268 That is, silk dyed with a gray or black dye prepared from the shell of the acorn of *tsurubami* 橡; see n. 153.

269 The *Ootono-hogai* 大殿祭 is called 'Luck-wishing of the Great Palace' by E. Satow in his 'Ancient Japanese Rituals' (*TASJ*, 1st series, VII) in which the ritual is translated. This is supposed to have been a celebration originating long before any legal codes, but it is not mentioned in the various ceremonial procedures (Kōnin, Jōgan). The ceremonies include the blessing of all parts of the Palace, and the Consort's Palace. Also, as seen in Bk. V, it was performed in the palaces of the Consecrated Princess. For text of the ritual, see Philippi, *Norito,* pp. 41-3.

270 It is difficult to know from the position of the phrase '*yū-kazura tasuki wo tsuketaru*' whether it is the four *kambe* who wear the bark-cloth headdress and sleeve-ties, or the Nakatomi, Imbe officials, and so forth. The *Kokushi taikei* edition applies the phrase to the *kambe*.

Sen'yō Gate and are waiting inside the Palace. Entering together they proceed to the carpet of split-bamboo matting on the east side of the hall. Then each of the Maidens takes a box. The Nakatomi, the Imbe and the Maidens in succession enter the Great Hall. The Imbe take the beads and hang them up in the four corners of the Hall. The Maidens scatter rice, sake and finely cut bark-cloth in the four corners of the Hall and then withdraw. The Nakatomi wait on the south side of the Great Hall. The Imbe move to the southeast and in a low voice recite the ritual. That done, they proceed to the august bathhouse and hang up the beads in the four corners of it. Next they hang them in the four corners of the august privy and then in the four corners of the august household shrine and finally in the four corners of the Throne Hall.[271] The Sacred Maidens each time scatter rice, sake and bark-cloth as before. (One of them goes to the Shōmei Gate and scatters rice and sake.) They withdraw through the Immei Gate. Next the Chief Diviner leads the Imbe to the august kitchen and they hang the bark-cloth up and scatter rice and sake as before. When this is over, the Bureau of Palace Storehouses has charge of bestowing emoluments. (For amounts see the Procedures for Palace Storehouse Bureau.) They return to their respective offices, and leading the petty officials and below, they all proceed to the Depuration Hall[272] in the Ministry of the Imperial Household (see the *Gishiki* for this matter).

Festival of the Sacred Fire and Courtyard Fire[273] (repeated in the Middle Palace):
4 *shaku* each of five colors of silk, 2 *hiki* of pongee, 4 *shaku* of colored hemp-cloth, 2 *kin* each of bark-cloth and hemp, 2 skeins of silk thread, 2 *mochi* of floss silk, 2 *tan* of plain cloth, 2 *tan* of tax cloth, 4 mattocks, 2 *to* each of rice, sake, and salt, 2 *kin* each of abalone, bonito, dried meat and *wakame*, 2 food-mats, 8 saucers, 2 gourds and 10 bundles of oak.
The above is conducted by the Chief Diviner at the Palace Table Office after the *Ootono-hogai* is finished.

For Court Dress for Sacred Maidens offering the *Jinkonjiki* (not furnished in the 12th month):
for Sacred Maidens, 4 *hiki* of stiff silk, 1 *jō* 1 *shaku* of pongee, 2 *mochi* of floss silk, 6 *shaku* of fine-weave cloth, 6 *kin* of safflower, 130 *mon* in coin (same for Sacred Maidens of the Middle Palace); for each of the Sacred Maidens of Igazuri, Mikado, Ikushima and Tōgū,[274] 3 *hiki* of stiff silk, 9 *shaku* of pongee, 1 *mochi* of floss silk, 6 *shaku* of fine-weave cloth, 1 *kin* of safflower and 130 *mon* in coin.

271 The Shishin-den 紫宸殿, the ceremonial hall of the Imperial Palace containing the thrones of Emperor and Empress. D. C. Holtom, *Enthronement Ceremonies*, pp. 72–3.

272 The Gesai-den 解齋殿, where participants are released from abstinence. After important festivals like the *Daijō-sai, Niiname-sai* and *Jinkonjiki,* and the presenting of offerings at the Grand Shrines, this is the release from abstinence *(mono-imi)* after the ceremonies are completed. For the sovereign the procedure is: on a given day

after the festival, there is a hand-washing stand of white wood set up to the south of the sleeping quarter of the Residential Hall (Seiryō-den 清涼殿) where ceremonial hand washing takes place. *Nihon rekishi daijiten.*

273 In connection with the *Jinkonjiki* ceremonies offerings are made to the sacred fire for cooking the ritual foods and to the fire made to light nighttime ceremonies outdoors.

274 The *tōgū* 東宮, East Palace, is that of the Heir Apparent.

Emoluments for persons offering the *Jinkonjiki*:

One Nakatomi official is given 4 *hiki* of stiff silk, one Imbe official 3 *hiki* of stiff silk, one Chief Diviner 1 *hiki* of stiff silk, to one *uneme*[275] who serves the august food to His Majesty, 4 *hiki* of stiff silk, to the Sacred Maiden 3 *hiki* of stiff silk (same to the Maiden in the Middle Palace), 2 *hiki* to each of the Igazuri, Mikado, Ikushima and Tōgū Sacred Maidens.

The Great Purification on the Last Day of the 6th Month (repeated in the 12th month):[276]

2 *shaku* each of five colors of thin pongee, 1 *jō* 5 *shaku* of scarlet silk, 2 *hiki* of stiff silk, 2 swords ornamented with gold, 2 each of gilded and silvered effigies[277] (the foregoing are kept by the recorders of Yamato and Kawachi), 3 *tan* of tax cloth, 5 *kin* 2 *ryō* of bark-cloth, 20 *kin* 10 *ryō* of hemp, 12 *ryō* of nettle hemp, 6 swords ornamented in black,[278] 6 bows, 200 arrows, 6 mattocks, 3 pairs of deer antlers, 6 deerskins, 2 *to* of rice, 6 *to* of sake, 4 *soku* of rice-in-ear, 2 *kin* of abalone, 7 *kin* of bonito, 1 *koku* 5 *to* of dried meats, 40 *kin* of *wakame*, 6 *to* of salt, 6 water bottles, 6 gourds, 20 bundles of oak, 6 horses, 5 *tan* of tax cloth for reciting the rituals, one short *tatami*.

For the above, before the monkey hour on the last day, the host of officials from Princes-of-the-Blood and on down assemble at the Suzaku Gate, and the Diviners recite the ritual. (See the *Gishiki* for this matter.)

Miagamono: [Thank Offerings]:

2 iron effigies, 2 side swords ornamented in gold, 1 *jō* 1 *shaku* of five colors of thin pongee, 3 *ryō* of silk thread, 2 *kin* of Aki bark-cloth, 1 *kin* of common bark-cloth, 2 *kin* of hemp, 2 *tan* of tax cloth, 2 august garments, 2 divided skirts, 2 quilts (for the rest, see Procedures for the Needlework Bureau),[279] 4 mattocks, 2 *to* each of rice and sake, 2 *kin* of abalone, 2 *kin* of bonito, 4 *shō* of dried meat, 2 *kin* of *wakame*, 4 *shō* of salt, 2 each of water basins, jars and saucers, 2 gourds, 20 bundles of oak, 20 stalks of bamboo grass (each 2 *bu* in diameter, 8 *shaku* long); for lustrous robes for one Chief Diviner and 5 diviners, 3 *tan* 3 *jō* 6 *shaku* of tribute cloth.

Miagamono in the Middle Palace (repeated in the Palace of the Heir Apparent):

---

275 *Uneme* 采女 is thought to be derived from *yoneme* 米女, 'rice ladies', because these were the young women chosen for their beauty from various parts of the country who waited upon the sovereign personally and served him his food. The office of *uneme* was included in the Imperial Household Ministry and one in the Bureau of the Consecrated Imperial Princess. See Bk. v, below.

276 The *ōharae* 大祓, or 'great driving out', was a ceremony to symbolically remove all pollution and defilement from the nation as a whole. The *jingi-ryō* of the codes specifies this twice-yearly ceremony at which the Nakatomi offer up the symbolic offerings, the Recorders of East and West (Yamato and Kawachi Provinces) present swords, the Nakatomi recites the purification ritual and the host of officials, male and female, assemble at the purification place and the *urabe* perform rites of exorcism. Aida, *op. cit.*, p. 361.

277 Effigies or dolls, *hitokata* 人形, also 人象, were used in purification or exorcism. A simple human shape was cut out of paper, or in this case metal, to be held and rubbed in order to transmit to it the defilement from the person of the worshiper.

278 The swords listed here are written 横刀, and the decoration, *kurozukuri* 烏裝.

279 Procedures for the Needlework Bureau, the *nuidonoryō-shiki*, are in Bk. xIV of the *E-S.*

2 iron effigies, 1 *jō* 1 *shaku* each of five colors of thin pongee, 3 *ryō* of silk thread, 2 *kin* of Aki bark-cloth, 1 *kin* of common bark-cloth, 2 *kin* of hemp, 2 *tan* of tax cloth, 2 august garments, 2 skirts (divided skirts for Palace of the Heir Apparent), 2 quilts, 4 mattocks, 2 *to* each of rice and sake, 2 *kin* of abalone, 2 *kin* each of bonito and *wakame*, 4 *shō* of dried meat, 4 *shō* of salt, 2 each of water basins and jars, 2 saucers, 2 gourds, 20 bundles of oak, 20 stalks of bamboo; for lustrous robes for one Chief Diviner and five diviners, 3 *tan* 3 *jō* 6 *shaku* of tribute cloth (but for the Heir Apparent's Palace 8 items are reduced by half: common bark-cloth, hemp, rice, sake, abalone, dried meat, salt, and oak; the rest are the same as for the Middle Palace).

For the above, on the last day of the month the diviners don lustrous robes and one of them takes the symbolic offerings, two others the offerings of coarse cloth and two the offerings of soft cloth[280] and two take the large jar. The Chief Diviner, the scribes and members of the *kambe* form a guard at the left and right and advance in the lead. Next the Nakatomi official, then the symbolic offerings, then come the recorders of Yamato and Kawachi (each carrying a sword), next those bearing coarse offerings and then those bearing soft offerings (all wearing bark-cloth headdresses); they proceed to the Ensei Gate and wait, and the *ōdoneri* knock at the gate. The vice-minister of the Imperial Household enters and reports to the throne (for his words see the Procedures for the Imperial Household);[281] he withdraws and summons the Nakatomi. They give assent and then lead the recorders and the diviners of four provinces (the Chief Diviner is one of them), and wait on the south side of the Giyō-den.[282] The Nakatomi lead the *urabe* who bear the offerings of coarse cloth down the stairs and place them on the mats (the Bureau of Housekeeping having previously spread split-bamboo matting at the foot of the stairs, the Bureau of Needlework places the august garments of coarse cloth and soft cloth on top of the matting). Next the Nakatomi offer up the symbolic offerings and go to the rank-posting board.[283] The Imperial order is given to come forward. They give assent and advance to the foot of the stairs. A woman of the Nakatomi (a woman of the Nakatomi Uji who is able is chosen to report to the throne) ascends to the Palace, and presents the offerings one after another. When that is done she gives them to the Nakatomi. They take them and give them to one of the diviners who goes to the place of purification. Then again the vice-minister of the Imperial Household reports to the throne. (For the words see the Imperial Household Procedures.) He comes out and calls the Nakatomi. They give the verbal assent. The recorders of Yamato, raise up their swords and enter and go to the rank-posting board. The Imperial order is given for them to come forward. They reply with assent and come to the foot of the stairs and hand over the swords to the Nakatomi women. They take them

280 In this passage coarse cloth is called *arayo* 荒世 and soft cloth *nikoyo (nikiyo)* 和世. For the clothing, *aratae* 荒服 and *nikotae* 和服 respectively are used.

281 Procedures for the *kunai-shō* are in Bk. XXXI of the *E-S*.

282 The Giyō-den 宜陽殿 was one of the 17 halls within the Imperial Palace. It was located east of the Shishin-den (n. 271) and housed heirlooms and musical instruments and such. *Kogo jiten.*

283 The *hen'i* 版位 *(han'i, henni)* was a board listing all Court Ranks and promotions in rank, posted on festival occasions.

and offer them up; that done they go out. Next the recorders of Kawachi come forward and retreat in the same way as the ceremony above. The Chief Diviner spreads out the offering of coarse cloth and gives it to the Nakatomi. He takes it and gives it to the Nakatomi woman. She then respectfully measures the august person a total of five times, and when that is done the Chief Diviner offers up the jar.[284] The Nakatomi in turn take this and give it to the woman of the Nakatomi. She takes it and offers it up; that done she withdraws and gives it to the Nakatomi. He in turn gives it to the Chief Diviner. The Chief Diviner takes it and gives it to the diviner behind him. When the offering of coarse cloth has been taken care of, they withdraw. Then again, the Nakatomi take the offerings of soft cloth and come forward and retreat as was done with the coarse offering. The garments made from coarse cloth are bestowed on the *urabe* and the garments of soft cloth are bestowed on the Chief Diviner. When that is done, they all withdraw and they go to the river's edge and purify themselves, then leave. But in the Palace of the Consort a secretary of the Nakatomi or higher (the same in the Heir Apparent's Palace; if one is not available, an official of another office shall serve in dual capacity) offers up the symbolic offerings, enters the Office of the Palace and tells the ladies-in-waiting what to do. The woman of the Nakatomi presents the symbolic offerings and thank offerings. Presentation of the offerings of coarse cloth and soft cloth is the same as the above ceremony. In the Heir Apparent's Palace she enters the Office and gives instructions. That done, she comes out and summons the Nakatomi. He responds with assent and presents the symbolic offerings and goes forward to the center of the garden. The order is given for them to come forward. Saying 'Aye!' they ascend the south stairs and present the offering. When that is done they withdraw and hand over the offering to one of the *urabe* and then go to the purification courtyard. Once more, the [*jingi*] official leads the Chief Diviner in going forward and placing the offerings of coarse and soft cloth upon the straw matting. The official then ascends the stairs and in turn hands over the offerings to the woman of the Nakatomi who receives them. The rest of the ceremony is like that in the Palace. The Needlework Bureau has previously laid the garments of coarse and soft cloth on the matting at the foot of the stairs. The Palace Women lead their girl assistants and take the garments, consecrate them and then replace them on the matting. They are then bestowed on the Chief Diviner and other diviners as before.

Emoluments for the Persons who present Thank Offerings for the Purification:
for one Nakatomi official, 4 *hiki* stiff silk; for the Nakatomi woman, 4 *hiki* stiff silk (same at the Consort's Palace); for two each of recorders of Yamato and of Kawachi, 2 *hiki* stiff silk apiece; for the Nakatomi and Nakatomi woman who serve at the Heir Apparent's Palace, palace articles are bestowed.

Hoshizume Festival [*Chinka-sai*] (celebrated in the four corners of the Palace Precinct):[285]

---

284 The interlinear gloss says: a clay vessel inside which are small stones so it is like a bell.

285 The *Hoshizume* or *Hishizume no matsuri*

鎮火祭 (*Chinka-sai*) was a festival to ward off calamities of fire and traditionally was held in the four corners of the Imperial Palace.

4 *shaku* each of five colors of thin pongee, 4 *shaku* of colored hemp-cloth, 5 *ryō* of bark-cloth, 1 *kin* of hemp, 2 *tan* of tax cloth, 4 mattocks, 4 *shō* each of rice and sake, 1 *kin* 5 *ryō* each of abalone and bonito, 4 *shō* of dried meat, 1 *kin* 5 *ryō* of *wakame*, 2 *shō* of salt, 4 each of large jars, jars and saucers, 4 bundles of oak, 4 gourds, 4 armloads of straw.

The *Michiae Festival*[286] (held at the four corners of the Capital):

1 *jō* each of five colors of thin pongee, 4 *shaku* of colored hemp-cloth, 1 *kin* 10 *ryō* of bark-cloth, 7 *kin* of hemp, 2 *tan* of tax cloth, 4 mattocks, 2 oxhides, 4 each of monkeyskins, deerskins, bearskins, 4 *to* of sake, 4 *soku* of rice-in-ear, 2 *kin* 5 *ryō* of abalone, 5 *kin* of bonito, 8 *shō* of dried meat, 5 *kin* of *wakame*, 2 *shō* of salt, 4 each of water bottles and saucers, 8 bundles of oak, 4 gourds, two tribute straw-mats.

$$* \quad * \quad * \quad * \quad *$$

End of Book One of the *Engi-shiki*[287]

Enchō 5th Year [A.D. 927], 12th Month, 26th Day

Outer Rank, Junior 5th Rank Lower Grade, Left Great Secretary *omi* Achi no Sukune Tadayuki; Junior 5th Rank Upper Grade, Assistant Provincial Examiner and Senior Private Secretary, Provisional Governor of Kii, *omi* Tomo no Sukune Hisanaga; Junior 4th Rank Upper Grade, Chief of the *Jingi-kan*, *omi* Oonakatomi Ason Yasunori; the Major Counsellor Senior 3rd Rank, Chief of People's Affairs, *omi* Fujiwara Ason Kiyotsura; Great Minister of the Left, Senior 2nd Rank, Major Captain of the Left Palace Guards and Protector of the Heir Apparent *omi* Fujiwara Ason Tadahira.

---

[286] The *Michiae-matsuri* 道饗祭 or Banquet of the Roads, was a ceremony of placing food offerings at the crossroads outside the capital in order to waylay evil spirits. The deities to whom offerings were made were Yachimata-hiko 八衢彦, Yachimata-hime 八衢姫 and Kunado 久那斗.

Shintō daijiten, III, p. 304.

[287] The signatories are the chief editors of the *E-S*, with their traditional titles, Court Ranks, and government positions. The identical signatures appear at the end of each of the books of *jingi-shiki*, i.e., first ten books of the *E-S*.

ENGI-SHIKI, BOOK TWO

FESTIVALS OF THE FOUR SEASONS (PART II)

FESTIVALS OF THE NINTH MONTH

The Kanname Festival at the Grand Shrine of Ise :[288]

for 2 sets of symbolic offerings (provided by Bureau of the Imperial Treasury), 3 *hiki* of pongee, 8 skeins of silk thread, 1 *tan* 1 *jō* of colored hemp-cloth, 2 mats, 2 saddles, 4 horses, 1 *tan* 1 *jō* 4 *shaku* of cloth for the headstalls of their bridles.

The above offerings are for the presentation when the Sovereign goes to the Daigoku-kōden[289] at dawn on the 11th day of the month. (For this affair see the *Gishiki*). Imperial messengers and Princes of 5th Rank and above, one Nakatomi and one Imbe from the *Jingi-kan*—each receive an ensemble in the color prescribed for their rank. The five persons who present the symbolic offerings and their three attendants each receive 1 *tan* of plain cloth for pure robes. Only on the occasion of the first entry of the Consecrated Princess are august seats to be set up at the Daigoku-den. (For this affair see the *Gishiki*).

Festival of Deities Worshiped by the Sacred Maidens (the Sacred Maidens repeat this in the Palaces of the Consort and the Heir Apparent):

1 *hiki* 4 *jō* of pongee, 4 *jō* each of five colors of silk, 4 skeins of silk thread, 6 *mochi* of silk, 4 *shaku* of colored hemp-cloth, 5 *tan* of tribute cloth, 4 *tan* of tax cloth, 100 sheets of paper, 2 *kin* each of common bark-cloth and of hemp, 8 mattocks, 500 *mon* in coin, 1 *to* of sake, 6 *to* of rice, 4 *to* of glutinous rice, 8 *soku* of rice-in-ear, 2 *to* each of soybeans and red beans, 12 *kin* each of abalone, bonito, dried meats and *wakame*, 8 salmon, 4 *to* of salt, 2 white-wood boxes, 8 split-cypress-wood boxes, 8 food-boxes, 2 gourds, 4 each of jugs and cooking-pots, 8 large jars, 80 saucers, 50 bundles of oak, 2 seat-mats and 2 straw-mats, 8 food mats, 2 split-bamboo mats.

Festival of Deities Worshiped by the Mikado Sacred Maidens
(Requirements the same as for Festival of Deities.)

---

288 The *Kanname* or *Kamunie no matsuri* 神嘗祭, (Deity Food Festival) was celebrated at the Grand Shrine of Ise as a ceremony of 'divine tasting' of rice and sake from rice of the new crop in the 9th month. This is no longer celebrated at the Ise Shrines.

289 The Daigoku-den 大極殿 or Audience Hall of the Imperial Palace; the smaller building behind it was the Daigoku-kōden or Rear Hall of the Daigoku-den.

Festival of Deities Worshiped by the Igazuri Sacred Maidens:

1 *hiki* 2 *jō* 5 *shaku* of pongee, 2 *jō* 5 *shaku* of each of five colors of silk, 2 skeins of silk thread, 3 *mochi* of floss silk, 2 *shaku* of colored hemp-cloth, 2 *tan* of tribute cloth, 2 *tan* of tax cloth, 50 sheets of paper, 2 *kin* each of common bark-cloth and hemp, 5 mattocks, 200 *mon* in coin, 9 *shō* of sake 4 *to* of rice, 2 *to* of glutinous rice, 5 *soku* of rice-in-ear, 1 *to* each of soybeans and red beans, 6 *kin* each of abalone, bonito, dried meat and *wakame,* 5 salmon, 2 *to* of salt, 2 white-wood boxes, 5 split-cypress-wood boxes, 5 food-boxes, 2 gourds, 2 each of jugs and cooking-pots, 5 large jars, 50 saucers, 4 bundles of oak, 2 seat-mats, 2 straw-mats, 5 food-mats, 2 split-bamboo mats.

Festival of Deities Worshiped by the Ikushima Sacred Maidens:

1 *hiki* 1 *jō* of pongee, 1 *jō* each of five colors of silk, 1 skein silk thread, 3 *mochi* of floss silk, 2 *shaku* colored hemp-cloth, 3 *tan* of tribute cloth, 1 *tan* of tax cloth, 50 sheets of paper, 1 *kin* each of common bark-cloth and hemp, 2 mattocks, 200 *mon* in coin, 2 *to* each of rice and glutinous rice, 6 *shō* of sake, 1 *to* each of soybeans and red beans, 2 *soku* of rice-in-ear, 6 *kin* each of abalone, bonito, dried meat and *wakame,* 2 salmon, 2 *to* of salt, 2 each of white-wood boxes, split-cypress boxes and food-boxes, 2 gourds, 2 each of jugs and cooking-pots, 2 large jars, 20 saucers, 40 bundles of oak, 2 seat-mats, 2 straw-mats, 2 each of food-mats and split-bamboo mats.

The above are celebrated by the Sacred Maidens and those under them; all are celebrated at the Sacred Courtyard of the *Jingi-kan.*

FESTIVALS OF THE ELEVENTH MONTH

The Ainame Festival for 71 Deities[290]

Two at Futonoto Shrine[291] (in Nijō in the Left Capital):

4 *hiki* of pongee, 2 skeins 2 *ryō* of silk thread, 6 *mochi* of floss silk, 7 *tan* 3 *jō* 8 *shaku* of tribute cloth, 2 *tan* 2 *jō* 6 *shaku* of tax cloth, 3 *kin* 4 *ryō* of bark-cloth, 1 *kin* 4 *ryō* of abalone, 5 *kin* 4 *ryō* of bonito, 8 *kin* of dried meat, 6 *kin* of gel-idium,[292] 2 *shō* of salt, 4 *kin* of *wakame,* 2 round boxes, 4 each of shallow earthenware vessels, bottles, jars, water-jars, *yama-tsubaha, ko-tsubaha,*[293] covered jars, sake jugs, spouted vessels, *torosuki,*[294] pedestalled dishes, coverless dishes, short-stemmed dishes, dishes with sides, small dishes and ceramic mortars, 120 *soku* of rice-in-ear for the sake (from deity taxes).

290 The *Aimube* (or *Ainie* or *Ainame*) *matsuri* 相嘗祭 celebrated in the 11th month when the Sovereign made a ceremonial meal together with the deities to taste rice and sake made from the new crop. In the 4th year of Temmu Tennō (10th month) it is recorded that the sovereign sent offerings to the *Aimube* deities. Aida, *op. cit.,* p. 348.

291 'Shrine' is used to translate *yashiro*. The term is an anachronism throughout, as these later became *jinja.*

292 *Korumoha* 凝海藻 appears to be an old name for *tengusa* or *tokoroten* which belongs to *Gelidium,* a genus of red algae, which is a source of agar.

293 *Tsubaha* appears to be related to *tsubo* 壺, a jar, urn or crock. These two vessels are ceremonial or ritual urns. Cf. *tsubaha,* n. 232, above.

294 *Torosuki,* written phonetically, appears to be a ritual vessel for serving the festival food.

Kamo-no-wakeikazuchi Shrine, one deity:[295]

2 *hiki* of stiff silk, 1 skein 1 *ryō* silk thread, 3 *mochi* floss silk, 3 *tan* 4 *jō* of tribute cloth, 1 *tan* 1 *jō* 3 *shaku* of tax cloth, 13 *ryō* of bark-cloth, 10 *ryō* of abalone, 2 *kin* 10 *ryō* of bonito, 4 *kin* of dried meat, 2 *kin* of *wakame*, 3 *kin* of gelidium, 1 *shō* of salt, 1 round box, 2 each of shallow earthenware vessels, bottles, jars, water-jars, *yama-tsubaha*, *ko-tsubaha*, covered jars, sake jugs, spouted vessels, *torosuki*, pedestalled dishes, coverless dishes, short-stemmed dishes, dishes with sides, small dishes and ceramic mortars, 50 *soku* of rice-in-ear for the sake (from deity taxes).

Kamo-no-mioya Shrine, two deities:[296]

4 *hiki* of stiff silk, 2 skeins 2 *ryō* of silk thread, 6 *mochi* of floss silk, 7 *tan* 3 *jō* 8 *shaku* of tribute cloth, 2 *tan* 2 *jō* 6 *shaku* of tax cloth, 3 *kin* 4 *ryō* of bark-cloth, 1 *kin* 4 *ryō* of abalone, 5 *kin* 4 *ryō* of bonito, 4 *kin* of *wakame*, 6 *kin* of gelidium, 8 *kin* of dried meats, 2 *shō* of salt, 2 round boxes [remainder of list identical to that of Kamo-no-wakeikazuchi].[297]

Kamo-mitarashi Shrine, one deity:

2 *hiki* of stiff silk, 1 skein 1 *ryō* of silk thread, 3 *mochi* of floss silk, 3 *tan* 4 *shaku* of tribute cloth, 1 *tan* 1 *jō* 3 *shaku* of tax cloth, 13 *ryō* of bark-cloth, 10 *ryō* of abalone, 2 *kin* of bonito, 1 *shō* of salt, 1 round box, 2 *kin* each of *wakame* and gelidium [remainder of list identical to that of Kamo-no-wakeikazuchi].

Matsuno-o Shrine, two deities:[298]

[Requirements are identical to those of Kamo-no-wakeikazuchi Shrine, above].

Izumo Inoue Shrine, one deity:

[Requirements are identical to those for Kamo-no-wakeikazuchi, above.]

Minushi Shrine, two deities:

[Requirements are identical to those for Futonoto Shrine, above.]

Katayama Shrine, one deity:

[Requirements are identical to those for Kamo-no-wakeikazuchi, above.]

Konoshima Shrine, one deity:

---

295 The two Kamo Shrines, located in the Heian Capital, are of particular importance. In spite of the designation *yashiro* in this bk. II, these shrines were classed as 'middle' (in a great, middle, small classification) under the Taihō Code. The Kamo-no-wakeikazuchi 賀茂別雷 is the Upper Kamo (Kamigamo 上賀茂) Shrine venerating the 'Young and Powerful Deity' who was son of Tamayorihime-no-mikoto 玉依姫命. According to a modern account, this shrine holds an esoteric festival in which the resurrection of the deity is to be brought about. After that, the public festival held is the *Aoi-matsuri*. *Guide to the Kansai Area*, p. 29. Miyagi, *op. cit.*, II, p. 452.

296 The Lower Kamo (Shimogamo 下賀茂) Shrine is the Mioya 御租 (Divine Parents) Shrine in which the enshrined deities are Tamayorihime-no-mikoto and her father, Kamo-taketsunumi-no-mikoto 鴨建角身命. The Imperial Family paid reverence to these (and Wakeikazuchi-no-mikoto 別雷命) as tutelary deities of the Capital. In the reign of Saga Tennō 嵯峨天皇 (809-23) the institution of Sai-in (Itsuki-miko), an Imperial Princess appointed to serve the deities of the Kamo Shrines was established and lasted until the reign of Tsuchimikado 土御門 (1198-1210). This institution is treated in Book VI of the *E-S*.

297 Since this list contains offerings to 71 deities in 40 shrines, it seems permissible to abridge in the case of repeated lists of identical offerings.

298 The Matsuno-o 松尾 Shrine increased in importance from 'small' category to 'middle' to 'great'. Miyagi, II, p. 470. See n. 241, above. The Matsuno-o festival is 'middle' rank in the annual festivals of *E-S*, Bk. I.

[Requirements are identical to those for Kamo-no-wakeikazuchi, above.]

The above 8 shrines are located in Yamashiro Province.

Ooyamato Shrine, three deities:

6 *hiki* of stiff silk, 8 skeins 4 *shu* of silk thread, 12 *tan* 1 *jō* 6 *shaku* of tribute cloth, 3 *tan* 2 *shaku* of tax cloth, 8 *kin* 4 *ryō* of bark-cloth, 2 *kin* of abalone, 9 *kin* 4 *ryō* of bonito, 19 *kin* 14 *ryō* of dried fish, 13 *kin* 4 *ryō* each of *wakame* and gelidium, 2 *to* of salt, 3 round boxes, 4 each of shallow earthenware vessels, jugs, water-jars, *yama-tsubaha, ko-tsubaha,* covered jars, sake jugs, spouted vessels, *torosuki,* pedestalled dishes, dishes with sides, small dishes, coverless dishes, short-stemmed dishes and ceramic mortars, 200 *soku* of rice-in-ear for the sake (from deity taxes).

Isonokami Shrine, one deity:

2 *hiki* of stiff silk, 1 skein 1 *ryō* of silk thread, 3 *mochi* of floss silk, 3 *tan* 4 *jō* of tribute cloth, 1 *tan* 1 *jō* 3 *shaku* of tax cloth, 10 *kin* 10 *ryō* of abalone, 2 *kin* of *wakame,* 3 *kin* of gelidium, 2 *kin* 10 *ryō* of bonito, 4 *kin* of dried meat, 1 *shō* of salt, 1 round box [remainder of list same as for the Kamo-no-wakeikazuchi, above].

Oowa (Oomiwa) Shrine, one deity:[299]

3 *hiki* of stiff silk, 3 skeins 4 *ryō* 4 *shu* of silk thread, 6 *tan* 8 *shaku* of tribute cloth, 1 *tan* 1 *jō* 4 *shaku* of tax cloth, 4 *kin* 2 *ryō* of bark-cloth, 1 *kin* 5 *ryō* of abalone, 5 *kin* of bonito, 3 *to* of *yorito* fish,[300] 1 *to* of salt, 6 *kin* 10 *ryō* each of dried fish, *wakame* and gelidium, 2 round boxes, 2 each of shallow earthenware vessels, jugs, water-jars, *tsubaha, ko-tsubaha,* covered jars, sake jugs, spouted vessels, *torosuki,* pedestalled dishes, coverless dishes, small saucers, short-stemmed saucers, sided saucers and ceramic mortars, 200 *soku* of rice-in-ear for the sake (from deity taxes).

Unatari Shrine, one deity:

2 *hiki* of stiff silk, 1 skein 1 *ryō* 3 *bu* 2 *shu* of silk thread, 3 *tan* 4 *shaku* of tribute cloth, 1 *tan* 1 *jō* 4 *shaku* of tax cloth, 13 *ryō* of bark-cloth, 2 *kin* 10 *ryō* of *wakame,* 10 *ryō* of abalone, 2 *kin* 10 *ryō* of bonito, 4 *kin* of dried meat, 1 *shō* of salt, 1 round box [remainder of list identical to that for Kamo-no-wakeikazuchi, above].

Muraya Shrine, one deity:

1 *hiki* of stiff silk, 1 skein, 3 *bu* 2 *shu* of silk thread, 3 *tan* 4 *shaku* of tribute cloth, 1 *tan* 1 *jō* 3 *shaku* of tax cloth, 1 *kin* 10 *ryō* of bark-cloth, 10 *ryō* of abalone, 2 *kin* of bonito, 1 *kin* of dried meat, 1 *kin* 10 *ryō* of *wakame,* 1 *shō* of salt, 1 round box, 2 each of shallow earthenware vessels, jugs, water jars, *yama-tsubaha, ko-tsubaha,* covered jars, pedestalled dishes, coverless dishes, short-stemmed saucers, sided saucers, small saucers, sake jugs, spouted vessels, *torosuki* and ceramic mortars, 50 *soku* of rice-in-ear for the sake (from deity taxes).

Anashi Shrine, one deity:

---

[299] Concerning Oomiwa Shrine, see n. 228, above.

[300] *Yorito,* written phonetically, seems to be obsolete; the 'dried fish' in the next line is also unidentified.

2 *hiki* of stiff silk, 1 skein 1 *bu* of silk thread, 3 *tan* 4 *shaku* of tribute cloth, 1 *tan* 1 *jō* 4 *shaku* of tax cloth, 1 *kin* of bark-cloth, 10 *ryō* of abalone, 2 *kin* 10 *ryō* of bonito, 4 *kin* of dried meat, 2 *kin* 10 *ryō* of *wakame*, 1 *shō* of salt, 1 round box [remainder of list identical to that of Muraya Shrine].

Makimoku Shrine, one deity:

2 *hiki* of stiff silk, 1 skein 1 *ryō* 3 *bu* of silk thread, 3 *tan* 4 *shaku* of tribute cloth, 1 *tan* 1 *jō* 4 *shaku* of tax cloth, 13 *ryō* of bark-cloth, 10 *ryō* of abalone, 4 *kin* of dried meat, 2 *kin* 10 *ryō* each of bonito, and *wakame*, 1 *shō* of salt, 1 round box [remainder of list identical to that for Muraya Shrine].

Ike Shrine, one deity:

2 *hiki* of stiff silk, 1 skein 1 *ryō* 1 *bu* 3 *shu* of silk thread, 3 *tan* 4 *shaku* of tribute cloth, 1 *tan* 1 *jō* 4 *shaku* of tax cloth, 13 *ryō* of bark-cloth, 10 *ryō* of abalone, 2 *kin* 10 *ryō* each of bonito and *wakame*, 1 *shō* of salt, 1 round box [remainder of list identical to that for Muraya Shrine].

Oo-no-yashiro, two deities (多 Shrine, also written 大):

2 *hiki* of stiff silk, 3 skeins 4 *shu* of silk thread, 3 *tan* 4 *shaku* of tribute cloth, 1 *tan* 1 *jō* 3 *shaku* of tax cloth, 1 *kin* 10 *ryō* of bark-cloth, 1 *kin* 10 *ryō* of abalone, 2 *kin* 10 *ryō* of bonito, 4 *kin* of dried meat, 2 *kin* 10 *ryō* of *wakame*, 1 *shō* of salt, 2 round boxes [remainder of list identical to that for the Muraya Shrine].

Kazuragi-no-Kamo Shrine, two deities:

2 *hiki* of stiff silk, 3 skeins 4 *shu* of silk thread, 3 *tan* 4 *shaku* of tribute cloth, 1 *tan* 1 *jō* 3 *shaku* of tax cloth, 1 *kin* 10 *ryō* of bark-cloth, 4 *kin* of dried meat, 10 *ryō* of abalone, 2 *kin* 10 *ryō* of bonito, 2 *kin* 10 *ryō* of *wakame*, 4 *shō* of salt, 2 round boxes [remainder of list the same as that for Muraya Shrine except that rice-in-ear is 100 *soku*].

Asuka Shrine, four deities:

8 *hiki* of stiff silk, 12 skeins of silk thread, 12 *mochi* of floss silk, 12 *tan* of tribute cloth, 6 *tan* 8 *shaku* of tax cloth, 6 *kin* 8 *ryō* of bark-cloth, 2 *kin* 8 *ryō* of abalone, 8 *kin* 10 *ryō* of bonito, 2 *to* of dried meat, 8 *kin* 10 *ryō* of *wakame*, 4 *to* of salt, 4 round boxes, 8 each of shallow earthenware vessels, jugs, water-jars, *yama-tsubaha*, *ko-tsubaha*, covered jars, sake jugs, spouted vessels, *torosuki*, pedestalled dishes, coverless dishes, short-stemmed saucers, sided saucers, small saucers, sake cups, ceramic mortars, 200 *soku* of rice-in-ear for sake (108 *soku* of deity-tax rice, 92 *soku* regular tax).

Amakashi Shrine, four deities:

[Requirements the same as for Asuka Shrine, except that dried meat is 5 *shō* (instead of 2 *to*) and all rice-in-ear is from regular taxes.]

Takakamo Shrine, four deities:

[Requirements the same as for Asuka Shrine, except that abalone and bonito are omitted and in their stead are 8 *kin* 8 *ryō* of *wakame* and 8 *kin* 10 *ryō* of gelidium; all rice-in-ear from regular taxes.]

Takamahiko Shrine, one deity:

2 *hiki* stiff silk, 1 skein 1 *bu* 1 *shu* of silk thread, 3 *tan* 4 *shaku* of tribute cloth, 1 *tan* 1 *jō* 4 *shaku* of tax cloth, 3 *mochi* of floss silk, 13 *ryō* of bark-cloth, 10 *ryō* of abalone, 4 *kin* of dried meat, 2 *kin* 10 *ryō* of bonito, 1 *shō* of salt, 2 *kin* 10 *ryō*

each of *wakame* and gelidium, 1 round box [remainder of list the same as for Muraya Shrine].

Kanemitake Shrine, one deity:

2 *hiki* of stiff silk, 1 skein 1 *bu* of silk thread, 3 *mochi* of silk floss, 3 *tan* 4 *shaku* of tribute cloth, 1 *tan* 1 *jō* 4 *shaku* of tax cloth, 13 *ryō* of bark-cloth, 10 *ryō* of abalone, 2 *kin* 10 *ryō* of bonito, 4 *kin* of dried meat, 1 *shō* of salt, 2 *kin* 10 *ryō* each of *wakame* and gelidium, 1 round box [remainder of list the same as for Muraya Shrine].

Kazuragi-no-hitokotonushi Shrine, one deity:

2 *hiki* of stiff silk, 1 skein of silk thread, 3 *mochi* of floss silk, 3 *tan* 4 *shaku* of tribute cloth, 1 *tan* 1 *jō* 4 *shaku* of tax cloth, 13 *ryō* of bark-cloth, 1 *kin* 10 *ryō* of abalone, 4 *kin* of dried meat, 2 *kin* of bonito, 2 *kin* each of *wakame* and gelidium, 1 round box [remainder of list the same as for Muraya Shrine].

Honoikazuchi Shrine, two deities:

4 *hiki* of stiff silk, 2 skeins of silk thread, 6 *mochi* of floss silk, 6 *tan* 2 *jō* of tribute cloth, 2 *tan* 2 *jō* 8 *shaku* of tax cloth, 2 *kin* 4 *ryō* of bark-cloth, 2 *kin* 4 *ryō* of abalone, 5 *kin* 4 *ryō* of bonito, 4 *kin* of *wakame*, 6 *kin* of gelidium, 8 *kin* of dried meat, 2 *shō* of salt, 2 round boxes, 2 each of shallow earthenware vessels, jugs, water-jars, *yama-tsubaha*, *ko-tsubaha*, covered jars, sake jugs, spouted vessels, *torosuki*, pedestalled dishes, coverless dishes, short-stemmed saucers, sided saucers, small saucers, ceramic mortars, and 100 *soku* of rice-in-ear for sake (from deity taxes).

The 17 shrines above are in Yamato Province.

Hiraoka Shrine, four deities:[301]

8 *hiki* of stiff silk, 12 skeins of silk thread, 12 *mochi* of floss silk, 12 *tan* of tribute cloth, 6 *tan* of tax cloth, 6 *kin* 8 *ryō* of bark-cloth, 2 *kin* 8 *ryō* of abalone, 8 *kin* 8 *ryō* of bonito, 2 *to* of dried meat, 8 *kin* 8 *ryō* each of *wakame* and gelidium, 4 *to* of salt, 4 round boxes, 8 each of [same list of utensils as for Muraya Shrine], 200 *soku* of rice-in-ear for sake (from regular taxes).

Onchi Shrine, two deities:

2 *hiki* of stiff silk, 3 skeins 4 *shu* of silk thread, 3 *tan* 4 *shaku* of tribute cloth, 1 *tan* 1 *jō* 3 *shaku* of tax cloth, 1 *kin* 10 *ryō* of bark-cloth, 10 *ryō* of abalone, 2 *kin* 10 *ryō* of bonito, 4 *shō* of dried meat, 2 *kin* 6 *ryō* of *wakame*, 1 *shō* of salt, 2 round boxes, 2 each of [same list of utensils as for Muraya Shrine], 50 *soku* of rice-in-ear for the sake (from regular taxes).

Yuge Shrine, two deities:

4 *hiki* of stiff silk, 4 skeins of silk thread, 4 *mochi* of floss silk, 6 *tan* of tribute cloth, 4 *tan* of tax cloth, 2 *kin* of bark-cloth, 1 *kin* 4 *ryō* of abalone, 2 *kin* of bonito, 4 *shō* of dried meat, 4 *kin* of *wakame*, 4 *shō* of salt, 2 round boxes, 4 each of [same utensils as for Muraya Shrine], 200 *soku* of rice-in-ear for sake (from regular taxes).

The above 3 shrines are in Kawachi Province.

---

301 The Hiraoka Shrine also became a major shrine, and its festival was a national celebration held in the spring and fall, at which times Nakatomi officials of the *Jingi-kan* presented offerings. See n. 221.

Sumiyoshi Shrine, four deities:[302]

4 *hiki* 3 *jō* of stiff silk, 4 skeins 8 *ryō* 4 *shu* of silk thread, 3 *mochi* 3 *ryō* of floss silk, 3 *kin* 10 *ryō* of bark-cloth, 8 *tan* 3 *jō* 4 *shaku* of tribute cloth, 1 *tan* 1 *jō* 3 *shaku* of tax cloth, 2 *hiki* of pongee for pure robes for the *imubito*,[303] 2 *kin* 8 *ryō* of abalone, 6 *kin* 15 *ryō* of bonito, 1 *to* of dried meat, 5 *shō* of salt, 9 *kin* 10 *ryō* each of *wakame* and gelidium, 4 round boxes, 8 each of [same utensils as for Muraya Shrine], 200 *soku* of rice-in-ear for sake (from regular taxes).

Ooyosami Shrine, four deities:[304]

8 *hiki* of stiff silk, 12 skeins of silk thread, 12 *mochi* of floss silk, 12 *tan* of tribute cloth, 6 *tan* of tax cloth, 6 *kin* 8 *ryō* of bark-cloth, 2 *kin* 8 *ryō* of abalone, 5 *shō* of dried meat, 8 *kin* 10 *ryō* of bonito, 8 *kin* 8 *ryō* of *wakame*, 8 *kin* 10 *ryō* of gelidium, 4 *to* of salt, 4 round boxes, 8 each of [same utensils as for Muraya Shrine], 200 *soku* of rice-in-ear for sake (from regular taxes).

Naniwa-no-ōyashiro, two deities:

4 *hiki* of stiff silk, 6 skeins of silk thread, 6 *mochi* of floss silk, 6 *tan* of tribute cloth, 1 *tan* 2 *jō* 3 *shaku* of tax cloth, 2 *kin* of bark-cloth, 10 *ryō* of abalone, 5 *shō* of dried meat, 1 *to* of salt, 4 *kin* 4 *ryō* of bonito, 4 *kin* 4 *ryō* each of *wakame*, and gelidium, 2 round boxes, 6 each of [same utensils as for Muraya Shrine], 100 *soku* of rice-in-car for sake (from regular taxes).

Shitateru-hime Shrine, one deity (also called Himekoso Shrine):

2 *hiki* of stiff silk, 3 skeins of silk thread, 3 *mochi* of floss silk, 3 *tan* of tribute cloth, 1 *tan* 1 *jō* 7 *shaku* of tax cloth, 1 *kin* 8 *ryō* of bark-cloth, 10 *ryō* each of abalone and bonito, 5 *shō* of dried meat, 2 *kin* 10 *ryō* of *wakame*, 2 *kin* 2 *ryō* of gelidium, 1 *shō* of salt, 1 round box, 2 each of [same utensils as for Muraya Shrine], 50 *soku* of rice-in-ear for sake (from regular taxes).

Niiya Shrine, one deity:

2 *hiki* of stiff silk, 3 skeins of silk thread, 2 *mochi* of floss silk, 3 *tan* 4 *shaku* of tribute cloth, 1 *tan* 1 *jō* 3 *shaku* of tax cloth, 10 *kin* 3 *ryō* of bark-cloth, 10 *ryō* of abalone, 2 *kin* 10 *ryō* of bonito, 3 *kin* 10 *ryō* each of *wakame* and gelidium, 4 *shō* of dried meat, 4 *shō* of salt, 1 round box, 2 each of [same utensils as for Muraya Shrine], 100 *soku* of ricc-in-ear for sake (from regular taxes).

Hirota Shrine, one deity:[305]

2 *hiki* of stiff silk, 1 skein 1 *ryō* of silk thread, 3 *mochi* of floss silk, 3 *tan* 4 *shaku* of tribute cloth, 1 *tan* 1 *jō* 3 *shaku* of tax cloth, 1 *kin* 10 *ryō* of bark-cloth, 1 *kin* 10 *ryō* of abalone, 2 *kin* 10 *ryō* of bonito, 4 *kin* of dried meat, 1 *shō* of salt, 2 *kin* 10 *ryō* of *wakame*, 1 round box, 2 each of [same utensils as for Muraya Shrine], 50 *soku* of rice-in-ear for sake (from deity taxes).

[302] Sumiyoshi 住吉 Shrine in Naniwa was dedicated to three deities of the sea, patron gods of mariners, and to one manifestation of Jingū Kōgō 神功皇后, who is supposed to have set out from Naniwa to make her Korean conquest.

[303] *Imubito (imibito)* 齋人, participants who performed abstinence—other than the Imbe who were professional abstainers. If these can be distinguished from *omibito* (n. 262) it would be that they performed total as well as partial abstinence.

[304] Ooyosami 大依羅 Shrine in Settsu 攝津 Province (present Sumiyoshi-ku, Osaka) venerates Oonamuchi-no-mikoto 大己貴命, Tsukiyomi-no-mikoto 月讀命 and Emperor Suinin. Traditions also connect Yamato Takeru-no-mikoto 日本尊命 and Jingū Kōgō with it. *Shintō daijiten.*

[305] The Hirota Jinja 廣田神社, in present Nishinomiya, is also linked to Jingū Kōgō's Korean expedition, whereby her 'aramitama' or 'turbulent spirit' is said to be enshrined there.

Ikuta Shrine, one deity:

> 2 *hiki* of stiff silk, 1 skein 1 *ryō* of silk thread, 3 *mochi* of floss silk, 3 *tan* 4 *shaku* of tribute cloth, 1 *tan* 1 *jō* 3 *shaku* of tax cloth, 1 *kin* 10 *ryō* of bark-cloth, 1 *kin* 10 *ryō* of abalone, 2 *kin* 10 *ryō* of bonito, 4 *shō* of dried meat, 1 *shō* of salt, 2 *kin* 10 *ryō* of *wakame*, 1 round box, 2 each of [same utensils as for Muraya Shrine], 50 *soku* of rice-in-ear for sake (from deity taxes).

Nagata Shrine, one deity:

> 2 *hiki* of stiff silk, 1 skein of silk thread, 3 *mochi* of floss silk, 3 *tan* 4 *shaku* of tribute cloth, 1 *tan* 1 *jō* 3 *shaku* of tax cloth, 1 *kin* 10 *ryō* of bark-cloth, 1 *kin* 10 *ryō* of abalone, 2 *kin* 10 *ryō* of bonito, 4 *kin* of dried meat, 1 *shō* of salt, 1 round box, 2 *kin* 10 *ryō* of *wakame*, 2 each of [same utensils as for Muraya Shrine], 50 *soku* of rice-in-ear for sake (from deity taxes).

The foregoing eight shrines are in Settsu Province.

Hinokuma Shrine, one deity:

> 4 *hiki* of stiff silk, 3 skeins 4 *shu* of silk thread, 8 *mochi* 5 *ryō* of floss silk, 6 *tan* 8 *shaku* of tribute cloth, 2 *kin* 8 *ryō* of bark-cloth, 100 *soku* of rice-in-ear for sake (from deity taxes).

Kunikakasu Shrine, one deity:

> 4 *hiki* of stiff silk, 3 skeins 4 *shu* of silk thread, 8 *mochi* 5 *ryō* of floss silk, 6 *tan* 8 *shaku* of tribute cloth, 2 *kin* 8 *ryō* of bark-cloth, 100 *soku* of rice-in-ear for sake (from deity taxes).

Itakiso Shrine, one deity:

> 2 *hiki* of stiff silk, 3 skeins of silk thread, 3 *tan* 1 *jō* 7 *shaku* of tribute cloth, 13 *ryō* of bark-cloth, 50 *soku* of rice-in-ear for sake (from deity taxes).

Narukami Shrine, one deity:

> 1 *hiki* of stiff silk, 3 skeins of silk thread, 3 *tan* of tribute silk, 13 *ryō* of bark-cloth, 50 *soku* of rice-in-ear for sake (from deity taxes).

The foregoing four shrines are in Kii Province.

The above shrines which hold the *Ainame* festival as indicated, celebrate it on the first hare day of the 11th month. The various articles necessary are requested and received from the [*Jingi-*]*kan* and the *hafuribe* and others are assigned to distribute and offer them. Deity taxes and regular taxes are used for the rice-in-ear to make sake.

Mitama-shizume Festival [Chinkon-sai][306] (repeated in the Palace of the Consort, but clothing is not bestowed again):

---

306 The *Chinkon-sai* (also read *Oomitamafuri-no-matsuri*) or 'Pacification of Spirits', held on a tiger day in the 11th month, had as its purpose to prolong the life of the sovereign and pacify or soothe the ancestral spirits. It was held in the office of the Imperial Household Ministry (on the day before the *Daijō-sai* if that was held). The ancestral spirits worshiped included: Kami-musubi 神魂, Takami-musubi 高御魂, Iku-musubi 生魂, Taru-musubi 足魂, Tamatsume-musubi, 魂留魂, Oomiyanome 大宮女, Miketsu(tama) 御膳魂,

Kotoshironushi 辞代主—the eight deities worshiped in the *Jingi-kan*, plus Oonaobi-no-kami 大直毘神. The celebration includes the presentation of symbolic offerings, food offerings, and a dance done by the 'descendants' of Sarume-no-mikoto 猿女命 (or Ame-no-uzume-no-mikoto 天鈿女命) upon an inverted tub, as occurs in the myth of luring the Sun Goddess out of the Heavenly Rock Cave. While the dancer thumps the spear-end on the tub, counting up to ten, the chief of the *Jingi-kan* entwines the sacred bark-cloth and places it in★

Eight deities *(Kamimusubi, Takamimusubi, Ikumusubi, Tarumusubi, Tama-tsumemusubi, Oomiyanome, Miketsutama* and *Kotoshironushi).*

One presentation to Oonaobi-no-kami:

1 longsword, 1 bow, 2 quivers, 20 round bells, 20 *sanagi*,[307] 1 *hiki* of pongee, 5 *kin* of bark-cloth, 10 *kin* of hemp, 1 round box, 1 coarse box, 1 white-wood box, 1 cooked-rice box for the offering, 2 *soku* of rice-in-ear for the sacred meal, 1 offering-table, 1 large tub, 1 mortar, 2 pestles, 4 bundles of oak, 1 straw-mat, 1 Kara stove, 4 dippers, 2 jars, 4 cooking-pots, 1 leaf-mat for wrapping.

As to the above: the Sacred Maidens pound the rice in the Sacred Court-yard of the *Jingi-kan,* they put it in the coarse boxes for winnowing and cook it on the Kara stove; that done they put it in rush containers, enclose it in the boxes and place it on the offering-table. Two members of the *kambe* carry the table up to the place of worship and present it.

Required for Court dress for the *Jingi-kan* officials and those under them (duplicated for the Chief Diviner in the Middle Palace):

for 7 persons from Chief of the *Jingi-kan* down to Chief Ritualist and for one Chief Diviner (the foregoing get printed tunics)[308]; 2 masters of tor-toise divination, 2 *koto* players, 1 Sacred Maiden and 1 *kambe* each receive a blue printed tunic and 1 pair of trousers; 4 scribes, 13 *kambe*, 12 *urabe* and 3 official attendants[309] each receive a blue printed skirt (the foregoing provided by the Needlework Bureau); 1 Sacred Maiden (duplicated for Sacred Maidens of Middle Palace and Heir Apparent's Palace), 1 Mikado Sacred Maiden and 1 Ikushima Sacred Maiden each receive a blue printed tunic (3 *jō* of silk each for garment and for lining), 2 *mochi* of floss silk, 1 vest-and-train[310] (3 *jō* of silk each for garment and for lining), 2 *mochi* of floss silk, 1 unlined silk garment (3 *jō* of silk), 1 overskirt (3 *jō* of silk each for garment and lining, 1 *jō* for girdle), 2 *mochi* of floss silk, 1 underskirt (3 *jō* of silk each for garment and lining, 1 *jō* for girdle), 1 pair of trousers (3 *jō* 5 *shaku* of silk), 2 *mochi* of floss silk, 1 pair of unlined trousers (2 *jō* of silk), 1 skirt (2 *jō* of silk), 1 ceremonial outer garment[311] (2 *jō* of silk), 1 wide sash (4 *jō* of scarlet silk),

---

*a box, then a female official takes a sacred garment out of the august garment box and shakes it. Under the direction of the *jibu-shō,* singers and players then perform sacred music. Aida, *op. cit.,* p. 349. Hagenauer, 'La Danse rituelle dans la cérémonie du Chinkonsai'.

307 The interlinear gloss says *sanagi* 佐奈伎 is 'a thing like a spear' *(hoko* 戈*). Dainihon kokugo jiten* says it is a bell *(taku* 鐸*).* This appears to be the ceremonial spear used in the dance to beat the tub—*ukebune* 宇氣槽 in the text.

308 The first printed garment stated is *harisuri* 榛摺, the rest are *aozuri* 青摺; all are white gar-ments with a design in color made by rubbing on a plant dye. Alder *(hari* or *hannoki)* produced a reddish brown, while dark blue was produced from

wild indigo plant. The latter was favored for cere-monial wear in earlier times, but Saga Tennō re-vived its use and it was made regulation for cere-monies in his reign. T. Ema, *Shinshū yūsoku kojitsu,* pp. 98–9.

309 *Shibu* 使部, or *tsukawarebe*—official attend-ants—were petty officials attached to the *Dajō-kan* and the various ministries to perform clerical and menial tasks. R. K. Reischauer, *Early Japanese History,* B, p. 214.

310 The *shitakasane* 下襲 is a formal ladies garment with long train extending from the waist.

311 There are conflicting glosses for the term *hi* 帔; one says it is a head covering (reading *chikiri-kōburi),* the other calls it *uchikake,* which is a Court lady's ceremonial sleeveless outer cloak.

1 sash (3 *jō* of brocade), 1 *jō* of fine-weave cloth for binding their hair and for tying socks, 7 *shaku* of fine silk for scarves, 2 combs, and 1 pair of shoes. For 1 Igazuri Sacred Maiden: 1 blue printed tunic (2 *jō* 5 *shaku* of silk each for tunic and for lining), 1 *mochi* of floss silk, 1 vest-and-train (2 *jō* 5 *shaku* of silk each for garment and for lining), 1 *mochi* of floss silk, 1 unlined silk garment (2 *jō* 5 *shaku* of silk), 1 overskirt (3 *jō* of silk each for skirt and for lining, 1 *jō* for girdle), 1 *mochi* of floss silk, 1 underskirt (3 *jō* of silk each for skirt and for lining, 1 *jō* for girdle), 1 pair of trousers (1 *jō* 5 *shaku* of silk), 1 *mochi* of floss silk, 1 pair unlined trousers (1 *jō* of silk), 1 ceremonial outer garment (1 *jō* of silk), 1 wide sash (1 *jō* 5 *shaku* of scarlet silk), 1 sash (1 *jō* of brocade), a 6-*shaku* scarf, 5 *shaku* of fine-weave cloth to tie socks, 1 pair of shoes.

For the above, at the monkey hour on the middle tiger day (the *Mitama-shizume* in the Middle Palace is celebrated on the same day), those of 5th Rank and above and the top officials of the various offices gather at the Ministry of the Imperial Household. The Officers of Ceremonial[312] according to precedent inspect the procession. The Great Ministers, or else Imperial Advisers and above, take seats at the West Building. Officials of the *Jingi-kan* down to the *kambe* wear blue printed tunics (the *Jingi-kan* having previously ordered, prepared and distributed them). They enter ahead of the Sacred Maidens and others and take the high seats in the [Main] Building (the Sacred Maidens face south, the Chief of the *Jingi-kan* and down to official attendants face east in order of rank ascending southward); the ladies-in-waiting carry the august garments and come out from inside. Members of the Palace Table and Wine Offices prepare the various foods and enter at this time (repeated in the Middle Palace and Heir Apparent's Palace); the Needlework Bureau tells the Sarume to enter;[313] thereupon the Great Minister ascends to his seat (he faces north and goes up to the east); he summons the messenger and tells him to summon the Officers of Ceremonial; the messenger gives the verbal response and goes forth to summon them. Then an official of the Third Class[314] or higher goes forward to the posting-board for ranks; the Great Minister makes the announcements and causes the host of officials to enter. They make the verbal response, come out and enter (5th Rank and above go to seats in the building, and face north, 6th Rank and lower separate and go to seats in the East and West Buildings, respectively). The seating fixed, the Great Minister orders the messenger to summon the Civil

---

312 The *shikibu* 式部 were officials of the Ministry of Ceremonial, *shikibu-shō*, in charge of registers, central and local officials, promotions in rank, palace ceremonies, and so forth. R. K. Reischauer, *op. cit.*

313 The *sarume* 猿女 were the group who did the particular dance to soothe divine spirits. The *Kogoshūi* says the Sarume-no-kimi were descendants of Ame-no-uzume and Sarudahiko 猿田彦. It goes on to say: 'The sacred symbolic dance or pantomime was the hereditary duty of the Sarume family of *kimi* rank . . .' Katō and Hoshi-

no, *Kogoshūi*, pp. 29, 36. Holtom calls them 'singers and dancers' who were perhaps temple prostitutes or fertility maidens. Sarudahiko was the chief of the phallic deities. *National Faith of Japan*, p. 28.

314 Within each government bureau and office there were four classes of officials: the highest was *chōkan* 長官, the second was *jikan* 次官 or *suke* 助, the third *hangan* 判官 or *jō*, and the fourth, *sakan* 主典 or 目. This classification was separate from that of Court Rank or of government position. J. Murao, *Ritsuryō-sei no kichō*, p. 48.

Administrator who causes the chorus[315] to come forth. Again, he calls to the Ministry of the Treasury to bestow the bark-cloth for headdresses, all as [stated] in the ceremonial above. That done, the chief of the *Jingi-kan* summons the player of the august *koto* and his assistant (both persons make the response); next he summons the flute-player and his assistant (the two make the response together). Again, he orders them, saying: 'Play the august *koto* and flutes' (all four make the verbal response); first they perform one flute number, then they play the *koto,* and then the singers commence to sing. The *kambe* in the upper hall accompany them with hand clapping. The Sacred Maidens and the Sarume perform the dances according to precedent. When it is done one 5th Rank and one 6th Rank *Jingi-kan* official (a Nakatomi and an Imbe) and two chamberlains[316] of 5th Rank or higher, one secretary of the Imperial Household,[317] two *udoneri* and two *ōdoneri* go forward into the courtyard and dance. When they have finished they return to their original places. The secretaries give the order to the office-keeper[318] to call to the Imperial Household Ministry to bestow the drink and food. After drinking sake three times over, they clap their hands behind them and depart.

On the day of the snake at the monkey hour the Pacification of the August Spirit is held in the Palace of the Heir Apparent.

Niiname-no-matsuri[319]—*The Festival of the First-Fruits: 304 Deities Worshiped with Offerings on top of the Offering-tables* (all Great).

198 Shrines: for each presentation, 5 *shaku* of pongee, 1 *shaku* each of five colors of thin pongee, 1 *shaku* of colored hemp-cloth, 2 *ryō* of bark-cloth, 5 *ryō* of hemp, 1 each of *yokura-oki* and *yakura-oki,* 1 shield, 1 spearhead; for each shrine, 1 *jō* 4 *shaku* of tax cloth, 5 *shaku* of leaf-mat for wrapping.

For presentations to 106 deities:

to each deity the offerings are made according to the rule of the shrine; but tax cloth is omitted.

The above is carried out by the officials of the *Jingi-kan* in its Sacred Courtyard. (The host of officials do not make offerings.) However, the distribution of symbolic offerings and the requirements for articles to be made for offering to the deities and requirements for the ritual [recited] by the Nakatomi all duplicate the *Tsukinami* festival.

Festival of the Cook-house of the Sacred Fire:

---

315 That is, the *utame* 歌女, female chorus, also called *utabito* 歌者 in this passage, below.

316 Chamberlains, *jijū* 侍從, were officials who were in close attendance upon the sovereign and belonged to the Ministry of Central Affairs (*nakatsukasa-shō* 中務省). Senior chamberlains were eight in number and waited upon the sovereign personally. Assistants with more general duties numbered up to 92.

317 The *kunai no jō*: 宮內丞. The subsequent secretaries are the *benkan* (n. 251).

318 The *kanjō* or *kajō* 官掌.

319 *Niinae* or *Niiname-no-matsuri* 新嘗祭, is supposed to be the 'original' ceremony of offering the first fruits to Amaterasu-ō-mikami and other deities. The *Nihongi* has a reference to a feast in the 11th month of 3rd year of Seinei Tennō 清寧天皇 (A.D. 482) and speaks of the 'First Fruits' celebrations in the 11th month in the reigns of Kōgyoku 皇極 and Temmu 天武. The days of the month differ. Miyagi, I, p. 45.

4 *shaku* each of five colors of thin pongee, 2 *shaku* of colored hemp-cloth, 5 *ryō* of bark-cloth, 1 *kin* 5 *ryō* of hemp, 4 mattocks, 4 *shō* each of rice and sake, 2 *kin* of abalone, 4 *kin* each of bonito, *wakame* and assorted seaweeds, 2 *shō* of salt, 4 jars, 4 saucers, 1 food-mat, 2 *tan* of tax cloth.

The above are required when a new cook-house is to be built before the *Niiname* festival; a pacification ceremony, as the item states, is conducted by the Chief Diviner. The old building is dismantled and given to the Chief Diviner.

Required for presentation at the *Niiname*:

1 *jō* 2 *shaku* of ramie cloth, 2 *jō* 2 *shaku* of stiff silk, 4 *ryō* of silk thread, 3 *tan* 1 *jō* of tribute cloth, 1 *jō* 2 *shaku* of bleached cloth, 3 *jō* 2 *shaku* of fine-weave cloth, 3 *kin* 10 *ryō* of bark-cloth, 2 august knives with carved handles, 10 each of long and short knives,[320] 14 round boxes, 2 coarse boxes, 3 white-wood boxes, 2 *to* each of august cooked rice and rice for gruel, 2 *to* of millet, 5 shallow *sue* ware vessels, 6 shallow *sue* ware jars, 4 each of jars and sake jugs, 8 spouted vessels, 8 water bowls, 6 wash-basins, 20 sided saucers, 4 ritual water pitchers, 8 bowls, 4 chopping bowls, 2 mortars, 2 coverless clay bowls, 10 sake cups, 10 small saucers, 20 pedestalled dishes, 2 clay jars for hot water, 2 hand-basins, 4 wide-topped jars, 10 cooking-pots, 2 braziers, 8 *sue* ware saucers, 12 offering-tables, 2 short tables, 2 mallets, 2 chopping boards, 4 bales of oak, 18 gourds, 2 small gourds, 2 sun umbrellas, 2 ritual elongated basins,[267] 3 *shō* of oil; the Imperial Table Office provides various condiments.

The above are for the preceding item [*Niiname*]; the requirements for the festivals of *Miagamono ōtono*, Sacred Fire and Courtyard Fire all duplicate those for the *Jinkonjiki*.

FESTIVALS OF THE TWELFTH MONTH

Festival of Abstinence[321] *for Propitiation of August Imperial Spirits* (duplicated in the Middle Palace):

1 *hiki* of pongee, 1 *shaku* each of five colors of silk, 1 skein of silk thread, 1 *mochi* of silk floss, 1 *shaku* of colored hemp cloth, 3 tan of tribute cloth, 3 *tan* of tax cloth, 2 *kin* each of bark-cloth and hemp, 1 *to* each of rice and sake, 6 *kin* each of abalone, bonito, dried meat and *wakame*, 2 *shō* of salt, 1 shallow earthenware vessel, 1 water jar, 8 saucers, 1 gourd, 10 bundles of oak, 1 food-mat.

Festival of Abstinence for Propitiation of August Spirits of the Heir Apparent:

3 *jō* of pongee, 1 *shaku* each of five colors of silk, 6 *ryō* of silk thread, 1 *mochi* of floss silk, 1 *shaku* of colored hemp-cloth, 1 *tan* of tribute cloth, 1 *tan* of tax

---

320 The interlinear glosses indicate that the ceremonial knives are for cutting willows, the long and short knives for the *uneme* (n. 275) to prepare oak—i.e., for the sacred fire (*imibi* 忌火).

321 To follow up the ceremonies of Mitamashizume held in the 11th month in the palaces, these two festivals were held in the 12th month in the *iwaido* 齋戸 sanctuary in the Sai-in of the *Jingi-kan* and included the reciting of a special ritual. T. Kaneko, *Engi-shiki norito-kō*, p. 215. D. Philippi, *Norito*, no. XV.

cloth, 1 *kin* each of bark-cloth and hemp, 5 *shō* each of rice and sake, 3 *kin* each of abalone, bonito, dried meat and *wakame*, 2 *shō* of salt, 1 shallow earthenware vessel, 1 water jar, 4 saucers, 1 gourd, 5 bundles of oak, 1 food-mat.

The above take place in the Sacred Courtyard of the *Jingi-kan* and the Nakatomi conduct the ceremony.

Festival of the Sacred Fire and Courtyard Fire on the First Day of Every Month (Courtyard Fire is duplicated in the Middle Palace and Heir Apparent's Palace, but Sacred Fire is not celebrated):

4 *shaku* each of five colors of thin pongee, 2 *shaku* of colored hemp-cloth, 4 *ryō* of bark-cloth, 4 large *ryō* of hemp, 2 *tan* of tax cloth, 4 mattocks, 4 *shō* each of rice and sake, 2 *kin* each of abalone and bonito, 4 *shō* of dried meat, 2 *kin* of *wakame,* 2 *shō* of salt, 2 shallow earthenware vessels, 4 saucers, 2 water jars.

For the above the Chief Diviner goes to the Office of the Imperial Table to conduct the affair. But at the Heir Apparent's Palace the Palace Chefs conduct it.

August Symbolic Offerings on the Last Day of Each Month (not held in the 6th and 12th months):

4 iron effigies, 1 *kin* of Aki bark-cloth, 1 *kin* of hemp, 1 *jō* 4 *shaku* of tax cloth, 2 mattocks, 2 *shō* each of sake and rice, 2 *soku* of rice-in-ear, 1 *kin* each of abalone, bonito and *wakame*, 2 *shō* of dried meat, 1 *shō* of salt.

August Symbolic Offerings on the Last Day of Each Month in the Middle Palace (duplicated in the Heir Apparent's Palace):

4 iron effigies, 1 *kin* of Aki bark-cloth (10 *ryō* in Heir Apparent's Palace) 1 *kin* of hemp, 1 *jō* 4 *shaku* of tax cloth, 2 mattocks, 2 *shō* each of rice and sake, 2 *soku* of rice-in-ear, 1 *kin* each of abalone, bonito and *wakame*, 2 *shō* of dried meat, 1 *shō* of salt.

For the above, on that day the Nakatomi, leading the diviners, go forth and wait at the Ensei Gate (all are wearing ceremonial attire and bark-cloth headdresses). The *ōdoneri* knock at the gate. The Minister of the Imperial Household enters and speaks, he steps back and summons the Nakatomi; they give the verbal response, raise the symbolic offerings and enter, then go to the posting-board of ranks. An Imperial edict is pronounced and they all approach. They make the verbal response and ascend to the carpet of split-bamboo matting. They hand over the offerings to the ladies-in-waiting. They descend and wait at the foot of the stairs. The ladies-in-waiting step forward and present the symbolic offering. When that is done they return them to the Nakatomi. These take them and step backward. This ceremony is carried out in the same way on the last day of the 6th month in the Middle Palace and Heir Apparent's Palace.

Thank Offerings on the Last Day of Each Month (duplicated in the Middle Palace and the Heir Apparent's Palace, but not held on the 6th and 12th Months):

32 each of gold and silver effigies (8 each for the Palace of the Heir Apparent), 4 *shaku* of violet silk, 5 *shaku* each of five colors of silk, 1 skein of silk thread,

1 *tan* of tribute cloth, 1 *kin* each of bark-cloth, hemp and yellow-bark, 1 *to* of
rice, 6 *shō* 5 *gō* of sake, 2 salmon, 1 basket of assorted food-stuffs, 2 *shō* of salt,
2 saucers, 8 jars (4 for the Heir Apparent's Palace), 1 gourd, 10 bundles of oak, 1
food-mat, 4 model palanquins, 20 wands for appending the symbolic offerings.
For the above, Sacred Maidens conduct the affair.

      *   *   *   *   *

End of Book Two of the *Engi-shiki*
  Enchō 5th Year, 12th Month, 26th Day
    [same signatures as at end of Book One]

ENGI-SHIKI, BOOK THREE

EXTRAORDINARY FESTIVALS

As a rule, besides the regular festivals there are others which it is proper to celebrate. These are celebrated according to the circumstances. If the Secretaries do not arrange these it will not be easy to hold the regular festivals.

Festival of the Kantoki Deities :[322]

2 *hiki* of stiff silk, 6 *shaku* each of five colors of thin pongee, 6 *shaku* of colored hemp-cloth, 2 *tan* of tax cloth, 8 *ryō* of bark-cloth, 4 *kin* of hemp, 2 mattocks, 4 *kin* of abalone, 6 *kin* of bonito, 4 *kin* of dried meat, 4 *shō* of salt, 8 *kin* of *wakame*, 20 *kin* of assorted seaweeds, 2 *to* of rice, 4 *to* of sake, 4 *soku* of rice-in-ear, 2 each of jugs and bottles, 6 saucers, 2 waterbuckets, 2 chickens, 2 gourds, 20 bundles of oak, 2 food-mats, 1 palanquin, 1 *tan* of ordinary cloth for the pure robes (foregoing are required for the festival); 4 *kin* each of bark-cloth and hemp, 4 *tan* of tax cloth, 4 mattocks, 4 deerskins, 4 longswords, 4 bows, 8 arrows, 4 *to* of rice, 6 *to* of sake, 4 *soku* of rice-in-ear, 6 *kin* each of abalone and bonito and dried meat, 20 *kin* each of *wakame, arame* and assorted seaweeds, 4 *shō* of salt, 4 each of jugs and saucers, 4 gourds, 2 food-mats (the foregoing are for the purification).

Festival to Propitiate a Sounding Stove :[323]

1 *hiki* of stiff silk, 1 skein of silk thread, 4 *shaku* each of five colors of thin pongee, 1 *mochi* of floss silk, 1 *tan* ordinary cloth, 2 *tan* tax cloth, 2 *shaku* of colored hemp-cloth, 1 *kin* each of bark-cloth and hemp, 2 mattocks, 1 *to* each of rice and sake, 2 *soku* of rice-in-ear, 6 *kin* of abalone, 11 *kin* 10 *ryō* of bonito, 4 *kin* 6 *ryō* of dried meat, 6 *kin* of *wakame*, 3 *to* of salt, 1 jug, 2 saucers, 6 bundles of oak, 2 gourds, 2 food mats.

Festival of Propitiating the Water Deities :

2 *shaku* each of five colors of thin pongee, 2 *shaku* of colored hemp-cloth, 8 *ryō* of bark-cloth, 2 *kin* of hemp, 4 mattocks, 4 *shō* or rice, 8 *shō* of sake, 4 *soku* of rice-in-ear, 2 *kin* each of abalone and bonito, 1 *kin* 12 *ryō* of dried meat, 2 *shō* of salt, 4 bundles of oak, 2 jugs, 4 saucers, 2 leaf-mats for wrapping, 2 *tan* of ordinary cloth, 2 *tan* of tax cloth.

---

322 The Kantoki-no-kami 霹靂神; the name is said to mean *kamitoke* 雷解, signifying thunderbolt. *Kōgaku sōsho*, III, p. 36. This appears to be an emergency festival in contrast to the regular, annual one in Bk. I (n. 250).

323 This ceremony was for the purpose of quieting the cook-stove (*kama* 釜) which makes a noise (*naru* 鳴る).

Festival to the August Stove:

2 *shaku* each of five colors of thin pongee, 1 *shaku* of colored hemp-cloth, 3 *ryō* of bark-cloth, 6 *ryō* of hemp, 2 mattocks, 2 *shō* each of rice and sake, 1 *kin* of abalone, 2 *kin* 2 *ryō* of bonito, 14 *ryō* of dried meat, 2 *kin* 2 *ryō* of *wakame*, 1 *shō* 1 *gō* of salt, 3 each of saucers and jars, 1 *jō* 1 *shaku* of tax cloth.

Festival to the Sacred Wells :[324]

1 *hiki* of stiff silk, 4 *shaku* each of five colors of thin pongee, 1 skein of silk thread, 1 *mochi* of white silk, 8 *ryō* of bark-cloth, 1 *kin* of hemp, 1 *tan* of ordinary cloth, 1 *tan* of tax cloth, 2 mattocks, 2 *to* each of rice and sake, 4 *soku* of rice-in-ear, 2 *gō* of red beans, 1 *kin* of Azuma abalone, 2 *kin* of bonito, 4 *kin* of dried meat, 3 *kin* of *wakame*, 3 *shō* of salt, 2 shallow earthenware vessels, 1 jug, 2 saucers, 2 gourds, 1 leaf-mat for wrapping, 4 bundles of oak, 1 palanquin, 2 food-mats, 2 *jō* of tribute cloth for lustrous robes, two porters.

Festival to the Well of Birth :[325]

1 *hiki* stiff silk, 4 *shaku* each of five colors of thin pongee, 1 skein of silk thread, 1 *mochi* of white silk, 2 *shaku* of colored hemp-cloth, 1 *tan* ordinary cloth, 5 *ryō* of bark-cloth, 1 *kin* of hemp, 2 mattocks, 2 *to* each of rice and sake, 4 *soku* of rice-in-ear, 2 *gō* of red beans, 1 *kin* of Azuma abalone, 2 *kin* of bonito, 4 *kin* of dried meat, 3 *kin* of *wakame*, 3 *shō* of salt, 2 each of jugs and saucers, 2 shallow earthenware vessels, 2 gourds, 4 bundles of oak, 1 leaf-mat for wrapping, 1 *tan* of tax cloth, 2 *jō* of tribute cloth for pure robes, 1 palanquin, two porters.

Festival of Propitiating the Site for a Dwelling:

5 *hiki* of stiff silk, 5 *jō* each of five colors of thin pongee, 5 *jō* each of five colors of silk, 5 *jō* of colored hemp-cloth, 6 *tan* of ordinary cloth, 5 *ryō* each of bark-cloth and hemp, 10 mattocks, 5 *to* each of rice and sake, 36 *kin* of abalone, 69 *kin* 12 *ryō* of bonito, 18 *kin* of squid, 13 *kin* 2 *ryō* of dried meat, 30 *kin* of *wakame*, 30 *kin* assorted seaweeds, 3 *to* of salt, 5 each of jugs and saucers, 5 gourds, 10 bundles of oak, 2 palanquins, 5 seat-mats, 5 food-mats, 5 bamboo mats.

Festival of Propitiating the Lord of Earth (Dokū) :[326]

1 *jō* of stiff silk, 4 *shaku* each of five colors of thin pongee, 4 *shaku* of colored hemp-cloth, 1 *kin*, bark-cloth, 1 *kin* of hemp, 2 mattocks, 1 *tan* of ordinary cloth, 2 *tan* of tax cloth, 5 *shō* of rice, 5 *shō* of sake, 3 *kin* each of abalone and bonito, 3 *kin* of *wakame*, 2 *kin* of dried meat, 2 *shō* of salt, 1 jug, 4 saucers, 1 gourd, 10 bundles of oak, 1 food-mat.

---

324 There are five well deities worshiped by the Igazuri 座摩 Maidens in the *Jingi-kan*. *Kōgaku sōsho*, III, p. 37.

325 The *ubui* 産井 is the well from which the water is drawn to be heated for an infant's first bath. In this case, no doubt the Imperial Household is implied.

326 According to the *Wamyōshō*, the Earth Lord, Dokū 土公, for the 3 months of spring resides in the cookstove, for 3 months of summer resides in the gates, for 3 months of autumn in the wells and 3 months of winter in the courtyard. *Kōgaku sōsho, loc. cit.*

Festival for Sacred River Water :

4 *jō* 5 *shaku* of stiff silk, 6 *shaku* each of five colors of thin pongee, 2 *tan* of ordinary cloth, 2 *shaku* of colored hemp-cloth, 5 *mochi* of floss silk, 5 *ryō* of silk thread, 5 *kin* each of bark-cloth and hemp, 100 sheets of paper, 800 *mon* in coin, 5 mattocks, 5 *to* each of rice, sake and soy dregs, 5 *soku* of rice-in-ear, 2 *shō* each of soybeans and red beans, 3 *to* of glutinous rice, 6 *kin* each of abalone and bonito, 4 *kin* 6 *ryō* of dried meat, 5 salmon, 8 *kin* of *wakame*, 5 *shō* of salt, 2 white-wood boxes, 5 split-cypress-wood boxes, 50 saucers, 5 gourds, 1 bale of oak, 1 palanquin, 2 each of seat-mats, straw-mats and food-mats.

Festival of Propitiating the Ground for a New Palace :[327]

5 *ryō* each of gold and silver, 50 *kin* each of copper and iron, 50 crystal beads, 5 *hiki* each of five colors of silk, 5 *shaku* of colored hemp-cloth, 5 *tan* ordinary cloth, 25 *tan* of tax cloth, 50 *kin* each of bark-cloth and hemp, 5 longswords, 5 bows, 5 arrows, 6 mattocks, 1 large mattock,[328] 2 sickles, 5 deerskins, 5 *kin* of yellow-bark, 5 *koku* of rice, 5 bottles of clear sake (each holding 3 *to*), 250 *soku* of rice-in-ear, 5 *kin* of abalone, 5 baskets of bonito (each holding 11 *kin* 10 *ryō*), 5 baskets of dried meat (each holding 4 *kin* 6 *ryō*), 5 baskets of *wakame* (each holding 6 *kin*), 5 baskets assorted seaweeds (each holding 6 *kin*), 5 baskets of salt (3 *to* in each), 5 each of bottles and side-pouring bottles, 25 saucers, 5 gourds, 50 bundles of oak, 10 straw-mats, 2 robes of stiff silk, 1 robe of ordinary cloth, 2 black headbands, 5 horses.

Ceremonial Articles to be Presented to the Deities when Sacred Maidens Change Office :

for each sanctuary (1 *jō* 7 *shaku* long and 1 *jō* 2 *shaku* 5 *sun* wide), 4 robes for male deities, 8 *hiki* of scarlet silk for 4 quilts, 2 *hiki* of white silk for 4 under-shirts and 4 divided skirts; for female deities, 4 robes, 5 *hiki* 2 *jō* of violet silk for 4 skirts, 2 *jō* of green silk for the seats of the skirts, 1 *hiki* 2 *jō* of white silk for 4 undershirts, 54 *mochi* of floss silk, 3 *hiki* of scarlet silk for one curtain, 1 *hiki* of silk for two bed canopies and a curtain, 2 *ryō* each of scarlet and glossy silk thread for sewing, 2 *tan* of ordinary cloth each for a wall hanging and floor covering, 2 beds (6 *shaku* long, 3 *shaku* 3 *sun* wide), 2 yellow-edged *tatami* (same dimensions as beds), 2 Kara chests (lacquered and furnished with metal lock and staple).[329]

The above items from sanctuary on are renewed every time the Sacred Maidens change office, but when the Igazuri, Mikado and Ikushima Maidens make sacred offerings to the deities, only the sanctuary is renewed, not the ceremonial articles. The newly invested Sacred Maidens are furnished with a dwelling each (2 *jō* long and both sides of the roof each 2 *jō* long).

---

327 This is the first festival of Bk. III which Miyagi classes as an item, saying that it was held earlier than the Taika era. A mention of this ground-hallowing in the Capital in Wadō 和銅 1 (708) is found in the *Shoku-nihongi*. Miyagi, I, p. 47.

328 *Kuwa* or *ōguwa*, written 钁.

329 *Karabitsu* 韓櫃 were the large wooden chests, 'Chinese style', with six legs, capable of being carried hung from a pole by two porters. These served as trunks for clothing and other articles.

The August Cleansing[330] (same for the Middle Palace and Heir Apparent's Palace):
2 *tan* of ordinary cloth for 2 coarse garments,[331] 6 *shaku* each of five colors of thin pongee, 6 *shaku* each of five colors of silk, 3 *kin* of Aki bark-cloth, 1 *kin* ordinary bark-cloth, 2 *kin* of hemp, 4 mattocks, 10 sheets of yellow-bark, 2 *to* each of rice and sake, 4 *soku* of rice-in-ear, 6 *kin* each of abalone and bonito, 2 *kin* of dried meat, 6 *kin* of *wakame*, 6 *kin* of assorted seaweeds, 4 *shō* of salt, 8 each of jugs and saucers, 2 gourds, 10 bundles of oak, 4 food-mats, 2 palanquins, 2 *tan* of tax cloth for the rituals, 2 carrying poles, 4 porters.

August Thank Offerings in the Outer Quarter[332] (held once in every reign; same in the Middle Palace):
8 slaves,[333] 8 horses, 8 saddles, 30 *hiki* of figured silk, 8 *shaku* of colored hemp-cloth, 80 *tan* of ordinary cloth, 80 *kin* each of bark-cloth and hemp, 8 garments, 8 quilts, 8 curtains, 8 caps, 8 hat-crowns, 8 sashes, 8 pairs each of shoes and stockings, 8 deerskins, 80 mattocks, 8 *koku* of white rice, 8 jars of sake (3 *to* in each), 800 *soku* of rice-in-ear, 8 baskets each of abalone and bonito (6 *kin* in each), 8 baskets of assorted dried meats (4 *kin* 6 *ryō* in each), 8 baskets each of *wakame* and *arame* (6 *kin* in each), 8 baskets of *mirume*,[334] 8 *koku* of salt, 8 gourds, 80 sake cups, 8 jars, 8 bales of oak, 8 straw-mats, 8 food-mats, 1 short *tatami* mat, 1 bamboo mat.

Yachimata Festival[335] (same in the Middle Palace, but reduced by half for the Heir Apparent's Palace):
8 longswords, 8 bows, 8 quivers, 8 wrist-guards, 40 *hiki* of five colors of thin pongee, 8 baskets each of dried meat, *wakame*, *mirume* and *arame* (6 *kin* in each), 4 sets of shelves.

Festival for an Imperial Airing (not celebrated if there is no overnight stop):
symbolic offerings for deities of the route at each large shrine, 1 *shaku* each of five colors of thin pongee, 5 *shaku* of stiff silk, 1 skein of silk thread, 1 *mochi* of floss silk, 2 *ryō* of bark-cloth, 5 *ryō* of hemp, 5 *shaku* of leaf-mat for wrapping; for each small shrine, 1 *shaku* each of five colors of thin pongee, 3 *shaku* of stiff silk, 1 skein of silk thread, 1 *mochi* of floss silk, 2 *ryō* of bark-cloth, 5 *ryō* of hemp, 3 *shaku* of leaf-mat for wrapping.

Festival of Boundaries:
for each boundary line, 1 *shaku* of colored hemp-cloth, 5 *ryō* of bark-cloth, 8 *ryō* of hemp, 2 mattocks, 4 *shō* each of rice and sake, 2 *kin* each of abalone and bonito, 2 *kin* of dried meat, 2 *kin* of salt, 2 each of jars and saucers, 4 bundles of oak, 1 food-mat.

---

330 The *gokei* 御禊 (also read *oharae*) ceremony to drive out defilement from the persons of the Imperial Family. This was a ritual washing at a river.

331 Here *aratae no miso* is written 麁栲御服.

332 *Rajō* 羅城 outside the Palace. Gloss gives alternate written form as: 頼庄.

333 The Yōrō Code, in the section on Barriers and Markets, regulates the buying and selling of slaves, *nui* 奴婢. Aida, *Chūkai yōrōryō,* 1209–10.

334 *Mirume* 海松 or 水松布, *Codium tomentosum,* an edible marine alga.

335 A ceremony to the Wayside Deity, Yachimata 八衢, to ward off evil spirits of the road.

The Ootono-hogai :[336]

8 *ryō* of Aki bark-cloth, 1 8-legged table, 1 *shō* each of rice and sake, 1 round box, 1 each of jar and saucer.

Festival for the August Well and August Stove:

3 *shaku* each of five colors of thin pongee, 1 *shaku* of colored hemp-cloth, 3 *ryō* of bark-cloth, 2 *ryō* of hemp, 1 mattock, 1 *shō* each of rice and sake, 1 *kin* each of abalone and bonito, 1 *shō* of dried meat, 1 *kin* of *wakame*, 1 *shō* of salt, 1 each of jar and saucer, 1 food-mat, 4 bundles of oak.

Festival for the August Stove in the Middle Palace (same in the Palace of the Heir Apparent):

1 *shaku* each of five colors of thin pongee, 5 *sun* of colored hemp-cloth, 1 *ryō* of bark-cloth, 2 *ryō* of hemp, 1 mattock, 1 *shō* each of rice and sake, 1 *kin* each of abalone and bonito, 1 *kin* of dried meat, 1 *kin* of *wakame*, 1 *shō* of salt, 1 each of jar and saucer.

Festival of the Deities of Yasoshima[337] (same in the Middle Palace):

1 *hiki* 2 *jō* each of five colors of silk, 1 *hiki* 2 *jō* of pongee, 30 skeins of silk thread, 30 *mochi* of floss silk, 1 *tan* 3 *jō* 8 *shaku* of colored hemp-cloth, 30 *kin* each of bark-cloth and hemp, 10 *tan* of tax cloth, 200 sheets of paper, 120 sticks on which to fasten the offerings, 8 *tan* of tax cloth to make 8 coarse garments, 40 models of palanquins, 4 *jō* of violet silk for coverings, 40 mattocks, 3 strings of cash (two strings for scattering, one to be used to buy fresh fish and fruit), 80 each of gold and silver effigies, 80 gilded bells, 82 mirrors (2 of them 5 *sun*, 80 of them 1 *sun* in diam.), 100 beads, 1 longsword, 1 bow, 50 arrows, 1 quiver, 80 sheets of yellow-bark, 20 each of jugs and cooking-pots, 80 saucers, 2 *koku* each of rice and sake, 8 *to* of soy dregs, 6 bottles, 8 baskets each of abalone, bonito and *wakame*, 50 salmon, 5 baskets of salt, 2 bales of oak, 20 *soku* of rice-in-ear, 8 each of scat-mats and food-mats, 5 palanquins, 4 white-wood boxes, 10 gourds, 2 *hiki* of pongee for the ritual, 2 *tan* of tribute cloth.

Festival of Yasoshima in the Heir Apparent's Palace:

2 *jō* each of five colors of silk, 2 *jō* of pongee, 8 skeins of silk thread, 8 *mochi* of floss silk, 2 *jō* of colored hemp-cloth, 8 *kin* each of bark-cloth and hemp, 4 *tan* of tax cloth, 50 sheets of paper, 4 *tan* of tax cloth to make 8 coarse garments, 20 model palanquins, 2 *jō* of violet silk for coverings, 8 mattocks, 600 *mon* in coin (200 for scattering and 400 for cost of fresh fish and fruits), 60 sticks on which to fasten the offerings, 30 each of gold and silver effigies, 30 gilded bells, 40 mirrors (2 of them 5 *sun* and 38 of them 1 *sun* in diam.), 1 longsword, 1 bow, 50 arrows, 1 quiver, 20 sheets of yellow-bark, 8 each of jugs and cooking-pots, 40 saucers, 4 *to* each of rice and sake, 2 bottles, 2 baskets each of abalone, bonito, dried meat, *wakame* and salt, 2 each of seat-mats and straw-mats, 2

---

336 This ceremony of blessing the Palace was of course an extraordinary one, not the annual one of Bk. 11.

337 Yasoshima-no-kami, 八十島神, worshiped after the accession of a new sovereign. *Kōgaku sōsho*, 111, p. 40. See next note.

food-mats, 2 palanquins, 2 white-wood boxes, 2 gourds, 4 porters, 1 *hiki* of pongee and 2 *tan* of tribute cloth for [reciting] the ritual.

To the Four Deities of Sumiyoshi, the Four Deities of Ooyosami, the Two Deities of Watatsumi, Two Deities of Tarumi and the Two Deities of Sumuchi :[338]
for each presentation, 5 *shaku* each of 5 colors of silk, 5 *shaku* of stiff silk, 1 skein of silk thread, 1 *mochi* of floss silk, 1 *shaku* of colored hemp-cloth, 3 *shaku* of ordinary cloth for wrapping, 1 *hiki* of stiff silk for the chief of Sumi-yoshi Shrine, 2 *tan* of ordinary cloth for each of the *hafuri* of that shrine and the Ooyosami Shrine, 2 *tan* of ordinary cloth for each of the *hafuri* of Tarumi Shrine, 1 *tan* of ordinary cloth each for the *hafuri* of Watatsumi and Sumuchi Shrines, 2 *hiki* of stiff silk and 2 *tan* of ordinary cloth for each of the Ikushima Sacred Maidens, 10 bearers.
To celebrate the above, the Sacred Maidens of the Yasoshima Festival, the Sacred Maidens of Ikushima, together with one chief ritualist of the *Jingi-kan*, one *koto* player, two *kambe*, one lady-in-waiting, a member of the Bureau of Palace Storehouses and two *toneri* proceed to the harbor of Naniwa.[339]

Festival to the Deities of Epidemic at the Four Corners of the Palace (the same is to be done if the deities are to be propitiated at the four corners of the Capital):
1 *jō* 6 *shaku* each of five colors of thin pongee (to be divided equally among the four places, as are the following), 1 *jō* 6 *shaku* of colored hemp-cloth, 4 *kin* 8 *ryō* of bark-cloth, 8 *kin* of hemp, 8 *tan* of tax cloth, 16 mattocks, 4 each of oxhides, bearskins, deerskins and wild boarskins, 4 *to* each of rice and sake, 16 *soku* of rice-in-ear, 16 *kin* each of abalone and bonito, 2 *to* of dried meat, 16 *kin* each of *wakame* and assorted seaweeds, 2 *to* of salt, 4 jugs, 8 saucers, 4 gourds, 16 bundles of oak, 4 straw-mats, 4 armloads of straw, 4 *shimoto*[340] shelves (each 4 *shaku* high, 3 *shaku* 5 *sun* long), one carrying-pole.

Festival to the Deities of Epidemic at 10 Places on Boundaries of the Inner Provinces (the first on the Yamashiro-Oomi boundary, the second on the Yamashiro-Tamba boundary, third on the Yamashiro-Settsu boundary, the fourth on the Yamashiro-Kawachi boundary, the fifth on the Yamashiro-Yamato boundary, the sixth on the Yamashiro-Iga boundary, the seventh on the Yamato-Iga boundary, the eighth on the Yamato-Kii boundary, the ninth on the Izumi-Kii boundary, the tenth on the Settsu-Harima boundary):
for each of the boundaries, 4 *shaku* of colored hemp-cloth, 1 *kin* 2 *ryō* each of bark-cloth and hemp, 2 *tan* of tax cloth, 1 each of effigies of gold and iron, 4 mattocks, 1 each of oxhide, bearskin, deerskin and boarskin, 4 *soku* of rice-in-ear, 1 *to* each of rice and sake, 4 *kin* each of abalone, bonito, *wakame, arame*

---

338 For the four deities of Sumiyoshi see n. 302, and deities of Ooyosami, n. 304, above. The others are also sea gods: those of Watatsumi 海神, Tarumi 垂水神 and Sumuchi 住道神. All of these were worshiped in the Yasoshima festival, the first record of which was in Kajō 3 (850), and it continued on into the Kamakura and Muromachi periods.

Nihon rekishi daijiten.

339 Naniwa was a former capital and a town at the head of the Inland Sea on the site of present Osaka.

340 *Shimoto* 楉, a kind of tree; readings are *beni-ringo* 紅林檎 *(Pyrus)* or *sarugaki* 猿柿 *(Diospyrus lotus)*, a wild persimmon.

and assorted seaweeds, 5 *shō* of dried meat, 5 *shō* of salt, 1 water jug, 2 saucers, 1 gourd, 4 bundles of oak, 1 straw mat, 1 armload of straw, 1 palanquin, 1 carrying-pole, 2 bearers. (The Offices of the Capital requisition and provide forced labor.)

The 85 Deities worshiped in the Amagoi Festival (all Great):[341]
(In Yamashiro Province) [at these shrines 24 deities]:

1 at Kamo-no-wakeikazuchi	1 at Konoshima
2 at Kamo-no-mioya	1 at Hatsukashi
2 at Matsuno-o	1 at Otokuni
3 at Inari	1 at Waki
10 at Minushi	1 at Kifune
1 at Kabai	

(In Yamato Province) [at these shrines 36 deities]:

3 at Ooyamato	1 at Iware-no-yamanokuchi
1 at Oomiwa	1 at Miminashi-no-yamanokuchi
1 at Isonokami	1 at Yagyū-no-yamanokuchi
2 at Ooyashiro	1 at Tsuge-no-yamanokuchi
1 at Hitokotonushi	1 at Tsuge-no-mikomari
1 at Kataoka	1 at Hatsuse-no-yamanokuchi
1 at Hirose	1 at Osaka-no-yamanokuchi
2 at Tatsuta	1 at Uda-no-mikomari
1 at Kose-no-yamanokuchi	4 at Asuka
1 at Katsuragi-no-mikomari	1 at Asuka-no-yamanokuchi
1 at Kamo-no-yamanokuchi	1 at Unebi-no-yamanokuchi
1 at Taima-no-yamanokuchi	1 at Yoshino-no-yamanokuchi
1 at Osaka-no-yamanokuchi	1 at Yoshino-no-mikomari
1 at Ikoma-no-yamanokuchi	1 at Nibu-no-kawakami
1 at Ikoma	

(In Kawachi Province) [two shrines, 6 deities]:

4 at Hiraoka	2 at Onchi

(In Izumi Province):

1 at Ootori

(In Settsu Province) [at these shrines 18 deities]:

4 at Sumiyoshi	1 at Nagata
4 at Ooyosami	3 at Niiya
2 at Naniwa (Ooyashiro)	1 at Tarumi
1 at Hirota	1 at Natsugi
1 at Ikuta	

For each presentation, 5 *shaku* of stiff silk, 1 *shaku* each of five colors of thin pongee, 1 skein of silk thread, 1 *mochi* of floss silk, 2 *ryō* of bark-cloth, 5 *ryō* of

---

341 *Amagoi-matsuri* 祈雨祭 *(Kiu-sai),* to pray for rain in times of drought. Praying for rain is recorded in the *Nihongi* as far back as Empress Kōgyoku's first year (642) and there are many records of *amagoi* prayers for rain in the *Shoku-nihongi,* usually occurring in the 5th, 6th or 7th month when rain for water supply to growing rice was essential.

hemp, ½ mat for wrapping, 2 *tan* of tribute cloth for each shrine (for kneeling), 1 porter. A black horse each for Nibu-no-kawakami and Kifune; for the others add 1 *tan* of ordinary cloth. The same requirements for the festival when long rains do not stop,[342] except that white horses are used. At all times that symbolic offerings are presented to the deity of Nibu-no-kawakami the Chief Priest of Ooyamato Shrine follows the Fourth-Class Official in going to the shrine to make the offering.

Myōjin Festivals for 285 Deities :[343]
  (residing within the Imperial Household):
    1 in the Sono-no-kami Shrine   2 in the Kara-no-kami Shrine
  (In Yamashiro Province) [at these shrines]:
    1 at Kamo-no-wakeikazuchi   1 at Konoshima-ni-masu-Amateru-
    2 at Kamo-no-mioya   no-mitama
    2 at Matsuno-o   4 at Hirano
    3 at Inari   4 at Ume-no-miya
    1 at Kamo-no-kawa-ai   1 at Otokuni
    1 at Mii   1 at Sakatoke (also called Yamazaki)
    1 at Kadono-tsukiyomi
  (In Yamato Province) [at these shrines]:
    4 at Kasuga   2 at Kafuku-ikazuchi
    3 at Ooyamato   1 at Oomiwa
    1 at Isonokami   4 at Futodama
    2 at Oomasu (or Ooyashiro)   1 at Anashi
    4 at Asuka   3 at Takaya-abe
    1 at Takechi-no-miagata   1 at Oonamochi-no-mitama
    1 at Nibu-no-kawakami   1 at Kazuragi-no-honoikazuchi
    1 at Kane-no-mitake   1 at Kataoka
    2 at Kamo   1 at Hohata
    1 at Kazuragi-no-mitoshiro   1 at Hirose
    1 at Kazuragi-no-hitokotonushi   2 at Tatsuta
    4 at Takakamo   1 at Heguri-ni-masu-kiuji
    1 at Takamahiko
  (In Kawachi Province) [at these shrines]:
    2 at Onchi   2 at Morimoto
    4 at Hiraoka   1 at Asukabe
  (In Izumi Province):
    1 at Ootori Shrine
  (In Settsu Province) [at these shrines]:

---

342 What is alluded to is *amadome* 雨止, rain-stopping prayers to the deities of the list, or more properly, *Haregoi-matsuri* 祈晴祭 *(Kisei-sai)*, to pray for clearing weather.
343 The *myōjin* 名神 are principal deities whose shrines had become official *(kansha* 官社), many of them great shrines *(taisha* 大社). The corres-

ponding list in the *Jimmyō-chō* has 309 *myōjin*, showing an increase of principal deities during the compilation. Records of *myōjin* deities appear in the *Nihon-kōki* and *Shoku-nihon-kōki*, the later historical works of the Heian period. Miyagi, 1, pp. 51–5.

4 at Sumiyoshi   1 at Tarumi
4 at Ooyosami   1 at Hirota
2 at Naniwa-ikukunidama   1 at Ikuta
1 at Himekoso (or Shitateru-hime)   1 at Nagata
3 at Niiya
(In Ise Province) [at these shrines]:
  3 at Asaka   1 at Tado
(In Owari Province) [at these shrines]:
  1 at Oo   1 at Hisakimiko
  1 at Masuda   1 at Hikowakamiko
  1 at Ooagata   1 at Takakura-no-musubi-no-miko
  1 at Atsuta
(In Tōtoumi Province) [at these shrines]:
  1 at Tsunosakuhiko   1 at Kyōman
(In Suruga Province):
  1 at Asama
(In Izu Province):
  Mishima   Awa-no-mikoto
  Ikonahime-no-mikoto   Yanaihara
  Monoimina-no-mikoto
(In Sagami Province):
  Sabukawa Shrine
(In Musashi Province):
  Hikawa   Kanasana
(In Awa Province):
  Awa Shrine
(In Kamitsufusa Province):
  Tamasaki Shrine
(In Shimotsufusa Province):
  Katori-jingū
(In Hitachi Province):
  Kashima-jingū   Chikuwayama
  Ooarai-isosaki no Yakushi-bosatsu   Yoshida
  Shizu   Sakatsura-isosaki no Yakushi-
  Inada   bosatsu
(In Oomi Province):
  2 at Ono   2 at Kawata
  1 at Hie   1 at Mikami
  1 at Sakunado   1 at Okitsushima
  1 at Takabe   1 at Ikako
  1 at Mio
(In Mino Province):
  Nakayama-kanayamahiko
(In Shinano Province):
  2 at Namuhōtomi   1 at Ikushima-tarushima

1 at Hodaka
(In Kamitsuke Province):
  Nukisaki   Ikaho   Akagi
(In Shimotsuke Province):
  Futara
(In Michinoku Province) [Mutsu Prov.]:

Tsutsukowake	Hitsujisaki
Kamutamine (Karitane)	Ogamishi (Oroeshi)
Shibahiko	Kesema
Hanabushi	Taga
Shibahime	Izanami
Idachi	Unagorowake
Azumayanuma	Ootakayama
2 at Kawada*	Koimine
Mikami*	

    * lacking in some texts

(In Idewa Province) [Dewa Prov.]:
  Oomonoimi and Tsukiyama
(In Wakasa Province):
  2 at Wakasahiko
(In Echizen Province):
  7 at Kehi   1 at Oomushi
(In Noto Province):
  Keta
(In Echigo Province):
  Iyohiko
(In Tamba Province):
  Izumo   Make
  Ogawanotsuki   2 at Kushi-iwamado
(In Tango Province):

Ookawa	Oomushi	2 at Oomiyanome
Komori	Oomushi	

(In Tajima Province):

Awaka	Yama	Hosoki
Yabu—2	He	Watatsumi
Izushi—8	Ikazuchi	

(In Inaba Province):
  Ube
(In Oki Province):
  Yuranohime   Miwakasu-no-mikoto
  Usaka-no-mikoto   Ise-no-mikoto
(In Harima Province):
  Tarumi (or Watatsumi)—3   Ieshima
  Iibo-ni-masu-Amaterasu   Iwa
  Nakatomi-no-itachi

(In Mimasaka Province):
  Nakayama
(In Bizen Province):
  Annin (or Ani)
(In Bitchū Province):
  Kibitsuhiko
(In Aki Province):
  Hayatani   Ooie
  Itsukishima
(In Nagato Province):
  Sumiyoshi-no-aramitama—3
(In Kii Province):
  Nibutsuhime   Naru
  Hinokuma (or Hinomae)   Itachi
  Kunikakasu   Shima
  Itakeso   Shizuhi
  Ooyatsuhime   Susa
  Tsumatsuhime
(In Awaji Province):
  Awaji-Izanagi   Yamato-no-ōkunidama
(In Awa Province):
  Ooasahiko   Amanohiwashi
(In Sanuki Province):
  Awai
(In Iyo Province):
  Murayama   Noma
  Ooyamatsumi   Ajimi
(In Chikuzen Province):
  Munakata—3   Tsukushi
  Sumiyoshi—3   Kamado
  Shikaumi   Minagi—3
  Yahata
(In Chikugo Province):
  Takaranotamatare-no-mikoto   Toyohime
(In Buzen Province):
  Yahatahime
(In Hizen Province):
  Tajimanimasu
(In Higo Province):
  Takeiwatatsu-no-mikoto
(On Ikinoshima):
  Sumiyoshi   Nakatsu
  Hyōsu   Amanotanagao
  Tsukiyomi   Amanotanagahime
(On Tsushima-no-shima) [6 shrines]:

Watatsumi	Watatsumi
Watatsumi-no-miko	Futonotto
Takamimusubi	Sumiyoshi

For each presentation: 5 *shaku* of pongee, 1 *mochi* of floss silk, 1 skein of silk thread, 1 *shaku* each of five colors of thin pongee, 2 *ryō* of bark-cloth, 5 *ryō* of hemp, 20 straw-mats for wrapping, but if great prayers are held, then add 6 *jō* 5 *shaku* of pongee and substitute 1 *tan* of ordinary cloth for the skein of thread.

Festival for the Time of Despatching an Envoy to a Foreign Country (same for the day when the envoy returns):[344]

> 3 *hiki* 4 *jō* 8 *shaku* each of five colors of thin pongee, 4 *hiki* of pongee, 2 *tan* of colored hemp-cloth, 15 *kin* of bark-cloth, 15 *kin* of hemp, 16 *tan* of ordinary cloth, 6 *tan* of tax cloth for lustrous robes, 10 strings each of abalone and bonito, 20 salmon, 10 baskets of dried meat, 2 baskets of *wakame*, 2 *to* 4 *shō* 2 *gō* of *sushi*, 2 *shō* 4 *gō* 2 *shaku* of salt, 4 jugs, 5 jars, 200 saucers, 2 bales of oak, 2 *to* of white rice, 2 *koku* of cooked rice, 1 *koku* of sake (tables, sake-jars and cups, gourds and sieves to go with these), 20 leaf-mats.

The above [are required] when they are about to despatch the envoy. All the deities of heaven and earth are worshiped out in the fields. At the site of the festival the governor of that province sweeps clean the ground and the officials in charge prepare rush-mats and set out seats. The *Jingi-kan* requisitions and receives all the necessary articles from the [*Dajō-*]*kan*. The sake and foodstuffs are gathered by the officials in charge and assembled at the site of the festival. The *Jingi-kan* [officials] lead the *kambe* and the others (all wearing lustrous robes) and they conduct the festival. The ambassador himself recites the ritual. The *kambe* present the symbolic offerings. That done, the ambassador and those of lesser rank present each his own symbolic offering. (The *kambe* take them and offer them at the abode of the Deity.[345])

Festival for the Tree Spirit and the Mountain Deity when Building a Ship for the Envoys to T'ang:

> 280 beads in five colors, 4 golden bells, 4 mirrors, 1 skein of silk thread, 1 *hiki* 6 *shaku* of pongee, 1 *mochi* of floss silk, 1 *jō* 4 *shaku* each of five colors of thin pongee, 3 *shaku* of colored hemp-cloth, 1 *kin* 8 *ryō* of bark-cloth, 4 mattocks, 2 mats for wrapping (the foregoing to be requested from the Capital Store-

---

344 The term for envoy(s) is *shi* 使, *tsukai*, messenger. Here the term *taishi* 大使 occurs once and is translated 'ambassador'. The influence of the Great T'ang Empire upon Japan during Nara and Heian is seen in the importance given to these and the ensuing ceremonies. The sending of official envoys began in Shōtoku Taishi's regency in 607. Between 630 and 837 twelve official embassies to T'ang are recorded, the most notable of which was Kibi no Makibi 吉備眞備, who went in 717 to study, spent 17 years in China, returned, and later was sent as official envoy. G. B. Sansom, *Japan*, pp. 96–8. Services to the deities to des-

patch the envoys to T'ang is recorded in the *Shoku-nihongi* in Yōrō 1 (717), in Hōki 寶龜 8 (777) and in *Shoku-nihon-kōki* in Shōwa 承和 3 (836). Miyagi, 1, p. 54. That the *shiki* here use the phrase 'to a Foreign Country' shows some attempt to universalize the regulations, although the Great T'ang alone was the destination.

345 The *shinza* 神座 was the hallowed spot in which the deity resided, not necessarily a shrine building, as these ceremonies were held in specially selected locations—which are mentioned in the historical records.

houses), 1 *kin* 8 *ryō* of hemp, 1 *to* 4 *shō* of white rice, 6 *soku* of rice-in-ear, 1 *to* 4 *shō* of sake, 6 *kin* of abalone and bonito, 8 *kin* each of *wakame, arame, mirume* and assorted seaweeds (for the foregoing use regular taxes), 6 sake cups, 4 saucers, 3 gourds, 26 bundles of oak, 2 sets of shelves (for the foregoing use local products of the province), one envoy (of the Nakatomi Uji).

Festival for Opening of the Wharf for the Journey to T'ang (at Sumiyoshi Shrine): 4 *jō* of stiff silk for the symbolic offerings, 4 *shaku* each of five colors of thin pongee, 4 skeins of silk thread, 4 *mochi* of floss silk, 8 *ryō* of bark-cloth, 1 *kin* 4 *ryō* of hemp.
The above are for when the *Jingi-kan* sends the envoys to the shrine to make the celebration.

Festival to the Deities en route when Guests from T'ang arrive at the Capital: 5 *shaku* of pongee for symbolic offerings, 1 skein of silk thread, 1 *mochi* of floss silk, 1 *shaku* each of five colors of thin pongee, 2 *ryō* of bark-cloth, 3 *ryō* of hemp, 4 mats for wrapping (the foregoing symbolic offerings are provided for each deity); two envoys are sent (one for the inner provinces, one for the outer) both of them Nakatomi [Uji].

Festival to the Deities when a Foreign Guest is sent to the Boundary: 4 *shaku* each of five colors of thin pongee, 2 *shaku* of colored hemp-cloth, 2 *kin* each of bark-cloth and hemp, 4 *tan* of tax cloth, 4 mattocks, 2 each of oxhides, bearskins, deerskins and boarskins, 2 *to* of sake, 4 *shō* of rice, 2 *kin* each of abalone and bonito, 4 *kin* of *wakame*, 8 *kin* of dried meat, 4 *shō* of salt, 12 *soku* of rice-in-ear, 2 water jugs, 4 saucers, 2 gourds, 2 straw-mats, 4 arm-loads of straw, 8 bundles of oak (the foregoing are for the festival), 4 *ryō* of bark-cloth, 1 *kin* of hemp, 6 *shō* of sake, 4 *shō* of rice, 1 *kin* each of abalone and bonito, 2 *kin* of assorted seaweeds, 1 *kin* of dried meat, 1 *shō* of salt, 2 each of water jugs and saucers, 1 gourd, 2 food-mats, 10 bundles of oak, 1 palanquin, 1 carrying-pole, 2 porters (the foregoing are required for the purification).
The above are for when the foreign guest enters Japan and draws near to the boundary of the Inner Provinces and worships the deities of travel. The guest and his retinue at the moment they reach the capital are visited with the wand of purification, and when they have been purified they enter.

Festival for the Deity of the Barriers:[346] 1 *jō* 2 *shaku* each of five colors of thin pongee, 1 *jō* 2 *shaku* of colored hemp-cloth, 12 *kin* each of bark-cloth and hemp, 8 *tan* of tax cloth, 4 each of bear-skins, oxhides, deerskins and boarskins, 16 mattocks, 4 *to* each of rice and sake, 16 *soku* of rice-in-ear, 8 *kin* each of abalone and bonito and *wakame*, 2 *to* each of dried meat and salt, 4 water jugs, 8 saucers, 4 gourds, 12 bundles of oak, 4 straw-mats (from thin pongee on, the items are divided among the four places).

---

346 *Sae-no-kami:* 障神.

The above are used two days before the arrival of the guests to worship the deities of the barriers in the four corners of the Capital.

When the Local Chieftain of Izumo is Honored with Congratulatory Gifts:[347]

1 gold-ornamented sword, 20 skeins of silk thread, 10 *hiki* of stiff silk, 20 *tan* of tribute cloth, 20 mattocks.

When the above have been entrusted to the Local Chieftain, one Secretary and one Chief Ritualist go to the office of the *Jingi-kan*. (The seat for the Secretary is placed above the seat of the Chief [to the *Jingi-kan*], then the Secretary enters from the west and takes his place; the seat for the Chief Ritualist is spread in front, then the Chief Ritualist enters from the east and takes his place. Next the Chief of the *Jingi-kan* and down to the Secretary in turn take their seats, one Chief Ritualist and one 4th Class official of the Treasury enter from the south gate and take their seats (the seat of the Treasury official is spread in front). The Chief Ritualist calls the office-keepers and commands them to summon the Governor of Izumo and Local Chieftain of Izumo. The office-keepers lead the Governor and the Local Chieftain to the posting-board of ranks. (The Local Chieftain goes to the posting-board and the Governor stands behind him. The office-keepers stand to the west. But if the Governor is of 5th Rank or higher he takes a seat.) The Chief Ritualist summons the *kambe*. One of the *kambe* comes forward (he wears a bark-cloth headdress and sleeve-ties). He places the large sword below the offering-table and kneels there. At the hour of noon the Secretary proclaims, saying: 'Upon the name and title of the Local Chieftain of Izumo are at this time bestowed congratulatory gifts.' The Chieftain gives the verbal assent and bows twice, and twice again, and claps his hands twice. That done, he proceeds to the offering-table under which the sword is and kneels there. The *kambe* take the sword and confer it on him. They clap their hands and bestow it (clapping twice). As he retires he gives it to the stewards[348] and he goes to the posting-board. Next, the Treasury official[349] summons the Local Chieftain. The Chieftain goes and kneels below the [tables of] emoluments. One steward comes forward. First he takes the silk thread and offers it to the Chieftain. He claps his hands once. After receiving it he hands it to the steward. The steward retires and stands in his original place. The same is repeated with the stiff silk, the ordinary cloth and the mattocks. The Chieftain retires and goes to the posting-board. Once more he takes up the sword and he withdraws. (The stewards stand in front, the Chieftain behind them. Each time the Chieftain calls a name and bestows emoluments, the verbal response is made.) Then the Treasury official, the chief official,[350] the Chief Ritualist and the Secretary all withdraw.

When The Local Chieftain recites the Laudatory Ritual to the Deities:[351]

347 The Izumo-no-kuni-no-miyatsuko 出雲國造, Local Chieftain of Izumo Prov., had 5th Court Rank as well as his traditional title *(kabane)*. 'Congratulatory gifts' is used for *oisachi-mono* 負幸物, the gold-ornamented sword and other articles in the list.

348 *Shindori (shidori)* 後取.

349 The *sakan* 錄, a fourth-class official of the Ministry of Treasury, *ōkura-shō* 大藏省.

350 The ambiguous term *honkan* 本官 is used, probably signifying the officials of the *Jingi-kan*.

351 This is the recitation of the *kamu-yogoto* 神壽詞. A translation may be found in Philippi, *Norito*, pp. 72–5. Deities invoked include those of both Izumo and Yamato myths.

68 beads (8 red crystals, 16 white crystals, 44 blue crystals), one sword ornamented with gold and silver (2 *shaku* 6 *sun* 5 *bu* in length), 1 mirror (7 *sun*
7 *bu* in diam.), 2 *tan* of colored hemp-cloth (each 1 *jō* 4 *shaku* long and 2 *shaku*
2 *sun* wide; both to be put on the offering-table), 1 light roan horse with white
eyeballs,[352] 2 white swans (to be perched on the eaves), 50 loads of food-
offerings (each load being 10 basketfuls).

The above are for when the Local Chieftain is honored with congratulatory gifts.
He returns to his province to perform lustration and abstinence for one year.
(During the period of avoidance he is not to decide grave offenses, but if it
comes time to redistribute the *handen*[353] he must interrupt.) When it is over the
governor of the province leads the Chieftain, the various *hafuribe* and junior
members[354] up to Court. At a suitable spot outside the Capital they prepare
the articles to be offered. The Chief of the *Jingi-kan* personally inspects them. An
auspicious day having been previously divined, it is announced to the [*Jingi-*]
kan, submitted to the Throne and proclaimed to the officials in charge. Once
more a subsequent year of avoidance and again he comes up to Court and recites
the laudatory ritual. (See the *Gishiki* for this matter.)

The Local Chieftain always recites the Laudatory Ritual to the Deities at daybreak on that day, and the *Jingi-kan* tests the Chieftain's recital of it; 5 tribute
straw-mats are provided for seats. He reports to the *Jingi-kan* before the one-day
abstinence for the reciting of the Laudatory to the Deities. All from the Chieftain
down, including *hafuri, kambe*, district prefects,[355] junior members and various
functionaries[356] are presented with emoluments. But the number of such persons
is announced according to the occasion as there is no fixed number. The method
of emoluments is: for the Local Chieftain, 20 *hiki* of stiff silk, 60 *tan* of tribute
cloth, 50 *mochi* of floss silk; for the *hafuri* and *kambe*, regardless of whether they
have rank or not, 1 *tan* of tribute cloth apiece; for the district prefects 2 *tan*
apiece and for junior members 1 *tan* apiece.[357]

Each time articles for *miagamono* are to be sent before the 15th of each month
to the officials in charge; these receive them by the 27th day and prepare them
for presentation.

Each time the articles required for the various festivals and the two seasonal
Great Purifications are prepared on the 5th day.

---

[352] *Samitsukige-uma* 白眼鴇毛馬, *tsuki* being
defined as light pink.

[353] The *handen* 班田, or allotted rice-fields,
after the Taika Reforms were theoretically to be
redistributed every six years. Regulations concerning *handen* and other classifications of fields are
found in the latter part of *E-S*, XXII, *mimbu-shiki*
民部式, Pt. A. The text here seems to imply that
the civil duties of land distribution would take
precedence over the *jingi* abstinence obligations.

[354] *Shitei* 子弟, according to a source as old as
the *Chou Li*, meant the junior members of the
family: sons and younger brothers. Whether the

term refers to sons of the Chieftain or merely to
a class of pages is not certain.

[355] The *kōri-no-tsukasa* 郡司 (*gunshi*).

[356] *Goshiki-no-hito* 五色人, 'five kinds of persons', I have taken to be equivalent to *zōshiki-no-
hito*, n. 489.

[357] At this point the regulations for 'Extraordinary Festivals' end and are followed by a
succession of 57 *shiki* concerning taboos, defilements, offerings, taxes, sustenance to shrines,
divination and other matters relating to items in
the first five books of *E-S*.

Each time the recorders of Yamato and Kawachi[358] present [offerings of] swords at the Great Purification, officials of Fourth Class or above are to be used.

Each time the bamboo required for *miagamono* on the last day of the 6th and the 12th months is requested of the Secretaries before the 25th day and they order it to be gathered in Yamashiro Province.

At all times, for Chief Diviner, one of the diviners who qualifies is taken. It must be a diviner who excels in the divining arts of three provinces. (Five persons from Izu, five from Iki and ten from Tsushima.) If they use persons living in the Capital it will not be easy to fill the need from those who excel in arts of divination. Their food allowance per person per day is 2 *shō* of unpolished rice, 2 *shaku* of salt, and for the wives 1 *shō* 5 *gō* of rice and 1 *shaku* 5 *satsu* of salt. At all times there is one each: Sacred Maiden, Sacred Maiden of the Palace, and Ikushima Sacred Maiden (the Middle Palace and Heir Apparent's Palace have only one Sacred Maiden each); these offices are filled by ordinary young women who qualify; but their selection corresponds to that for Women of the Palace who have rank but no appointment. At all times, to fill the position of Sacred Maiden of Igazuri, they take female children of age 7 or over from the *uji* of Local Chieftains outside the Capital. When they reach the time for marriage it is announced to the Secretaries and a replacement is found.

At all times, to these various Sacred Maidens, 1 *hiki* of pongee for a summer garment is supplied to each, but nothing for winter. As for food, each receives per day 1 *shō* 5 *gō* of white rice and 1 *shaku* 5 *satsu* of salt.

At all times, for diviner's assistants they take male children of age 7 or over who do divining[359] to fill these positions; when they reach the time of marraige it is announced to the Secretaries, who then find a replacement.

At all times, if any of the Superintendents or Chief Priests of shrines must be released from duty because of going into mourning before their 6-year term is up, they are not to be replaced. Therefore the *hafuribe* are made to carry on their their duties. The day their mourning is ended they may return to office and complete their term. The *negi* and *hafuribe* once they have been put in office cannot easily be replaced.

At all times, members of *kambe* families may not easily leave the household.

At all times, if there is contact with defilement or evil, avoidance is practiced: for 30 days time after the death of a person (count from the day of burial), for 7 days after a birth, for 6 days after death of a domestic animal, for 3 days after the birth of one (avoidance does not apply to chickens), eating of meat is avoided for three days (the *Jingi-kan* regularly avoids it, but at the time of a festival the rest of the officials all avoid it).

At all times, when consoling in a bereavement, or calling upon the sick, or when

---

358 The *jingi-ryō* state that scholars (to the national university) must be scions of 5th Rank or higher, and the sons of *fubitobe* of Yamato and Kawachi (東西史部). Tradition said the *fubitobe* of Yamato were descendants of the scholar Achi-no-omi 阿知使主 (Achiki) and the *fubitobe* of Kawachi descended from Wani 王仁—the two scholars who brought Chinese learning to Japan about A.D. 400. Aida, *op. cit.*, pp. 588–9.

359 Diviner's assistants (*heza* 戸座) were young boys who aided in preparation for divining —*urahameru* or *ura-aeramu* 卜食—by gathering firewood, making fires to heat the tortoise shell and other tasks.

reaching a place where a mound is being built, or encountering a 37th-day Buddhist memorial service, even though one's person is not defiled he is not allowed to enter the Imperial Palace on that day.

At all times, in the case of reburial or a miscarriage at 4 months or more, there is 30 days of avoidance; in the case of an abortion of 3 months or less, 7 days of avoidance.

At all times, during the days of partial abstinence before and after the festivals of *Toshigoi, Kamo, Tsukinami, Kanname* and *Niiname*, monks, nuns and persons in mourning, as well as bands of robbers, may not enter the Imperial Palace. Even persons in light attire if they are practicing partial or total abstinence may not enter the Palace. This rule applies in like manner to abstinence days for all the remaining festivals. At all times, if persons request a leave on account of the death of a young child, should they be summoned before the time limit [of mourning] is up, they may not participate in festival affairs.

At all times, when ladies of the Palace become with child they must withdraw before the days of partial abstinence; if they have their menses they must withdraw before the day of a festival to their homes and hearths and may not go up to the Palace. For the lustration and fasting in the 3rd and 9th months they must withdraw outside the Palace.

At all times, if place A becomes defiled, person B who enters there (meaning takes a seat there; the same hereafter) and all persons in that place become defiled. If C enters B's premises, his body alone becomes defiled, not those of people on his own premises. If D enters C's premises he does not become defiled. Whoever has contact with death or burial, even if it is not a month of *kami* affairs, may not join the assembled officials, nor the guards, nor the place of chamberlains.

At all times, if an official of the Palace becomes defiled he may not interrupt festival proceedings. At all times, if a person has contact with a fire he must observe 7 days' avoidance of *kami* affairs. Every year the books of deity taxes and tribute and *corvée* taxes, the account books of *kambe* and registers of *hafuribe* must be examined and sent up to this *kan*; they are audited and exposed and a certification is affixed.[360]

Whenever there is damage to a provincial shrine it must be repaired, except for the Sumiyoshi Shrine in Settsu, the Katori Shrine in Shimōsa and Kashima Shrine in Hitachi, whose main sanctuaries are to be rebuilt once every 20 years,[361] the cost of which is to be met with deity taxes. If such are not available, then regular taxes are to be used.

At all times, within the perimeter of shrine precincts no trees may be cut nor the dead be buried.

---

[360] The procedure for checking the accounts of *kambe* (*shinko*) who provided support to the shrines and the registers of the *hafuri* who served the shrines was for the *kageyushi* 勘解由使, examiners, to look them over, after which they were transmitted to the *Jingi-kan* for the slow process of auditing.

[361] These three became 'great' shrines: Sumiyoshi Taisha, Kashima Jingū and Katori Jingū, and by tradition have their main buildings rebuilt at twenty-year intervals. (See n. 212, 213, 302.)

At no time may any Buddhist monk or any butcher live unlawfully on the south side of Kamo-no-mioya Shrine, even if it is outside the perimeter.[362]

At all times, tribute and *corvée* taxes from *kambe* are used to cover festival requirements and ceremonial articles to be offered to the deities; but the paddy tax is set aside as deity tax.

At all times, those who are in charge of the various *myōjin* and official shrines of the various deities must await the handing down of an official order;[363] moreover, they are to carry out the order handed down to the province and request the inner seal.

Whenever ladies-in-waiting prepare the symbolic offerings for the Shrine of the Great Deity, the officials of the *Jingi-kan* lead the *kambe* and on the appointed day at dawn they go up to the Shrine and conduct the affair jointly.[364]

At all times, for the *Toshigoi, Tsukinami, Jinkonjiki* and *Niiname* festivals, articles like boards for shields and wood for offering-stands[365] are requisitioned from the farmers of the *kambe* of the 5 Inner Provinces (200 shield boards from Yamashiro; 400 shield boards and 12,500 pieces of wood for offering-stands from Yamato; 390 shield boards and 12,000 pieces of wood for offering-stands from Settsu; besides, 240 shield boards and 12,000 pieces of wood for offering-stands from Kawachi, moreover, farmers who are quiver-weavers provide 1,832 pieces of wood for offering-stands and Izumi Province 111 shield boards).

At all times, the year's requirement of birch-cherry[366] for divination purposes is requisitioned from the Ufu Shrine in Yamato Province.

At all times, the year's requirement of auguring bamboo[367] is grown in a secluded place within the *Jingi-kan* and gathered as occasion demands.

At all times, the 1,364 arrowshafts which are needed for the purifications for festival during the year are to be presented by Yamato Province in lieu of deity taxes and sent up before the 10th month.

At all times, both Izu and Kii Provinces present in lieu of deity taxes a variety of 85 skins used for the festivals (Izu Province, 5 bearskins, 10 boarskins, 30 deerskins; Kii Prov., 5 bearskins, 5 boarskins and 30 deerskins). All are assigned to the tribute and tax envoy and forwarded to the [*Jingi-*]*kan* where he presents them together with the other officials.

At all times, Kai and Shinano Provinces furnish the 180 divers bows required for the *Toshigoi* festival (Kai Prov., 80 zelkova bows and Shinano Prov., 100 catalpa bows). All are sent by envoys before the 11th month.

---

362 By this and many of the *shiki* preceding it we get a list of what things constituted defilement —or offense to the deities of the Palace and the shrines—namely, illness, menses, pregnancy, blood, childbirth, slaughter, death, burial, period of mourning, and anything relating to Buddhism.

363 The *kampu* 官符 was an official notice or order handed down from the *Dajō-kan* or *Jingi-kan* to subordinate officials.

364 One would expect to find this regulation concerning the Shrine of the Great Deity in Ise to be placed at the end of Bk. IV, which deals with the Ise Shrines.

365 *Okikura* 置座, the dais or stand on which offerings were placed for presentation. There appear to have been types made of four or eight boards, respectively, called *yokura-oki* and *yakura-oki*, see n. 157 above.

366 *Hahaka* 婆波加 or 波波加, the birch cherry, of which leaf, bark and branches were used to make the fire to heat tortoise shell or deer bones for divination purposes.

367 *Samashidake* 兆竹.

At all times, the three provinces of Tajima, Inaba and Mimasaka send up bows, arrows and swords in lieu of deity taxes.

At all times, the 1,244 poles for spearhandles are provided by Sanuki Province and before the 11th month are sent up by means of transport laborers.

At all times, both Inaba and Hōki Provinces are made to send up 88 unfinished boxes required for the *Ainame* festival (44 boxes from each) to be sent each year before the 10th month in lieu of deity taxes, and delivered by a messenger.

At all times, Izumo, Province is made to send up 60 *mifuki* beads (36 for the three *Ootono* festivals and 24 for other occasions). Every year before the 10th month the jewel-makers of Ou District are ordered to make these and send them up by messenger.

At all times, 378 straw-mats are to be sent up from Settsu Province in lieu of deity taxes to the [*Jingi-*]*kan* to fill the requirements for annual festivals.

At all times, the total number of tortoise-shells to be used during the year is fixed at 50 (Kii Prov. provides 17 from medium males,[368] Awa Prov. provides 13 from medium males and 6 in lieu [of taxes] and Tosa Prov. 10 from medium males and 4 in lieu). However, as for the 13 shells required when the Consecrated Princess enters the No-no-miya, on such occasions the Secretaries are requested to order the provinces which produce these to send them up each month to the *Jingi-kan*.[369]

At all times, the various deity tax goods and articles in lieu of taxes from the provinces and tribute and tax goods from the unattached workers[370] of Watarai, Iino and Take Districts, Ise Province, are all turned over to the *Jingi-kan* and offered up by the officials in charge.

At all times, the tribute, tax and paddy-tax rice from sustenance households of Sanuki Province for the Sono and Kara Shrines are sent up to the *Jingi-kan* and used to meet requirements for repairs to the shrines.

At all times, the grains which are deity taxes for three shrines—Kamo-no-mioya, Wakeikazuchi and Atsuta—may not be used for any other purpose. Even though the need for these shrines is filled, the matter is reported to the secretaries and answer awaited.

At all times, sustenance tax grain for the Matsuno-o Shrine from Inaba Province is stopped from being collected by this *kan*; it is gathered at the shrine and used for offerings to the deities.

At all times, the tribute, tax and levies of grain for the Hiraoka Shrine from the sustenance households of Musashi Province are stopped from being collected by this *kan*; they are gathered at the shrine to meet requirements for repair of the shrine.

At all times, for the Isonokami Shrine the sustenance grain levy from Bingo

368 It is hard to determine what *chūnan* 中男 means—whether referring to the men who prepare the shells, or the age, or the size of the tortoises.

369 For ceremonies on entering the No-no-miya, see Bk. v on the Consecrated Princess, and n. 494.

370 *Rōnin* 浪人 would seem to indicate those who are not members of *kambe* households in these three deity districts (see below). Tsuchiya says both *kambe* and other commoners were called *rōnin*. In Bk. v I call them 'floating workers'.

Province is gathered at the shrine house to be used for the summer and winter festivals.

At all times, for the Sumiyoshi Shrine the sustenance grain levies from Nagato Province are transported by forced labor to the shrine; after transport costs the remainder is made available for forced labor to repair the shrine; but the forced labor from sustenance households of Toyora District, being cheap, remains to supply the Mikage Shrine.[371]

At all times, as regards ceremonial dress for the musicians of Katori Shrine, the governor of the province is made to furnish these; but if he should fail to do so, they seize his certifying document.[372] (For 6 musicians there are required 6 tunics, 6 cloaks, 6 undergarments, 6 sets of white trousers, 6 pairs of socks; for eight dancing girls, 8 lined robes, 8 unlined robes, 8 pairs of trousers, 8 skirts, 8 silk sashes and 8 pairs of socks.)

At all times, for the Isonokami Shrine, the gate key and the Kara keys[373] are kept in the *Jingi-kan* storehouse. When the time of festival draws near, *kan* officials consisting of one each of *kambe* and *urabe* are sent to open the gates, clean the precinct and prepare for the festival. Besides the keys to the main sanctuary, keys for the Tomo and Saeki buildings are also kept in the storehouse, which cannot readily be opened.

At all times, the keys to the storehouses of Kasuga, Hirose and Tatsuta Shrines are kept in the [*Jingi-*]*kan* storehouse and officials who represent the *kan* at festivals request the keys when the time of festival is near and when it is over return them to storage.

At all times, at the Atsuta Shrine in Owari Province, in spring and autumn of each year when the 64 kneeling monks repeat 1,000 sections of the *Vajracchedika Sūtra* by skipping recitation,[374] their alms and masses for the dead are provided for from deity sustenance.[375]

At all times, as regards emoluments for members of the *kan*: for required horses, essential articles as well as ceremonial dress for *kan* officials participating in *kami* affairs, also for the seasonal emoluments and horse requirements for the Chief Diviner, players of the divine *koto,* and elders of tortoise divination, and for monthly rations and for clothing of diviners and Sacred Maidens—deity taxes are to be used (except that monthly rations for the Chief Diviner are provided from paddies belonging to the *kan*). At all times, the rice allotments for diviners who are not present are supplied from provisions within the *kan*.

---

371 Toyora 豐浦 District in Kawachi Province. Mikage 御陰 Shrine was an auxiliary of the Kamo-no-mioya Shrine and located in the foothills of Mt. Hiei 比叡山.

372 The document, *geyu* 解由, which the new governor drew up to certify that the outgoing governor's records were in proper order. In case the governor had failed in any respect in his obligations, his certifying document could be held up until amends were made.

373 The first character may mean a lock or a

key 鑰, probably here a key; the second, *karakagi* 匙, the grooved pin type for a Chinese padlock.

374 The method of reading sutras by *tendoku* 轉讀 was reading and skipping alternately because of the length of the text, in this case the *Kongō-hannya-kyō* 金剛般若經.

375 After the mention of prohibitions against contact with anything Buddhist, it is astonishing to find that deity taxes are used to finance the recitation of a sutra at so prominent a national shrine as the Atsuta 熱田.

At all times, rice allotments for two recorders, one office-keeper and four *kambe* are supplied from deity tax goods, each of them getting 1 *to* 5 *shō* of white rice per month. At all times, to the caretaker of the sanctuary of Hirano one forced laborer of Yamashiro Province is provided.

At all times, to the caretaker of the sanctuaries of Sono and Kara Shrines one sustenance laborer is provided; his monthly allotments are provided out of deity sustenance tax rice in the amount of 6 *to* per month.

At all times the superintendency of Yawata Shrine is filled from either the Ooga or the Usa Uji, and it may not be filled from any other *uji*.[376]

At all times if a *negi* or *hafuri* should quarrel with someone and strike him, or if he violate another, the details of the matter shall be forwarded to this *kan* and the Governor of the Province shall not readily judge the case.

At all times regarding seasonal emoluments for various shrine superintendents and *negi*: at the Grand Shrine of Ise the *negi* correspond to Junior 7th Rank officials, and the *negi* of the Watarai Shrine to Junior 8th Rank (both are supplied from deity taxes from the Deity Districts[377]); the Superintendent of Katori Shrine in Shimotsuke Province, the Superintendent of Kashima Shrine in Hitachi Province and Superintendent of Kehi Shrine in Echizen Province all correspond to Junior 8th Rank officials (all are provided for from sustenance goods); while the Superintendant of Keta Shrine in Noto Province corresponds to *shōso* rank[378] (he is provided for from deity sustenance).

*   *   *   *   *

End of Book Three of the *Engi-shiki*
   Enchō 5th Year, 12th Month, 26th Day
   [same signatures as at end of Book One]

---

[376] The Yawata Jingū or Hachiman Jingū 八幡神宮 dedicated to Hachiman, supposed to be the deified Oojin Tennō 應神天皇.

[377] The three deity districts, *shingun* 神郡, of Ise to support the Grand Shrine were: Watarai 度會, Take 多氣 and Iino 飯野.

[378] *Daiso* 大初 and *shōso* 少初, the lowest pair of Court Ranks in the scale.

ENGI-SHIKI, BOOK FOUR

THE SHRINE OF THE GREAT DEITY IN ISE[379]

At the Shrine of the Great Deity (located on the upper reaches of the Isuzu River, Uji Village, Watarai District, Ise Province) there are three deities:

Amaterasu-ō-mikami

two *aidono* deities[380]

[There are:] one *negi* (an official of Jr. 7th Rank), 4 *ō-uchindo*,[381] 9 *mono-imi* (one boy and eight girls), 9 fathers[382] and 9 *ko-uchindo*.

One deity at the Aramatsuri Shrine (of the Turbulent Spirit of the Great Deity,[383] located 24 *jō* north of the Great Shrine).

2 *uchindo*, 1 *mono-imi* and 1 father are to be furnished to the above two shrines for the *Toshigoi, Tsukinami, Kanname* and *Kammiso* festivals.[384]

Two deities at the Izanagi Shrine (located 3 *ri* north of the Great Shrine):

Izanagi-no-mikoto

Izanami-no-mikoto[385]

At the Tsukiyomi Shrine two deities:

---

[379] The *Oo-mikami-no-miya*, meaning the shrine to the Great Deity, Amaterasu-ō-mikami. Whenever the text says 'the Great Shrine' it means this one. Sometimes the text uses 'both Great Shrines', meaning this one and the Watarai Shrine. A large portion of the material in Bk. IV stems from an earlier work, the Handbook of Ceremonial Procedures for the Two Great Shrines, which is referred to as the *Gishiki-chō*, see n. 95 above. Of the 59 items of *shiki* in Bk. IV, 23 are based upon the text of the *Gishiki-chō*. Miyagi, II, p. 356.

[380] The *aidono* 相殿, 'same hall', deities are those worshiped together with the main deity. Here, according to tradition, the deity on the left is Ame-no-tajikara-no-mikoto, and the one on the right Yorozuhata-toyoakitsuhime-no-mikoto, Mother of the Heavenly Grandson of Amaterasu-ō-mikami.

[381] The *uchindo* (*uchibito*) 內人, 'penetrants', were those whose duties associated them with the intimate matters of preparing offerings and food for the deities. They were shrine officials serving under the *negi* and supervised the *mono-imi* who helped them (see n. 204 above). Besides *uchindo* there were great and small *uchindo*: the *ō-uchindo*

and *ko-uchindo*, respectively.

[382] Because the *mono-imi* were so young, their fathers accompanied them as they performed their shrine duties.

[383] In the 13th century Saka Jūbutsu 坂十佛 wrote: 'To the northeast of the Oomiya [Great Shrine] is a place called the Aramatsuri-no-miya 荒祭の宮 where dwells the violent spirit of the Deity.' *Ise daijingū sankeiki*, p. 53. The belief was that as many as four different spirits might be embodied in an august being: namely, the *niki-mi-tama* 和御魂—'august gentle spirit', *ara-mitama* 荒御魂—'august turbulent spirit', *saki-mitama* 幸御魂—'august lucky spirit' and *kushi-mitama* 奇御魂—'august wondrous spirit'. It is the *ara-mitama* of the Sun Goddess which is enshrined in the Ara-matsuri Shrine.

[384] The *Toshigoi, Tsukinami* and *Kanname* festivals are national celebrations covered in Bk. I; the *Kammiso* 神御衣, or Festival of Deity Raiment, is celebrated only at the Great Shrine.

[385] Izanagi and Izanami were the male and female creator gods of the myths who produced the three chief deities: the Sun Goddess (Amaterasu-ō-mikami), the Moon God (Tsukiyomi-no-*

Tsukiyomi-no-mikoto

Aramitama-no-mikoto[386]

One deity at the Takihara Shrine (a distant shrine to the Great Deity, located in the mountains on the boundary between Ise and Shima Provinces, 90 *ri* west of the Great Shrine).

One deity at the Takihara-no-nami Shrine (a distant shrine to the Great Deity, located in the precinct of the Takihara Shrine).

One deity at the Izawa Shrine (a distant shrine to the Great Deity, located in Tōshi District, Shima Prov., 83 *ri* south of the Great Shrine).

These separate shrines[387] each provide for the *Toshigoi, Tsukinami* and *Kan-name* festivals (except that Takihara-no-nami and Izawa do not participate in the *Tsukinami*): 2 *uchindo* (one of 8th Rank or higher and hereditary[388]), 1 *mono-imi* and 1 father. But at the Tsukiyomi Shrine one Sacred Maiden who is an *uchindo* is added.

Four deities at the Watarai Shrine (located in Yamadanohara, Numaki Village, Watarai Dist., 7 *ri* west of the Great Shrine):

Toyouke-no-ōkami[389]

three *aidono* deities

One *negi* (Jr. 8th Rank), 4 *ō-uchindo*, 6 *mono-imi*, 6 fathers, 8 *ko-uchindo*.

At the Taka Shrine (of the Turbulent Spirit of Toyouke-no-ōkami, located 60 *jō* south of that deity's shrine) 2 *negi*, 1 *mono-imi* and 1 father. The two foregoing shrines furnish the said personnel for the *Toshigoi, Tsukinami* and *Kanname* festivals.

At all times *negi, ō-uchindo* and *ko-uchindo* and *mono-imi* for both of the Great Shrines, as well as the *uchindo* and *mono-imi* for separate shrines shall be people from Watarai District. (However, the 2 *uchindo*, the *mono-imi* and father are to be from the *kambe* of Shima Province.)

The small shrines enshrining 40 deities:[390]

[A] Auxiliaries of the Shrine of the Great Deity enshrining 24 deities:

Asakuma   Ookunidama-hime

---

*mikoto), and the Storm (or Volcano?) God, Susa-no'o-no-mikoto. There is also one of the small auxiliary shrines which is dedicated to Izanami. See n. 106 above.

386 The two enshrinements here are the Moon God, Tsukiyomi, and his *ara-mitama* or turbulent spirit.

387 The separate shrines are *bekkū* 別宮.

388 The term is *onshison* 陰子孫. According to the system of *on'isei* 陰位制, children of high-ranking nobles attained rank automatically at age 21. The son of a royal prince became Junior 4th Rank Lower Grade; the heir of a nobleman of 1st Rank became Jr. 5th Rank Lower Grade; the son of a noble of 3rd Rank became Jr. 6th Rank Upper Grade, and so forth. This secured the filling of administrative positions by the uppermost class of nobility. J. Murao, *Ritsuryō-sei no kichō*, pp. 51–2.

389 The Watarai-no-miya, now known as the Outer Shrine (*gekū* 外宮), enshrining the Goddess of Food, variously known as Toyouke-no-ōkami 豊受大神, Ukemochi-no-kami 保食の神 or Mi-ketsu-no-kami 御食津神, the guardian deity of food *(mike)*. The three other deities *(aidono)* are not named. The *ara-mitama* of the goddess is enshrined in the Taka-no-miya, a separate shrine.

390 All these auxiliaries have the designation *yashiro* 社 which (as in Bk. III) is translated 'shrines'. However, all of this list of shrines attained *kansha* (official shrine) status and are so listed in the *Jimmyō-chō*, where all have the designation *jinja* 神社. Again, this shows that the shrines and deities list of Bks. IX and X was put together later than Bk. IV, which used as sources the *Kōnin-shiki* as well as the *Gishiki-chō* (of 804 A.D.).

Sonō	Enokami
Kamo	Kamusaki
Tanoe	Awa-ōji (or Awanomiko)
Kano	Kugutsuhime
Yuta	Narahara
Ootsuchi-no-mioya	Oihara
Kunitsu-mioya	Mifune
Kuchira	Sakatekuninari
Izanami	Satakuninari
Tsunaga	Takihara
Oomizu	Kawara

[B] Auxiliaries of the Watarai Shrine enshrining 16 deities:

Tsukiyomi	Kiyonoite
Kusanagi	Takakawara
Oomanokuninari	Kawara-(no-ō)
Watarai-no-kuni-no-mikami	Kawaranofuchi
Watarai-no-ōkunidamahime	Yamasue
Tanoe-no-ōmizu	Usunono
Shitomi	Omata
Ookawachi	Mike

The above shrines participate in the *Toshigoi* and *Kanname* festivals.

Every time on the first day of the year, the *negi*, the *uchindo* and so on, worship at each of the shrines, making presentations of sacred sake steeped with herbs.[391] (The herbs therefor are sent by the Provincial Government.) That done, they all gather at the august kitchens. The Superintendent of the Great Shrines then leads the *negi*, *uchindo* and others of the various shrines and the officials of the deity districts in making obeisance to the shrines from a distance (first to the Watarai Shrine, then to the Shrine of the Great Deity, then to the other shrines). That done, they make obeisance to the Sovereign's Court. Following this a feast is bestowed. On the third day at dawn they respectfully offer congratulations to the Consecrated Princess.

In all cases the offerings for the *Toshigoi* festival in the 2nd month are: (The kinds of offerings are listed in the Festivals of Four Seasons). On the day the Imperial Messenger comes he is led by the Superintendent of the Great Shrines and first goes to worship at the Watarai Shrine, then presents offerings at the Shrine of the Great Deity, all according to the usual procedure . . . (At the Taka and Aramatsuri Shrines the Messenger personally presents offerings; at the other shrines the *negi* and others are caused to make the presentations.) At the two Great Shrines and their auxiliaries the offerings to be made to each deity include: 3 *shaku* of stiff silk, 2 *ryō* 2 *bu* each of bark-cloth and hemp. The Superintendent of the Great Shrines apportions them and the *negi* inspect them and distribute them among the shrines.

---

[391] The reference is to *byakusan* 白散, a preparation which is drunk at the New Year, in which five kinds of medicinal herbs were soaked in sake, a white paper placed over the cup and the contents strained for drinking. See n. 567 below for details of this compound.

The Festival of Deity Raiment in the 4th and 9th months[392]

At the Shrine of the Great Deity: 24 *hiki* of soft raiment[393] (8 *hiki* are 1 ½ *shaku* wide, 8 are 1.2 *shaku* wide, 8 are 1 *shaku* wide, all are 4 *jō* in length), 16 strands of silk each for hair bands, necklaces, bracelets, jeweled foot-thongs, ties for socks; 64 strands of sewing thread (each 5 *shaku* long), 1 long knife, 16 each of short knives, awls, needles and spearheads, 2 decorated *sakaki*[394] hung with silk thread, 2 Kara chests (one for the garments and one for the hardware), 1 box (to carry the silk thread and silk ties), 80 *hiki* of coarse raiment (40 are 1.6 *shaku* wide, 40 are 1 *shaku* wide, all are 4 *jō* long), 20 each of knives and needles, 1 Kara chest (for both garments and knives). At the Aramatsuri Shrine: 13 *hiki* of soft material, 8 strands of silk thread each for hair bands, necklaces, bracelets, jeweled foot-thongs, and ties for socks, 40 strands of sewing thread, 8 each of knives, awls, needles and spears, one decorated *sakaki* branch hung with silk thread, 2 Kara chests, 1 box, 40 *hiki* of coarse material, 12 each of knives and needles, 1 Kara chest.

Members of the Hatori Uji cleanse and purify the above soft materials and members of the Omi Uji[395] do the same for the coarse raiment, and starting on the first day of the month in which the festival is held, they commence to weave, and on the 14th day present the raiment for the festival. The procedure is: the Superintendent of the Great Shrines, the *negi*, the *uchindo*, and others, lead the 8 weaver women. All wear lustrous garments, carry decorated *sakaki* and form a line behind the [bearers of] august raiment. The Superintendent of the Great Shrines recites the ritual. When it is finished they all bow two times twice, clap inaudibly twice, then kneel and draw back, bow two times twice, clap inaudibly twice and bow once more, then withdraw. They proceed to the Aramatsuri Shrine and offer up the august raiment. The ceremony is the same as at the Shrine of the Great Deity except that they bow two times twice, clap inaudibly two times twice and then withdraw. On this day the *kasanui uchindo*[396] and others make offerings of straw raincoats and sedge hats—3 sets at the Shrine of the Great Deity, 1 set at the Aramatsuri Shrine, 2 sets at the Izanagi Shrine, 2 sets at the Tsukiyomi Shrine, 2 sets at the Takihara Shrine, 1 set at Takihara-no-nami Shrine, 1 set at Izawa Shrine, 2 sets at the Asakuma Shrine 1 set each at the small shrines of Sonō, Kamo, Tanoe, Kano and Izanami; 8 sets at the Watarai Shrine.

Requirements for the Hatori to make Deity Raiment twice a year for the *Hata-*

---

392 The *Kammiso-sai*.

393 *Nikitae-miso* 和妙衣, raiment of soft material—namely, silk. The raiment of coarse material, *aratae-miso* 荒妙衣, is made of hemp-cloth. In the *Nihongi* the story of the ceremonies to lure the Sun Goddess out of the Heavenly Rock Cave mentions 'blue soft offerings and white soft offerings' that were made. These were probably reference to finely woven hemp-cloth, resembling linen, and to soft bark-cloth (the blue), respectively. In time, these changed to silk and hemp-cloth. Aston, *Nihongi*, I, p. 44.

394 This is a *tamagushi* 玉串, a branch of *sakaki* ornamented and then festooned with silk or streamers of bark-cloth and carried aloft in the procession.

395 The Hatori Uji, 服部氏, meaning 'loom weavers' (*hata-ori* 機織), and the Omi Uji whose name (o-umi 麻績) meant 'spinners of hemp', were the families organized to do the spinning and weaving of stuffs for the ceremonial raiments. 'Weaver women' are *hataori-me* or *hatoribe-me* 服織女.

396 The name *kasanui* 笠縫 means makers of shade hats and umbrellas of sedge-grass or of silk. *Kasanui uchindo* made these articles for presentation to the deities.

dono festival,[397] and for other purposes: 100 skeins of silk thread, 2 *jō* 1 *shaku* of colored hempen cloth (this item to be requested from the official storehouses),[398] 13 *kin* 4 *ryō* 2 *bu* each of bark-cloth and hemp (the foregoing items are for the festival), 4 *hiki* 4 *jō* 2 *shaku* of stiff silk, 4 *mochi* of floss silk, 9 *tan* 1 *jō* of tribute cloth, 79 *tan* of commercial cloth, 6 bars of iron, 4 whetstones (this item to be requested from the official storehouse), 1 *to* of oil, 1 *koku* of salt, 656 *soku* of rice-in-ear (the foregoing are for the festival in the 9th month), 4 wall hangings,[399] 4 seat-mats, 1 *shō* 2 *gō* of rice per day for two *kambe*.

Requirements for the Omi for the *Hatadono* festival and for other purposes: 30 headdresses of hemp (2 *shaku* makes a headdress), 4 *jō* of stiff silk, 3 *jō* of colored hempen cloth, 13 *kin* 4 *ryō* 2 *bu* of bark-cloth (foregoing items are for the festival), 79 *tan* of commercial cloth, 2 whetstones, 9 *shō* of oil, 1 *koku* of salt, 397 *soku* of rice-in-ear (foregoing are for the festival in the 9th month).

The various items specified above as 'requirements' for weaving Deity Raiment all come from the tribute, *corvée* and paddy taxes[400] of 22 households of Hatori and 22 households of Omi, each furnishing a portion. The Superintendent of the Great Shrines inspects all this. If there is more than can be transported, it is recorded in an account book and reported. If any household defaults, the Superintendent of the Great Shrines measures the deficiency and sees that it is supplied [from elsewhere].

Whenever the Festival of Deity Raiment in the 4th month is held, purification is performed on the last day of the preceding month. (Same for the festival in the 9th month).

The Tsukinami Festival in the 6th Month (same in the 12th month)

For the Shrine of the Great Deity: 40 skeins of bright red thread,[401] 7 large *kin* of bark-cloth, 12 large *kin* of hemp,[402] 10 *koku* of rice for sake, 3.3 *koku* of rice, 20 jugs of deity sake (3 *to* per jug; 15 jars from this province, 2 jars from Iga Prov., one each from Owari, Mikawa and Tōtoumi Provinces; all brewed from deity-tax rice),[403] 20 loads of various foodstuffs (presented to accompany the sake). For various offerings: 15 *koku* of rice, 1 *koku* 4 *to* of salt and one bar of iron. For the Watarai Shrine: 30 skeins of bright red thread, 4 large *kin* of bark-cloth, 10 large *kin* of hemp, 10 *koku* of rice for sake, 2 *koku* of rice, 8 jugs of deity sake (3 jugs from this province, the others from 4 provinces, as above), 8 loads of various food-

---

397 *Hatadono* 機殿 means 'weaving hall', which presumably perpetuates the tradition of the Sun Goddess weaving in her august weaving hall.

398 The *kanko* 官庫, or storehouses of the *Jingi-kan.*

399 That is, *kabeshiro* 壁代, a large curtain put up to screen part of the ceremonies and participants.

400 These were *chō, yō* and *so*, respectively. The standard tax for all households was the *so* or land tax. Where it was specifically rice lands it was called *denso*, paddy tax. The laws of Taika (A.D. 646) had set this tax at 2 *soku* 束 2 *wa* 把 of rice-in-ear per *tan* of paddy—amounting to a tax

ratio of about 1:23. In addition to the land tax or paddy tax, the *chō* (or *tsuki* 調) had to be paid in other products—'tribute'—and the third category, *yō* (*chikarashiro* 庸) was paid in lieu of forced labor, hence '*corvée*' tax. See n. 187 and n. 193.

401 The term *akahiki-ito* 赤引絲 (in *Gishiki-chō* : 明曳糸) appears to be thread of red color and particular lustre taken from special silkworms in spring; used for deity raiment.

402 'Large' measure usually means ten times the standard; 70 *kin* of hemp and 180 *kin* of bark-cloth would be commensurate with the large amounts of thread; and or rice and sake.

403 For deity taxes, *shinzei*, see n. 235.

stuffs. For various offerings: 10 *koku* of rice, 1.4 *koku* of salt and one bar of iron. (The same items are used for this festival at the auxiliary shrines.)

The above is celebrated on the 16th day of the month at Watarai Shrine and on the 17th day at the Shrine of the Great Deity. The procedure is that after sundown of the 15th the *negi*, at the head of the *uchindo* and *mono-imi*, lay out for display the various sacred articles for the deities. When this is done, at the hour of the boar [10 p.m.] they present the evening food offering.[404] Then at the hour of the ox [2 a.m.] they present the morning food offering. After that, *negi, uchindo* and others perform the sacred song and dance. At dawn of the 16th day the Consecrated Royal Princess enters the Watarai Shrine. When she reaches the east side of the gate of the board fence[405] she alights from her palanquin. She enters the gate of the outer shrine fence[406] and takes her place in the East Hall. Inside the gate there is a hall to the east and one to the west. In the East Hall is set up the seat for the Consecrated Princess; to left and right of it are set places for the Palace women.[407] In the West Hall are set the places for girl attendants. When all have entered, the Superintendent of the Shrine bears the bark-cloth headdress, enters the gate of the outer shrine fence and, facing north, he kneels. A Palace woman followed by girl attendants comes out to receive it and then presents it to the Consecrated Princess. She claps her hands, receives and puts on the headdress. The Superintendent also carries the ornamented *sakaki* branch (a *sakaki* decked with bark-cloth has the name *futo-tamagushi*),[408] and enters through the same gate and kneels. The Palace woman again receives this and presents it to the Consecrated Princess. She takes it, raises it aloft and enters the gate of the inner shrine fence, and takes her seat there. (The Palace woman and girl attendant follow her.) Leaving her seat, she moves forward and bows twice two times. (The Palace woman does not bow.) That done, she bestows the ornamented *sakaki* branch on the Palace woman, who on receiving it bestows it on the *mono-imi*, who on receiving it bears it and stands at the west side of the gate of the shrine fence. The Consecrated Princess then returns to her original place. Afterward the *negi* put on their lustrous garments (both garment and bonnet are of raw silk). The Superintendent dons ceremonial robes of color prescribed for his rank[409] and he bears the ornamented *sakaki* branch. The *negi* are standing in front (the *negi* of the Great Shrine stand on the left and the *uchindo* of Uji[410] on the right). Next is the Superintendent of the Shrine, then the various offerings and the horses forming a procession in single file. Next, the Imperial Messenger[411] arrives and enters the gate of the outer shrine fence. When he reaches the gate of the inner shrine fence everyone kneels

404 *Mike* 御饌, august food; food offered to the deities.

405 The board fence, *itagaki* 板垣, surrounding the entire shrine precinct.

406 Within the board fence are three successive enclosures: the outer *tamagaki* 外玉垣, the inner *tamagaki* 內玉垣 and the *mizugaki* 瑞垣.

407 *Myōbu* 命婦 were the noblewomen of 5th Rank or higher who served in the Imperial Palace.

408 *Futo-tamagushi* 太玉串: a more ornate

and larger *tamagushi* than that mentioned above. (See n. 394.)

409 For 'color prescribed for rank', see n. 191.

410 That is, *uchindo* from the village of Uji 宇治.

411 A member of the Nakatomi Uji ('liturgists') who is sent as the messenger from the Imperial House to the Shrine of the Great Deity for the *Tsukinami* festival.

together. First the Imperial Messenger pronounces the sovereign's message, then the Superintendent recites the ritual.[412] When this is finished the *mono-imi* and *uchindo* raise the offering-tables with offerings upon them. They enter and place them in the storehouse inside the shrine fence. The Consecrated Princess and the host of officials and attendants bow twice and clap the hands eight times. After that they clap inaudibly and bow twice. They do the whole thing twice. When it is completed the host of officials withdraw. Thereupon Imperial Messenger, Superintendent of the Shrine and attendants turn towards the Taka Shrine (the Consecrated Princess does not). They bow twice two times. They clap hands inaudibly twice. They withdraw and go to the Depuration Hall.[413] They are served with sake and food. When they have finished they go in the gate of the outer shrine fence and the *Yamato-mai*[414] is performed. First the Superintendent of the Shrine, then the *negi, ō-uchindo,* the Imperial Messenger with the offerings, then the chief priest of the Bureau of the Consecrated Princess, and an official who is no less than a Secretary of that Bureau. (One sake-serving maiden carries the oak leaves, one carries the sake. Every time a dance is completed the dancer is served oak-leaf sake. But on days when the Consecrated Princess participates the afore-mentioned serving maids are replaced by *uneme* or a girl attendant is used. On days when the Princess does not attend, wives and daughters of the *negi* or of the *uchindo* do the serving.) Next come the wives of the *negi* and of the *ō-uchindo.* When it is over, four girl attendants of the Consecrated Princess perform *Gosechi* Dances.[415] Then the *Torikona*[416] is danced. On the 17th they go to worship at the Shrine of the Great Deity where the procedure is the same as at the Watarai Shrine. (Obeisance to the Aramatsuri Shrine is the same as at the Taka Shrine.)

For the Kanname Festival in the 9th Month (but the number of offerings from the Imperial Court is stated in the *shiki* for the Bureau of Palace Storehouses[417]):
    3 *hiki* of august raiment for the Shrine of the Great Deity (the *negi* have already in the 5th month collected silk thread as tribute from sustenance households, performed cleansing and purification and caused the thread to be woven

---

412 A translation of the text of this ritual is found in Philippi, *Norito,* pp. 36–40, 'Monthly Festival of the Sixth Month'.

413 See n. 272.

414 *Yamato-mai* 倭舞 is a traditional dance associated with *kami* worship. It was anciently performed for the important festivals: the *Daijō-sai* of the Enthronement, the *Chinkon-sai,* and others, and then became a part of the *gagaku* 雅樂 (court music) repertoire in the group called *utamai* 歌舞. The usual performers consisted of two dancers, two singers, one each of players of the *shakubyōshi* 笏拍子 (wooden clappers), *fue* 笛 (a kind of flute), *hichiriki* 篳篥 (fife) and sometimes of the *wagon* 和琴 (so-called native Japanese zither).

415 *Gosechi-mai* 五節舞 were Court dances

(*bugaku* 舞樂) performed by five young dancing ladies or girls on ox, tiger, hare and dragon days of the 11th month to celebrate the *Niiname-sai* (Festival of First Fruits) and also for the *Daijō-sai.* Tradition said these dances originated when Temmu Tennō was playing his august zither and a Heavenly Maid descended to dance for him.

416 *Torikona* (or *tokona*) 鳥子名 was a traditional dance of the Great Shrine said to have been inaugurated when the '800 Myriad Deities' danced for joy at the re-appearance of the Sun Goddess from out of the Heavenly Rock Cave. The dance is no longer performed today, though there is said to be an effort afoot to revive it.

417 The procedures for the Bureau of Palace Storehouses, *uchinokura-ryō* 內藏寮, are in *E-S,* Bk. xv.

into garments), 113 *hiki* 1 *jō* 2 *shaku* of initial tribute silks[418] (106 *hiki* for the Shrine of the Great Deity, 1 *hiki* for each of the 6 separate shrines and 1 *hiki* 1 *jō* 2 *shaku* for each of the 24 small shrines), 1 *hiki* of stiff silk for the five colored silk offerings, 3 *hiki* 2 *jō* of stiff silk for the curtain across the gate, 3 skeins of silk thread, 53 *mochi* of floss silk, 1 *tan* of ordinary cloth, 10 *kin* of bark-cloth, 18 *kin* of hemp, 20 *kin* of dried meat, 12 *kin* of dried bêche-de-mer,[419] 14 *kin* of bonito, 12 *kin* of abalone, 6 *koku* of salt, 6 *shō* of oil, 20 *kin* of *wakame* (the foregoing items are initial tribute goods of sustenance households of various provinces), 3 *koku* 3 *to* of rice, 10 *koku* of rice for sake, 25 *koku* of rice for various offerings, 1 *koku* of salt, 23 jugs of sacred sake (15 jugs from this province, 1 jug from the *mono-imi* of the *nekura*[420] of Watarai Shrine, 1 jug each from Hatori and Omi, 2 jugs from Iga Province and one each from Owari, Mikawa and Tōtoumi Provinces; all brewed from deity tax rice), 230 *soku* of rice-in-ear as small tax[421] (of which 1 *wa* equals a *soku*; 100 *soku* from the Kan'omi, 80 *soku* from the Kanhatori,[422] 10 *soku* from sustenance households of Iino District and 40 *soku* from sustenance households of Iga Province), 100 *soku* of rice-in-ear as great tax (of which 5 *wa* equal 1 *soku*; 100 *soku* from Kan'omi, and 80 *soku* from Kanhatori), 1222 *soku* of *hakari* taxes[423] (1,082 *soku* for the Shrine of the Great Deity, 50 *soku* for the Aramatsuri Shrine, 30 *soku* for the Tsukiyomi Shrine, 20 *soku* for the Takihara Shrine, 20 *soku* for Takihara-no-nami Shrine, 10 for the Takimatsuri[424] and 10 for Asakuma Shrine; deity taxes are used for all, as they are for items below), 1 *tan* of ordinary cloth, 20 *tatami* mats, 20 short *tatami*, 24 seat-mats, 23 food-mats, 3 large curtains, 1 large jar, 2 shallow vessels, 3 *sue* ware bowls, 3 sake cups (each provided with a stand), 3 each of stemmed dishes, flat dishes and sake jugs, one bar of iron, one whetstone, 10 tables, 80 split-cypress-wood boxes with legs and 200 without, 10 short tables, 8 high tables, 20 dippers, 20 gourds, 4,500 clay dishes of various sorts.

Lustrous Robes for Negi and Uchindo, and so forth :

For two persons, one *negi* and one *ōmono-imi,* each 3 *hiki* of stiff silk, 3 *mochi*

---

418 Namely, *mitsugi-nozaki* 調荷前, first products (*hatsumono* 初物) of the season collected from the sustenance households (*fuko* 封戸) of various provinces, consisting of: silks, ordinary cloth (of hemp), and other farm products to be presented first at the Shrine of the Great Deity and then at shrines of other deities. *Dai Nihon kokugo jiten.*

419 *Iriko* 熬海鼠—dried sea-slug or bêche-de-mer.

420 *Nekura* 根倉, a small storehouse of the Watarai Shrine.

421 *Ochikara* 小税, 'small tax', was one-tenth of the standard unit, *soku*, consisting of one *wa* only.

422 Kan'omi and Kanhatori are the designations for the *kambe* families of Omi and Hatori

who were engaged in the weaving of the stuffs of silk and hemp for deity raiment. (See n. 395.) As seen here, they also contributed support in kind.

423 The ratios stated are somewhat confusing, as *hakari-jikara* 斤税, 'measured tax', is said to mean the same as 'great tax', *daizei* 大税, which had 10 *wa* to the *soku*. In the preceding line a special ratio of 5 *wa* to the *soku* is stated which is only relatively 'great'. Great tax is regular tax.

424 The *Taki-matsuri* 瀧祭, though listed in the *Gishiki-chō* as a shrine, had no building. Thus it is not listed in this Bk. IV as an auxiliary of the Great Shrine, nor is it in the *Jimmyō-chō* (Bk. IX). Nevertheless, as a sacred place of worship it receives support rice for its *mono-imi* workers.

of floss silk. For four *ō-uchindo*, each 2 *hiki* of stiff silk, 2 *mochi* of floss silk. For three *mono-imi* who serve as shrine keeper, ground-hallower and salt-burner, each 1 *hiki* 3 *jō* of stiff silk and 1 *mochi* of floss silk. For the four fathers of the one *ōmono-imi* and the 3 *mono-imi* who serve as shrine-keeper, ground-hallower and salt-burner, together with the five *mono-imi* for brewing sacred sake, for ordinary sake, for cutting trees,[425] for the Takimatsuri, and for making clay utensils—plus their fathers and nine others: the maker of sacred boxes, maker of bark-cloth, sacred metalsmith, maker of *sue* ware utensils, sacred sedge-hat maker, *hinomi* Sacred Maiden[426] and two *uchindo* who feed the sacred horses—for every one: 1 *hiki* of silk and 1 *mochi* of floss silk. For two *uchindo* of the Aramatsuri Shrine: 3 *hiki* of silk (1 *hiki* 3 *jō* apiece), and 3 *mochi* of floss silk (1 ½ *mochi* each). For one *mono-imi*: 1 *hiki* 3 *jō* of silk and 1 *mochi* of floss silk. For his father: 1 *hiki* of silk and 1 *mochi* of floss silk. The *uchindo* and the others of the Tsukiyomi Shrine receive the same as the *uchindo* and others of the Aramatsuri Shrine, except that the *uchindo* Sacred Maiden is given 1 *hiki* of stiff silk and 1 *mochi* of floss silk. The two *uchindo* of the Izawa Shrine and a *mono-imi* and father—4 persons in all—receive 1 *hiki* of stiff silk and 1 *mochi* of floss silk apiece.

For the Watarai Shrine:

2 *hiki* of august garments (the *negi* having already collected silk thread from sustenance households and had it purified and woven, as above), 55 *hiki* 4 *jō* 8 *shaku* of initial tribute silks (54 *hiki* for [Watarai] Shrine, 1 *hiki* for the Taka Shrine, 4 *jō* 8 *shaku* for the 16 small shrines. 1 *hiki* of stiff silk for the five-colored offerings, 2 *hiki* 3 *jō* of stiff silk for the curtain across the gate, 2 *hiki* of stiff silk for the Sacred Food Hall,[427] 2 skeins of silk thread, 52 *mochi* of floss silk, 1 *tan* of plain cloth, 6 *kin* of bark-cloth, 15 *kin* of hemp, 20 *kin* of dried meat, 8 *kin* of dried bêche-de-mer, 10 *kin* of bonito, 8 *kin* of abalone, 4 *koku* of salt, 15 *kin* of *wakame* root, 2 *koku* of rice and 10 *koku* of sake rice for the festival, 25 *koku* of rice for various offerings, 5 *to* of salt, 20 jugs of deity sake (12 from the local province, from the other provinces same as for the Shrine of the Great Deity), 120 *soku* of rice-in-ear of lesser tax (40 *soku* from the Kanhatori and 80 *soku* from Kan'omi), 80 *soku* of greater tax (40 from Kanhatori and 40 from Kan'omi), 800 *soku* of *hakari* tax (790 *soku* for the [Watarai] Shrine and 10 for the Taka Shrine; 20 *tatami* mats, 20 short *tatami*, 20 seat-mats, 23 food-mats, 3 large curtains, 3 each of *sue* ware bowls, sake cups, sake stands, high stands and sake jars; 1 bar of iron and 1 whetstone.

Lustrous Robes for Negi, Uchindo, and so forth [at the Watarai Shrine]:

425 The expression Yamage 山向 *(yamamuki)* refers to the members of the Yamagebe Uji 山向部氏, a *mono-imi* family who went into the Yusuki mountain to cut 'heavenly 8-branched *sakaki*' for shrine ceremonies. Also, once in 20 years they went thither to cut wood for sacred containers for treasures of the Great Shrine at the rebuilding. *Daijingū-gishikikai*, I, pp. 778–9.

426 The *hinomi* 日祈 were a certain group of *uchindo* (*uchibito*) who prayed to the sun and wind. Duties of the *hinomi uchindo* are given shortly below in the text. In this list there are only 8 persons, as *hinomi-no-mikannagi* is to be taken as one. The list for Watarai (below) totals eight.

427 The *mike-dono* 御饌殿, in which food offerings are prepared.

3 *hiki* of stiff silk and 3 *mochi* of floss silk for the *negi*; 2 *hiki* of stiff silk and 2 *mochi* of floss silk apiece for 4 *ō-uchindo* and 1 *ōmono-imi*; 1 *hiki* 3 *jō* of stiff silk and 1 *mochi* of floss silk each for 2 *mono-imi* who help with sacred cooking and salt burning; 1 *hiki* of silk and 1 *mochi* of floss silk each for 3 *mono-imi* who serve at the *nekura*, in rush cutting and clay-utensil making, and for each of the fathers of the 5 *mono-imi* and 1 *ōmono-imi*, as well as for 8 *uchindo*, including bark-cloth maker, Sacred Maiden, sacred metalsmith, sedge-hat maker, *sue* ware maker, sacred-box maker and the two who feed the sacred horses. At the Taka Shrine 2 *uchindo* each gets 1 *hiki* 3 *jō* of stiff silk and 1½ *mochi* of floss silk, 1 *mono-imi* gets 1 *hiki* 3 *jō* of stiff silk and 1 *mochi* of floss silk and the father gets 1 *hiki* of silk and 1 *mochi* of floss silk.

The [*Kanname*] above is held at the Watarai Shrine on the 16th day of the 9th month and at the Shrine of the Great Deity on the 17th day. The *negi* and *ō-uchindo* are all clothed in lustrous robes. They are divided left and right and the Superintendent of the Shrines stands between them. Next the Messengers who are Imbe[428] present symbolic offerings, then come the horses, then the Messenger Nakatomi and the Messenger Prince all enter and go to the posting-board in the inner courtyard. The Messenger Nakatomi recites the ritual. When he is finished the Superintendent of the Shrines also recites a ritual. The remainder of the ceremony is the same as that of the *Tsukinami* festival.

At the three times of the festivals (6th, 9th and 12th months) purification is performed beforehand on the last day of the preceding month. For this are required each time: 1 horse, 13 mattocks, 13 *kin* of hemp and 1 *tan* of commercial cloth for the priests.

At each time the *negi*, *uchindo* and others attached to the Watarai Shrine, according to precedent, present the sacred food offerings in the morning and evening at the Shrine of the Great Deity and the Watarai Shrine and do not present them at any other shrine. The annual requirements for the Sacred Food Hall are: 2 *hiki* of stiff silk, 8 *tan* of plain cloth, 3 Azuma seat-mats, 2 *tan* of unlined cloth for food [preparation] and 3 food-mats, all provided by the Superintendent of the Shrines.

Every year in the 7th month the *hinomi uchindo* requires 4 *jō* of stiff silk in praying for the calming of winds and rains (5 *shaku* each at the Shrine of the Great Deity and the Watarai Shrine, 3 *shaku* for each of the ten deities enshrined in the Aramatsuri, Tsukiyomi, Aramitama, Izanagi, Izanami, Takihara, Ko-asakuma, Taka, Kugu and Kaze-no-kami Shrines), 15 *kin* 5 *ryō* 5 *bu* each of bark-cloth and hemp (3 *kin* at the Great Shrine, 2 *kin* at the Watarai Shrine, 4 *kin* for each of the ten auxiliaries and 6 *kin* 5 *ryō* 6 *bu*—2 *ryō* 2 *bu* each—for each of the 40 deities of Watarai District). The Superintendent of the Great Shrines supplies all of these.

Every year, for the purpose of procuring handles for spades and mattocks to be used for tilling the deity rice paddies, in the 3rd month the *Yamanokuchi* and

428 There are three types of official messenger participating in these ceremonies: the Imbe who present symbolic offerings, the Nakatomi who recites the *norito*, and a prince representing the sovereign or the Imperial Family.

Konomoto[429] festivals are first held and then the foregoing are procured. For this are required 80 each of iron effigies, mirrors and spears.

Once in every 20 years the Main Sanctuary and treasure houses and outer Hall for Offerings of the Shrine of the Great Deity are to be rebuilt (the interval for rebuilding the sacred halls of the Watarai Shrine, the separate shrines and the auxiliary small shrines is the same).[430] For all of them new lumber is selected for the construction. Other than these, the various buildings use old and new lumber combined. (For the precincts of the shrines two lots are marked out and when the time comes, the move is from one to the other.) The divine treasures of the old shrines are moved to the new buildings. But such things as the pongee and floss silk are divided among the Superintendent, the *negi, uchindo* and so forth of the Great Shrines, and also the Master of Ceremonies from the *Jingi-kan.*

Whenever the time is fulfilled for the Shrine of the Great Deity to be rebuilt Imperial Messengers are sent down (including a 3rd Class and a 4th Class official—the 3rd coming from the Nakatomi or Imbe Uji). With the onset of winter they commence the construction of the 7 buildings of the Shrine of the Great Deity and the 12 small shrines (of Asakuma, Sonō, Kamo, Tanoe, Kano, Yuta, Tsukiyomi, Kusanagi, Ooma, Sumarome, Sana and Kushida). Provisions for the messengers come from deity taxes. The rations for the forced laborers and laborers from sustenance households come from deity taxes when available. If deity taxes are not sufficient then regular taxes are used. Other shrines not on the list are repaired by the Office of the Great Shrines.

[Required for] Festival of the Deity of Yamanokuchi:

40 each of iron effigies, mirrors and spears (the Watarai Shrine gets half as many of each of these 3 items; same proportions for the rest of the festival items), 20 long knives, 1 adze, 1 sickle, 5 *shaku* each of five colors of thin pongee, 2 *kin* each of bark-cloth and hemp, 1 *to* each of rice and sake, 2 *kin* each of bonito and abalone, 1 *to* of assorted dried meats, 2 *to* of assorted seaweeds, 2 *shō* of salt, 2 chickens (male and female), 10 hen's eggs, 50 each of *sue* ware and clay vessels, 5 *tan* of tax cloth for lustrous robes for the *uchindo* (1 *tan* less at the Watarai Shrine).

Festival for Selecting the Central Pillar[431] *for the Main Sanctuary:*

40 each of iron effigies, mirrors and spears, 20 long knives, 4 axes (at the Watarai Shrine, 3 axes fewer, but 1 more adze), 2 sickles, 1 short knife, 1 plane, 5 *shaku* each of five colors of thin pongee, 2 *kin* each of bark-cloth and hemp,

---

[429] The Yamanokuchi 山口 (entrance to the mountain) deity is worshiped in six different localities in connection with getting the timber for the shrine buildings. *Konomoto* 木本 may be the foot of the tree or the source of the wood.

[430] The rule requiring the shrines to be rebuilt every 20 years is not laid down in the *jingi-ryō* of the codes. It is first stated in the *Gishiki-chō* of A.D. 804. The first rebuilding is reported in the

reign of Empress Jitō 持統 in the 7th century and the practice has continued with few interruptions till the present; the most recent rebuilding was the 59th, in 1953. See n. 117.

[431] *Shin-no-mihashira* 心柱, the 'heart pillar', which is the central support of the Main Sanctuary, has a symbolic significance as source and center of life. Its sanctity is matched only by that of the sacred mirror itself.

1 *to* each of rice and sake, 2 *kin* each of bonito and abalone, 1 *to* of assorted dried meats, 2 *to* assorted seaweeds, 2 *shō* of salt, 2 chickens, 10 eggs, 20 each of *sue* ware and clay vessels, 4 *tan* of tax cloth for lustrous robes for the *uchindo*, 1 *tan* for lustrous robes for the messenger who is an Imbe.

For the above, the Imbe who is messenger for the building of the shrines personally leads the *uchindo* and workmen to the foot of the trees in the mountains and they hold the festival.

Festival to Propitiate the Land for the Shrines (subsequent propitiation is the same, except that lustrous robes and mattocks are omitted):
from iron effigies through short knives the list is the same as for the Festival of the Central Pillar, then add: 2 mattocks, 1 *jō* each of 5 colors of thin pongee, 2 *kin* each of bark-cloth and hemp, 2 *to* of sake, 2.5 *to* of rice, 2.5 *to* of assorted dried meats, 3 *kin* each of bonito and abalone, 2.5 *to* of assorted seaweeds, 2 *shō* of salt, 2 chickens, 20 eggs, 20 each of *sue* vessels and clay vessels; for lustrous robes for the *negi, uchindo* and *mono-imi*, 5 persons in all, 2 *hiki* of stiff silk (1 less for Watarai Shrine), 80 *tan* of tax cloth for lustrous robes for the 80 *negi* and *uchindo* who level the land for the Main Sanctuary (half that for Watarai Shrine).

Required for Propitiation of the Ground for the Auxiliary Shrines of the Great Shrine :
40 each of iron effigies, mirrors and spears and long knives, 4 each of axes, adzes, and sickles, 8 mattocks, 4 *kin* each of bark-cloth and hemp, 2 *jō* each of five colors of thin pongee, 2 *to* each of rice, sake and dried meat, 4 *kin* each of bonito and abalone, 4 *to* of seaweeds, 4 *shō* of salt, 8 chickens, 40 eggs (equal number for each of the shrines), 13 *tan* of tax cloth for lustrous robes for 13 *uchindo* and others.

Required for Propitiation of the Ground for Auxiliary Shrines of Watarai Shrine :
10 each of iron effigies, mirrors, spears and long knives, 1 each of scythe, sickle and knife, 2 mattocks, 1 *kin* each of bark-cloth and hemp, 5 *shaku* each of five colors of thin pongee, 5 *shō* each of rice, sake and dried meat, 1 *kin* each of bonito and abalone, 1 *to* of seaweeds, 1 *shō* of salt, 2 chickens, 10 eggs, 10 each of *sue* and clay vessels; 3 *tan* of tax cloth for lustrous robes for three *uchindo*.
When the above festival of propitiation is over, the ground-hallower *mono-imi* sweeps clean the ground and digs a hole for the Central Pillar; then the *negi* erect the pillar. On the day the ground is made level for the building a dark-blue cloth curtain is raised around the sanctuary to prevent the workmen from coming and looking in.

Festival for the Building of the August Boat-shaped Coffers :[432]
40 each of iron effigies, mirrors, spears; 2 chisels, 2 saws, 2 planes, 10 long knives, 3 sickles (1 less at Watarai), 2 each of two kinds of adzes,[433] 2 awls (omit

---

[432] *Mifunashiro* 御船代, 'august boat shape', is the ceremonial box of large size made to hold the sacred object of each shrine. From the dimensions given one can see that these coffers are not only large but of considerable thickness.

[433] The two different types, or sizes, of adze are: *tatsuki* 鐏 and *te-ono* 手鐏.

at Watarai), 2 knives, 2 axes, 5 *shaku* each of five colors of thin pongee, 2 *kin* each of bark-cloth and hemp, 1 *to* each of sake and rice, 2 *kin* each of bonito and abalone, 1 *to* of dried fish, 2 *to* of assorted seaweeds, 2 *shō* of salt, 4 chickens, 20 eggs, 20 each of *sue* and clay vessels (the last four in half amount for Watarai), 6 *tan* of tax cloth for lustrous robes for *uchindo* (reduce by 1 for Watarai), 2 *tan* for lustrous robes for the builders of the garden.

Various Things to be Made:
3 august boat-shaped coffers for the Shrine of the Great Deity (one for the main shrine, 7 *shaku* 3 *sun* long, 5 *shaku* 7 *sun* inside; 2 *shaku* 5 *sun* wide, 2 *shaku* inside; 2 *shaku* 1 *sun* high, 1 *shaku* 4 *sun* inside; two for the *aidono* deities, each 7 *shaku* 6 *sun* long, 7 *shaku* 6 *bu* inside; 1 *shaku* 5 *sun* wide, 1 *shaku* 5 *bu* inside; 1 *shaku* 7 *sun* high, 1 *shaku* inside depth). One august container[434] (for Main Sanctuary, 2.1 *shaku* high, 1.4 *shaku* deep, inner diam. 1.63 *shaku*, outer diam. 2 *shaku*). Four august boat-shaped coffers for Watarai Shrine (one for Main Sanctuary, 7.5 *shaku* long, 5.8 *shaku* inside length, 2.5 *shaku* wide, 2 *shaku* inside, 2.1 *shaku* high, 9 *sun* inside depth; two for the *aidono* deities, each 4.3 *shaku* long, 3.9 *shaku* inside, 1.5 *shaku* wide, 1.1 inside, 1.7 *shaku* high, 1 *shaku* deep; one for the Taka Shrine, 4 *shaku* long, 1.5 *shaku* wide). Onc august container (for the main shrine, diam. 1.5 *shaku*, height the same). One *Yamatogoto*[435] for the Shrine of the Great Deity, 5 lampstands, 1 Kara chest to hold the keys, and 2 tables for offerings, 3 couches[436] (one for the Great Deity and two for the *aidono* deities), 1 ceiling canopy, 2 short couches. [Same for the Watarai Shrine except that one couch is added.]
For each of the above festivals, from *Yamanokuchi* on, are required: 9 *jō* each of 5 colors of thin pongee, 32 *kin* each of bark-cloth and hemp, 16 bars of iron, 16 mattocks, 3 *hiki* of stiff silk, 203 *tan* of tax cloth, 8 *tan* of dark-blue cloth—all requested by the messenger in charge of shrine construction from the storehouses of the capital. Other items are furnished by the Superintendent of the Shrine of the Great Deity.

The Messengers who conduct the making of Sacred Treasures and Ceremonial Articles:
one Secretary of 5th Rank or higher, one chief ritualist of the *Jingi-kan*, two scribes, one office-keeper, four persons qualified for this work who are at least 4th Class officials of *Jingi-kan* or *Dajō-kan*, 4 scribes, 21 girl attendants, 2 maidservants, 6 messengers of various kinds, 63 workmen of various kinds; besides these, various persons who can be called up according to need to serve as messengers in charge of work in order to complete everything. To each one, from girl attendants upward, are furnished lustrous robes: to men, 4 *jō* 5 *shaku* of stiff silk; to women, 1 *hiki* 1 *jō*. To the workmen and others of higher status, males are provided with 2 *jō* 6 *shaku* of ordinary cloth each and females 2 *jō*. The chefs

---

434 *Mihishiro* 御樋代, 'august box shape', is a cylindrical container made to hold the sacred mirror.

435 *Yamato-goto* 和琴, *wagon*, the so-called native Japanese zither, as opposed to Korean or

Chinese *chin*. See n. 414.

436 The word bed, *toko* 床, is used for these and the short couches. Whether these are the symbolic couch-thrones for the use of the deities can only be conjectured.

and cooks of 5th Rank and under are given provisions according to precedent. This is done the first time in the Sacred Courtyard of the *Jingi-kan* on the first day of the 7th month.

Fittings for Ornamentation of the Shrine:

132 clamps for suspending the curtains inside the Main Sanctuary (back 1 *sun* long, 2½ *bu* wide; stem 1 *sun* long, 2½ *bu* thick, length of foot 1 *sun*, thickness 2 *bu*), 2 door-pulls (diameter of ring 3.6 *sun*), 2 metal plates (floral design, 3 *sun* in diam.), 2 metal covers for the backs of door-pulls (floral design, 1.9 *sun* in diam., 3 holes in each), 6 crab-eye nails,[437] 3 clamps (back 2.4 *sun* long, 6 *bu* wide, stem 3 *sun* long, base 1.7 *sun* long, 4 *bu* thick, 3 *bu* wide), 8 metal plates for the clamps (floral design, 1.5 *sun* in diam.), and besides these, 8 floral metal plates for covering the clamps on the outside (1.9 *sun* in diam., each having 3 holes), 24 crab-eye nails, 1 keyhole plate[438] (6.1 *sun* long, 3.6 *sun* wide; the hole: 1.9 *bu* long and 6 *bu* wide), 8 crab-eye nails, 5 metal plates to cover nailheads (1.6 *sun* in diam., cast with 3 prongs), 8 metal studs for the tops and bottoms of doors of the Main Sanctuary (each 3 *sun* in diam., cast with 3 prongs on each), 3 curtain rings (each 1.5 *sun* long, hole 4 *bu* in diam., head 6 *bu* in diam.), 3 metal plates (each 1.2 *sun* in diam.), 1 padlock (tube 4.5 *sun* long, mouth 1.7 *sun* in diam., from curve to end 2.7 *sun*, tube 2 *sun* wide and 2 *sun* thick, from tongue stem to curve 1.4 *sun*, tongue 5 *bu* in diam. 8 *sun* long), 2 staples for the lock (loop 1.3 *sun* in diam., base 1.5 *sun* long, width of base 1 *sun*, diam. of eye 6 *bu*, base 7 *bu* wide, 2½ *bu* thick, stem 3 *sun* long), 2 metal plates[439] (floral design, each 1.5 *sun* in diam.), one Kara key (1 *shaku* 5 *bu* long, 6 *bu* wide), one key[440] (3.47 *shaku* long, handle 3.5 *sun* long, width of metal on handle 8 *bu*, diam. of handle at base 1.1 *sun*, binding for end of handle 8 *bu* long, length from handle to bit 5.8 *sun*, metal of bit 7 *bu* wide, from middle to bottom 6 *bu*, from bit to bottom 2 *shaku* 8 *bu*, 3 *bu* thick, flowered grip ornaments[441] on middle of handle, metal ring on end of handle). Two metal fittings for the ends of the ridge pole (7.5 *sun* long, 6.5 *sun* wide, 8 holes in each), 16 crab-eye nails (each 1.5 *sun* long, diam. of head 1½ *bu*), 4 metal caps for the beam ends (each 7.5 *sun* long, 6.5 *sun* wide, 8 holes in each), 32 crab-eye nails (1.5 *sun* long, diam. of head 1½ *bu*), 86 metal plates for rafter ends (3.1 *sun* square, 4 holes in each), 344 crab-eye nails (1.5 *sun* long, diam. of head 1½ *bu*), 4 metal strips for the gables (each 7 *shaku* long, 3 *sun* wide, 4 holes in each), 16 crab-eye nails (each 2 *sun* long, diam. of head 1¼ *bu*), 24 metal caps for round timbers (each 2.1 *sun* in diam., cast-iron prongs 1.5 *sun* long), 16 metal caps for ends of the projecting timbers (each 1.6 *sun* in diam. with 3 prongs, 1.5 *sun* long), 14 borders for the gables (each 4 *sun* in

---

[437] A small nail with semi-spherical head used for its decorative effect. Unless otherwise specified, these nails measure 1 *sun* in length, 1½ *bu* in head diameter.

[438] The *kiji-tategane* 雉子楯金, a type of decorated metal plate on which the lock, latch or fastener of a door or gate was mounted.

[439] A metal plate called *kuraigane* 位金.

[440] The first key is *karakagi*, the type for a Chinese-style padlock, the other is *kagi*. See n. 373. These ceremonial keys are of great size.

[441] *Menuki* 目抜, a type of decoration later used on sword handles; indicates the elaborate style of the key.

diam. with 3 prongs), 12 metal studs for trimming the barge-boards (1.5 *sun* in diam. each with 3 prongs), 20 metal caps for tops of the gables (3 *sun* in diam., 3 prongs on each), 10 metal caps for the ends of the round beams[442] at the top of the balcony (each 1.6 *sun* in diam., 4 sun long, 4 holes), 40 nails (each 1 *sun* long, head thickness 1 ½ *bu*, diam. 1 ½ *sun*), 10 metal plates for the ends of the middle beams of the balcony (each 7 *sun* long, 2.8 *sun* wide, 6 holes, flower-embossed), 60 crab-eye nails, 10 metal caps for ends of the low level beams of the balcony (each 7 *sun* long, 3.8 *sun* wide, 6 holes each, floral embossed), 60 crab-eye nails, 4 metal hinges for the balcony rail (each 1.4 *shaku* long, each half 7 *sun* long, 3.6 *sun* wide, 14 holes in each, embossed floral design), 56 crab-eye nails (1 *sun* long, head 1 ½ *bu* in diam.), 26 metal studs for the stay-boards of the balcony (each 3 *sun* in diam., 3 prongs each), 150 covers for nails that hold down the split-bamboo carpeting for the balcony (2.1 *sun* in diam. 3 prongs each), 92 studs for the balcony (21 with diam. 2.1 *sun,* 71 with diam. 3 *sun,* 3 prongs on each), 18 balls for the uprights of the balcony rail (4 red, 3 white, 3 blue, 4 yellow, 4 black, 3.4 *sun* high, 3.7 *sun* in diam.), 18 nails to affix the balls (2 *sun* long), 18 floral mounts for the balls (each 5.5 sun in diam. with 6 flowers, one hole in each), 18 metal plates to go under the floral mounts (7 *sun* long, 4.7 *sun* wide, with five holes), 104 crab-eye nails, 6 balls for the sacred stairway[443] (2 red, 1 white, 2 blue, 1 ycllow, each 3.4 *sun* high, 3 *sun* 1.7 *bu* in diam.), 6 nails to affix the balls (2 *sun* long), 6 metal-plate floral mounts for the balls of the sacred stairway (each 5.6 *sun* in diam.), 6 metal plates to go under the mounts (7 *sun* long, 4 *sun* wide, with 4 flower-shaped holes in each), 24 crab-eye nails, 6 nails to hold the floral mounts (2 *sun* long), 28 metal studs for the sacred stairway (3 *sun* in diam., 3 prongs on each), 2 metal hinges for the corner posts (1.2 *shaku* long, 3.7 *sun* wide, half-length 6 *sun,* 14 holes in each), 56 crab-eye nails, 14 studs to cover thc nails in the cross-boards at the corner posts (3 *sun* in diam., 3 prongs on each), 100 metal studs to cover the nails in the board floor (2.1 *sun* in diam., 3 prongs on each), 5 metal plates to cover the nails which hold the ring fasteners on the august north gatc (each 1.5 *sun* in diam., 3 prongs each), 8 studs (each 3 *sun* in diam., 3 prongs on each), 1 metal plate (4 *sun* long, 3 *sun* wide, with 6 holes, 5 *bu* across), 6 crab-eye nails, 6 metal plates for around the clamps (2.1 *sun* in diam., 3 holes in each), 18 crab-eye nails, three clamps (2.4 *sun* at the back, width 6 *bu,* base 1.7 *sun* long, 4 *bu* thick, pin length 3 *sun,* width 3 *bu*), 6 metal plates (1.5 *sun* in diam.), 3 curtain rings (2.1 *sun* in length, head 6 *bu* in diam.), 3 metal plates (each 1.2 *sun* in diam.), 66 metal studs for the 3 august thatched gates to the south (3 *sun* in diam., 3 prongs each), 8 metal studs for the august gate of the guard (3 *sun* in diam., 3 prongs each), 15 metal plates to cover the hinge nails on three august gates (1 ½ *sun* in diam., 3 prongs on each), 12 rings for the curtains at four august gates (each 1.5 *sun* long, head 3 *bu* in diam.), 12 metal plates (1 ½ *sun* in diam.), 28 metal studs to cover the nails

---

442 The full term for these is 'duck roost round beams': *kamoi-marogeta* 鴨居丸桁.

443 The *mihashi* 御階, steps up to the doors of the Main Sanctuary.

on the gables of the two treasure houses[444] (each 3 *sun* in diam., 3 prongs). For two of the four sacred couches, 36 gilded flower-headed nails (7 *bu* in diam., 1 *sun* long), 8 gold hinges (1 *shaku* 7 *bu*, half-length 6 *sun*, other half 4 *sun* 7 *bu*, width 1.9 *sun*, with hammered floral border, 14 holes in each), 112 crab-eye nails, for two [hinges] 32 flathead gold nails (length 1 *sun*). For the entire lot are needed: 131 *kin* 3 *ryō* 2 *bu* of finished copper, 171 *kin* of semi-finished copper, 8 *kin* 4 *ryō* of gold plate and 1 *ryō* 2 *bu* 1 *shu* of silver.

The Twenty-one Deity Treasures :[445]

two gilt-bronze spindles[446] (each 1.16 *shaku* high, base 3.5 *sun* in diam.), two gilt-bronze shuttles[447] (each 3.6 *sun* in diam. of opening, 2.8 *sun* diameter of container and 2.2 *sun* deep), two gilt bronze reels[448] (each 9.6 *sun* long, fingers 5.8 *sun* long), two gilt-bronze beaters[449] (each with stem 9.3 *sun* long and ring diam. 1.1 *sun*), one silvered-copper spindle (1.16 *shaku* high, diam. of base 3.5 *sun*), one silvered-copper shuttle (opening 3.6 *sun* in diam., container 2.8 *sun* in diam., 2.2 *sun* deep), one silvered-copper reel (9.6 *sun* long, fingers 5.8 *sun* long) two silvered-copper beaters (stems 9.3 *sun*, ring 1.1 *sun* in diam.), 24 catalpa bows (each less than 8 *shaku* but more than 7 long, lacquered in red, with grip wound round with green twine), 1,480 common arrows (each 2.3 *shaku* long, iron heads 2.5 *sun.* long, crow feathers, tip painted with gold lacquer, bow-notch painted with cinnabar),[450] 768 more arrows (2.4 *shaku* long, forked arrowheads, eagle feathers on the shafts, painted with shades of vermilion lacquer), one side-sword wound with ornaments (handle 7 *sun* long, scabbard 3 *shaku* 6 *sun*, side of handle gilded copper for 3.8 *sun*, one edge 1.5 *sun* wide, the other 1 *sun*), a flat ring on top of handle (1.5 *sun* in diam., 13 *chō* of beaded winding-band with 5 colors of beads showing on the four sides), 1 *jō* of 5-colored braid, 4 *shaku* of *ashisue* braid,[451] a length of 2 *shaku* of gold wire for around the handle (with 8 bells and 2 amber beads attached), a small fish of gold (6 *sun* long and 2.5 *sun* wide), a length of 6 *shaku* of violet braid on which to hang it, one sword-case made of *dai-ungen* brocade,[452] lining of scarlet silk damask (length of each 7 *shaku*). //1 Sugaru side-sword[453] (handle 6 *sun* long, scabbard 3 *shaku* long, decorated with gold and silver, handle wound with feathers of crested ibis, leather of hand-grip 1 *shaku* 4 *sun*

444 The *hōden* 寶殿, or *takaradono*, small buildings in which to store the shrine treasures.

445 In those days the *shimpō* 神寶, 'deity treasures', were solely for the Shrine of the Great Deity, but in recent times a set of treasures for the Watarai Shrine also have been accrued. To keep up the renewal of these treasures for both shrines (every 20 years) has become a matter of great outlay because of the expense and difficulty of having so many unique hand-made articles fashioned.

446 *Tatari* 多多利.

447 This is the *oke* 麻笥, derived from *o-umi-no-ke*, 'box for spun hemp-fibre'.

448 The *kasehi* 賀世比.

449 *Saitsue* 鏑: an implement 'shaped like a hoe', presumably the beater-in for use at the loom.

450 *Shusa* 朱沙: 'vermilion sand', that is, native mercuric sulfide used as a pigment.

451 *Ashisue* 阿志須惠, possibly related to *ashitsuo* 足津緒, a cord for the foot.

452 *Dai-ungen* 大暈繝 and *shō-ungen* 小暈繝 are two types of polychrome woven cloth with colors in gradation, having large and small figure patterns, respectively.

453 *Sugaru* 須我流 is thought to be derived from *sue* 末, 'end', and *karu* 枯る, 嗄る, 'to dry, to wither', and refer to the baking of the metal. *Kōgaku sōsho*, III, p. 71.

long, lining of *shō-ungen* brocade 1 *sun* wide), 6 gold mirror holders, handle of each bound with *shō-ungen* brocade (3.1 *sun* long, 1.5 *sun* wide), 4 embossed teat buttons with 1 *jō* of five-colored braid, 4 *shaku* of *ashisue* braid, one golden fish (6 *sun* long, 2.5 *sun* wide) with 6 *shaku* of violet braid, one sword-case (outside of *dai-ungen* brocade, lining of scarlet silk damask, both 7 *shaku* long)//[454] 20 assorted side-swords (cherry-wood handles 6.5 *sun* long, scabbards 2.7 *shaku* long, lacquered and wound with scarlet silk and colored hempen cloth and set with crow feathers) bound at the joints with *shō-ungen* brocade and *ashisue* braid (each 3.3 *shaku* long and 1.2 *sun* wide), with sashes of scarlet and dark-blue silk 9 *shaku* in length (2.5 sun wide), 24 cypress quivers (each 2.4 *shaku* long, upper width 6 *sun*, lower 4 *sun*) outside covered with brocade and inside lined with scarlet silk, straps at four places all of violet leather (each 2 *shaku* long and 1.3 *sun* wide), 480 arrows (fitted with crow feathers), 20 bulrush quivers (each 2 *shaku* long, upper width 4.5 *sun*, lower width 4 *sun*, made of cypress wood with bulrushes woven over it, top covered with deerskin painted inside with vermilion, straps at four places, all of violet leather, 2 *shaku* long and 1 *sun* wide), 1,000 arrows (fitted with crow feathers), 24 leather quivers (each 1.8 *shaku* long, top width 4.5 *sun*, lower width 3.8 *sun*, covered with tribute cloth painted with black lacquer, 4 straps all of violet leather, each 2 *shaku* long, 1 *sun* wide), 768 arrows (fitted with eagle feathers), 24 wrist-shields (sewn of deerskin with *sumi* designs on Chinese-white background[455] to be placed in two offering boxes 1 *shaku* 6.5 *sun* in diam., 1.45 *shaku* deep), one strap for each made of violet leather (1.7 *shaku* long, 2 *bu* wide), 24 shields (each 4.45 *shaku* long, top width 1.35 *shaku*, lower width 1.4 *shaku*, 1 *sun* thick), 24 spears (each 1 *jō* 2 *sun* long, metal head 8.5 *sun*, width 1.5 *sun*, diam. 1.4 *sun*, metal bottom 2.8 *sun* long, 1.4 *sun* in diam., bottom painted with gold lacquer). One kite-tail *koto*[456] (8.8 *shaku* long, head end 1 *shaku* wide, other end 1.7 *shaku* wide, width of kite-tail 1.8 *shaku*).

For the whole lot there is needed: 49 *kin* 5 *ryō* of finished copper, 172 *kin* 14 *ryō* of semi-finished copper, 9 *kin* 7 *ryō* 8.4 *bu* of gold for plating, 4 *ryō* 1 *bu* of gold, 7 *ryō* 5 *shu* of silver, 34 pieces of silver leaf, 5 *kin* of solder, 15 bars 1 *ryō* 2 *bu* of iron, 4 *to* 2 *gō* of lacquer, 1 *shō* 2 *gō* of gold lacquer (this includes the silver and copper needed for the silk umbrellas, sunshades[457] and mirrors mentioned below), 3 *gō* of perilla oil, 5 *gō* of oil, 2 *shō* of lampblack, 2,250 arrowshafts, 3,080 crow feathers, 800 eagle feathers, 1 *ryō* 2 *bu* of cinnabar, two *chūenshi*,[458] 1.2 *ryō* each of prussian blue, gold yellow and blue-black, 1 *hiki* 8 *shaku* of brocade, 1 *jō* 4 *shaku* of *dai-ungen* brocade and 8.5 *shaku* of *shō-ungen*, 1 *jō* 2 *shaku* of colored hempen cloth, 1 *jō* 4 *shaku* of scarlet damask,

---

454　The passage between diagonals is missing from some texts of *E-S*.

455　The design is in black China ink on background of *gofun* 胡粉, a mixture of lime and silica (from shells).

456　The *shibi-no-ongoto* (or *tobino-o-goto*) was then a six-stringed instrument, the end of which is designed like a tail of a large bird. A modern one can be seen in the Museum of the Shrines (*chōko-kan* 徴古館), but it has 13 strings.

457　The *sashiba* 翳 is a shade or screen with a very long handle. These may also be seen in the museum.

458　*Chūenshi* 中烟子 is the residue from making lampblack by burning pine wood. It is believed to have been used as an ingredient in lacquer.

1 *hiki* 3 *jō* 7 *shaku* of scarlet silk, 4 *jō* 5 *shaku* of dark-blue silk, 5 *shaku* of
stiff silk, 14 *ryō* 4 *bu* of gloss silk thread, as follows: 9 *ryō* 2.2 *bu* dark violet, 1
kin 3.2 *ryō* lavender, 3 *ryō* 8 *shu* dark purple, 2 *ryō* 8 *shu* light purple; 1 skein
pale-blue thread, 1 *kin* 4 *ryō* 3 *bu* raw silk thread, 2 *mochi* of floss silk, 1 *tan*
3 *jō* of tribute cloth, 18 hides dyed violet, 1 ½ deerskins, 6 pairs of deer antlers,
1 *kin* of ramie, 9 cypress logs, 13 slats for the loom, one plank, one piece of
black persimmon wood (2 *shaku* long, 4 by 4 *sun*), one armload of bulrushes.

Ceremonial Articles for the Shrine of the Great Deity:
2 silk umbrellas covered with lavender silk damask, lined with scarlet damask
(3 *jō* for the covering, lining proportionate), the top and points covered with
brocade (1 *jō* for each umbrella) and hung with lavender braided tassels (8
ryō for each umbrella, but amount of thread must be carefully estimated and
requested at the time needed; same for what follows), 4 scarlet cords (2 for the
silk umbrellas, 2 for the sedge umbrellas, each 2 *jō* long), 2 violet fans, 2 sedge
umbrellas, 2 sedge fans, 3 silk wall-coverings (one 6 *shaku* long 6 widths wide,
one 4 *jō* 5 *shaku* long 6 widths, and one 9 *shaku* long and 2 widths wide), a
silk canopy to cover the ceiling (3 *jō* 6.3 *shaku* long, 9 widths wide), 2 silk curtains for the mosquito net inside (1 *jō* 3 *sun* high, 12 widths wide), 1 curtain
(7.3 *shaku* long and 4 widths wide), 1 spread lined with linen to spread under
the bed (2 *jō* 8 *shaku* long, 6 widths wide), 1 silk-lined spread (1 *jō* 2 *sun* long,
4 widths wide), 2 silk quilts bound with raw silk (9 *shaku* long, 4 widths wide,
one filled with 20 *mochi* of floss silk, other not filled), one eyelet brocade quilt
with scarlet lining (9 *shaku* long, 4 widths wide, 20 *mochi* of floss silk for
filling), one small figured violet quilt (5 *shaku* long, 2 widths wide, 8 *mochi* of
floss silk for filling), one small figured scarlet quilt (same size as above), one
double brocade quilt (same size as above), 1 *hiki* of small figured scarlet silk
(for folding and spreading), 3 silk quilts (two 1 *jō* long, 4 widths wide, 2 *mochi*
floss silk for each; one 9 *shaku* long 4 widths, no filling), one 5-eyelet brocade
quilt (1 *jō* long, 5 widths wide, scarlet lining, 20 *mochi* of floss silk for filling),
one spread lined with linen for under the bed (9 *shaku* long, 4 widths wide),
one silk-lined curtain (same size as above), 2 small figured violet jackets (3.5
shaku long, white lining, each filled with 1 *mochi* of floss silk), 2 small figured
dark-blue jackets (3.5 *shaku* long, lined and filled as above), 4 silk jackets
(length, lining and filling as above), 4 silk skirts (5 *shaku* long, with pale-blue
lining), 2 skirts of violet silk gauze (same length and color of lining), 6 violet
sashes (7 *shaku* long, 1.8 *sun* wide), 8 silk scarves (5 *shaku* long, 2 widths wide),
8 white silk veils (2 *jō* 5 *shaku* long, 2 widths wide), 4 linen headbands (5 *shaku*
long), 4 white silk headbands (same length), 20 sashes (6 violet, 14 dark green,
each 7 *shaku* long, 1.8 *sun* wide), 2 pairs of brocade shoes (9.5 *sun* long), 8 pairs
of socks (9.5 *sun* long, 7.5 *sun* high), 8 white silk pinafores (2 *shaku* long, 1 *shaku*
5 *bu* wide), 1 willow box[459] to hold them (1.5 *shaku* sq.), one comb case (1 *shaku*
sq., lined with raw silk; to hold 8 combs), 2 mirrors (each 9 *sun* in diam.),

---

459 *Yanagibako* or *yanaibako* 柳筥 was a box made of split willow wood bound together
with vines and used for sacred and ceremonial articles.

a pulley box for them covered with brocade and lined with scarlet silk, 8 violet silk hair-ribbons (5 *shaku* long), 1 willow box to hold them (1 *shaku* sq.), 8 silk hair-ties (3 *shaku* long), 1 *ryō* 3 *bu* of pearls[460] (divided up and wrapped in white silk), 2 white boxes in which to keep them (1 *shaku* sq. and covered with a bag of raw pongee), 2 brocade pillows (each 5.5 *sun* long, 3.8 *sun* wide and 2.4 *sun* thick), 1 willow box for them (1.5 *shaku* sq.), 23 *tan* 3 *jō* of ordinary cloth to roll out as carpet for the august route, 8 Kara chests to contain the ceremonial articles (ceremonial articles for the auxiliary shrines likewise to be contained therein).

Ceremonial Articles for the Aidono Deities:
for the deity on the left one silk bag (7 *shaku* 2 *sun* long, 2 widths wide), for the deity on the right one bag (4.2 *shaku* long, 2 widths wide), 2 stiff silk curtains (6.3 *shaku* long, 4 widths wide), 4 curtains for the 4 gates (for the gate of the inner shrine fence: 7.8 *shaku* long, 4 widths wide; for the gate of the low fence of bamboo:[461] 8.8 *shaku* long, 5 widths wide; for the Tamagushi gate:[462] 8.8 *shaku* long, 5 widths wide; for the gate of the outer shrine fence: 7.4 *shaku* long and 3 widths wide).

Ceremonial Articles for the Aramatsuri Shrine:
one sedge umbrella (4.5 *shaku* in diam.), a scarlet bag trimmed with gold to put it in), 2 *jō* of scarlet cord, 1 mosquito net (7.6 *shaku* long, 12 widths wide), an inside mosquito net (7 *shaku* long, 2 widths wide), 1 covering of fine-weave cloth[463] (8 *shaku* long, 2 widths wide), one stiff silk quilt, one plain silk quilt (each 7 *shaku* long, 3 widths wide, filled with 8 *mochi* of floss silk), 1 scarlet wadded jacket, 1 brocade wadded jacket, 1 wadded jacket of stiff silk (all 2 *shaku* long), 1 brocade skirt, 1 plain silk skirt (each 2 *shaku* at the waist and 4 *shaku* length of bottom), 1 glossy silk drape for the boxes (9 *shaku* long, 4 widths wide), 1 stiff silk curtain (6 *shaku* long, 3 widths wide), 1 comb case (to hold 4 combs), 2 strands of violet silk for tying the hair (4 *shaku* each), 2 violet sashes (4 *shaku* long).

Ceremonial Articles for the Two Deities of the Izanagi Shrine:
2 stiff silk spreads (each 1 *jō* long, 3 widths wide), 2 curtains (each 6 *shaku* long, 3 widths wide), 2 quilts of stiff silk (each 7 *shaku* long, 3 widths wide), 2 plain silk quilts (same size as above), 2 blue tie-dyed wadded silk jackets (each 2 *shaku* long, lined with plain silk), 2 unlined silk jackets (same length), 2 pairs of wadded trousers of plain silk (each 1.6 *shaku* long), 1 skirt of thin violet silk, 1 plain silk skirt (each 1.6 *shaku* at the waist, bottom of skirt 4 *shaku* long), 4 dark green sashes (4 *shaku* long), 4 strands of violet silk for tying the hair (each 4 *shaku* long), 2 comb cases (each to hold 8 combs).

---

460 Text says only 'white beads' 白玉, which may or may not be pearls.

461 The *masegaki* or *hamugaki* 蕃垣, a low fence made of bamboo. This no longer survives but has the form of a gate that stands between the two gates of the inner fences.

462 That is, the gate through which the *tamagushi* and *futo-tamagushi* are borne. See n. 394, n. 408.

463 Some texts say *kabeshiro* 壁代, though here *tsuchishiro* 土代, a carpeting, is indicated; the same is true in subsequent passages.

Ceremonial Articles for the Two Deities of Tsukiyomi Shrine:

2 covers of stiff silk (one 1 *jō* long, the other 8 *shaku*, both 3 widths wide), 2 curtains (one 6 *shaku* long, 3 widths wide, the other 5 *shaku* long, 2 widths), 2 quilts of stiff silk (each 7 *shaku* long, 3 widths), 2 quilts of plain silk (same length and width as above), 2 blue tie-dyed wadded jackets (each 2 *shaku* long, lined with plain silk), 2 unlined jackets of stiff silk (same size as above), 2 pairs of wadded trousers of plain silk (each 1.6 *shaku* long), 4 dark green sashes, (4 *shaku* long), 4 strands of violet silk for tying the hair (4 *shaku* long), 2 comb cases (each to hold 4 combs).

Ceremonial Articles for Takihara Shrine:

2 mosquito nets of stiff silk (one 7.6 *shaku* long, 12 widths wide, the other 7 *shaku* long, 2 widths wide), 1 curtain of stiff silk (6 *shaku* long, 3 widths wide), 1 covering for the floor (7.7 *shaku* long, 3 widths wide), 1 scarlet jacket, 1 unlined violet jacket, 1 jacket of plain silk (these each 2 *shaku* long), 1 *tachikae*[464] skirt, 1 skirt of plain silk, 1 skirt of thin violet silk (these each 2 *shaku* at the waist, skirt bottom 4 *shaku* long), 1 quilt of plain silk, 1 quilt of stiff silk (each 7 *shaku* long, 3 widths wide), 1 stiff silk curtain (7 *shaku* 7 *sun* long, 3 widths wide), 1 ceiling canopy of raw silk (7 *shaku* 6 *sun* long, 12 widths wide), 1 comb case (to hold 8 combs), 2 strands of violet silk to bind the hair (4 *shaku* long), 2 dark-green sashes (4 *shaku* long).

Ceremonial Articles for Takihara-no-nami Shrine:

for the Main Sanctuary, 2 mosquito nets of stiff silk (one 5 *jō* long, 10 widths wide, the other 5 *shaku* 4 *sun* long and 2 widths wide), 1 covering of fine-weave cloth (7 *shaku* 7 *sun* long, 2 widths wide), 2 scarlet jackets (each 2 *shaku* long), 1 skirt of thin violet silk, 1 plain silk skirt (each 2 *shaku* long), 1 plain silk quilt, 1 stiff silk quilt (each 6 *shaku* long and 3 widths wide), 1 stiff silk curtain (6 *shaku* long and 3 widths wide), 1 comb case (to hold 4 combs), 2 strands of violet silk to bind the hair (4 *shaku* long), 2 dark-green sashes (each 4 shaku long).

Ceremonial Articles for Izawa Shrine:

2 stiff silk mosquito nets for the Main Sanctuary (one 7 *shaku* 6 *sun* long, 12 widths wide; the other 7 *shaku* long, 2 widths wide), 1 quilt of stiff silk, 1 quilt of plain silk (each 7 *shaku* long, 3 widths wide), 1 floor covering of fine-weave cloth (8 *shaku* long, 2 widths wide), 1 unlined scarlet jacket, 1 unlined plain silk jacket (each 2 *shaku* long), 1 plain silk skirt, 1 brocade skirt, 1 dark-blue skirt (each 2 *shaku* long), 1 curtain of stiff silk (6 *shaku* long, 3 widths wide), 1 comb case (to hold 4 combs), 2 strands of violet silk to bind the hair (each 4 *shaku* long), 2 dark-green sashes (4 *shaku* long).

Ceremonial Articles for the Watarai Shrine:

1 violet silk umbrella, 1 sedge umbrella, 1 violet sunshade, 2 large curtains of stiff silk (one 6 *jō* long and 6 widths wide; the other 1 *jō* 8 *shaku* long, same

---

464 *Tachikae* 裁替: tailored or cut short.

width), 1 canopy to cover the ceiling (2 *jō* 5 *shaku* long, 9 widths wide), 2 mosquito-net canopies (one 1 *jō* 4 *sun* high, 19 widths wide; the other the same height, 5 widths wide), 1 curtain (7 *shaku* 3 *sun* long, 4 widths wide), 1 wall curtain for over the doors (8.5 *shaku* long, 2 widths), 1 lined stiff silk curtain (1 *jō* long, 4 widths wide), 1 cover of lined linen for the floor (2 *jō* long, 5 widths wide), 1 quilt of plain silk (8 *shaku* long, 4 widths wide), 2 quilts of embroidered brocade (each 8 *shaku* long, 4 widths wide), 2 small-figured silk-damask quilts for inside the august coffer (each 8 *shaku* long, 2 widths wide), 1 quilted silk coverlet for on top (8 *shaku* long, 4 widths wide), 1 small-figured violet-damask quilt (same size as above), 1 scarlet brocade jacket, 1 dark-blue jacket, 1 small-figured dark-green damask jacket, 1 jacket of stiff silk (each of these 3 *shaku* long, with 1 *kin* of wadding), 1 jacket of Kure[465] brocade, 1 small-figured violet-damask jacket, 1 jacket of small-figured silk damask, 1 scarlet jacket (each of these 3.5 *shaku* long, with 1 *kin* of wadding), 1 scarlet skirt, 2 skirts of plain silk, 1 dark-blue skirt, 1 skirt of stiff silk (each 5 *shaku* high, train length 2 *jō*, waist 1 *jō* 3 *shaku*), 1 skirt of Kure brocade, 1 skirt of small-figured violet damask, 1 dark-blue skirt, 1 skirt of colored hempen cloth (each of these 3.5 *shaku* high, train length 2 *jō* 5 *shaku*, waist 7 *shaku*), 4 scarves of stiff silk (each 2.5 *shaku* long), 4 veils[466] of plain or stiff silk (each 2 *jō* 5 *shaku* long), 2 plain silk head bands (each 5 *shaku* long), 4 plain silk pinafores (each 2 *shaku* long), 2 pillows, 1 comb case (to hold 4 combs), 4 strands of violet silk thread to bind the hair (each 3 *shaku* long), 2 violet sashes (each 7 *shaku* long, 2 *sun* wide), 2 pairs brocade socks, 2 pairs brocade shoes, 18 *tan* of tribute cloth for carpeting for the august route, 3 willow boxes (each 1.6 *shaku* sq.), 1 long curtain (6 *jō* long and 3 widths wide), 4 Kara chests in which to put the ceremonial articles (ceremonial articles for the auxiliary shrines included).

Ceremonial Articles for the Three Aidono Deities [at Watarai Shrine]:
3 quilts of plain silk, 3 quilts of stiff silk (each 3.5 *shaku* long, 2 widths wide, 5 *kin* of floss silk for wadding), 3 jackets of plain silk, 6 jackets of stiff silk (each of these 2.7 *shaku* long with 6 *ryō* of floss silk for wadding), 9 skirts of stiff silk (each 2 *shaku* high, train length 1 *jō*, waist 3 *shaku*), 2 curtains of stiff silk (each 7.2 *shaku* long, 4 widths wide), 3 curtains for the gates (each 9 *shaku* long, 5 widths wide), 2 spears (each 1 *jō* 2 *shaku* long), 2 shields (4.6 *shaku* high, 1.4 *shaku* wide), 2 bows, 2 quivers, 60 arrows, 2 wrist shields.

Ceremonial Articles for the Taka Shrine:
2 mosquito-net curtains of stiff silk (one 5.4 *shaku* long, 2 widths wide, the other 5 *shaku* long, 10 widths wide), 1 ceiling canopy (8 *shaku* long, 3 widths wide), 1 unlined linen curtain (6 *shaku* long, 2 widths wide), 1 quilt of plain silk, 1 quilt of stiff silk (each 4.5 *shaku* long, 2 widths wide, 5 *kin* of floss silk for wadding), 1 scarlet jacket, 1 jacket of stiff silk, 1 skirt of violet thin silk, 1 skirt

---

465 *Kure* or *Wu* 吳 (China), from which this textile technique came.

466 *Osui* 忍比: a long veil worn in Nara and Heian times by women or men. It was made of very thin silk, was draped over the hat and hung nearly to the ground.

of plain silk, 1 comb case (to hold 4 combs), 2 strands of violet silk thread to bind the hair, 2 sashes (each 4 *shaku* long), 1 curtain of stiff silk (6 *shaku* long).

Ceremonial Articles of Dress for Negi and Uchindo for the Shrine Removal Ceremony:
at the Shrine of the Great Deity, 5 lustrous robes of stiff silk (3 for men, 2 for women), 60 lustrous robes of plain cloth (30 for men, 30 for women), 2 lustrous robes of stiff silk for the Watarai Shrine (1 man, 1 woman), 60 lustrous robes of plain cloth (30 for men, 30 for women).

When the various materials for the foregoing ceremonial articles of dress are ready, then one Master of the Secretaries,[467] one 4th Class official,[468] two scribes, one office-keeper, two official attendants, one Chief Ritualist and a scribe of the *Jingi-kan,* a *kambe* and a diviner lead the way to the Shrine of the Great Deity. Their porters all wear colored unlined tunics. The Watarai Shrine is decorated on the 14th day of the 9th month. On the 15th day, the sacred effigies are moved. The same day the Shrine of the Great Deity is decorated and on the 16th its sacred effigies are moved. (First the Master of Ceremonies[469] announces the decorating. But if the Master of Ceremonies cannot do so, the Superintendent of the Shrines makes the announcement. Thereupon the decorating of the shrines is carried out.)

At all times, when ceremonial articles are sent to Ise for the Great Deity the Shrines must be purified and cleansed inside beforehand. Moreover, members of the Nakatomi Uji are sent, being despatched to the Capital, the Inner Provinces, as well as Oomi and Ise Provinces and the Office of the Great Shrines. (One to the Left and Right Offices of the Capital,[470] one to the 5 Inner Provinces, one to Oomi, Ise and the Shrine Offices.) They cleanse and purify all alike beforehand. (The same applies to the Toyouke [Watarai] Shrine.)

Every 10 days at both of the Great Shrines, the *negi* (chief guards[471]) and the *ō-uchindo* lead the fathers of the *mono-imi,* the *ko-uchindo* and people from sustenance households[472] in taking up watch to guard the deities.

At all times, menservants of sustenance households are on duty: 3 at the Great Shrine, 2 at the Toyouke Shrine, 1 each at the Aramatsuri, Tsukiyomi, Takihara, Takihara-no-nami, Izanagi, Izawa and Taka Shrines, 16 at the august kitchens, 48 at the Itsuki-no-miya, 10 with the Master of Ceremonies.

At all times, for each of the two Great Shrines 2 august horses are to be fed and stabled. They are chosen from among the horses presented as offerings. They are cared for and fed regularly. The rest of the horses are all put out in the sacred pasture.

At all times, when paraphernalia are set out in preparation for festivals, the

---

467 The *ben no daibu:* 辨大夫.

468 That is, a *sōkan (sakan)* 史 of the *Dajō-kan.*

469 The *saishu* 祭主, or Master of Ceremonies, was an official of the capital appointed for the occasion.

470 The Capital for administrative purposes was divided into an Office of the Left and office of the Right.

471 Here *chōban* 長番 is used as a category of *negi.*

472 *Hebito* 戸人, members of sustenance households *(fuko)* which supported or worked for the Great Shrines. It is recorded in A.D. 806 that there were 1,300 such households attached to the Ise Shrines.

various laborers under the *kambe* are made to prepare such things as pine wood, kindling and charcoal, and there must be no deficiencies.

At all times, the various buildings of the Shrines and the residence of the Consecrated Imperial Princess when she comes to worship at the Great Shrines must be repaired, if damaged, by the laborers sent by the Superintendent of the Great Shrines and the *kambe,* for there must be no disrepair.

At all times, when the Princess and Ministers are unable to present offerings to the Great Deity, it is permitted to the Three Great Ones and the Heir Apparent only to make their offerings at a special time.

At all times, the farmers of the 3 deity districts and the *kambe* are not supposed to enter public service, if any of them clandestinely enter public service they are put to work in the Great Shrine, and for events on the first day of the month they are sent to the *Jingi-kan*, but may not serve central officials nor those of local governments.[473]

At all times, one diviner is set up in the Office of the Great Shrines and is caused to conduct divination for the various events throughout the year. His clothing and rations are furnished out of deity sustenance goods.

At all times, when the envoy from the post-station enters the boundary of the Shrine of the Great Deity, as soon as he reaches the stream of Shitai[474] in Iitaka District he silences the sound of his bell.

At all times, on the day when the Consecrated Imperial Princess comes to worship, the Superintendent of the Great Shrines sees to the matter of the pontoon bridge over the Kushida River in Iitaka District and has persons from the deity districts build it for the occasion. (The same is done for the day she returns to the capital.)

At all times, when the Consecrated Imperial Princess comes to worship at the Great Shrines on the three seasonal festivals[475] and goes to the place of four purifications,[476] the offices of the 3 deity districts all make offerings. The rice for this purpose comes from the regular taxes collected by the provincial government from the public district.[477] They pound, clean and send it. Servants and horses are provided by the offices of the three districts (each time 50 men and 80 horses).

At all times, on the day after the *Kanname* festival, 100 *hiki* of deity sustenance tribute silk is presented to the Consecrated Princess.

At all times, for the *Kanname* festival a messenger to present offerings is selected from Princes of 5th Rank or higher, according to the reading of cracks in the tortoise shell, and four times during the year the messenger serves as Master of Ceremonies. If for any reason this is not possible, then a nobleman of 5th Rank or higher in the

---

473 *Naigai-kan* 內外官, 'inner/outer officials', refers to the highest-ranking officials of the *Dajō-kan*. Miyagi, II, p. 387. The outer officials were those holding provincial appointment; the inner, in the Capital.

474 An old name for the river now called Miyagawa which flows through Watarai District.

475 Three festivals, *miori no matsuri* 三節祭, held on the 16th and 17th days of the sixth, ninth

and twelfth months.

476 The four important festivals for which purification *(o-harae)* was performed were the *Toshigoi*, the *Kanname* and the two *Tsukinami* festivals of 6th and 12th months. To these four festivals an Imperial Messenger was sent to present offerings from the Imperial Court.

477 'Public district' refers to Take District of Ise Province.

Jingi-kan or from among the many officials, or a member of the Nakatomi Uji who is without assignment is chosen. If this is not possible, someone of 6th Rank. When the Consecrated Princess comes for the first time then it absolutely has to be someone of 5th Rank or higher.

At all times, the messengers who present offerings at the *Kanname* festival are given emoluments. To a Prince of 4th Rank are given 12 *hiki* of stiff silk (8 *hiki* to his escorts), to a Prince of the 5th Rank are given 10 *hiki* (6 hiki to his escort), and the same is given to Nakatomi and Imbe. Nakatomi and Imbe of 6th Rank and below are given 8 *hiki* (4 *hiki* to their escorts), to diviners [*urabe*] of 6th Rank and below are given 4 *hiki* (2 *hiki* to escorts; but if diviners perform official duties they receive 1 more *hiki*), for those of Beginning Rank[478] and below 3 *hiki* (1 *hiki* for escorts). At the *Toshigoi* and the [two] *Tsukinami* festivals, the Messenger of 6th Rank and below is given 6 *hiki* (2 *hiki* for escorts), and to Provincial Governors present—if of 4th Rank they receive 6 *hiki*, if of 5th Rank they receive 5 *hiki*. Their deputy receives 4 *hiki*, their 4th Class official: 3 *hiki*, and their scribe: 2 *hiki*.

At all times, for extraordinary occasions emoluments are given to messengers who present the offerings. To those of 4th Rank are given 12 *hiki* of stiff silk (8 for the escort), to those of 5th Rank, 10 *hiki* (6 for the escort), to Nakatomi and Imbe of 6th Rank or lower 6 *hiki* each (2 hiki for escorts), for diviners of 6th Rank and below same as at the *Kanname* festival. Provincial Governors in attendance receive the same as in the preceding.

At all times, at the *Toshigoi* and *Tsukinami* festivals when messengers come to worship, the diviner of the Office of the Great Shrines goes to the Take River to purify himself by lustration. If he fails so to do he is deprived of his clothing.

At all times, two officials of the Great Shrines—one chief priest of the shrines an official of Senior 6th Rank Upper Grade and one assistant priest,[479] an official of Senior 7th Rank Upper Grade—are given yearly salaries out of deity taxes. The emoluments for 5th Court Rank *negi* of the Shrine of the Great Deity and the Toyouke Shrine are likewise furnished from deity taxes. The noblemen[480] procure these from the people of the deity districts.

At all times, the Superintendent of the Great Shrines changes office to correspond with that of the provincial governor. In the first year they serve, they are given 1,000 *soku* of rice-in-ear. Every year they are given 50 *hiki* of stiff silk and 100 *koku* of rice. (An official serving as provisional governor[481] receives the same on a *pro rata* basis.) If an Imbe from the *Jingi-kan* of 5th Rank or higher serves as the Master of Ceremonies, he is given 10,000 *soku* of rice-in-ear in his first year. When this is used up he may not receive any more.

At all times, the *negi* at both the Great Shrines receive 2 *shō* of table rice on each day of the 4th and 6th months (not provided in other months). Four *mono-imi* of

---

478 *So-i* 初位, which had *dai* and *shō* divisions; see n. 378.

479 These two chief officials of the Great Shrines, *daigūji* 大宮司 and *shōgūji* 少宮司, respectively, are what I have translated as Superintendent and Assistant Superintendent of the Great Shrines.

480 These are *tsukaibito* 資人, noblemen who aided in government procurement of tax goods.

481 Namely the *gon-no-kuni-no-tsukasa* 權國司, which has little relevance to the main point here that Superintendents of the Great Shrines have terms of office and status the same as provincial governors.

the Shrine of the Great Deity and three of the Watarai Shrine are provided with food throughout the year: 8 *gō* of rice each per diem. But menservants are fed on the same basis as when they work in the capital.

At all times, on the days of post-festival feasts of the three seasons,[482] the rule for emoluments for *negi* and *uchindo* is: to a *negi* of 5th Rank is given 1 quilt (requiring 1 *hiki* 1 *jō* 3 *shaku* of stiff silk and 5 *mochi* of floss silk), to a *negi* of 6th Rank is given 1 over-garment (requiring 1 *hiki* of stiff silk and 1 *mochi* of floss silk), to the *ō-uchindo* and to the *uchindo* and *mono-imi* of the different shrines is given 1 summer garment each, to two dancers of the *Gosechi* dances 1 *hiki* of stiff silk apiece, and to 4 maidens who serve sake, 3 *jō* of stiff silk apiece.

The foregoing are supplied from goods in the storehouse of the Bureau on days when the Consecrated Imperial Princess participates, but at times when she does not participate in worship, they are furnished from deity sustenance goods.

At all times, on the days of breaking abstinence and holding feasts after the festivals of the three seasons, the ceremonial dress for 18 young boys and girls who dance the *Torikona* is green-print jackets and skirts. These are printed beforehand and provided to them when the festival draws near. For these 12 *tan* of cloth are required. (For boys: 2 *jō* 8 *shaku* apiece, for girls 2 *jō* 5 *shaku*.) For 2 *koto* players, 2 flute players and 3 leaders of the singing are required 3 *tan* 2 *jō* of plain cloth (2 *jō* apiece). This is furnished to each individual at the end of the year.

At all times, there must be 10 supervisers of the august kitchens and one overseer, 3 keepers of the keys, one kitchen matron—all selected from farmers of the 3 deity districts and the *kambe* of the 6 localities.[483] Their clothing and food is furnished out of deity sustenance goods.

At all times, the tribute, taxes and paddy tax from the *kambe* of the 3 deity districts and the 6 localities and of other provinces, as shown on the tribute records and tax registers at the place the provincial government collects them, are counted by the Superintendent of the Great Shrines, the count is given to the provincial governor and forwarded to both the Bureau of Census and the Bureau of Taxation.[484]

At all times, in the 3 deity districts the overseeing of the inspection of allotted fields which are unfit because of losses, as well as overseeing of statistics of deaths due to epidemic, is jointly carried out by the Superintendent of the Great Shrines and the Governor of the Province. They segregate those fields and combine their yield in one place, the matters connected with this being originally handled in Uji Village in Watarai District. The Provincial Government first removes the name [of the owner] and then after taking the readings of the tortoise shell, administers them. If the Imperial Messenger arrives he stops outside the boundary of the deity districts and after the tortoise omens have been read he enters. (If there is no reading of the tortoise omens he performs his duties outside the boundaries.)

482 The *naorai* 直會 is the feasting held after the taboos of the festival celebration are over with. See n. 475.

483 The six localities were lands or villages of sustenance households *(fuko)* in the districts of Iitaka 飯高, Ichishi 壹志, Ano 安濃, Kawawa 河曲, Suzuka 鈴鹿 and Kuwana 桑名, serving as prebend or benefice to the Great Shrines.

484 The Bureau of Census, *kazue-ryō* 主計寮, and Bureau of Taxation, *chikara-ryō* 主税寮, were both under the Ministry of People's Affairs, *mimbu-shō*.

At all times, unless the order of the *Jingi-kan* carries the seal of the Master of Ceremonies, the Superintendent of the Shrines and the other officials may not conduct the ceremonies.

At all times, if the annual harvest fails to ripen, resulting in decrease in tribute and taxes, first the portion of yield for offerings to the deities is set aside, and what is left over is measured out for salaries to the officials of the Great Shrines and for emoluments to the various messengers. If there is nothing left over, then of course nothing is furnished to them.

At no time may the *kambe* of the 3 deity districts and the 6 localities and of the other provinces obtain loans at interest on regular taxes.

At all times, if there is damage to shrines, ditches, ponds, dams or government post-station buildings within the 3 deity districts, or if mulberry and lacquer growing are not promoted, this will delay the honorable dismissal document of the Superintendent of the Great Shrines.[485]

At all times, the buildings of the Bureau of the Consecrated Princess are caused to be repaired in advance by the Superintendent of the Great Shrines. At no time may anyone bearing arms come within the boundaries of the Great Shrines.[486]

At all times, when recommendation for rank for the *negi, ō-uchindo* and others of the two Great Shrines is made (namely, *negi* who are in charge and *ō-uchindo* and others who serve as guards), the Superintendent of the Great Shrines reviews such recommendations and presents them to the *Jingi-kan* before the 25th day of the 9th month. The *Jingi-kan* affixes its seal thereon and forwards them to the *Dajō-kan*. They are then turned over to the *shikibu-shō*.[487] The same is done for the officials of Rank without appointment and the descendants of noblemen in the 3 deity districts, as well as for the Kan'omi and Kanhatori.

At all times, when patents of rank are bestowed by gracious proclamation upon *negi, uchindo, hafuri* and so on of the deity districts, depending on their number, the *shikibu-shō* sends them to the *Jingi-kan* which passes them to the messenger to the four festivals for him to confer. Then the messenger, leading one chief ritualist of the *Jingi-kan*, first announces the conferral of ranks, then proceeds to the no. 1 building of the post-festival feasting compound, takes a seat facing south, then places the patents of rank upon the offering table and the Chief Ritualist calls out the name. (In front of the building, they face east as their names are called. The *negi* and *uchindo* ascend to the north and face east in rows.) When this is finished, they worship the Great Deity. (They clap their hands twice.) Then turning to the north, they worship the Sovereign.[488] However, at the Watarai Shrine

485 The *geyu* (see n. 372) or document of dismissal, would be drawn up and certified by the incoming Superintendent, just as a new governor did this for the outgoing predecessor. This further illustrates the equality of status of the Superintendent of the Shrines with the provincial governors.

486 The boundaries of the Shrines are not exactly specified here. The Shitai creek, mentioned above, formed the boundary of the Shrines area on the west, but other outer boundaries do not appear in the procedures.

487 The *shikibu-shō* 式部省 was the Ministry of Ceremonial, one of the eight ministries of the *Dajō-kan*.

488 This carries out the Chinese notion of the sovereign facing south as he rules the land. Actually, the two Great Shrines lie east of the Court and Capital.

this is done facing to the west. The rest of the procedure is the same as at the Shrine of the Great Deity. If the patent of 5th Rank is being conferred on one of the *negi* it is done in the middle row.

At any time when *negi*, *ō-uchindo*, various functionaries,[489] fathers of *mono-imi*, or *ko-uchindo* are in mourning for parents, they dare not have contact with defilement. They wear plain clothing for a period of 49 days, and when they have cleansed and purified themselves they may return to their duties. During the time they are in mourning habit they serve in the outer compound and do not participate in presentations of festival items; moreover, they do not enter the inner compound. (It is the same for mourning for either parent.) However, if the father of a *mono-imi* dies, the child is relieved of his duties; if the child dies, the father is relieved of his duties, and there is no specified time for either to return to his duties.

At no time may the *ō-uchindo*, *ko-uchindo*, *mono-imi* and functionaries of the august kitchens of the two Great Shrines easily turn over the office which they hold. (The same is true for the *uchindo*, *mono-imi*, *koto* players, flute players, leaders of singing, weavers and *kambe* of the separate shrines.)

Every time articles are offered at the festivals, if they are not listed in the *shiki*, then ancient custom is relied on so that the existing precedent is not altered. For clothing and food for the officials and the functionaries of the august kitchens, they measure the time worked and bestow accordingly. It is not permitted to spend deity goods vainly. There are 32 persons who assist in various roles at the Shrine of the Great Deity (namely, 1 *negi*, 4 *ō-uchindo*, 9 *mono-imi*, 9 fathers of *mono-imi*, 9 *ko-uchindo*) and 25 persons at the 6 auxiliary shrines (at each: 2 *uchindo*, 1 *mono-imi*, 1 father; at the Tsukiyomi Shrine 1 *uchindo* who is a Sacred Maiden is added), and 25 persons at the Watarai Shrine (1 *negi*, 4 *ō-uchindo*, 6 *mono-imi*, 6 fathers and 8 *ko-uchindo*) and four persons at its auxiliary shrines (2 *uchindo*, 1 *mono-imi*, 1 father).

The persons of the above positions all are exempt from tribute and *corvée* taxes; this includes the 18 grooms (12 for the Great Shrine and 6 for the Watarai). Fifty each of Kanhatori and Kan'omi remit tribute but are exempted from *corvée* tax.

Deity paddies: 36 *chō* 1 *tan*:

2 *chō* in Uda District, Yamato Province;

2 *chō* in Iga District, Iga Province;

32 *chō* 1 *tan* in Ise Province (1 *chō* each in Kuwana and Suzuka Districts, 3 *chō* each in Ano and Ichishi Districts, 2 *chō* in Iitaka District, 11 *chō* 6 *tan* in Iino District, 10 *chō* 5 *tan* in Watarai District).

The foregoing are deity paddies itemized; 5 *chō* 4 *tan* of the area for Watarai District is subdivided (2 *chō* 4 *tan* for the Shrine of the Great Deity and 3 *chō* for the Watarai Shrine). The office of this district supervises the seeding and they harvest the young rice shoots to be offered on three occasions at the Shrine of the Great Deity and for evening and morning food-offering at the Watarai Shrine.

---

489 *Zōshiki-no-hito* 雑色人 meant functionaries without rank who serve in various capacities in various bureaus and offices. See n. 356.

The rest is given over to requirements for festivals and taxed according to the value of the yield of the land.

Sustenance Households:

this province [Ise]: (1,831)

Watarai Dist.   Take Dist.   Iino Dist.

Iitaka Dist. 36 households	Ichishi Dist. 28 households
Ano Dist. 35 households	Suzuka Dist. 10 households
Kawawa Dist. 38 households	Kuwana Dist. 5 households

other provinces:

Yamato province 15 households	Shima Province 66 households
Mikawa Province 20 households	Iga Province 20 households
Owari Province 40 households	Oomi Province 40 households

Tribute and taxes from the above provinces are all inspected by the Office of the Great Shrines and they are used as offerings as specified. The land tax from this province [of Ise] is gathered into government buildings here and is distributed according to the occasion. If in some year the grain fails to ripen, or if 7 *bu,* or more, of the paddies are a loss, the decrease in tax rice is forgiven and noted in the register and sent to the officials in charge.

*   *   *   *   *

End of Book Four of the *Engi-shiki*

Enchō 5th Year, 12th Month, 26th Day

[same signatures as at end of Book One]

ENGI-SHIKI, BOOK FIVE

BUREAU OF THE
CONSECRATED IMPERIAL PRINCESS[490]

At all times, when a Sovereign accedes to the throne he appoints a Consecrated Princess to the Shrine of the Great Deity in Ise Province. That is to say, an unmarried Imperial Princess[491] is chosen by means of divination.[492] (If an Imperial Princess is not available another princess, in order of succession, is determined by divination and appointed.) When this is done an Imperial Messenger is despatched to her residence to announce the fact of her appointment. One person of the rank of Assistant Chief of the *Jingi-kan*, or higher, leads his assistants and follows the Imperial Messenger in making the call. The diviners perform purification of the area. Members of the *kambe* deck *sakaki* branches with bark-cloth and set them up around the four sides and at the inner and outer gates of her residence. (The officials in charge prepare the *sakaki* and bark-cloth, while the staff of the household prepare the scatter-rice, sake and fish items for the purification.) After this

490 These are the *saiguryō-shiki*, procedures for the Bureau of the Consecrated Imperial Princess. The other reading is *Itsuki-no-miya-no-tsukasa*, *itsuki-no-miya* being the usual title of the Princess. In the text she is also called *itsuki-no-miko*, meaning 'taboo' or consecrated Princess, or *itsuki-no-hime-miko*, equivalent to consecrated Imperial Princess. This Princess was selected to serve as the personal representative of the Sovereign at festivals held at the Shrine of the Great Deity (the Sun Goddess) in the Province of Ise. Because of the importance given to the Shrine by the Imperial House, a whole government bureau grew up around the Consecrated Princess. The structure of the Bureau was:

A Chief of the Bureau, an official of 5th Court Rank

The Deity Office (*kanzukasa*), consisting of: 1 Nakatomi (liturgist), 1 Imbe, 1 Chief Diviner

The *Toneri*-nobles Office (*Tonerizukasa* 舍人監) consisting of: 1 Chief of *toneri*, 1 4th Class Official (ritualist), *miya-no-toneri* and *ryō-no-toneri*.

The Offices of:
Accountants (*kura-be* 藏部)

Chefs (*kashihade-be* 膳部)
Brewers (*saka-be* 酒部)
Water-carriers (*moitori-be* 水取部)
Uneme ladies (采部)
Caretakers (*tonomori* 主殿)
Compounders of Medicines (*yaku-be* 藥部)
Housekeepers (*kanimori* 掃部)

This Bureau was under the *Jingi-kan* but is one of those which were *ryōge* 令外, or outside the codes.

491 That the princess must be a virgin is here specified, but no age limit is given. Some were but infants when they were appointed. Even though 3 years lapsed before they reached the residence in Ise, nevertheless their extremely youthful years seem to undermine the importance of their function. Of course, it is not so utterly strange when we see how many children of young age participated in the arts of divination and on the staffs of the Great Shrines—as seen in Bk. IV.

492 Divination for selecting the appointee and for selecting the auspicious days was done under supervision of the Bureau of Divination, *on'yō-ryō* 陰陽寮 of the Ministry of Central Affairs, *nakatsukasa-shō*.

is done, a day and time is chosen for all the officials to perform Great Purification (same procedure as for the twice yearly [Great Purification] ceremony).

Required for the Purification:

 4 great *kin* each of bark-cloth and hemp, 4 deerhides, 4 pairs deer antlers, 4 broadswords, 4 bows, 4 arrows, 4 mattocks, 1 *kin* of ramie, 1 *tan* of tax cloth, 4 *to* each of rice and sake, 4 *soku* of rice-in-ear, 8 *kin* each of abalone and bonito, 30 *kin* of dried meat, 26 *kin* of *wakame*, 10 *kin* of *arame* and 8 *kin* of assorted seaweeds, 4 *to* of salt, 4 water buckets, 4 gourds, 5 *tan* of tax cloth for kneeling cushions, 1 short *tatami*, 2 mats, 2 horses.

(The foregoing are sent by the respective officials in charge to the place of purification.) Moreover, a messenger is sent to present offerings at the Shrine of the Great Deity and to announce the fact of the selection by divination of the Consecrated Princess. (The procedure is the same as for the messenger to the *Kanname* festival.)

At all times, when the selection of a Consecrated Imperial Princess has been made, a suitable place within the Imperial Palace is selected by divination for the Shosai-in.[493] It is cleansed and purified. Then she enters it and dwells in abstinence in this compound until the 7th month of the following year. Then an undefiled moor away from the Palace is determined by divination and the No-no-miya[494] is built there. On an auspicious day in the first 10 days of the 8th month she goes down to the river for purification and lustration.[495] Then she enters the No-no-miya and lives in abstinence in that compound until one year from the time she entered it. On an auspicious day in the first 10 days of the 9th month, she goes down to the river for purification and lustration, and then she goes to enter the Itsuki-no-miya in the Province of Ise.

At all times, *sakaki* branches hung with bark-cloth are set up at all the gates of the Itsuki-no-miya. (They are renewed each month, using 1 *kin* of bark-cloth and 1.8 *kin* of hemp.)

At all times, certain words are taboo for the Princess. The inner seven words are:[496] the Buddha is the 'Central One', the sutras are 'dyed paper', a pagoda is a 'yew tree',[497] a temple is a 'tiled roof', a monk is a 'long-hair', a nun is a 'female long-hair', a Buddhist meal is 'short rations'. Besides these there are the outer seven words: death is called 'getting well', illness is 'slumber', weeping is 'shedding

---

493 The Shosai-in 初齋院, or Court of Beginning Abstinence, was where her initial period of preparation for duty began. Usually it was within the Palace precinct.

494 The No-no-miya, which Waley calls the 'Palace in the Fields', was the first edifice built especially for the princess and in which her isolation from Court life began in earnest as she was prepared for sacred duties.

495 Elaborate purification of both body and spirit was required in order to fit her for service to the Great Deity. Lustration was performed in one of the clear, running rivers of the Capital. The Katsura and Kamo Rivers are mentioned as being used. Later, on her progress to Ise Province,

she bathes in six other rivers.

496 Here are two lists of taboo words and their substitutions, each in the magic number of 7 (plus 2). The first list has key words having to do with Buddhism, a foreign faith which was offensive to the native deities. The second list includes taboos or words connected with them which constituted defilements offensive to the deities. If we compare this list with the defilements defined in the procedures at the end of Bk. III, we can easily imagine that there may have been more taboo words than the total of sixteen which make up these lists.

497 *Araragi* 蘭 has other meanings, but yew seems likely.

brine', blood is 'sweat', to strike is 'to caress', meat is called 'mushrooms',[498] a tomb is a 'clod of earth'. There are also other taboo words: a Buddhist Hall is called 'incense burner' and an upāsaka is called 'bow-notch'.[499]

At all times, when the Princess is about to enter the Shosai-in she goes to the river's edge for purification. (The Bureau of Divination is made to select the day and time, and the same is done when she is about to enter the No-no-miya and the Itsuki-no-miya in Ise.) Two days before the lustration a secretary leads the Commissioners of the Shosai-in[500] and those under them, followed by members of the Bureau of Divination and the host of officials, to the river's edge to determine the particular spot and announce the location. When the appointed day arrives the Consecrated Princess mounts into a carriage and is conveyed to the spot, with 12 running pages, 24 carriage attendants, 10 porters, 3 Kara chests of foods, two loads of various utensils for the same, 1 Kara chest each for toilet articles and ornaments, 2 Kara chests of clothing and 6 Kara chests full of articles for emoluments. (The bearers are all Palace Guards.) Also, 6 chefs, 2 *toneri*, 14 supervisors of portage, 6 escorts of the Sovereign's Private Office, a lady-in-waiting and the lady Commissioner of the Residence, with attendants, all follow after her carriage. (The ladies and attendants and the members of the Sovereign's Private Office and those higher all ride in their own carriages; while the *uneme*, girl attendants and those under them ride in carriages from the Mount Bureau.)[501] One Imperial Envoy who is an Imperial Adviser, one Commissioner of the Residence, two courtiers of 4th Rank, two courtiers of 5th Rank, and four of 6th Rank form her vanguard. Two each of Left and Right Inner Palace Guards, two each of Left and Right Military Guards, two each of Left and Right Gatekeepers, ten each of Left and Right Fire Chiefs[502] are in attendance. The Officials of the Left Offices of the Capital, leading attendants down to men-at-arms, go to meet her. The Governor of Yamashiro Province, leading the Prefects of the Districts, goes to meet her at the road which bounds the Capital. One Secretary, one Chief Ritualist, two scribes and one office-keeper, at the head of the host of officials in attendance, arrive at the site of lustration and the affair takes place. The Consecrated Princess goes behind the curtain, goes down to the stream and performs her lustration. A Nakatomi of the *Jingi-kan* presents the symbolic offerings.[503] The chief diviner recites the purification ritual. When this is done the Imperial Messenger and those below are given food and emoluments. (The Secretary makes a record of those in attendance and turns it over to the Commissioners of the Residence.) By this time [the Princess] has returned and

---

498 Or simply 'vegetables'.

499 *Tsunohazu* 角筈 may be the notch in the arrow, or the notches in the end of the bow for the string. The implication may be that the upāsaka, or lay Buddhist, is restricted by rules, since *hazu* also has the meaning of necessity or obligation.

500 'Commissioners' is used for convenience in translating *in-no-bettō* 院別當. These were officials—one male and one female—in charge of administering the day-to-day affairs of the residence of the princess.

501 The Left and Right Mount Bureaus, called *samaryō* and *umaryō*, are treated in Bk. XLVIII of *E-S.*

502 The Inner Palace Guards are *konoe* 近衞, the Military Guards, *hyōe* 兵衞, and the Fire Chiefs, *kachō* 火長.

503 *Nakatomi wa onusa wo tatematsuru* 中臣 麻進. The Nakatomi raises and waves the purification wand to hallow the air, the ground, the river, to keep all defilement from the area where the princess does the ritual bath.

re-enters the Shosai-in. Then a well for her august menage is selected by divination and *sakaki* branches are set up around it.

Required for the Purification:

> 2 *shaku* each of five colors of pongee, 3 large *ryō* of Aki bark-cloth, 4 large *ryō* of bark-cloth, 1 large *kin* of hemp, 4 mattocks, 2 iron effigies, 1 *tan* of tribute cloth for coarse garments, 2 covered boxes, 1 *to* each of *sake* and rice, 2 *kin* each of abalone and bonito, 4 *kin* of *wakame*, 4 *kin* of dried meat, 4 *shō* of salt, 1 water bucket, 4 each of stands and jugs, 4 bundles of oak, 2 gourds, 4 sheets of yellow-bark, 2 rush mats, 1 palanquin, 2 *tan* of tax cloth for reciting the rituals, 1 short *tatami*, 2 porters and 2 carrying poles.

Requirements for Purifying and Cleansing the Residence when the Princess enters the Shosai-in:

> 2 *tan* of tax cloth, 3 *kin* of bark-cloth, 4 *kin* of hemp, 2 swords with black scabbards, 2 bows, 40 arrows, 4 head of deer antlers, 4 deerskins, 4 mattocks, 4 *to* each of rice, sake, dried meat and salt, 5 *kin* each of abalone and bonito, 9 *kin* each of *wakame*, *arame* and assorted seaweeds, 20 bundles of oak, 4 *soku* of rice-in-ear, 4 shallow jars, 4 gourds, 1 palanquin, 2 leaf-mats, 2 horses, 5 *tan* of tax cloth for reciting the ritual, 1 short *tatami*, two porters.

Ootono-hogai [Blessing of the Great Hall] (for the No-no-miya; repeated at the Itsuki-no-miya in Ise):[504]

> 2 *ryō* of silk thread, 7 *ryō* of Aki bark-cloth, 2 *shō* each of rice and sake, 1 large jar, 4 covered boxes, 2 small saucers, 2 offering-tables (3 *shaku* in height), 2 *hiki* of pongee each as emolument to the Nakatomi and the Imbe, 1 *hiki* for the chief diviner, 1 *tan* of tribute cloth for each of four *kambe* who present the offering-tables (only two at the No-no-miya).

Festivals of the Sacred Fire, the Courtyard Fire,[505] *the August Stoves, and the God of the Well* (to be celebrated when she first moves into the No-no-miya; same are required for the ceremonies to the two stoves on the first day of each month):

> 4 *shaku* each of five colors of thin pongee, 2 *shaku* of colored hempen cloth, 8 *ryō* of bark-cloth, 1 *kin* of hemp, 1 *tan* of tax cloth, 2 mattocks, 2 *shō* each of rice and sake, 2 *kin* each of abalone and bonito and *wakame*, 2 *shō* of dried meat, 1 *shō* of salt, 2 bundles of oak, 1 large jar and 1 stand (the foregoing are for the festival to the God of the Well).

Festival for the Courtyard Fire on the First of the Month:

> 4 *shaku* each of five colors of thin pongee, 2 *shaku* of colored hempen cloth, 8 *ryō* of bark-cloth, 1 *kin* of hemp, 2 *tan* of tax cloth, 4 mattocks, 4 *shō* each

---

[504] The *Ootono-hogai* 大殿祭 has been called the blessing or luck-wishing of the Great Palace. But it is plain from these procedures that this ceremony of bringing good fortune to the Imperial Palace and the Middle, or Consort's Palace, was also used for blessing the temporary palaces of the Consecrated Imperial Princess. See n. 269.

[505] The *imibi* is the sacred fire for cooking the foods for the princess and the *niwabi* 庭火, 'courtyard fires', are the outdoor fires or torches for lighting the compound. See Festival of Sacred Fire and Courtyard Fire for the Imperial Palace treated in Bk. 1 (n. 273).

of rice and sake, 2 *kin* of abalone, 3 *kin* each of bonito and *wakame,* 4 *shō* of dried meat, 2 *shō* 2 *gō* of salt, 2 bundles of oak, 2 each of large jars and saucers, 1 water jug.

Required for the exorcism on the last day of the month (at the No-no-miya and same at the Itsuki-no-miya):
1 *jō* 4 *shaku* of tax cloth, 4 *ryō* of Aki bark-cloth and 8 *ryō* of hemp for the symbolic offerings, 2 iron effigies, 2 mattocks, 2 *shō* each of rice and sake, 2 *soku* of rice-in-ear, 1 *kin* each of abalone, bonito and *wakame,* 2 *shō* of dried meat, 1 *shō* 1 *gō* of salt, 1 jar and 1 saucer.

Required for extraordinary purification:
8 *ryō* of bark-cloth and 2 *kin* of hemp.

Ceremonial articles for the Shosai-in:
10 *hiki* of white silk, 2 *hiki* of scarlet Azuma pongee, 2 *hiki* of lined silk, 2 *hiki* of white figured silk, 8 *hiki* of Azuma pongee, 200 *mochi* of floss silk, 2 *tan* of fine-weave cloth, 50 *tan* of bleached cloth, 10 large *kin* of safflower, 1 *koku* 8 *to* of gardenias, a curtain frame of white wood (8 *shaku* high and 1 *jō* square), 6 *kichō*[506] (two 4 *shaku* high, two 3 *shaku* high and two 2 *shaku* high), four 5-*shaku* screens, one gilded carriage, two small portable screens. 2 large sunshades (to be put in flat, decorated boxes), 2 sedge hats (one a sun hat to be put in a green bag; one a rain hat to be put in an oiled silk bag, both with ties[507]), 2 offering jars (both with handles and ties), 1 shoe box, 1 carriage rest, 4 chests of foodstuffs (rests and carrying-poles for each), 1 silver box for boiled rice, 1 silver water cup, 1 silver sake cup, 1 silver saucepan, 4 silver spoons, 2 lacquered casks, 1 hot-water bucket (with stand), 1 wash-basin, 1 spouted vessel, 1 mesh spatter-guard, 1 *chōboku,*[508] 1 large jar, 4 black lacquered lampstands, 1 lightweight curtain, 1 bed, 12 paperweights, 10 Kara chests (foregoing are for the offerings), 64 *hiki* of pongee, 6 *hiki* of yellow pongee, 32 *hiki* of plain silk, 180 *mochi* of floss silk, 86 *tan* of tribute silk (foregoing for the ceremonial dress for noblewomen and down to *toneri*); 24 carriage attendants, 10 porters, 34 ceremonial outfits and 34 medicine bags.

For the Commissioners of the Shosai-in and those under them:
Two Commissioners who are nobles of the 5th Rank (one a noblewoman), one Nakatomi, one Imbe, one chief diviner, one *udoneri,* two *ōdoneri,* ten *miya-no-toneri,* three chefs, three caretakers, one cook, three water-carriers, one brewer, three housekeepers, two *uneme,* two palace girl attendants, three wet-nurses,[509] fourteen girl attendants to the Princess, one diviner's assistant, two children who kindle the fire, four sweepers, twelve menservants, eight

---

506 *Kichō* 几帳—'screens of state' Waley calls them—were silk curtains hung from wood frames used to screen royalty and nobility within their palaces.

507 *Shibe* 志部 is taken to be a variant of *shime* 締, a closing.

508 *Chōboku* 雕木, stand for the slop-jar of the privy.

509 *Menoto* 乳母 were needed if the princess happened to be an infant; but these women had become female bureaucrats of some influence, attached to this bureau.

maidservants. However, when entering the No-no-miya the following are added: one *udoneri*, two *ōdoneri*, four *kambe* (namely, two *murajibe*[510] of the Nakatomi and two *murajibe* of the Imbe), three diviners, ten *miya-no-toneri*, two each of cooks and brewers, four *uneme*, 25 girl attendants to the Princess, two bath attendants, two privy attendants[511] and eight maidservants.

Food Allotments:

for the 5th Rank, 2 *shō* of rice, 1 *shō* of sake, 2 *ryō* each of Azuma abalone and Oki abalone and of squid, 1 *ryō* 3 *bu* of sushi, one-third of a salmon, 2 *ryō* of *wakame*, 5 spoonfuls of salt, 1 *gō* of soy sauce, 2 spoonfuls of vinegar, 1 *gō* of pickling dregs. For Nakatomi and Imbe, 2 *shō* of rice, 6 *gō* of sake, 3 *ryō* 2 *bu* of sushi, one-third of a salmon, 2 *ryō* of *wakame*, 4 spoonfuls of salt, 3 spoonfuls of soy sauce, 2 spoonfuls of vinegar, 1 *gō* of pickling dregs. For *ōdoneri*, palace girl attendants and girl attendants to the Princess, 1 *shō* 6 *gō* of rice, same amounts of sake, fish and salt as for the Nakatomi. For the *miya-no-toneri*, same amount of rice as for *ōdoneri*, one-sixth of a salmon, 3 *ryō* 2 *bu* of sushi, 4 spoonfuls of salt, 3 spoonfuls of soy sauce, 2 *ryō* of *wakame*. For the persons of the various corporations:[512] same amount of rice as for *miya-no-toneri*, 3 *ryō* 2 *bu* of sushi, 4 spoonfuls of salt, 2 *ryō* of *wakame*, 1 *gō* of pickling dregs. For *udoneri* and chief diviner, rice from the main supply and other items the same as for the Nakatomi. For *uneme*, rice from the main supply, other items the same as for the *miya-no-toneri*. For the diviners, rice from the main supply, other items the same as for the members of corporations. For diviners' assistants and children who kindle the fires, 1 *shō* 2 *gō* of rice, other items the same as for persons of the corporations. For sweepers and maidservants, rice from the main supply, 1 *gō* of pickling dregs, 1 *ryō* of seaweeds, 1 spoonful of salt.

The numbers of persons above are counted and the amounts of foods issued every month. However, any officials of 5th Rank and below who are engaged in official duties may be provided for out of the main supply.

Festival of Propitiation of the ground for the No-no-miya (same for later Propitiations):

5 *shaku* each of five colors of thin pongee, 5 *shaku* of colored hempen cloth, 1 *tan* of tribute cloth, 5 *tan* of tax cloth, 1 large *kin* of bark-cloth, 2 *kin* of hemp, 5 mattocks, 5 *shō* each of rice and sake, 5 *kin* each of abalone, bonito, *wakame* and assorted seaweeds, 5 *shō* each of dried meat and salt, 5 each of jars and stands, 2 gourds, 20 bundles of oak, 5 food-mats and one seat-mat.

---

510 *Murajibe* 連部, the so-called hereditary corporations of persons who held the noble rank of *muraji*. (See n. 78.) As such titles were superseded by the Chinese style system of Court Ranks in the 7th century, we can conclude that the use of the term here is to signify that members of the highest ranks of Nakatomi and Imbe are called for.

511 Since the robes of many layers of costly silks worn by princess and noblewoman required particular care, mistresses were needed for the task of robing and disrobing the princess for the bath or the privy, both of which are thought to have been rather large rooms for this reason.

512 *Moromoro no tomobe* (or *tomokko*) 諸伴部, appears to mean members of various occupational groups *(be)* not including Imbe and *urabe* who are specified by name. Members of *tomobe* were exempt from tribute *(chō)* and forced labor *(yōeki)*. Miyagi, II, p. 297.

Required for the Purification on Completion of the No-no-miya:
>2 *tan* of tax cloth, 3 *kin* of bark-cloth, 4 *kin* of hemp, 2 side-swords with black scabbards, 2 bows, 40 arrows, 4 head of deer antlers, 4 mattocks, 4 *to* each of rice and sake, 4 *soku* of rice-in-ear, 5 *kin* each of abalone and bonito, 4 *to* of assorted dried meats, 9 *kin* each of *wakame* and *arame*, 4 *to* of salt, 4 shallow jars, 4 gourds, 20 bundles of oak, one palanquin, 2 leaf mats, 2 horses, 5 *tan* of tax cloth for reciting the rituals.

For Lustration at the River when the Princess moves to the No-no-miya:
>On the appointed day the Princess rides in a palanquin. (An official of the housekeepers directs the scribes in preparing the palanquin two days before the lustration.) [There are] eight captains of the palanquin, forty bearers, twenty ladies on horseback (including two wet-nurses, six secretaries of the Sovereign's Private Office,[513] four *uneme*, four young girls, two housekeepers, two privy attendants), then one Great Counselor and one Middle Counselor[514] as Imperial Messengers, two Imperial Advisers, four courtiers each of the 4th Rank and the 5th Rank. When the lustration ceremony has been completed the foods and emoluments are given. (Imperial Messengers and those down through 5th Rank are feasted by the Bureau of Palace Storehouses[515] and those of the 6th Rank and below are fed by the Palace Table Office.)[516] When they have finished they return home. For those who have reason to remain at the No-no-miya emoluments are again bestowed. (The rest of the procedure is the same as for the first lustration).

Required for the Purification:
>1 *shaku* each of five colors of pongee, 1 *tan* of plain cloth for coarse garments, 1 covered box, 4 *ryō* of bark-cloth, 1 *kin* of hemp, 2 iron effigies, 4 sheets of yellow-bark, 2 *kin* each of abalone, bonito and *wakame*, 4 *shō* of dried meat, 2 *shō* of salt, 4 *shō* each of rice and sake, 1 large jar, 2 food mats, 4 bundles of oak, 4 shallow jars, 4 stands, 1 palanquin, 2 gourds, 4 mattocks, 2 *tan* of tribute cloth for reciting the rituals, two porters, two carrying-poles.

Required for cleansing and purifying the No-no-miya when the Consecrated Princess removes thither:
>2 *tan* of tax cloth, 2 *kin* each of bark-cloth and hemp, 2 deerskins, 2 mattocks, 2 *to* each of rice and sake, 4 *soku* of rice-in-ear, 5 *kin* each of abalone, bonito, 2 *to* of assorted dried meats, 10 *kin* each of *wakame* and *arame*, 4 *shō* of salt, 2 shallow jars, 2 gourds, 4 bundles of oak, 1 palanquin, 2 leaf-mats for wrapping, 1 *tatami*, two large jars, 5 *tan* of tribute cloth for reciting the rituals, 2 porters.

For Twenty-one Deities at the Toshigoi Festival in the 2nd Month (four presentations to Oomiyanome-no-kami, eight presentations to the Gods of the August Gates,

---

513 That is, *kurōdo* 藏人.
514 One *dainagon* and one *chūnagon*, respectively.
515 The *kura-ryō*, or *uchi-no-kura-no-ryō*

內藏寮 under the Ministry of Central Affairs *(nakatsukasa-shō)*.
516 The *daizen-shiki* 大膳職 under the Ministry of the Imperial Household *(kunai-shō)*. See n. 281.

one to the God of the Sacred Fire, one to the God of the Courtyard Fire, two to the Gods of the Stoves, two to the Gods of the Sacred Wells, and one to the God of the Ground):[517]

> for each presentation: 5 *shaku* of silk, 1 *shaku* each of five colors of thin pongee, 1 *shaku* of colored hempen cloth, 2 *ryō* of bark-cloth, 5 *ryō* of hemp, 1 spear, 1 mattock, 4 *shō* of sake, 6 *ryō* each of abalone, bonito and *wakame*, 2 *shō* of dried meat, 1 *shō* of salt, 1 jar and 1 stand.
>
> The foregoing requirements are presented to the deities as stated, but for the Oomiyanome-no-kami a horse is added. For all of the festivals there must be 2 jugs, 2 gourds, 1 *jō* of matting to wrap the tribute, 1 short *tatami*, 5 *tan* of tax cloth for reciting the rituals, and 1 *tan* 1 *jō* 5 *shaku* of tribute cloth for lustrous robes for three Imbe who prepare the offerings.

Festivals of the 6th Month (repeated in the 12th month):

> *Tsukinami* festival—the above are the articles to be used: the same as for the *Toshigoi* festival, except that the mattocks are omitted.
>
> *Ootono-hogai*—the requirements for offerings and the emoluments for the Nakatomi and others are the same as the above, except that the boxes[518] are reduced by two.

Required for Miagamono [Thank Offerings]:

> 2 *shaku* each of five colors of thin pongee, 3 *ryō* of silk thread, 2 *shaku* of colored hempen cloth, 1 *kin* of Aki bark-cloth, 8 *ryō* of common bark-cloth, 6 *ryō* of hemp, 4 mattocks, 2 iron effigies, 2 *tan* of tax cloth, 1 *tan* of cloth for two august garments of plain cloth, 1 *tan* of cloth to make two skirts, 2 *tan* of cloth to make two quilts (4 *mochi* of floss silk for each as filling, for other details see the procedures for the Needlework Bureau),[519] two drapes, 1 *tan* 2 *shaku* of cloth for making two pinafores, 7 *shaku* of silk for two sashes, 2 pairs of shoes, 6 covered boxes (two are 2 *shaku* sq., four are 1 *shaku* 5 *sun* sq.), 4 *to* each of rice and sake, 1 *kin* each of abalone, bonito and *wakame*, 1 *to* of dried meat, 2 *shō* of salt, 2 each of water buckets, jars and stands, 1 leaf-mat (for wrapping, 20 stalks of Ogawa bamboo, 4 *tan* of tribute cloth (to provide lustrous robes for 6 *urabe* diviners, 2 *jō* 8 *shaku* apiece), for two Nakatomi (one male and one female) 2 *hiki* of silk for each as emolument.

Great Purification on the last day of 6th month at the No-no-miya (repeated in the 12th month):

> 2 *tan* of tax cloth, 2 *kin* of bark-cloth, 8 *ryō* of ramie, 4 *kin* of hemp, 2 broadswords, 2 bows, 100 arrows, 2 mattocks, 2 crow feathers, 2 head of deer antlers, 2 deerskins, 2 *to* each of rice and sake, 4 *soku* of rice-in-ear, 2 *kin* of abalone, 4 *kin* of bonito, 10 *kin* each of *wakame* and *arame*, 2 *to* each of dried meat and

---

517 Here the deity is *tokoro-nushi* 地主, who is propitiated in the ground-hallowing ceremonies. This has no apparent connection with the Earth Lord, Dokū. (See n. 326).

518 As no boxes (*hako* 筥) appear in the lists

immediately preceding, the reference is not clear.

519 The *nuidono-ryō* 縫殿寮 under the Ministry of Central Affairs. The *nuidono-shiki* appear in Bk. XIV of the *E-S*.

salt, 2 water jars, 2 gourds, 2 mats, 2 horses (4 horses on the days it is held in the Province), 2 *tan* of tax cloth and one short *tatami* for reciting the ritual.

Festival of Fire Propitiation at the No-no-miya :
4 *shaku* each of five colors of thin pongee, 4 *shaku* of colored hempen cloth, 2 *tan* of tax cloth, 5 *ryō* of bark-cloth, 1 *kin* of hemp, 4 mattocks, 4 *shō* of sake, 1 *kin* 5 *ryō* each of abalone and bonito, 4 *shō* of dried meat, 2 *shō* of salt, 1 *kin* 5 *ryō* of *wakame,* 4 large jars, 4 each of jugs and stands, 4 bundles of oak, 4 gourds and 1 mat.

Festival of Waylaying Spirits before the No-no-miya :[520]
1 *jō* each of five colors of thin pongee, 4 *shaku* of colored hempen cloth, 2 *tan* of tax cloth, 1 *kin* 10 *ryō* of bark-cloth, 7 *kin* 5 *ryō* of hemp, 4 mattocks, 2 each of oxhides, boarskins, deerskins and bearskins, 4 *to* each of rice and sake, 4 *soku* of rice-in-ear, 2 *kin* 5 *ryō* of abalone, 5 *kin* of bonito, 8 *shō* of dried meat, 2 *shō* of salt, 5 *kin* of *wakame,* 4 shallow jars, 4 stands, 4 bales of straw, 1 mat.

Festivals of the 11th Month :
Twenty-eight deities of the *Niiname* festival [Festival of First-fruits]: the two deities of the Sacred Fire and Courtyard Fire of the Kitchen; the two deities of the Sacred Fire and Courtyard Fire of the Water-carriers; one deity of the Cook-stove of the Caretakers, one deity of the Water of the August River, one deity of the Brewers, one August Food Deity of the Chefs, one deity of the Stove of the Cooks, the remainder of deities being those worshiped at the *Toshigoi* and *Tsukinami* festivals.

For each deity :
5 *shaku* of silk, 1 *shaku* each of colored hempen cloth and of five colors of thin pongee, 1 *jō* 4 *shaku* of tax cloth, 2 *ryō* of bark-cloth, 5 *ryō* of hemp, 4 *shō* of sake, 6 *ryō* each of abalone, bonito, *wakame* and *arame,* 2 *shō* of dried meat, 1 *shō* of salt, 1 each of large jar and saucer, one horse. (For the Oomiyanome-no-kami: 2 jugs, 2 gourds, and one short *tatami.*)
The above are the required articles for offerings to the deities. But at the *Toshigoi* festival each deity is also presented with a spear. And at all of the festivals there must be 6 leaf-mats, 5 *tan* of tax cloth for reciting the rituals, 1 *tan* 3 *jō* 5 *shaku* of cloth for lustrous robes for the three Imbe who prepare the offerings.

Requirements for the Festival of First-fruits :
2 *jō* of stiff silk, 2 *ryō* of silk thread, 1 *jō* 2 *shaku* of ramie cloth, 1 *jō* 2 *shaku* of bleached cloth, 1 *jō* 6 *shaku* of linen, 3 *tan* 1 *jō* of tribute cloth, 2 *kin* 4 *ryō* of bark-cloth, 2 knives, 10 long-knives, 4 *to* of rice, 2 *to* of millet, 14 covered boxes (1 *shaku* 5 *sun* in diam.), 2 coarse boxes, 3 white-wood boxes, 10 tables, 2 short tables, 2 clay braziers, 2 mallets and 2 blocks, 10 each of clay platters, bowls and pots, 8 *sue* ware bowls, 20 platters, 8 kettles, 5 shallow earthenware vessels, 5 flat-edge jars, 4 each of ritual clay urns and water pitchers,[521] 4 each

---

520 That is the *Michiae* festival for the No-no-miya. For *Michiae,* see n. 286.

521 For ritual water pitcher, see n. 266.

of clay shallow jars and *sue* ware chopping bowls, 8 spouted vessels, 2 each of clay hand-basins and *sue* ware hand-basins, 6 wash basins, 10 sake cups, 20 uncovered bowls (10 of them *sue* ware), 20 high stands (10 of them *sue* ware), 4 shallow jars, 4 sake jugs, 20 box-stands, 2 *sue* mortars, 2 ritual elongated basins,[522] 18 gourds (2 small), 3 *shō* of oil, 4 *ryō* of oak, 2 sunshades.

Ootono-hogai (same as above)

Monthly Requirements to be Requested by the Kanzukasa[523] of the No-no-miya :
20 sheets of paper, one brush, 1 tortoise shell, 5 sheets of birch-cherry (the tortoise shell and birch-cherry are the ones used by the *Jingi-kan*).

Festival of Propitiation at the Newly-built Kitchen :
2 *jō* of silk, 2 *shaku* each of five colors of thin pongee, 2 *shaku* of colored hempen cloth, 2 *kin* each of bark-cloth and hemp, 4 mattocks, 4 *shō* each of rice and sake, 4 *soku* of rice-in-ear, 4 *kin* each of abalone and bonito, 5 *shō* of dried meat, 4 *kin* each of *wakame* and assorted seaweed, 2 *kin* of salt, 4 each of large jars and stands, 4 bundles of oak, 1 mat, 2 *tan* of tax cloth for reciting the rituals.

Festival to the Sacred Fire and Courtyard Fire of the Newly-built Kitchen :
4 *shaku* each of five colors of thin pongee, 4 *shaku* of colored hempen cloth, 2 *hiki* of silk, 2 skeins of silk twist, 2 *tan* of tribute cloth, 2 *tan* of tax cloth, 2 *kin* each of bark-cloth and hemp, 2 *to* each of rice and sake, 2 *kin* each of abalone, bonito, dried meat, *wakame* and salt, 4 spades. One diviner's assistant (a child chosen from the *uji* of the Kamo no Agatanushi[524] of Otagi District, Yamashiro Prov.) Two children to kindle the fires (young girls chosen from the Hata Uji of Kadono District, same province).[525]
The above commence their duty when the Princess enters the Shosai-in and continue until she removes to the Shrine of the Great Deity; when she enters the Itsuki-no-miya of Ise they all retire.

Ceremonial Articles for Removing to the No-no-miya :
2 *hiki* of white silk, 50 *mochi* of floss silk, 25 *kin* of safflower, 1 white-wood curtain frame, 4 screens of state (two 3 *shaku* high and two 2 *shaku*), four 5-*shaku* screens, 1 palanquin, 2 woven rush sunshades, two umbrellas (one placed in a green bag, the other in a pongee bag), 1 embroidered fan, 4 red lacquered tray tables, 1 *chōboku* (the foregoing are required furnishings), 72 *hiki* of silk, 10 *tan* of linen, 120 *tan* of tribute cloth, 4,000 *mon* in coins (foregoing are ceremonial articles for noblewomen and on down to bath

---

522 The presence of the ritual basins (*ebihata-bune*) here would seem to indicate that these and the other special ritual vessels just mentioned are not exclusively for the use of the sovereign, but are for the use of the Consecrated Princess at these *Niiname* festivals.

523 This presumably means the 'deity office' or *kanzukasa* of the princess' Bureau (*saigū-ryō*).

524 That is, coming from the branch of the Kamo Uji who in earlier times held the position

of *agata-nushi* 県主 in Otagi District and later married into the Hata Uji of continental origin and established the line of hereditary priests of the Kamo Shrines. Lewin, *Aya und Hata*, 173.

525 Kadono District is the seat of the earliest settlement of the main branch of the Hata Uji. An offshoot of the Hata became the hereditary priests of the Matsuno-o Shrine after it was founded in the 8th century. Lewin, *op. cit.*, p. 81; pp. 174-5.

attendants), 6 robes of color prescribed for Rank (for six persons: Commissioners of 5th Rank, *udoneri*, Nakatomi and Imbe), 25 *tan* 1 *jō* 2 *shaku* of tribute cloth (for ceremonial dress for diviners down to and including sweepers[526]), red clothing and plain cloth sashes for the eight chiefs of the palanquins; pink, unlined tunics, crimson cloaks, plain cloth sashes, cloth trousers, hats and gaiters for the forty bearers of the palanquin, and also 40 yellow-cloth unlined tunics, 40 pairs of trousers, 40 cloth sashes (for twenty porters each from the Left and Right Offices of the Capital, who return there after the procession is over).

Supplies for the Year:

72 *hiki* 5 *jō* 5 *sun* of stiff silk, 15 *hiki* of *chōken*,[527] 10 *hiki* of white stiff silk, 20 *hiki* of plain silk, 2 *hiki* of white silk damask, 172 *mochi* of floss silk, 5 *tan* 4 *jō* of ramie cloth, 1 *tan* 2 *jō* 2 *shaku* of fine-weave cloth, 10 *kin* of silk thread (foregoing are for august winter garments, worn from the 9th month through the 2nd month), 60 *hiki* of stiff silk, 30 *hiki* of plain silk, 100 *mochi* of floss silk (foregoing are for august summer garments, worn from the 3rd month through the 8th month), 1 short curtain, 11 wall curtains, 3 curtains (the Needlework Bureau sews these and presents them annually, but frames for the curtains are made by the Bureau of Skilled Artisans[528] and presented just once), 1 *koku* 8 *to* of gardenias, 26 *kin* of safflower, 8 *to* of vinegar, 4 split-bamboo blinds, 2 seat-mats, 3 *tatami* bound on both edges, 1 short *tatami*, 10 *tatami* bound in green (foregoing are for fall and winter use), the same kind are required for spring and summer use, but are made of thin matting (the Bureau of Housekeeping makes these and presents them at the two seasons, but the Office of Hayato[529] presents the split-bamboo screens), 7 *tatami* bound in white cloth, 3 short *tatami* (foregoing are for the wet-nurses), 3 *tatami* bound in yellow cloth, 90 crushed-straw *tatami*, 13 short *tatami*, 2 long *tatami*, 108 seat-mats, 2 long mats, 223 tribute mats, 75 bamboo mats (foregoing for use of members of the *Jingi-kan* and below), 1 *hiki* 4 *shaku* of oiled pongee, 1 *hiki* 4 *shaku* of pongee for lining (to cover the tables of the chefs, brewers and water-carriers), 1 *hiki* 1 *jō* 9 *shaku* 5 *sun* of stiff silk (1 *jō* 1 *shaku* 5 *sun* for 10 sieves for the chefs; 1 *jō* 4 *shaku* for 6 sieves for the brewers and to cover the sacred sake; 5 *jō* for 20 sieves for the water-carriers and to cover the tables, and 4 *shaku* for 4 sieves for the diviners' assistants), 6 *shaku* of white stiff silk (for use by the brewers), 7 *ryō* of silk thread (3 *ryō* for the chefs, 2 *ryō* each for water-

---

[526] *Imaryō* or *imamairi* 今良, sweepers in the Palace.

[527] *Chōken* 長絹 was a kind of silk used for the courtiers' costumes known as *suikan* 水干, *nōshi* 直衣 and *kariginu* 狩衣.

[528] The *uchi-no-takumi-ryō* (or *takumi-ryō*) 内匠寮 under the Ministry of Central Affairs treated in Bk. XVII of *E-S*.

[529] The *hayato* 隼人 in protohistoric times were a tribe of South Kyushu. After the latter half of the 5th century they came under the rule of the Yamato people and were by them organized into a corporation of guards (*hayato-be*) of the Palace Gates; they also were made to perform songs and dances for the Court, and to make bamboo wares. The *hayato-no-tsukasa* 隼人司 was the office which supervised the *hayato* and had instruction in song and dance. The Taihō Code included this office under the Headquarters of the Gate Guards (*emon-fu* 衛門府); but by the time the *E-S* were compiled it was under the Ministry of War (*hyōbu-shō* 兵部省). *Nihon rekishi daijiten.*

carriers and brewers), 8 *tan* 2 *jō* 8 *shaku* of fine-weave cloth (6 *tan* 2 *jō* 4 *shaku* for the chefs, 2 *tan* 4 *shaku* for the brewers), 1 *tan* of Mōda cloth[530] (for the water-carriers), 1 *tan* 2 *shaku* of bleached cloth (1 *jō* 2 *shaku* for the brewers, 3 *jō* for the water-carriers), 7 *tan* 9 *shaku* of tribute cloth (4 *tan* 8 *shaku* for the chefs, 3 *jō* 1 *shaku* for the brewers, 1 *tan* 1 *jō* 9 *shaku* for the water-carriers, and 3 *jō* 1 *shaku* for the diviners' assistants), 6 Azuma straw-mats (2 for the water-carriers and 2 for diviners' assistants), 5 tribute Kara chests (1 for the *kanzukasa*, 2 for the chefs, 1 for the brewers, 1 for the water-carriers), 5 each of board boxes and rush boxes, 14 split-cypress-wood chests (8 for the chefs, 2 for the water-carriers and 4 for the diviners' assistants), 23 dippers (8 for the chefs, 3 for the brewers, 10 for the water-carriers, 2 for the diviners' assistants), 182 wooden trays (162 for the chefs, 20 for the brewers), 6 each of large water jars and water buckets (of each 2 for the chefs, 1 for the brewers, 2 for the water-carriers and 1 for the diviners' assistants), 3 large baskets (1 for brewers, 2 for water-carriers), 11 water buckets (4 for the chefs, 2 for brewers, 4 for water-carriers and 1 for the diviners' assistants), 2 large boxes (for the diviners' assistants), 50 sake jug stands, 105 sake cups (for the brewers), 30 willow boxes (9 of them are 1 *shaku* 5 *sun* square, 11 are 1 *shaku* square, 5 are 1 *shaku* 2 *sun* square, 5 are 1 *shaku* 2 *sun* long and 5 *sun* wide; 1 is for the *kanzukasa*, 20 for the chefs, 5 for the brewers, 2 for the water-carriers and 2 for diviners' assistants). For covering the food offerings: 1 *hiki* 1 *jō* 5 *shaku* of silk and 12 *mochi* of floss silk (for the chefs), 2 whetstones (for the same), 1 silver cup, 1 silver bowl, 1 silver spoon, 1 silver saucepan (all for sacred use and permanent), 2 palm leaves (for use by the diviners' assistants), 3 jars (one to contain 1 *to*, two to contain 5 *shō* each), 16 *sue* ware hand-basins, 8 mortars, 5 jars (one to contain 2 *shō*, the other four 1 *shō* apiece), 14 chopping bowls, 6 salt saucers, 30 bowls, 2 casks, 30 platters, two large ceremonial jars, 28 roughhewn boxes, two abalone slicers, 2 choppers, 11 knives (10 with blades 5 *sun* long and 3 *bu* wide, one with blade 1 *shaku* long and 1 *sun* wide), two Kara stoves, 1 bronze portable cook-stove (for permanent use), 11 wooden [jar] covers, one iron brazier (for permanent use), one clay brazier, one axe, 2 hatchets, 6 sake tubs, 4 cauldrons (one holding 1 *koku*, 2 holding 5 *to* each, one for roasting, holding 5 *to*), 3 dust-baskets, 4 bamboo mats, 32 small gourds, 1 steamer (to hold 2 *koku* of rice), 3 round tubs, 3 wash tubs, 3 offering-tables (each 3 *shaku* long, 8 *sun* high and 1 *shaku* 8 *sun* wide), 5 outside tables (each 4 *shaku* long, 2 *shaku* wide, 2 *shaku* 8 *sun* high). For the water: 2 tables and one each: spouted vessel and hand basin, 2 tables for hand washing, 1 table for sake (the foregoing 5 tables 3 *shaku* long, 1 *shaku* 8 *sun* wide and 1 *shaku* 8 *sun* high), 8 shelf tables, 6 cutting tables, 1 sake pitcher, 2 salt mortars, 4 tables for oak wood, 1 whetstone, 3 small axes, 3 chisels (the three foregoing required by the *kanzukasa*), 8 mattocks (for cleaning up), 5 *koku* of salt (for pickling a variety of vegetables), 5 large jars, 5 shallow earthenware vessels (both for permanent use), 10 jugs, 1 *to* 2 *shō* of oil, 120 dishes for oil, 40 dish-stands, 2 squat jars (for use the night of last day of the 12th month), 3 sticks of ink.

---

530 A kind of tribute cloth from Mōda 望陀 District of Kazusa 上總 Province.

Monthly Requirements (for short months reduce by one-thirtieth):

39 *soku* 1 *wa* 6 *bu* of rice-in-ear, 17 *soku* 8 *wa* of millet (both are pounded in mortars and presented by the Bureau of Palace Kitchens[531] each month), 24 *kin* 6 *ryō* of Azuma abalone, 11 *kin* 4 *ryō* each of various abalone and boiled bonito, 7 *kin* 8 *ryō* each of squid and salted and pressed trout, 15 *kin* of sharkskin, 1 *to* 5 *shō* of sardine sauce, 1 *to* 5 *shō* each of preserved abalone and mussel sushi, 24 *kin* 6 *ryō* of bonito, 7 *kin* 8 *ryō* each of dried and salted sea-bream and salmon, 90 large mackerel, 6 *to* of *sushi* of assorted fish, 3 *shō* each of mustard and of dried bonito, money to buy seasonings (according to prevailing prices), 2 *kin* 13 *ryō* each of laver and codium, 11 *kin* 4 *ryō* each of *wakame* and gelidium, 3 *to* each of salt and pounded chestnuts, 6 *to* of raw chestnuts, 6 *shō* of fermented beans, 2 *to* 4 *shō* of pickles, 30 pieces of pickled melon, 1 *to* 2 *shō* of fermented bean paste, 1 *to* 5 *shō* of barley sugar, 3 *to* each of glutinous rice, soybeans, red beans, wheat, sorghum, sesame seeds and *mino*,[532] 2 *to* 2 *shō* of rice, 1 *to* 2 *shō* of vinegar, 2 *koku* 4 *to* of sake, 1 *to* 5 *shō* broth lees, 2 *to* 4 *shō* of oil (6 *shō* of oil for foods, 1 *to* 8 *shō* of oil for lamps), 10 shallow jars, 30 cooking pots, 10 great bowls, 200 bowls, 400 uncovered dishes, 600 flat dishes, 380 hollow stands, 15 each of sake cups and sake jug stands, 70 bowls, 60 dishstands for mixed foods, 4 *shaku* 3 *sun* 5 *bu* of plain cloth, 300 bundles of pine torches, 5,400 *kin* of kindling wood, 24 *koku* of rough charcoal, 30 armloads of straw, 70 sheets of paper (50 for general use and 20 for the *kanzukasa*), 3 writing brushes (2 for general use, 1 for the *kanzukasa*), one tortoise shell, 20 stalks of bamboo.

Required for the Three Occasions in the First Month :[533]

3 *kin* each of Azuma abalone, bonito, Oki abalone, boiled bonito, dried birdsflesh, squid and dried and salted sea-bream, three dried and salted salmon, 3 salmon, 2 *kin* each of sliced abalone and dried bêche-de-mer, 1 *kin* each of laver and *wakame*, 3 *shō* of salt, 1 *shō* 5 *gō* each of pickles, bean paste and vinegar, 6 *to* of sake, 9 *shō* of glutinous rice, 3 *shō* each of soybeans, red beans, millet and sorghum, 6 *shō* each of wheat, sesame and raw chestnuts, 3 *shō* dried rice, 3 skewers of dried persimmons, 3 *shō* of pounded chestnuts (foregoing are for offerings), 1 *koku* of [ordinary] rice, 1 *koku* of glutinous rice, 2 *to* soybeans, 3 *to* of red beans, 1 *to* of oil, 3 *to* each of assorted dried meats and of sushi, 20 *kin* each of abalone and bonito, 1 *koku* of sake (foregoing required for members of the *Jingi-kan* and below), 13 *tan* 3 *jō* 6 *shaku* of tribute cloth (2 *jō* apiece for unlined tunics for 4 chefs, for 3 each of water-carriers, brewers, and cooks, and for 2 housekeepers; 8 *shaku* for their aprons and sleeve-bands,[534]

---

531 The *ōi-ryō* 大炊寮, Bureau of Palace Kitchens under the Ministry of the Imperial Household.

532 *Mino* 篁子, also called *minogome* or *tamugi,* was a wild grain related to wheat. Makino gives *Glyceria acutiflora Torr.*

533 The three occasions of the New Year were, according to the miscellaneous laws (*zōryō* 雑令), the 1st, 7th and 16th days. These were the important feast days. On the 7th day of the 1st month the conferral of Court Ranks, 5th Rank and up, was customarily held. Miyagi, II, pp. 569, 577.

4 *shaku* each for three girl attendants for their sleeve-bands, and 8 *shaku* for apron and sleeve-bands for one servant).

Occasions of the 5th Month:

1 *to* 5 *shō* of glutinous rice, 3 *shō* of long beans,[535] 2 *to* of sake, money for seasonings (according to seasonal price; foregoing are for offerings), 5 *to* of glutinous rice, 1 *koku* of [ordinary] rice, 1 *to* 5 *shō* of long beans (foregoing required for members of the *Jingi-kan* and down), 7 *tan* 1 *jō* 8 *shaku* of tribute cloth (4 *tan* 1 *jō* 8 *shaku* are for unlined tunics and sleeve-bands for 3 chefs, 2 water-carriers, 2 brewers; 3 *jō* 2 *shaku* are for aprons and sleeve-bands for two *uneme* and two girl attendants, 1 *tan* 2 *jō* 2 *shaku* are for aprons and sleeve-bands for two menservants and three maidservants; 1 *jō* is used to cover the water jars and two thread boxes; 1 *jō* is for wiping-cloths).

Occasions of the 7th Month (same for the 9th Month):

for offerings, 2 *to* of sake, money for seasonings (according to prevailing price); for the members of the *Jingi-kan* and below: 20 salmon, 100 musk-melons.[536]

At all times, when the Consecrated Imperial Princess has completed three years of abstinence, in the first 10 days of the 4th month officials of ceremonial dress are appointed: two of 5th rank (one at least an Assistant Chief in the *Jingi-kan*, the other at least a Minor Secretary of Left or Right), four persons of 6th rank or lower (at least of the Fourth Class of civil official), 6 scribes from various Offices, 10 petty officials (6 persons of rank without assignment, and 4 whose parents have rank), 40 artisans (chosen from among chiefs or less of the bureaus and offices of skilled artisans, carpenters and Hayato, and various corporations), 20 builders (menservants are used), 20 girl attendants, 2 servants.

In the same ten-day period the affair begins in the Sai-in of the *Jingi-kan*. Those of 5th Rank and above are furnished with lustrous garments; for scribes and above, each gets: 4 *jō* 5 *shaku* of stiff silk, girl attendants each 3 *jō*; female artisans and above each get 2 *jō* 6 *shaku* of plain cloth. There is no custom of goods bestowed on builders and servants. Food is given according to the usual custom.

Various Articles to be made:

1 palanquin, 2 small tables (white wood), 1 palanquin, 1 canopy, 2 sunshades, 2 umbrellas (one for sun, one for rain), 1 frame for a bed, 1 bed (white wood), 2 august saddles, 1 saddle for noblewoman (foregoing with fur saddle-blanket), 4 saddles for girl attendants (with crape leather saddle-blankets), 4 dotted curtains, 1 curtain-frame (1 *jō* 2 *shaku* square, height 7 *shaku* 5 *sun*), 88 courtiers' hats, 88 cords for fastening them, 57 printed garments of light-green cloth, 96 garments of light-green cloth, 153 cloth trousers, 153 cloth sashes, 80 wide

---

534 *Chihaya* are broad bands, 襷 used here, while *tasuki* 襷 are narrow; both are used to tie back long sleeves.

535 *Sasage* 大角豆, long beans.
536 *Hosochi* 熟苽, muskmelon.

sashes, 88 prs. of leggings and 88 prs. of puttees,[537] 88 aprons, 1 bathtub, 1 stool (lacquered), 1 small tub, 1 *chōboku,* 1 Kara chest to contain all these, 1 light curtain, 1 dark-blue pongee curtain, four 4-*shaku* folding screens, 1 Kara chest for medicines, 1 stool (lacquered), 1 silver rice-box, 1 silver sake cup, 1 silver saucepan, 1 silver water bowl, 1 silver spoon, 1 slat box, 1 small food-chest, 6 chests for foods, 6 stools, 1 Kara chest for the august kitchen, 3 eating-tables, 1 sake table, 1 gruel table, 1 cutting table, 1 white-wood chest (with stand), 7 willow boxes, 4 coarse boxes, 1 piece of ramie cloth, 5 silk sieves, 2 tax-cloth sieves, 7 bags, 3 wiping-cloths (each 1 *jō* long), 2 lacquered casks, 1 lacquered spouted vessel, 2 lacquered hand-basins, 2 pulley buckets, 3 presentation bottles, 7 wooden platters, 4 large jars, 2 squat jars, 2 *sue* ware bottles, 2 hand-basins, 2 wash-bowls, 2 kettles for cooking mixed foods, 2 chopstick vases, 3 dippers, 4 gourds, 1 chopping knife, 30 cypress carrying-poles, 1 thin silk wall-curtain, 3 *shaku* 4 *sun* of treasure brocade, 5 *jō* 7 *shaku* of brocade, 1 *hiki* of violet tie-dyed silk, 3 *jō* 8 *shaku* of deep-violet silk damask, 1 *hiki* 5 *jō* 1 *shaku* 1 *sun* of lavender silk damask, 1 *jō* 8 *shaku* of deep-violet silk, 1 *hiki* 1 *jō* 3½ *shaku* of oiled pongee, 2 *hiki* 3 *jō* of thin gloss silk, 12 *kin* 5 *ryō* of violet silk thread, 5 violet leather skins, 2 wild-dog hides, 7 bearskins, 1 small *kin* of kudzu, 4 large *ryō* of white kudzu, 11 small *ryō* 1 *bu* 2 *shu* of refined gold, 5 large *kin* 11 *ryō* of silver, 5 small *kin* 3 *ryō* of quick-silver, 2 blue whetstones, 7 *ryō* of bleached rattan, 2 jujube-wood saddle frames (the foregoing are requested from the Imperial Storehouses), 6 *hiki* 1 *jō* of lined material, 17 *hiki* 5 *jō* 8 *shaku* 9 *sun* of scarlet silk, 2 *jō* 9 *shaku* 1 *sun* of scarlet Azuma pongee, 5 *hiki* 9 *sun* of green silk, 6 *hiki* 4 *jō* 3 *shaku* of light-green silk, 4 *hiki* 2 *jō* 2 *shaku* of dark-blue Azuma pongee, 8 *hiki* 5 *jō* 9 *shaku* 3 *sun* of yellow silk, 3 *jō* 1 *shaku* 3 *sun* of raw-silk damask, 1 *hiki* 3 *jō* 1 *shaku* 2 *sun* of white silk damask, 8 *shaku* of plain silk, 2 *hiki* of acorn-dyed Azuma pongee,[538] 21 *hiki* 2 *jō* 2 *shaku* of plain silk, 14 *hiki* 5 *jō* 5 *shaku* 7 *sun* of raw pongee, 3 *jō* 2 *shaku* 2 *sun* of Azuma pongee, 3 *jō* 7 *shaku* of dyed silk damask, 19 *kin* 1 *ryō* of scarlet silk thread, 1 *kin* 1 *ryō* of green silk thread, 4 *ryō* of dark-blue silk thread, 1 *kin* 3 *ryō* of light-green silk thread, 14 *ryō* of yellow silk thread, 8 *ryō* of acorn-dyed silk thread, 2 *kin* 9 *ryō* 2 *bu* of glossy silk thread,[539] 1 *kin* 2 *ryō* of raw silk thread, 53 *mochi* 1 *ryō* of tribute floss silk, 1 *jō* 7 *shaku* of light-green linen, 2 *tan* 1 *jō* 4 *shaku* of dark-blue tribute cloth, 63 *tan* 3 *jō* 1 *shaku* of light-green tribute cloth, 1 *tan* 1 *jō* of linen, 105 *tan* 3 *jō* 5 *shaku* of tribute cloth, 3 *jō* of ramie cloth, 17 *tan* 1 *jō* 6 *shaku* of commercial cloth, 4 bales of indigo plant,[540] 21 large *kin* 2 *ryō* of safflower, 3 *to* 9 *shō* 5 *shaku* of lacquer juice, 1 large *kin* 8 *ryō* of processed hemp, 2 small *kin* 2 *bu* of ramie, 3 Azuma straw-mats, 2 Izumo straw-mats, 11 Kadono straw-mats, four leaf-mats, 3 cured hides, 1 oxhide,

---

[537] Both leg coverings are *hagimaki,* but the first (脛巾) is perhaps a gaiter, the second (脛繩) is evidently to be wound around the leg like puttees.

[538] The acorn of *tsurubami* (see n. 268) produced a gray dye.

[539] *Ren* 練, a heat treating to produce high gloss in silk thread.

[540] The *ai* 藍, *polygonum tinctorium* or wild indigo, the leaves of which are used to produce a dark-blue dye. See n. 308.

1 large *kin* of glue, 1 *kin* of equisetum, 7 Iyo whetstones, 40 sheets of gold leaf, 57 great *kin* 7 *ryō* of finished copper, 118 *kin* of semi-finished copper, 51 *kin* 4 *ryō* of iron, 7 tribute Kara chests, 73 sheets of thin paper, 324 sheets of paper, 2 sticks of ink, 10 writing brushes, 9 *shō* 1 *gō* of lampblack, 5 *kin* of rattan, 4 *shō* 5 *gō* of oil (1 *shō* 5 *gō* of perilla oil, 2 *shō* of *hosoki*[541] oil, 1 *shō* of sesame oil), 4 coarse boxes, 8 *shō* 2 *gō* of glutinous rice, 1 *to* 2 *shō* 2 *gō* of wheat, 3 *to* 5 *shō* of vinegar, 15 cryptomeria logs, 20 bundles of oak, 4 gourds, 100 arrows, 10 cross-cuts of magnolia wood (each 1 *shaku* in diam., 3 *sun* thick), 16 pieces of cherry wood (each 2 *shaku* 5 *sun* long, 3 by 3 *sun*), 34 zelkova timbers (one 3 *shaku* long, 8 *sun* diam., 3 *sun* thick; one 1.2 *shaku* long, 9 *sun* in diam.; four logs each 3 *shaku* long and 1 *sun* 2 *bu* square; two logs 1 *shaku* 8 *sun* long, 8 *sun* in diam.; two logs each 1 *shaku* 7 *sun* long, 1 *shaku* in diam.; three, each 1 *shaku* long, 8 *sun* in diam.; four, each 1 *shaku* 8 *sun* square, 8 *sun* thick; one 9 *sun* square; four 1 *shaku* 8 *sun* long, 1 *sun* 2 *bu* square; twelve, each 6 *shaku* long, 3 *sun* 5 *bu* square), 370 bamboo arrowshafts, 5 cypress timbers, 15 split-bamboo mats, 10 walking planks, 4 cross beams 5 by 6 *sun*, 4 boards, 45 shoots of *chisaki*,[542] 20 bundles of rushes, 22 *koku* 2 *to* of hard charcoal and 94 *koku* 1 *to* of soft charcoal, 40 needles, 88 hats (the foregoing are requested from the *Jingi-kan*).

At all times, two august horses [for the Princess] and the six horses for the girl attendants are supplied by the Left and Right Mount Bureaus. If one is lost by death, a replacement may be requested.

At all times, the Consecrated Imperial Princess performs cleansing and abstinence for three years while she is at the capital, and on the first day of each month she dons the bark-cloth headdress, enters the Abstinence Hall and makes distant obeisance to the Great Deity. At that time symbolic offerings are presented first, then the bark-cloth of the headdress. For this purpose are required: 4 *ryō* of Aki bark-cloth and 2 *kin* of hemp (this includes what is required for Commissioners and below). The Commissioners, Masters and below take the readings of the tortoise shell, and they bow together two times twice. However, they do not participate [on the first day of] the 6th, 9th and 12th months, but on the 16th and 17th they come to worship and they bow two times twice. The principals clap their hands twice. The Consecrated Princess does not clap her hands. When her time of abstinence is completed, she goes to the Shrine of the Great Deity in the Province of Ise. Then the inner and outer buildings the fences and so on of her No-no-miya are given to the Nakatomi of the *Jingi-kan*; the furnishings and ceremonial articles from the halls she has vacated are given to the Nakatomi of the *kanzukasa*, the various articles within her sleeping apartment are given to the Imbe of the *kanzukasa*, but the gold and silver utensils, the kettles, large jars, and so on, are retained for the residence of the Princess.

At all times, when the moment approaches for the Consecrated Imperial Princess to go to Ise, before the 7th month a secretary and a scribe of the Bureau are sent

---

541 *Hosoki* 榠椒, also called *inuzanshō* 犬山椒, which Makino gives as *Fagara schinifolia Engl.,* a kind of pepper.

542 *Chisaki* 松楊 *(chisha-no-ki), Ehretia acuminata.* (Here it is written 知佐木.)

to the Itsuki-no-miya and to the [Office of the] Province to attend to a variety of preparations.

At all times, when the Consecrated Princess leaves the No-no-miya to progress to the Shrine of the Great Deity, she first goes to the edge of the river to perform lustration (day and time to be chosen as above).

Required for the Purification:
1 *shaku* each of five colors of pongee, 1 *tan* of cloth for coarse garments, one covered box (1.5 *shaku* long), 1.4 *kin* of bark-cloth, 3 *kin* of hemp, 2 iron effigies, 4 sheets of yellow-bark, 4 *kin* each of abalone, bonito and *wakame*, 4 *shō* of dried meat, 2 *shō* of salt, 4 *to* each of rice and sake, 4 jugs to put them in, 1 large jar, 2 food-mats, 4 bundles of oak, 2 shallow jars, one palanquin, 2 gourds, 2 *soku* of rice-in-ear, 4 mattocks, 2 *tan* of tax cloth for reciting the rituals, 2 porters, 2 carrying-poles.

At all times, when the Consecrated Princess is about to enter the Shrine of the Great Deity, whether in the 7th month or 8th month, there are sent at the same time the Messengers for the Great Purification (one each of representatives of the Left and Right Capital, one for the five Inner Provinces and one for each of the Seven Circuits).

At all times, when the Consecrated Princess is about to enter the Shrine of the Great Deity, Great Purification is held at the Imperial Palace on the last day of the 8th month, for which are required:
2 *tan* of tax cloth, 4 *kin* each of bark-cloth and hemp, 4 deerskins, 4 pairs of deer antlers, 4 broadswords, 4 bows, 4 arrows, 4 mattocks, 1 *kin* of ramie, 1 short *tatami*, 4 *to* each of sake and rice, 4 *soku* of rice-in-ear, 8 *kin* each of abalone and bonito, 26 *kin* of *wakame*, 10 *kin* of *arame*, 8 *kin* assorted seaweeds, 7 *to* dried meat, 4 *to* of salt, 4 water buckets, 4 gourds, 2 mats, 2 horses, 5 *tan* of tax cloth for kneeling cushions for reciting the ritual.

At all times, when there is some kind of damage to the Itsuki-no-miya, the governor of the province causes it to be repaired. If damage is excessive, a messenger is sent in advance and then repairs are made.

At all times, when the Consecrated Princess is about to enter the Shrine of the Great Deity, from the first day till the 30th of the 9th month, sacred lanterns are lighted for the North Star in the Capital, in the inner provinces and in Ise and Oomi Provinces, and the conduct of mourning and funerals is suspended.

The temporary shrines on her journey are always at Kōfu, Kōga, and Tarumi in Oomi Province, and at Suzuka and Ichishi in Ise Province, five places in all. The governors of each province oversee construction of these according to custom. The rice-in-ear which is due from these is 15,000 *soku* from Oomi and 23,000 *soku* from Ise. All the needed paraphernalia and offerings are to come out of these amounts.

At all times, when the Consecrated Princess leaves the capital farewell envoys must be appointed:
one Imperial Adviser (or a Middle Counselor may serve), 1 Secretary, 1 scribe, 1 official of 6th rank or lower. Then ceremonial dress is bestowed on messengers and the officials of the Itsuki-no-miya and those under them. For

messengers of 4th Rank, 10 *tan* of cloth, for those of 5th Rank, 5 *tan* of cloth, for those of 6th Rank, 1 *hiki* of pongee, 1 *mochi* of floss silk and 1 *tan* of cloth; however, to the Imbe are given 3 *tan*, to the chief of the Itsuki-no-miya 10 *hiki* of stiff silk, 20 *mochi* of floss silk, 20 *tan* of cloth, and to the assistant chief 8 *hiki* of silk, 15 *mochi* of floss silk, 15 *tan* of cloth. And to the Nakatomi and diviners of the *kanzukasa*, the secretary of the Bureau, the chief of the office of *toneri* and chief of the office of chefs are given 4 *hiki* of silk, 6 *mochi* of floss silk and 5 *tan* of cloth apiece. To 4th-class officials of the Bureau, and to the chiefs of the treasurers, cooks, brewers, water-carriers, palace women care-takers, medicine makers, housekeepers, gatekeepers, equerries and 3rd-class officials of both offices[543] are given 3 *hiki* of stiff silk, 5 *mochi* of floss silk, 4 *tan* of plain cloth. The chief diviner and the 4th-class officials of the *toneri,* treasury, chefs and gatekeepers, each are given 2 *hiki* pongee, 4 *mochi* of floss silk, 3 *tan* of plain cloth. Scribes, *ōdoneri, ryō-no-toneri* and watchmen of the various offices each are given 1 *hiki* of stiff silk, 2 *mochi* of floss silk, 2 *tan* of plain cloth. The official attendants of the bureau each get 2 *tan* of plain cloth; hostlers and sweepers, each 1 *tan* of plain cloth; [the Princess's] ladies-in-waiting, 20 *hiki* of silk damask of various colors, 40 *mochi* of floss silk, 20 *tan* of plain cloth; the wet-nurses each 14 *hiki* of silk damask of various colors, 20 *mochi* of floss silk, 13 *tan* of plain cloth; girl attendants of 1st class each 10 *hiki* of silk of various colors, 10 *mochi* of floss silk, 5 *tan* of plain cloth; girl attendants of 2nd class each 8 *hiki* of silk of various colors, 7 *mochi* of floss silk, 4 *tan* of plain cloth; those of 3rd class each 6 *hiki* of stiff silk, 5 *mochi* of floss silk, 3 *tan* of plain cloth; the caretakers each 4 *hiki* of silk of various colors, 4 *mochi* of floss silk, 2 *tan* of plain cloth; maidservants each 2 *hiki* 2 *jō* 5 *shaku* of silk of various colors, 1 *tan* of *sayomi* cloth,[544] 4 *mochi* of floss silk; diviners' assistants and children who kindle the fires each 2 *hiki* stiff silk, 4 *mochi* floss silk, 2 *tan* plain cloth and 1.5 *jō* of blue cloth.

At all times, horses are provided for the group of officials and their attendants who accompany [her]:

2 each for the Nakatomi, Imbe, and chief diviner of the *kanzukasa*; 4 horses for the chiefs, 3 horses for their assistants, 2 each for the officials of 4th class and higher, and 2 each for the guards; 4 each for the noblewomen, 3 each for wet-nurses and girl attendants, 1 each for the chiefs of the palanquin and for the caretakers. Horses are not supplied to retainers of messengers, grooms, maidservants, chief diviners or other diviners. To her escorts of 4th Rank are furnished 6 horses, to those of 5th Rank 5 horses. The rest [may receive] according to the number of horses available. Petty officials of the Palace do not require [horses] as they will have been sent them in advance.

Messengers for the Kanname Festival in the 9th Month :
According to the usual custom they come to worship on the 11th day [of the month]. However, when it is a time that the Consecrated Princess has come to

---

543 Probably 'both offices' refers to the *Itsuki-no-miya-no-tsukasa (saigū-ryō)* and its *kanzukasa*.

544 *Sayomi* 賽布 is a kind of coarse cloth made from inner bark of the *shina* 科 tree. (See n. 242.)

worship, her escorts come to worship. The requirements for their offerings and their lustrous robes are the same as is customary. Moreover, one Nakatomi as envoy is sent ahead to the two provinces of Oomi and Ise in order to cleanse and purify [the route] in advance of her coming.

The 18 Days of Abstinence:
Usual abstinence is for 3 days, while this time abstinence is observed from the 1st to the 18th of the month. However, avoidance of mourning and burial is observed for the entire month.

At all times, on the day for departure of the Consecrated Imperial Princess, the officials concerned set forth seat-mats in the Daigoku-kōden.[545] The Sovereign progresses to the Kōden. (No instruction.) A *Jingi-kan* Nakatomi of the 4th Rank presents the symbolic offerings. The chief ritualist passes the offering to a chamberlain of 5th Rank or higher. At the moment she arrives at the Daigokuden the Consecrated Imperial Princess alights from her palanquin, enters the Hall and takes the seat of honor. When the ceremony is finished she starts out for the Shrine of the Great Deity. (The affair is to be found in the *Gishiki*.)[546]

Her august lustration is performed in rivers in six places (in Yamashiro Province; in the Seta and Kōga Rivers in Oomi Province; in the Suzuka, Shitai Stream and Take River in Ise Province).

[Required:]

> 6 *tan* of tax cloth for her six outfits of coarse garments, 12 iron effigies, 6 *kin* each of bark-cloth and hemp, 6 *kin* each of sake and rice, 6 *kin* each of abalone and bonito, 6 *shō* of dried meat, 6 *shō* of salt, 6 *kin* each of *wakame* and assorted seaweeds, 6 jugs, 4 boxes (each 1 *shaku* 7 *sun* long), high-quality lacquer boxes (to hold abalone, bonito, etc.) 1 seat-mat, three porters.

At all times, when the Consecrated Imperial Princess is en route and she arrives at the boundaries of Yamashiro, Oomi and Ise and at the rivers of Seta, Suzuka, Shitai and Take, two each of *kambe* and diviners are sent ahead to propitiate and purify the places. Needed for this are:

> 12 iron effigies, 6 jackets of plain cloth, 6 skirts (1 *tan* of tax cloth for each jacket and skirt), 6 *kin* each of bark-cloth and hemp, 6 *shō* each of rice and sake, 6 *kin* each of abalone and bonito, 6 *shō* of dried meat and salt, 6 *kin* each

---

545 That is, the *kōden* 後殿 of the Daigoku-den, the Rear Hall of the Imperial Audience Hall. See n. 289.

546 The reference is presumably to the *Engi-Gishiki* (Engi Ceremonial Procedures) which is not extant. As the procedures for the Saigū are outside the codes and are not described in the chronicles, we do not have the details of this unique farewell audience. It is mentioned in the *Genji monogatari* ('The Sacred Tree' chapter) and in the *Ookagami*, an historical narrative covering mid-9th to early 11th century. On this occasion the sovereign personally placed the *wakare no mikushi* (or *ogushi*) 別の御櫛, 'the august comb

(or the little comb) of parting' in the hair of the princess. The *Ookagami* passage gives an impression that the comb was a token or talisman to be kept by the princess while she was away from the Capital in a sort of exile in Ise at the Shrine of the Great Deity. Perhaps the comb invested her with some divine or magic power imparted from the person of the sovereign. The words he spoke on the occasion were something like this: 'Now, as thine honoured self goest down to Ise, take thou this keepsake, and turn not thine eyes back hither when thou goest.' T. Yamagishi, ed., *Ookagami*, pp. 64–5.

of *wakame* and assorted seaweeds, 6 baskets of assorted foods, 6 covered jars, 4 boxes (1 *shaku* 7 *sun* sq.), 1 seat-mat, 1 food-mat, three porters.

Requirements for offerings at the small shrines en route:

1 *hiki* of stiff silk, 5 skeins of silk thread, 5 *mochi* of floss silk, 1 *kin* of bark-cloth, 2 *kin* of hemp. Also, for the *Ootono-hogai* for the 5 temporary shrines en route: 40 sheets of Aki bark-cloth, 1 *kin* of ordinary bark-cloth; also, required for offerings to be prepared en route: 1 *hiki* of pongee, 5 *mochi* of floss silk, 5 skeins of silk thread, 1 large *kin* each of bark-cloth and hemp, 1 tortoise shell for divining. All of these the *kanzukasa* requests, retains and presents. Materials for the propitiation and purification are requested from the storehouses of the capital.

115 deities to be worshiped by the Itsuki-no-miya[547] *at the Toshigoi Festival:*

Of the large shrines 17 presentations to deities (worshiped within the Itsuki-no-miya):

4 to Oomiyanome-no-kami   8 to the Deities of the Gates
2 to the Deities of the Wells   2 to Deities of the Divining-place
1 to the Ground Deity

For each:

5 *shaku* of stiff silk, 1 *shaku* each of 5 colors of thin pongee, 1 *shaku* of colored hempen cloth, 2 *ryō* of bark-cloth, 5 *ryō* of hemp, 1.4 *jō* of tax cloth, 1 mattock, 1 shield, 1 each of *yakura-oki* and *yokura-oki*, 5 *ryō* each of abalone and bonito, 2 *shō* of dried meat, 1 *shō* of salt, 6 *ryō* each of *wakame*, *arame* and assorted seaweeds, 2 *shō* of sake, 1 jar and for the Oomiyanome-no-kami the addition of one horse, and for deities of the August Gates two spears.

For the 98 small shrines (in Take and Watarai Districts):

Those of

Sumarume	Sanaka—2	Kushida
Uni (有貳)	Omi	Hatori-itoma
Ookamuyama—(2)	Nanami	Unisakura
Uni (宇尒)	Hatori-otoma—2	Kishi
Amenokaguyama	Anashi	Nagareta
Ishida	Takenosasafue	Isawa
Mure	Ookunidama	Sakikurisu—2
Hitsukura	Isonokami	Kushida-tsukimoto
Ushiniwa	Oogushi	Kasuya
Takenokami	Takenonaka	Io-umi—2
Hayashi	Ookanokami	Moruyama
Hatake—3	Hichi	Ooyodo
Osaya	Kuninari	Oowake
Ooka	Ironokami	

(the above are in Take District)

Asakuma	Aramitama-no-mikoto	Izanagi

---

[547] Here the sacred residence of the princess in Ise, and its staff, rather than the princess herself, is indicated.

Sonau	Kano	Izanami
Satanokuninari	Kamo	Tanoe
Kusanagi	Iso	Takihara
Tsukiyomi	Yuta	Narahara
Oomizu	Tsunaga-no-ōmizu	Ookunidama-hime
Miarushi	Ootsuchi-no-mioya	Tanoue-ōmizu
Kunitsu-mioya	Sakate-no-kuninari	Awa-no-miko
Kawara-no-kuninari	Kukutsu-hime	Ooma-no-kuninari
E (江)	Kansaki	Enomura
Kuchira	Watarai-no-kuni	Watarai-no-
Koyonoite	Shitomi	ōkunidama-hime
Yamasue	Sugihara	Kawara
Usonono	Omata	Kawara-no-ō
Oomikami-no-mifune	Ikazuchi (or Raiden)	Kawara-no-fuchi
Ookōchi		Ogihara (or Haibara)

(the above are in Watarai District)

For each:

3 *shaku* of stiff silk, 2 *ryō* of bark-cloth, 5 *ryō* of hemp, 1.4 *jō* of tax cloth, 1 shield, one each *yakura-oki* and *yokura-oki*, 6 *ryō* each of abalone and bonito, 5 *gō* each of dried meat and salt, 1.2 *ryō* each of *wakame*, *arame* and assorted seaweeds, 1 *shō* of sake, 1 jar. For the whole are needed: 3 brewing jars, 3 gourds, 5 food-mats, 5 *tan* of tax cloth for reciting the rituals, 3 *tan* of cloth for lustrous robes for the Imbe who present the symbolic offerings.

The foregoing all are celebrated on the 4th day of the 2nd month [*Toshigoi* festival] while the articles offered to the deities, as well as cloth for the robes and the rituals for the *Tsukinami* festivals of 6th and 12th months, for the *Hoshizume*, *Michiae*, *Ootono*, *Miagamono*, Great Purification and for the festivals to the Sacred Fire and Courtyard Fire on the 1st of the month are all the same as those while she is at the capital.

Requirements for Lustration of the Consecrated Imperial Princess at three seasonal festivals :[548]

6 *shaku* each of 5 colors of pongee, 15 sheets of Aki bark-cloth, 3 *kin* each of ordinary bark-cloth and hemp, 6 *tan* of tax cloth, 3 sets of plain-cloth jackets and skirts (tax cloth), 12 mattocks, 3 boxes, 6 *kin* each of abalone and bonito, 6 *kin* each of *wakame* and assorted seaweeds, 1.2 *to* each of dried meat and salt, 3 *to* each rice and sake, 12 *soku* of rice-in-ear, 12 jars, 6 stands, 18 bundles of oak, 3 gourds, 3 palanquins, 6 food-mats, 15 *ryō* of yellow-bark (the foregoing for the lustration on the last day of the month), 9 *shaku* each of 5 colors of thin pongee, 9 *shaku* of colored hempen cloth, 27 sheets of Aki bark-cloth, 6 *kin* each of ordinary bark-cloth and hemp, 9 jackets and skirts of plain cloth (tax cloth), 18 iron effigies, 9 boxes, 9 *kin* each of abalone and bonito,

---

548 *Sanji-no-matsuri* 三時祭, presumably the same three festival times as *miori no matsuri* (n. 475), meaning the festivals of the 6th, 9th and 12th months, when food offerings were presented on the 16th & 17th days at Ise Shrines.

9 *shō* each of dried meat and salt, 9 *kin* each of *wakame* and assorted seaweeds, 9 baskets of assorted foods, 2.7 *to* each of rice and sake, 9 *soku* of rice-in-ear, 3 bales of straw (the foregoing are required for the lustration on the arrival day and for festivals at the boundaries).

The above are for performing lustration at the nearby river on the last day of the 5th month and the 11th month. On the last day of the 8th month she goes to the harbor of Ono[549] and performs lustration. For the festivals of the 3 seasons on the 15th day of the month the Consecrated Imperial Princess enters a detached palace and on her way celebrations are held at two places on the boundaries (outside the wall on the east of her palace and at the boundary between Take and Watarai Districts; requirements for these celebrations are as listed above). When she arrives at the lustration hall[550] (the Office of the Shrines and the Office of Housekeeping provide the ceremonial articles), the Nakatomi of the *kanzukasa* conducts the lustration ceremony. (Materials required are kept by the Office of the Shrine.) The Office of the Great Shrines provides the august food for the Consecrated Princess, at the same time bestowing sake and fish on Imperial Messengers and their assistants. Next the *kanzukasa* make the offerings for the *Ootono-hogai* for the Inner Compound. (Articles required for this are kept by the Office of the Shrines.) After this the Consecrated Princess moves into the Inner Compound. (Ceremonial dress and articles are the same as for the lustration hall.) They present the evening food offering. (The *kanzukasa* take the required articles and give them to the officials concerned; but male and female officials take charge of dividing and preparing the offerings.) After [they present] the food offering on the morning of the 16th, the Consecrated Princess goes to worship at the Watarai Shrine. The poor people along her route are relieved with alms as usual. She performs lustration in the Watarai River, and enters the shrine. When she reaches the east post of the gate of the board fence she alights from her palanquin. She enters the gate of the outer shrine fence and goes to the east hall. (The *negi* and members of the Office of Housekeepers present the ceremonial articles.) The Superintendent of the Shrines takes the bark-cloth for her headdress, goes through the gate of the outer shrine fence and kneels. The noblewoman comes forth, receives it and presents it. The Consecrated Princess claps her hands, then receives the headdress and puts it on. Then the Superintendent of the Shrines takes the ornamented sacred *sakaki* branch[551] and comes through the same gate and kneels down. The lady-in-waiting again receives this and presents it; the Consecrated Princess claps her hands, takes the ornamented *sakaki* and raising it aloft she enters the gate of the inner shrine fence and takes her seat inside. (Two ladies-in-waiting or girl attendants escort her.) Leaving her seat she moves forward and bows two times twice. When that is done, she hands over the ornamented *sakaki* to the lady-in-waiting who receives it and in turn hands it to the *mono-imi,* who receives it, takes it and stands it up by the west post of the gate of the innermost fence. The Consecrated Princess returns and takes her original seat. The Superintendent

---

549 Harbor of Ono 尾野.
550 The *misogi-dono* 禊殿.

551 That is, the *futo-tamagushi* (n. 408).

of the Shrines recites the ritual. When it is finished the *mono-imi* and *uchindo* set the offerings upon the offering-tables. The Consecrated Princess and the host of officials and their attendants bow twice, clap their hands 8 times, then they clap their hands inaudibly and bow twice. This is repeated. When finished, the host of officials withdraw. They go to the Depuration Hall and are served with sake and food. When that is over, they enter the outer shrine fence gate and the *Yamato-mai*[552] is performed. First the Superintendent of the Shrines and his retinue, then the members of the *kanzukasa* and of the Bureau of the Consecrated Princess successively dance. Next four of the girl attendants of the Princess perform the *Gosechi-mai*.[553] When they have finished, the distributing of emoluments is carried out. After that the Consecrated Princess returns to her detached palace. The Nakatomi of the *kanzukasa* stay at the south gate to present the symbolic offerings. On the 17th day [of the month] she goes to the Shrine of the Great Deity, per-forming lustration in the Mimosuso River. From then on the rest of the procedure is the same as at the Watarai Shrine. (For this see the *Daijingū-shiki*.) On this day the Superintendent of the Shrine offers the goods and bestows the emoluments. Also, the envoys who bear the offerings similarly bestow emoluments. All of them individually carry this out. On the 18th, the Consecrated Princess returns to her palace. The Nakatomi of the *kanzukasa* stay at the south gate to present the symbolic offerings. At the same time they make the offerings for the *Ootono-hogai* and bestow emoluments on the officials of the provincial government who reverently participate.

Festival to the Deities of Divination on the last day of each month (the festivals for the Deities of Divination when the Consecrated Princess comes to worship at the three seasonal festivals are the same as this):
[Required:]
    4 *shō* each of rice and sake, 1 *kin* each of bonito and *wakame*, 2 *shō* of dried meat and 1 *shō* of salt.
For the purification on the last day of the 10th month the requirements are always the same as for the purifications for the festivals of 3 seasons.

115 deities of the Festival of First-fruits (17 Greater and 98 Lesser):
the various articles presented for this are the same as for the *Toshigoi* festival. But those for festivals of propitiating the Cooking Hall and of the Sacred Fire and Courtyard Fire and *Ootono* are all the same as they are when [she is] at the Capital.

Required for Offerings at the First-fruits (eight men and ten women perform divi-nation):
    2 *jō* of stiff silk, 2 *ryō* of silk thread, 1.2 *jō* of ramie, 1.6 *jō* of linen, 1.2 *jō* of bleached cloth, 3 *tan* 1 *jō* of tribute cloth, 2 *kin* 4 *ryō* of bark-cloth, 10 clay plates, 2 hand-basins, 10 bowls without covers, 10 pedestalled plates, 6 wash-basins, 10 cooking pots, 4 jars, 2 ewers for hand-washing (provided by the

---

552 For *Yamato-mai* dance, see n. 414.
553 For *Gosechi* dances, see n. 415.
554 These procedures for the 'three festivals'

at times when the Consecrated Princess is in residence in Ise are given in Bk. iv, 'Procedures for the Shrine of the Great Deity.'

Bureau), 14 boxes, 2 coarse boxes, 3 white-wood chests, 10 offering tables, 2 *to* of rice for offering purposes, 2 *to* of rice for making gruel, 2 *to* of millet, 20 *soku* of rice-in-ear for making both clear and turbid sacred sake, 1 *koku* of sacred sake, 18 gourds, 4 sake jugs, 4 *hyō* of oak wood, 2 swords with lacquered, incised hilts, 10 long knives, 2 clay braziers, 2 wooden mallets, 2 chopping blocks, 2 ritual elongated basins, 2 loads of *hikage-no-kazura*,[555] 2 litters (furnished by the province), 5 shallow earthenware dishes, 5 flat-edged jars, 4 ritual clay urns, 8 spouted vessels, 8 small dish-stands, 2 mortars of *sue* ware, 20 box-stands, 8 *sue* ware dishes, 4 ritual water-pitchers, 6 jars, 8 *sue* ware bowls, 20 plates, 10 high stands, 10 sake cups, 3 *shō* of oil, 2 short tables, 4 chopping bowls (the foregoing furnished by Mino Province), 2 *kin* 10 *ryō* of Azuma abalone, 2 *kin* each of thin abalone and Oki abalone, 5 *kin* of bonito, 10 *kin* of boiled bonito, 10 *ryō* each of squid and shellfish, 2 *shō* of sushi abalone, 2 *kin* of dried codium, 1 *kin* of laver,[556] 1 *shō* of abalone wrapped in codium, 2 *shō* each of trout boiled in salt water and pickled carp, 2 *ryō* of dried ginger, 2 *shō* each of clear sake and turbid sake, 1 *shō* each of ordinary rice and glutinous rice, 2 *shō* each of soybeans, red beans, wheat and sesame seeds, 4 *soku* of glutinous rice-in-ear, 1 *shō* of cooked and dried glutinous rice, 2 *shō* each of cooked and dried millet, *mino* and sorghum, 5 *shō* each of acorns and water-chestnuts, 1 *shō* each of lotus nuts and dried jujubes, 1 *shō* of raw chestnuts, 6 *shō* of pounded chestnuts, 2 *shō* of dried persimmons, 10 *kage*[557] of oranges, 3 *hyō* of dried oak, 1 load of *yuzuruha*[558] (the foregoing furnished by the Bureau), 1 palanquin (provided by the province).

The above are requested by the *kanzukasa* and the chefs.

4 *soku* of rice-in-ear, 4 *soku* of millet (foregoing provided by the Bureau).

The above are requested by the cooks.

1 shaku of fine-weave cloth, 2 sake-cup stands, 20 hollow stands, 15 dishes without covers (provided by the Bureau), 2 food-mats (provided by the province).

The brewers request the above.

5.1 *jō* of stiff silk, 6 *tan* 2.85 *jō* of bleached cloth, 6 *shaku* of ramie cloth, 10 *ryō* of silk thread, 2 sieves, 2 thread boxes, 1 *shimoto* table, 2 clay platters, 1 *shō* of oil, 1 *shō* of red beans (foregoing furnished by the Bureau), one each: bathtub, round tub and foot tub; 1 shelf table, 5 board covers, 2 white-wood chests, 1 box, 1 rough-made box, 2 lampstands, 3 gourds, 1 *ryō* of fragrant herbs (these furnished by the province), 1 Ike ceremonial jar and 4 large ceremonial jars, 4 chopping bowls, 1 oil jar, 2 each of stands and dishes for oil, 1 metal bowl, 1 *sue* ware bowl (these are furnished by Mino Province).

The above are requested by the Caretakers.

1.2 *jō* of *harae* cloth,[559] 1 box, 12 *tatami* with white binding, 8 short *tatami*, 2

---

555 For *hikage no kazura* 日陰鬘, a vine, Makino gives *Lycopodium clavatum, L.*

556 Here the familiar *nori* 紫菜 is mentioned.

557 *Kage*, a measure not used elsewhere, may neam a basket cover or a basket used to measure fruit.

558 *Yuzuruha* 弓絃葉. Brinkley gives *Daphniphyllum macropodum.*

559 *Harae-nuno* 祓布, hempen cloth for exorcising ceremonies, perhaps.

slanted pillows, 2 folded-mat *tatami* (these are furnished by the Bureau).
The above are requested by the Housekeepers.

   5 *hiki* pongee, 2.5 *jō* white stiff silk, 20 *mochi* of floss silk, 3 *jō* of variegated
   silk, 2 *jō* of linen, 1 *tan* 1.4 *jō* of bleached cloth, 6 boxes, 1 comb (boxwood),
   1 comb table, 1 knife, 1 hat, 1 *tsumato*,[560] 1 pair of shoes, 1 Izumo seat-mat.
The above are for the sacramental garments[561] for the Consecrated Imperial
Princess.

   14 *hiki* 3 *jō* of stiff silk (10 *hiki* for quilts, 4 *hiki* 3 *jō* for printed blue robes),
   190 *mochi* of floss silk, 67 *tan* 3.4 *jō* of tribute cloth, 6 *kin* of safflower (foregoing are required for the printed blue robes), 6 *tan* 6 *shaku* of bleached cloth
   (foregoing for sleeve-cords and sleeve-bands for the Chefs and the girl attendants).

The above are for sacred robes for *omibito* which the Bureau supplies according
to precedent. Their emolument consists of one garment bestowed on New Year's
Day.

Spring Festival for the Various Offices (same for Fall Festival)

Festival to Deities of the Chefs:
   1 *shaku* each of 5 colors of thin pongee, 1 *shaku* of colored hempen cloth, 1
   kin each of bark-cloth and hemp, 1 *tan* of tax cloth, 1 mattock, 5 *to* of rice,
   4 *to* of sake, 1 *to* of glutinous rice, 2 *shō* each of soybeans and red beans, 12
   kin of dried meat, 2 *kin* of abalone, 3 *kin* each of bonito, dried bêche-de-mer
   and *wakame*, 3 *to* of sushi, 5 *shō* of salt, 1 *shō* each of soy sauce and vinegar,
   1 food-mat.

Festival to the Deities of the Cooks:
   3 *sun* each 5 colors of thin pongee, 3 *sun* of colored hempen cloth, 1 *kin* each
   of bark-cloth and hemp, 1 *tan* of tax cloth, 1 mattock, 4 *to* of sake, 3 *shō* each of
   rice and glutinous rice, 1 *kin* each of abalone, bonito and dried meat, 2 *kin*
   of *wakame*, 2 *shō* of sushi, 1 *shō* of salt, 2 *shō* each of soybeans and red beans.

Festival to the Deities of the Brewers:
   6 *sun* each of 5 colors of thin pongee, 6 *sun* of colored hempen cloth, 8 *ryō*
   each of bark-cloth and hemp, 1 *tan* of tax cloth, 1 mattock, 6 *shō* each of rice
   and sake, 4 *shō* of glutinous rice, 1 *shō* each of soybeans and red beans, 1 *kin*
   each of abalone and bonito, 4 *shō* each of sushi and dried meat, 1 *shō* of salt, 5
   plates, 1 food mat.

Festival to the Deities of the Water-Carriers:
   6 *sun* each of 5 colors of thin pongee, 6 *sun* of colored hempen cloth, 8 *ryō* of
   bark-cloth, 4 *ryō* of hemp, 1 *tan* of tax cloth, 1 mattock, 2 *shō* each of rice and
   sake, 8 *ryō* each of abalone and bonito, 1 *shō* of sushi, 8 *ryō* of *wakame*, 5 *gō*
   of salt.

---

560 *Tsumato*, perhaps a nail polisher or shar-
pener (爪磨).

561 The term *kamu-imi-no-miso* 神忌御服
would be 'deity-taboo august garments'.

Festival to the Deity of the Icehouse:
> 1 *shaku* each of 5 colors of thin pongee, 1 *shaku* colored hempen cloth, 4 *ryō*
> of bark-cloth, 3 *ryō* of hemp, 1 mattock 6 *shō* of rice, 1 *shō* each of glutinous
> rice and sake, 2 *shō* each of soybeans and red beans, 8 *ryō* of abalone, 1 *kin* of
> bonito, 6 *shō* each of sushi and dried meat.

Festival to the Deities of the Cook-stove, Mountain of the Charcoal Stove, of House-
holds, of the Sacred Rivers and Ponds:
> 1 *shaku* each of 5 colors of thin pongee, 1 *shaku* of colored hempen cloth, 4
> *ryō* each of bark-cloth and hemp, 1 *tan* of tax cloth, 2 mattocks, 4 *shō* of rice,
> 6 *shō* of sake, 1 *shō* each of soybeans and red beans, 1 *kin* each of abalone,
> bonito and *wakame*, 6 *shō* each of dried meat and sushi, 2 *shō* of salt, 4 food
> mats.

Offerings to be presented at the Two Great Shrines in the 12th Month
For each shrine:
> 1 *hiki* stiff silk, 1 skein of silk thread, 1 *mochi* of floss silk, 1 *tan* of tax cloth,
> 1 *kin* each of bark-cloth and hemp.

The *kanzukasa* requests and offers the above.

Offerings for 17 Deities within the Itsuki-no-miya:
> For each:
> > 5 *shaku* stiff silk, 1 skein silk thread, 1 *mochi* floss silk, 1.4 *jō* tax cloth, 2 *ryō*
> > of bark-cloth, 5 *ryō* of hemp.

Furnishing the Itsuki-no-miya:
> 2 board beds for the Consecrated Imperial Princess, 2 violet-bound *tatami*,
> 2 yellow-bound *tatami*, 6 green-bound *tatami*, 20 seat-mats. For officials of
> 5th rank and noblewomen, 2 board beds and 2 yellow-bound *tatami* each. For
> each of the wet-nurses, 1 board bed and 1 green-bound *tatami*. For the Assist-
> ant Chief of the Bureau: 1 board bed and 1 *shimoto* bed and 2 folded-mat
> *tatami*. For the rest of the personnel and girl attendants, each 1 *tatami* bed
> and for each of the guards 1 *tatami*.

The above are provided when the Consecrated Imperial Princess goes to the
province. The first year the province provides them; in subsequent years the
offices of the Bureau prepare them.
> 4 curtains, 2 short curtains of dark-blue cloth, 10 wall-coverings made of
> bulrushes.

The above are provided from goods in the capital storehouses, and when they
are torn they may be replaced.
> 40 great jars of sake (3.4 *koku* of rice per jar), 5 great jars of vinegar (3.7 *koku*
> per jar) and 6 great jars of soy sauce (3 *koku* of soybeans per jar).

In the first year in which the Consecrated Imperial Princess is present the
governor of the province will have already set aside and stored the rice, soybeans,
salt and so forth to be provided to her Bureau. If great jars get cracked or broken
Owari Province provides and sends more.

Supplies for the Year:

13 *hiki* 1.7 *shaku* of stiff silk to make the curtains to cover the walls of the sleeping room, 37 *mochi* of floss silk, 15 *tan* 2.2 *jō* of tribute cloth to make the canopy, 1 *tan* 2.3 *jō* of tribute cloth for the horizontal timbers, 8 *tan* of tax cloth for sun screens, 3 *tan* 3.9 *jō* of linen for blinds, 7 *hiki* 2.4 *jō* of stiff silk for curtains, 30 *mochi* of floss silk, 2 *hiki* of stiff silk for curtains around the bed, 10 *mochi* of floss silk, 2 *hiki* 2 *jō* of stiff silk for a cover over the bed, 3 *hiki* 1.67 *jō* stiff silk for the mattress, 24 *mochi* of floss silk, 12 *hiki* of *chōken* silk for the quilts, 84 *mochi* of tribute floss silk, 110 *hiki* of stiff silk for clothing, 180 *mochi* of floss silk, 1 *hiki* of pongee for socks, 40 skeins of silk thread, 24 pairs of shoes (foregoing are provided by the Bureau).

The Office of *uneme* sews and puts together the above; if anything down to and including cloth for blinds becomes soiled, it is changed.

1 *hiki* 4 *jō* of lined cloth, 5.7 *jō* of scarlet silk, 1 *hiki* 3 *shaku* of oiled pongee, 3.4 *jō* of stiff silk, 1.6 *jō* of linen, 2.4 *jō* of bleached cloth, 1 *mochi* of floss silk, 1 skein of silk thread, 1 *kin* of hemp, 2 great water jars, 3 boxes for the jars, 4 Kara stoves, 2 long knives, 5 short knives, 1 whetstone (the Bureau provides these), 1 table for foods and 1 table for fruit, 3 boxes, 2 board boxes, 1 chopstick box, 5 coarse boxes, 2 short tables, 2 tables for oak wood, 2 great tables, 3 Kara chests, 8 white-wood chests, 2 tables with removable legs, 2 horizontal boxes, 10 jugs, 1 tub, 2 round tubs, 8 seat mats, 6 reed-mats, 1 mortar, 2 pestles, 20 gourds, 20 box dippers, 2 shallow baskets, 4 palanquins (foregoing provided by the province).

The above are requested by the Office of Chefs.

8 *shaku* of lined cloth, 1.2 *jō* of scarlet silk, 8 *shaku* of oiled pongee, 1 *tan* of tribute cloth (these are provided by the Bureau), 1 mortar operated by foot, 2 pestles, 2 shallow baskets, 1 shallow tub, 3 white-wood boxes, 2 tables with removable legs (these provided by the province).

The above are requested by the Office of Cooks.

4.19 *jō* of lined cloth, 2.99 *jō* of scarlet silk, 5 *jō* of oiled pongee, 1.9 *jō* of stiff silk, 2 *tan* 7 *shaku* of linen, 3 *tan* 3 *jō* 5 *sun* of tribute cloth, 3 *jō* of tax cloth, 48 sake cups, 20 dishes without covers, 1 wash-basin, 2 *ryō* of silk thread, 2 mattocks, 10 large bamboo baskets (these are provided by the Bureau), 2 tables with removable legs, 3 Kara chests, 1 white-wood chest, 2 sake tubs, 1 tub with sideboard, 2 great tables, 20 gourds, 10 box dippers, 2 large baskets, 2 shallow baskets, 4 reed-mats, 4 food-mats (these are provided by the province).

The above are requested by the Office of Brewers.

3 *jō* 6 *sun* of lined silk, 2 *jō* 4 *shaku* 7 *sun* of scarlet floss silk, 4 *jō* 4 *shaku* of oiled pongee, 2 *jō* 4 *shaku* of stiff silk, 1 *jō* 2 *shaku* of thin silk, 1 *ryō* of silk thread, 3 *jō* 4 *shaku* of bleached cloth, 3.4 *jō* of linen cloth, 1 *jō* of hand-woven ramie, 1 hatchet, 2 small knives, 2 [each] large water-jars and buckets (these are provided by the Bureau), 1 jar, 30 *sue* ware bowls, 2 mortars, 10 plates (these are provided by Mino Province), 2 outside tables, 1 white-wood hand-washing tub, 4 each of wooden covers and stands for the water supply [jars], 2 great tables, 1 box, 2 coarse boxes, 1 clay brazier, 2 white-wood boxes, 5

M

gourds, 5 box dippers, 10 shallow baskets (foregoing provided by the province).
The above are requested by the Office of Water-Carriers.

2.63 *jō* of lined cloth, 4 *hiki* 3.7 *jō* of scarlet silk, 2 *hiki* 5.92 *jō* of oiled pongee,
6 *shaku* white pongee, 5.35 *jō* of stiff silk, 9 *tan* 2.17 *jō* of bleached cloth, 6
shaku of hand-woven ramie, 2.9 *jō* of tribute cloth, 2 *bu* of silk thread, 1 *shimoto*
table, 3 each of dish-stands and dishes for oil, 1 iron pot for hot coals, 5 bars
of iron, 2 mattocks (foregoing are supplied by the Bureau), 1 bathtub, 1
washing platform, 2 great tables, 5 wooden covers, 1 shampoo tub, 1 foot tub,
1 washtub, 2 Kara chests, 2 lampstands, 2 white-wood chests, 2 boxes, 2 rough-
made boxes, 3 gourds (foregoing provided by the province), 1 Ike ceremonial
jar, 4 large ceremonial jars, 1 spouted vessel, 1 large jar, 2 jugs, 4 chopping-
bowls (foregoing provided by Mino Province).
The above are requested by the Office of Caretakers.

1 *jō* 7 *shaku* 6 *sun* each of brocade and scarlet silk, 1 *hiki* 4 *shaku* of oiled pongee,
1 *jō* 2 *shaku* of *harae* cloth (foregoing provided by the Bureau), 1 box (provided
by the province).
The above are requested by the Office of Housekeepers.

Seventeen and one-third Doses of Compounded Medicines:

2 doses each of four-flavor *richū*[562] pills and seven-vapor[563] pills; 1 dose
each of Chinese pepper[564] pills, herbaceous peony pills and *onbaku*[565] pills,
1/3 dose of rhinoceros-horn pills, 2 doses each of deity-bright ointment and
panacea ointment, 3 doses each of bugbane ointment and *zokufu*[566] ointment,
52 doses of deity-bright *byakusan*,[567] 2 doses of *toshōsan*[568] and 2 doses of
toso.[569]

Pharmacopoeia required:

6 *ryō* 1 *bu* of cinnamon, 55 croton seeds, 10 *ryō* 3 *bu* 2 *shu* of licorice, 4 *bu* 2 *shu*
of rhinoceros horn, 5 *shō* of honey, 7 *ryō* 4 *shu* of Epsom salts, 1 *ryō* 2 *bu* 4 *shu* of
bōfū,[570] 2 *ryō* 3 *bu* 4 *shu* of ephedra, 9 *ryō* 1 *bu* of potentilla, 1 *ryō* 3 *bu* of gypsum,
7 *ryō* 3 *bu* of hemlock parsley, 1 *kin* 4 *ryō* 2 *bu* 4 *shu* of rhubarb, 10 *ryō* of ginseng,
2 *ryō* 2 *bu* of aster, 5 *ryō* of bupleurum, 10 *ryō* 2 *bu* 2 *shu* of *koganebana*,[571]
1 *ryō* 2 *shu* of *ōren*,[572] 2 *bu* 1 *shu* of gleditsia, 6 *ryō* of herbaceous peony, 6 *ryō*

---

562 *Shimirichū*, a compound of four flavors or
ingredients. See App. VII.

563 *Shichiki-gan*, made of 'seven vapors' or
liquids?

564 A compound of Chinese pepper, *Kara-
hajikami*, or 'Fagara of Wu', according to E.
Schafer, *Golden Peaches*, 149.

565 That is, *ombyaku-gan*, 'warm, white medicine'.

566 *zokufukō*

567 The *byakusan* herbs included spices and
plants, such as cinnamon, pepper, *toso* and *bōfū* (n.
570)—listed separately here—all used for their
beneficial effect on the health. The *byakusan* were
drunk in sake at the New Year as a ritual (see
n. 391).

568 *Toshōsan* is a compound of herbs put into
sake and drunk to ward off certain illnesses. It
contained a wild pepper, a bitter herb, *bōfū*, *kikyō*
(campanula), dried ginger, *byakujutsu* (*Atractylis
ovata*) and cassia root or bark for a bitter brew.
Dainihon kokugo jiten.

569 *Toso*, spices and herbs used in the sake for
New Year's which was believed to promote health
and longevity. Nowadays *toso* is used to mean
the sake steeped in these herbs. See U.A. Casal,
The Five Sacred Festivals, pp. 19–20.

570 *Bōfū*, *Siler divaricatum.*

571 *Koganebana* or *ōgon*, 'flower of gold',
Scutellaria baicalensis George.

572 *Kakumagusa* or *ōren* is *Coctis japonica*
Makino.

1 *bu* of *kurokusa*,[573] 15 *ryō* of forsythia, 11 *ryō* 2 *bu* of *hakushimu*,[574] 4 *ryō* 1 *bu* of thistle, 9 *kin* 15 *ryō* of aconite, 7 *ryō* 2 *bu* of dried ginger, 64 *kin* 8 *ryō* of fat of wild boar, 7 *kin* 10 *ryō* 2 *bu* of *okera*,[575] 14 *kin* 4 *ryō* of aconite,[576] 2 *ryō* 2 *bu* of *hosogumi*,[577] 9 *kin* 5 *ryō* 2 *bu* of campanula, 7 *kin* 14 *ryō* of wild ginger root, 1 *kin* 6 *ryō* of Chinese ginger, 2 *ryō* 2 *bu* of iris root, 2 *ryō* 2 *bu* of fungus, 2 *kin* 2 *bu* of *saru-hajikami*,[578] 2 *ryō* of peach kernels, 12 *ryō* 1 *bu* 2 *shu* of thorny-lime fruits, 2 *ryō* 1 *bu* of shadflower, 2 *ryō* 3 *bu* 2 *shu* of apricot kernels, 2 *bu* 2 *shu* of magnolia bark, 120 gardenia seeds, 11 *ryō* 2 *shu* of bugbane, 2 *bu* of dried indigo plant, 1 *gō* 1 *shaku* of fermented bean sauce, 2 *kin* 1 *bu* of angelica, 2 *kin* 1 *bu* of angelica *(dahurica)*,[579] 4 *ryō* 2 *bu* of *yamazeri*,[580] 1 *kin* 1 *bu* of *sakutaku*,[581] 4 *ryō* 1 *bu* of pokeweed, 3 *kin* 5 *ryō* of *insō*,[582] 4 *ryō* 1 *bu* of *kibanaōgi*,[583] 4 *ryō* 1 *bu* of tree peony, 4 *ryō* 1 *bu* of burnet, 5 *ryō* 1 *bu* of euphorbia, 3 *ryō* 3 *bu* of scrophularia, 3 *ryō* 1 *bu* of anemone, 9 *ryō* 1 *bu* of azalea, 1 *ryō* 1 *bu* of wild persimmon,* 2 *to* 5 *shō* of vinegar, 1 whetstone, 9 *shaku* 6 *sun* of lined silk, 9 *shaku* 6 *sun* of oiled pongee, 4 *jō* 1 *shaku* of plain silk, 1 *jō* 5 *sun* of scarlet silk, 8 *shaku* of stiff silk, 3 *shaku* of thin silk, 3 *jō* 5 *shaku* of plain cloth, 2 *ryō* of silk thread, 7 *ryō* of bark-cloth, 84 sheets of paper (the foregoing supplied by the Bureau), 4 each of *sue* ware jars and chopping bowls, 1 *sue* hand-basin, 2 *sue* bowls, 2 plates (foregoing supplied by Mino Province), 2 boxes, 2 tables, 1 split-cypress-wood chest, 1 white-wood chest, 1 great table, 1 thread box, 1 dipper, 1 large box (foregoing supplied by this province), 1 knife for cutting herbs, 1 iron mortar, 1 pestle, 1 copper pot, 1 copper measure (from the knife on are for permanent use), 1 *hiki* of stiff silk for the lustrous robe to be worn while compounding drugs, 2 *mochi* of floss silk (for permanent use), 2 *jō* of tribute cloth (to be used fresh). When the *toso* is supplied for New Year's the noblewomen and their attendants partake of it; 10 *hiki* of plain silk for clothing for children and on up, 20 *mochi* of floss silk (the color of the silk to be that of the vital principle of the Consecrated Princess). (The foregoing all provided by the Bureau.)

The above are requested by the Office of Medicine Makers.[584]

2 *jō* 7 *shaku* 6 *sun* each of scarlet silk, violet silk and oiled pongee, 30 *kin* of hemp (foregoing provided by the Bureau).

The above are requested by the Office of Equerries.[585]

---

* [Here ends the list of pharmacopoeia.]

573 *Kurokusa* or *rōro, Echinops latifolius* Tausch.

574 *Hakushimu* or *byakuren, Ampelopsis japonica* Makino.

575 *Okera* or *byakujutsu* (see n. 568), *Atractylodes japonica* Koidzumi.

576 Two terms are given which mean aconite, so possibly one is intended for the herb and the other the root. Or, they are two different varieties.

577 *Hosogumi* or *hange, Pinellia ternata* Breitenbach.

578 *Saruhajikami*, a pepper, *Polypodium vulgare.*

579 *Zenkō* or *sengo ;* the first may be *angelica*

decursiva, and the second *dahurica*. (See list, Appendix VII.)

580 *Yamazeri* or *tōki, Ligusticum acutilobum* Siebold et Zuccharini.

581 *Sakutaku* or *sakuteki*, a wild plant resembling the elder tree, the dried juice of which is used as a diuretic and diaphoretic. (Morohashi, *Daikanwa-jiten.*)

582 *Insō* or *minogome, Glyceria acutiflora* Torr. (?)

583 *Kibanaōgi, Astralagus membranaceus* Bunge.

584 The *kusuri-be-no-tsukasa* 藥部司.

585 The *mebu-no-tsukasa* 馬部司 of the Bureau.

At all times, requirements for each month and for each season for the Conse-crated Princess are the same as when she is in the Capital. Officials of the [*Jingi-*]*kan* include 26 persons of 4th official class and above, 101 watchmen, 1 noblewoman, 3 wet-nurses, 39 girl attendants, 2 privy attendants, 2 bath attendants (for each person: 2 *shō* of rice, 2 *shaku* of salt), 15 menservants, 25 servants on horseback, 8 grooms (servants from the Deity Districts and from among *kambe* are used), 8 sweepers (for each person: 2 *shō* of rice and 2 *shaku* of salt), 10 maidservants, 273 persons in her retinue (for each person: 1.5 *shō* of rice and 1.5 *shaku* of salt), 1 diviner's assistant, 2 girls to kindle fires (for each child: 1.4 *shō* of rice, 1.4 *shaku* of salt), 4 persons from the chief diviners and *urabe* (for each: 1.5 *shō* of rice, 1.5 *shaku* of salt).

Every New Year's Day the Consecrated Imperial Princess makes distant obei-sance to the Shrine of the Great Deity. When that is done, the south gate of her palace is opened and from outside the gate the Chief and all under him respectfully congratulate the Princess. The method of emoluments is thus: for the Chief, 4 *hiki* of stiff silk, 20 *mochi* of floss silk, for the Assistant Chief, 2 *hiki* of stiff silk, 8 *mochi* of floss silk, for the Secretary of the Bureau, 2 *hiki* of stiff silk; for the Nakatomi, Imbe, *toneri,* treasury inspectors, chefs and chief of the gatekeepers of the *kanzukasa* each: 1 *hiki* of stiff silk, 2 *tan* of plain cloth; for the 2nd and 3rd class officials and *toneri* of the Bureau and for the chiefs of other offices, each: 1 *hiki* of stiff silk, 1 *tan* of plain cloth; for the chief diviner and 4th class officials of other offices, each: 1 *hiki* of stiff silk; for the watchmen, each 1 *tan* of plain cloth; the noblewomen receive the same as the Chief of the Bureau; those of 'Outer Ranks' receive 3 *hiki* of stiff silk, 10 *mochi* of floss silk; the wet-nurses and girl attendants of high rank, each: 2 *hiki* of stiff silk; the girl attendants of middle rank: 1 *hiki* of stiff silk; the girl attendants of lower rank, 1 *tan* of plain cloth and 1 skein of silk thread. For the rest of various ranks, each: 1 *tan* of tax cloth. To the Superintendent of the Shrine of the Great Deity, who respectfully congratulates the Princess on the 3rd day, is given one august garment; to the *negi* is given a quilt; to the Chief of the District 1 *tan* of plain cloth, to each of the *uchindo* 1 skein of silk thread. But on the 7th day the Chief of the Bureau is given 1 quilt, and on the 16th day one printed blue tunic and one pair of trousers.

At all times, when the Consecrated Princess goes to worship at the Great Shrine in the 6th month ceremonial dress is bestowed on her escorts (same in the 12th month). From 4th class officials of the offices and up each one receives 3 *jō* 5 *shaku* of stiff silk (for the officials who serve the food the cloth for trousers is added). The 6 *kambe,* 3 diviners, 8 chefs, 3 cooks, 4 brewers, 4 water-carriers, 6 accountants, 6 caretakers, 4 housekeepers, 4 sweepers, each receive 2 *jō* of plain cloth; 1 diviner's assistant gets 1.4 *jō* of plain cloth; of the 4 girls who perform the dances, each gets 1 *hiki* of stiff silk; the remainder do not receive anything.

At all times, when she participates in the festivals of the 9th month, ceremonial dress is bestowed on the noblewoman who is her escort, and on those serving her; namely, to those of 5th rank, 4 *hiki* of stiff silk and 10 *mochi* of floss silk; to those of Outer Ranks, 2 *hiki* 3 *jō* of stiff silk and 5 *mochi* of floss silk; to wet-nurses, each: 2 *hiki* 3 *jō* of stiff silk and 2 *mochi* of floss silk; to one girl attendant of high rank, 1 wet-nurse of high rank, and 23 persons of middle rank and below each: 1 *hiki* 3 *jō* of stiff silk and 2 *mochi* of floss silk. The remainder receive nothing.

At all times, when spring and autumn emoluments are given to the officials of the Bureau, deity taxes from the province are used. The summer and winter garments are given by the Bureau itself. In summer each man receives 4 *jō* 5 *shaku* of stiff silk, each woman 1 *hiki* of stiff silk, but girl attendants of middle class and below each get 3 *jō* of stiff silk, sweeping maidens and maidservants each 3 *jō* of silk and 2 *tan* of tax cloth, children who kindle the fire each get 2 *hiki* of stiff silk and 2 *jō* of tribute cloth. In winter each man receives 1 *hiki* 3 *jō* of stiff silk and 4 *mochi* of floss silk, women each 1 *hiki* of stiff silk and 2 *mochi* of floss silk, sweeping maids each get 1 *hiki* of stiff silk, 1 *tan* of plain cloth and 2 *mochi* of floss silk, children who kindle the fire each get 4 *jō* of stiff silk, 1 *tan* of plain cloth and 2 *mochi* of floss silk, maidservants each get 1 *hiki* of stiff silk, 2 *mochi* of floss silk and 1 *tan* of tax cloth; the rest, down to servants on horseback, receive 1 *tan* of tax cloth in summer, 1 *tan* of tax cloth and 2 *mochi* of floss silk in winter.

At all times, when the Consecrated Princess is in the province, in the first year 700 *soku* of regular tax rice for her august table are allotted for the year. The district each month pounds it and sends it to the Bureau. For subsequent years her supply comes from paddies which purvey,[586] of which there are 2 *chō* (1 in Take and 1 in Watarai Dist.), and 4 *chō* of additional purveying paddies (3 in Take and 1 in Iino Dist.). Of cultivated paddies[587] there are 27 *chō*, 8 *tan* 117 *bu* (17 *chō* 71 *bu* are in Take District, and 10 *chō* 8 *tan* 46 *bu* in Iino District). Besides these the rice from the purveying paddies is sent up to the Bureau as rent payment in kind and used to make up deficiencies in the august supply. The cultivated paddies according to the value of the land pay a percentage for the year to be used by the Bureau for various purposes.[588]

At all times, the various goods sent as tribute and taxes from the provinces as well as goods requested from the storehouses of the capital are accumulated and stored in the storehouses of the Bureau to be distributed for various uses. Namely, 700 *hiki* of stiff silk and pongee (300 *hiki* from Ise, 20 *hiki* of *chōken* silk from Owari, 30 *hiki* of white stiff silk from Mikawa, 150 *hiki* of stiff silk from Tōtoumi, 100 *hiki* from Suruga, 50 *hiki* from Sagami, 50 *hiki* from Mino); 300 skeins of silk thread (200 skeins as tribute from Owari, 100 skeins as tax from Tōtoumi); 1,100 *mochi* of tax floss silk (from Sagami); 1,000 *tan* of plain cloth (100 *tan* of linen from Shimōsa, 100 *tan* of tribute cloth from Hitachi, 500 *tan* from Sagami, 300 *tan* from Shimōsa); 850 *tan* of tax cloth (650 *tan* from Kazusa, 200 *tan* from Suruga); 2 *hiki* of colored hempen cloth (Hitachi); 300 *kin* of bark-cloth (262 from Izu, 38 from Tōtomi); 400 *kin* of hemp, 100 *kin* of processed hemp (Shimōsa); 8 bearskins

---

586 That is, the *kuden* 供田 which are assigned to the support of the Bureau of the Consecrated Princess.

587 Cultivated paddies are *konden* 墾田 (also called *myōden* 名田).

588 After the Yōrō Codes the land tax was referred to as *chinso—chin* 賃 being the value of the land before its cultivation, and *so* 租 the rate at

which it was taxed. The *so* on public paddies came to 20% of the rice-in-ear yield in one year, this amount being collected and forwarded to granaries in the Capital. In the present case, these are *konden* assigned to the Bureau of the Consecrated Princess *(saigū-ryō)*, to which bureau the annual *so* was paid. *Nihon rekishi daijiten.*

(Shinano); 12 tortoise shells (Shima); 30 pairs of shoes, 1,000 sheets of paper (foregoing from Ise); 228 writing brushes (100 from Ise, 100 from Owari, 28 from Mino); 3 *hiki* 3 *jō* of lined cloth, 7 *hiki* 3 *jō* of scarlet silk, 1 *jō* 7 *shaku* 6 *sun* of brocade, 8 *hiki* 1 *jō* of oiled pongee, 56 types of medicinal plants (itemized above); 600 *mochi* of white silk floss, 235 mattocks, 50 bars of iron, 8 whetstones, 19 inksticks (foregoing from Capital storehouse); 1,667.5 *koku* of *corvée* tax rice[589] (342 *koku* from Iga, 473.2 *koku* from Ise, 559.3 *koku* from Mikawa, 293 *koku* from Mino); 1,334.8 *koku* of pounded rice (534.8 from Ise, including 395 *koku* of unpolished rice, 200 *koku* from Owari, 200 *koku* from Mikawa, 400 from Mino); 10 *koku* of glutinous rice, 10 *koku* of wheat, 3.6 *koku* of millet, 6 *koku* each of soybeans and red beans, 1 *koku* of sesame seed, 1 *koku* of *mino* (foregoing from Ise); 1 *koku* of sorghum (Mikawa); 80 *koku* of salt (15 from Shima, 65 from Owari); 3 *koku* of sesame seed oil (Tōtoumi); 4.4 *to* of *hosoki* oil (Ise); 300 *kin* of Azuma abalone (from Awa); 500 *kin* of bonito (288 *kin* from Shima, 220 *kin* from Izu); 140 *kin* of boiled bonito (Suruga); 4 *to* of bonito in sauce (Izu), 3 *to* of boar lard, 120 salmon cut in strips, dried and salted (foregoing from Shinano); 2 *koku* of trout cooked in brine, 1 *koku* trout for sushi (Ise); 3 *koku* of salted carp (Oomi); 10 *kin* of dried birds-flesh (Owari); 90 *kin* of sea-bream cut in strips, salted and dried, 1.8 *koku* of sea-mussel sushi, 100 *kin* of sea-bream dried flat (foregoing from Mikawa); 5 *koku* of assorted dried meats (2 *koku* from Shima, 2 from Owari, 1 from Tōtoumi); 7 *to* of pickled abalone (Sagami); 10 *koku* of small-fish sushi (5 *koku* each from Ise and Owari); 100 *kin* of dried bêche-de-mer, 2 *koku* of sushi abalone, 344 *kin* of assorted abalone, 309 *kin* 14 *ryō* of *wakame*, 340 *kin* of codium (foregoing from Shima). 10 armloads of *mizubuki*[590] (Owari); 1 *to* of dried sweet-arrowroot[591] (Ise); 5 *to* of mustard seed (Shinano); 2 *to* of wild horseradish (Hida); 696 *sue* ware dishes (Mino); 2 *soku* of rice-in-ear per day for value of food offerings (Ise); 120 *soku* of fodder rice (Office of the Great Shrine provides this at 40 *soku* for each of the three seasonal festivals); 4,800 bales of fodder (half obtained by the Office of the Great Shrine as reaped by floating workers in the Deity Districts, half obtained by provincial Government as reaped by floating workers within the province).

Whenever the officials of the Bureau go up to the capital on public business they may ride post-horses. For those of 5th Rank, 4 horses allowed, from 8th Rank up to 5th, 3 horses, Beginning Rank and under, 2 horses (same for women officials).

On the day the Princess arrives in the province, a young boy of the Isobe Uji of Futami Village in Watarai District is chosen to divine and becomes a diviner's assistant; and a young girl from the same district is chosen to kindle the fire for the divination. But when either has to go into mourning or grows up, a change is made. When she has already served in the No-no-miya and has entered the Itsuki-no-miya, the list of the various functionaries, maidservants and upward, is reported every month in the last ten days to the *kanzukasa*. Thereupon the omens are read for these. Again in the 6th, 9th, 11th and 12th months omens are again read for them. The indications are furnished in advance of the festivals (but divina-

589 Here *chikarashiro-yone* 庸米 is specified.
590 *Mizubuki* 茨菜, *Euryale ferox* Sieb.
591 *Amazuru-iori* or *amakazura-iori* 甘葛煎,

parched arrowroot or kudzu. For kudzu powder used as a medicine, see Schafer and Wallacker, no. 365.

tion for the festivals is not done at the No-no-miya). Officers of the Bureau and other officials, when the reading of omens is completed, form a line and go to the board with the posted lists of ranks. At this time an official of the Nakatomi calls out commands and the bamboo divining-sticks are broken and they all perform purification and cleansing. Together they give a verbal response and then retire.

Ladies-in-waiting, *uneme,* girl attendants and below remain in their places, and hear the instructions. Those who do not pass the reading of omens are forbidden to enter the palace. (They are forbidden from the inner compound of the No-no-miya, and from entering the Itsuki-no-miya.)

At all times, when the Consecrated Princess performs lustration before going to worship in a festival, the list of officials 4th class and up of the provincial government is sent to the Itsuki-no-miya to submit to divination before they arrive. One person reverently obtains the results thereof. On the 15th day of each of the three months of the festivals, the number of officials is announced (an official of 5th rank or higher who obtains the omens acts as secretary and announces the names; 6th rank and below announce themselves).

At no time may the farmers of the sustenance households of the Great Shrine directly assist the *ryō-no-toneri.*[592]

At all times, the protection of the Deity Hall in the inner compound is of chief concern to the *kanzukasa.* If any harm comes to it, they forfeit their compensation.

Whenever the builders have completed work on the buildings of the inner compound or of other offices, the officers of the Bureau go around each season to inspect them. If any official in residence has suffered harm, compensation shall be withheld. Officers of the Bureau, if they be negligent and not perform their duty in the tours of inspection, shall be subject to the rule of censure.[593] The same applies to members of the offices.

It is required that the inner courtyard be cleaned by the various officials on the last day of every month. The officers of the Bureau take turns in making inspection tours. If there has been laxity, the rule of censure is applied as above.

August food offerings are made every morning and evening. If any deficiency occurs the officers of the Bureau and the members of the Chefs' Office both are punished.

There shall always be rows of pine and willow trees planted along the moat on the four sides. This and the cleaning around the perimeter of the great fence and in the great courtyard shall be maintained by the Office of Gatekeepers. If there is any damage to the trees or any laxity in the cleaning, those officials shall be punished, again according to the above rule.

Of the 48 menservants, 6 are assigned to build the Bureau and the august kitchen. One officer of the Bureau is the chief steward of these matters. He inspects the articles prepared and in consequence of any injury must make the repairs thereof. The 3rd-class official of the Bureau receives the account book for this and if there is light injury due to misperformance or great injury due to disorderliness, then the officer who is chief steward is removed from his post. But if there is some

---

592 This seems to be a provision against graft whereby noblemen of *toneri* class may not collect private income locally.

593 The *kenseki no hō* 譴責之法.

unusual, extraordinary damage, he may plead for disposition of his case.

At all times, the regulations for the various articles presented within the Bureau, whether left over or not yet used, require that they be entered in a seasonal account book and at the beginning of each of the four seasons a messenger is sent up to report to the *Jingi-kan*. However, the seasonal account books of the officials under the jurisdiction of the Bureau are examined by the officers of the Bureau, stamped with its seal, and sent up.

The monthly compensation of the male and female members of the various offices and the clothing allotments for the functionaries, according to the amounts forwarded by this province and the other provinces, without fixing upward or downward, are distributed at regular intervals. First, however, to the female officials and then to the male officials.

There are always 8 august horses from the Office of Equerries whose annual requirement of fodder rice and of hay does not have to be moved to the Bureau but is presented to the Office of Equerries, and is rationed daily as needed. However, the account book is inspected each season and the seal of the Bureau stamped upon it.

At all times, on the day of purification[594] for the Festival of First-fruits the Superintendent of the Great Shrine leads the *negi*, the *uchindo*, the supervisors of the tables of the august kitchen, officials of the three Deity Districts, the *kambe*, the singers, and so forth, to assemble for worship. The feast and emoluments are bestowed on each of them in order. (The Chief of the Bureau and those under him also bestow emoluments.)

The various functionaries and those supervising them who always have contact with outside people must perform higher purification.[595]

At any time that the officials of the Bureau, of the various offices or of the palace of the princess practices a Buddhist rite, has an illicit relation, or marries secretly, that person must perform middle purification.

If at any time within the enclosure someone suffers the defilement of letting the fire go out, persons of that building as a consequence must be cleansed and purified and may not enter the palace of the Princess for 7 days.

At all times, when there is a change in succession of Consecrated Princess and she returns to the capital, a messenger is sent ahead to present offerings, as is done in the beginning of her term. If the messenger encounters mourning or the death of parents in the province, he sends one Nakatomi to inform of the situation and the offerings are not presented.

At all times, when the Consecrated Princess does return to the Capital she takes the seal of her Bureau to Yamashiro Province and causes it to be presented. (After the Bureau entrusts it to that Office, it asks for its use.) The seal of the *kanzukasa* and the official documents of the different heads all are presented to the *Jingi-kan* and prepared for later inspection.

At all times, when the Consecrated Princess returns to the Capital (if she is returning owing to some cause[596] she does not use the route which she took in the

594 *Harae-kiyomi* 祓清.
595 There were three different degrees of

purification *(harae)*—great, middle and small, as well as 'high'.

beginning), a delegation is sent to meet her respectfully; one person of the 5th and one of the 6th Rank, reverently await her at the boundary between Oomi and Ise Provinces. One Secretary, leading one scribe and one office-keeper, comes to meet the Consecrated Princess to supervise her return back home.[597] The officers of the Bureau have the sacred garments of the Princess and such things as her palanquin sent by messengers [since] she changes everything when she is at the provincial border. (Her clothing and such is given to the Imbe; the palanquin and such are given to the Nakatomi, and each one of these gets an august horse with saddle.) The temporary shrines and the provisions for them are the same as on her journey down to the province.

At all times, when the Consecrated Princess returns to the Capital, she leaves behind a variety of things. These are distributed to the officials of her Bureau and those under them and to the farmers in proximity to her palace. The furnishings of her sleeping quarters are given to the Imbe and the furnishings of her reception hall are given to the Nakatomi; but the gold and silver vessels and utensils are presented to the family of the Consecrated Princess. Moreover, the curtains and hangings, the stoves, brewing jars and such, that are for permanent use, are all given to the care of the government of the province.

*   *   *   *   *

End of Book Five of the *Engi-shiki*
   Enchō 5th Year, 12th Month, 26th Day
    [same signatures as at end of Book One]

---

596 That is, if she returns without finishing her term of office, owing to the death of a parent, illness, an indiscretion, or whatever.

597 'Supervise' does not give the meaning implicit in *kengyō* 檢校, which signified that at the time of changes of office (as here the princess is going out of office) officials from another bureau would step in to help with the extra duties involved. Regulations for these changes are spelled out in the *kōtai-shiki*, 'procedures for change of office'. But the *Engi-kōtai-shiki* do not include procedures for the *saigū-ryō*. Cf. *Kokushi taikei*, 1904 ed., XIII, pp. 63 ff. See n. 102 above.

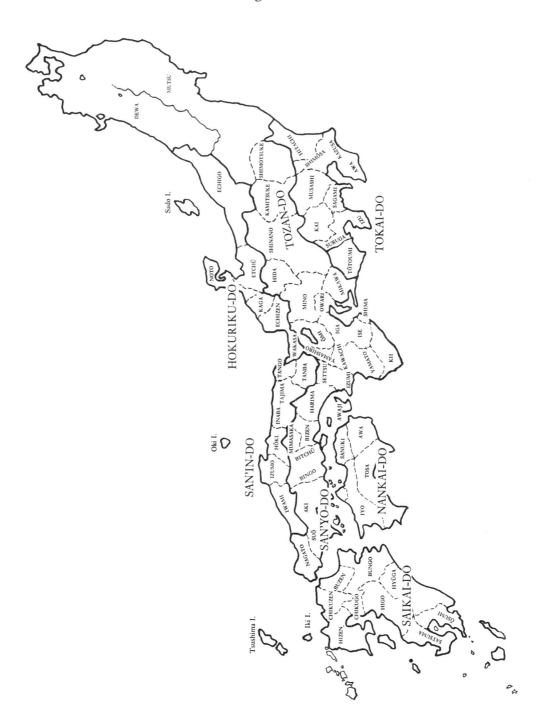

Plate II Map showing the Provinces and Circuits in the time of the *Engi-shiki*

TABLE OF MEASUREMENTS

I MEASURE OF LENGTH (for cloth, etc.):

    1 *bu* 分　　= 0.15 inch

    10 *bu* 分　　= 1 *sun*　　= 1.5 in.

    10 *sun* 寸　= 1 *shaku* = 1.243 ft.

    10 *shaku* 尺 = 1 *jō* 丈　= 4.14 yds.

    1 *tan* 反 or 段 = varies from 2 *jō* 8 *shaku* up to 4 *jō*, according to textile type

    1 *hiki* 疋 or 匹 = 2 *tan* (50 to 80 *shaku*)

    1 *ryō* 兩　= 1 *hiki* or 2 *tan* ('a double')

II CAPACITY:

    1 *tsubu* (or *ka*) 顆　= a grain (of rice, cereal, etc.)

    1 *satsu* 撮　　　　= a pinch (0.0048 oz.)

    10 *satsu*　　　　= 1 *sai*　(0.048 oz.)

    10 *sai* 才　　　　= 1 *shaku*　　　= 0.03 pint

    10 *shaku* 勺　　= 1 *gō*　　　　= 0.3 pint

    10 *gō* 合　　　= 1 *shō*　　　= 3.18 pints

    10 *shō* 升　　　= 1 *to*　　　　= *c.* 4 gals.

    10 *to* 斗　　　= 1 *koku* 石 or 斛 = *c.* 4.9 bushels

    1 *wa* (or *taba*) 把　= 'a bundle'

    1 *soku* (or *tsuka*) 束 = 10 *wa* (except in 'small tax', when it equals one *wa*)

    1 *hyō* 俵, a bale　　= 4 *to*

  Variables:

    1 *tan* 擔 'a burden'

    1 *i* 圍 'an armload'

    1 *kago* 籠 'basketful'

III WEIGHT:

    12 *bu* 分　= 1 *shu*

    24 *shu* 銖　= 1 *ryō*

    16 *ryō* 兩　= 1 *kin* 斤　= 1.32 lbs.

    1 *mochi* (or *ton*) 屯　　= 10 *ryō* (*c.* 13 oz.)

                  Wamyōshō says: 6 *ryō* (*c.* 7.8 oz.) = 1 *mochi*

    1 *ko* 絇　= 1 skein of thread:

          fine thread, 1 *ko* = 4 *ryō*

          medium thread, 1 *ko* = 5 *ryō*

          coarse thread, 1 *ko* = 7 *ryō*

IV LINEAR MEASURE:

    1 *chō* 町　= 60 *ken* 間　(*c.* 119 yds.)

    1 *ri* 里　= 36 *chō* 町　(*c.* 2.44 miles)

V AREA:

    1 *tan* 段 or 端 = 9.9 ares; 0.24 acre

    1 *chō* 町　= 10 *tan* or 3,000 *tsubo* (*c.* 2.45 acres)

VI COINAGE:

    1 *mon* 文　= a copper coin

    1 *kan* 貫　= 1,000 *mon* = 'a string of cash'

APPENDIX I

CONTENTS OF THE *ENGI-SHIKI*

(1) Memorial Presenting *Engi kyaku* and *shiki* to the Throne
(2) Preface to the *Engi-shiki*
Book (巻)

I	Jingi I: Festivals of Four Seasons (A)
II	Jingi II: Festivals of Four Seasons (B)
III	Jingi III: Extraordinary Festivals
IV	Jingi IV: The Shrine of the Great Deity in Ise
V	Jingi V: Bureau of the Consecrated Imperial Princess
VI	Jingi VI: The Office of the Princess Consecrated to the Kamo Shrines
VII	Jingi VII: Great New Food Festival for the Enthronement
VIII	Jingi VIII: Rituals *(Norito)*
IX	Jingi IX: Register of Deities (A)
X	Jingi X: Register of Deities (B)
XI	The Great Council of State *(Dajō-kan)*
XII	The Ministry of Central Affairs *(Nakatsukasa-shō)*
XIII	Office of the Middle Palace *(Chūgū-shiki)*
XIV	Bureau of Needlework
XV	Bureau of Palace Storehouses
XVI	Bureau of Divination
XVII	Bureau of Skilled Artisans
XVIII	Ministry of Ceremonial *(Shikibu-shō)* (A)
XIX	Ministry of Ceremonial (B)
XX	Bureau of Higher Education
XXI	Ministry of Civil Administration *(Jibu-shō)*
XXII	and XXIII: Ministry of People's Affairs (A) and (B) *(Mimbu-shō)*
XXIV	and XXV: Bureau of Census
XXVI	and XXVII: Bureau of Taxation
XXVIII	Ministry of War *(Hyōbu-shō)*
XXIX	Ministry of Justice *(Gyōbu-shō)*
XXX	Ministry of the Treasury *(Ookura-shō)*
XXXI	Ministry of the Imperial Household *(Kunai-shō)*
XXXII	and XXXIII: Office of the Palace Table (A) and (B)
XXXIV	Bureau of Carpentry
XXXV	Bureau of the Palace Kitchen
XXXVI	Bureau of Palace Caretakers
XXXVII	Bureau of Medicines
XXXVIII	Bureau of Housekeeping
XXXIX	Offices of the Imperial Family and Emperor's Table
XL	Offices of Sake, of *Uneme* and of Water
XLI	Board of Police
XLII	Left and Right Offices of the Capital
XLIII	The Quarters of the Heir Apparent
XLIV	Investigators of Outgoing Officials
XLV	Left and Right Divisions of the Inner Palace Guards
XLVI	Left and Right Divisions of the Outer Palace Guards
XLVII	Left and Right Divisions of the Middle Palace Guards

XLVIII   Left and Right Mount Bureaus
  XLIX   Bureau of Military Storehouses
     L   Miscellaneous Procedures

APPENDIX II
THE TWENTY-ONE ITEMS
OF BOOK ONE OF THE *ENGI-SHIKI*

after E. Miyagi, *Engi-shiki no kenkyū*

 1 Great, Middle and Small Festival Celebrations
 2 Days of Festivals
 3 Toshigoi Festival
 4 Kasuga Festival
 5 Ooharano Festival
 6 Sono and Kara Festivals
 7 Hiraoka Festival
 8 Hanashizume Festival
 9 Oomi Festival
10 Kaze-no-kami Festival
11 Hirano Festival
12 Miagamono (Thank Offerings)
13 Divining the August Person (of the Sovereign)
14 Tsukinami Festival
15 Jinkonjiki (Deity Food Ritual)
16 Ootono-hogai (Blessing the Palace)
17 Ooharae (Great Purification)
18 Miagamono (Thank Offerings) [after the Purification]
19 Miagamono in the Middle Palace
20 Hoshizume Festival (Fire Propitiation)
21 Michiae Festival (Banquet of the Roads)

APPENDIX III
THE EIGHT ITEMS
OF BOOK TWO OF THE *ENGI-SHIKI*

after E. Miyagi, *Engi-shiki no kenkyū*

 1 The Kanname Festival of Ise
 2 The Ainame Festival
 3 Mitamashizume Festival *(Chinkon-sai)*
 4 Niiname Festival (First Fruits Festival)
 5 Festival to the Sacred Fire and Courtyard Fires on the First Day (of each Month)
 6 Symbolic Offerings on the Last Day of the Month
 7 Symbolic Offerings for the Middle Palace
 8 Miagamono (Thank Offerings) on the Last Day of each Month

APPENDIX IV
THE THIRTY-FOUR ITEMS
OF BOOK THREE OF THE *ENGI-SHIKI*

after E. Miyagi, *Engi-shiki no kenkyū*

1 Propitiation of Ground for a new Palace
2 Festival for the Yasoshima Deities
3 Yasoshima Deities in the Heir Apparent's Palace
4 Propitiation of Deities of Epidemics at the Four Corners of the Palace
5 To the Deities of Epidemics at the Boundaries of the Inner Provinces
6 Amagoi Festival
7 Festivals to the Myōjin (Principal Deities)
8 Despatching Envoys to a Foreign Country
9 Congratulatory Gifts
10 Laudatory Ritual to the Deities
11 Recitation of the Laudatory Ritual at Daybreak
12 The Recorders of Yamato and Kawachi
13 Chief Diviner and Urabe (Diviners)
14 Sacred Maidens
15 Superintendents and Chief Priests who encounter Mourning
16 Avoidance of Defilement
17 Mourning
18 Reburial and Miscarriage
19 Partial and Total Abstinence
20 Pregnancy and Menstruation
21 Death of a Young Child
22 Contact with Defilement
23 Defilement of an Official
24 Contact with Fire
25 Register and Accounts of Deity Taxes
26 Repairs to Shrines
27 Shrine Precincts
28 Tribute and Corvée Taxes from Kambe
29 Various Bows for Festival Offerings
30 Court Dress for Musicians of Katori Shrine
31 Emoluments for Personnel of the Jingi-kan
32 The Yawata Jingū
33 If Negi Quarrel
34 Correspondence of Ranks for Shrine Superintendents and Negi

APPENDIX V
THE THIRTY-EIGHT ITEMS
OF BOOK FOUR OF THE *ENGI-SHIKI*

after E. Miyagi, *Engi-shiki no kenkyū*

   1 Shrine of the Great Deity; its separate shrines; staff
   2 Shrine of Toyouke-no-ōkami; its separate shrines; staff
   3 On who are *negi, uchindo* and *mono-imi*
   4 The auxiliary minor shrines
   5 Celebration of the First Day of the New Year
   6 The Toshigoi Festival (Prayers of the New Year)
   7 The Kammiso Festival (Offerings of Deity Raiment)
   8 Purification before the Kammiso Festival
   9 The Tsukinami Festival (in the 6th and 12th months)
 10 The Kanname Festival at both Great Shrines
 11 Requirements for Purification at Festivals of 3 Seasons
 12 Yearly Requirements for presenting Sacred Food Offerings
 13 *Hinomi* (Prayers to Sun and Wind by the *hinomi uchindo*)
 14 Handles for the tools used in cultivating Deity Paddies
 15 The Construction of the Shrines
 16 The Re-building at Twenty-Year Intervals
*17 Envoys who conduct the making of Sacred Treasures and Ceremonial Articles for the Shrines
 18 The Twenty-one Sacred Treasures
 19 Ceremonial Articles for the Shrines
*20 Ceremonial Articles for the Shrine Removal Ceremonies
 21 Guard Duty
 22 Sacred Horses
 23 Utensils and Fuel
*24 Repair of Buildings
 25 On Who may present Offerings
 26 Requirements for Purification
*27 Messenger who presents offerings from the Imperial Court
*28 Superintendent of the Shrines
*29 Annual Stipend of the Superintendent
 30 Rice Allowance for Petitioners *(negi)*
 31 Emoluments at the Festivals of Three Seasons
*32 Tribute, Commuted Taxes and Rice Tax *(chō, yō* and *so)*
*33 Deity Households *(shinko* or *kambe)*
*34 Honorable Dismissal Document of the Superintendent of the Shrines
*35 Buildings of the Bureau (of the Consecrated Princess)
 36 Articles offered at Festivals
 37 Deity Paddies *(shinden* or *jinden)*
*38 Sustenance Households *(fugo)*

(cf. Miyagi, I, Appendix, 3.)

* Indicates item introduced in Book IV and not covered in the *Gishiki-chō*.

APPENDIX VI
THE TWENTY ITEMS
OF BOOK FIVE OF THE *ENGI-SHIKI*

after E. Miyagi, *Engi-shiki no kenkyū*
Saigūryō-shiki

1 Appointment of a Princess
2 Requirements for Purification
3 Purification and Lustration
4 Taboo Words
5 Lustration at the River
6 Procedure at Termination of Purification
7 Leaving the No-no-miya
8 Envoy for the Great Purification
9 Taboos in Oomi and Ise Provinces
10 Temporary Shrines along the Route to Ise
11 Farewell Envoys
12 Beginning of the Term of Service
13 Lustration for the Festivals of Three Seasons
14 Supplies for the Year (includes list of medicinals)
15 First Day of the New Year
16 Various Articles of Tribute and Commuted Taxes
17 Outside Contact
18 Secret Marriage
19 Succession of the Consecrated Princess
20 Messengers to Meet the Returning Princess

(cf. Miyagi, I, Appendix, 4)

APPENDIX VII
LIST OF MEDICINALS
IN BOOK FIVE OF THE *ENGI-SHIKI*

NO.*	CHAR.**	JAPANESE NAMES	WESTERN NAMES
2	七氣丸	*shichiki-gan*	a compound, 'seven vapors'
62	商陸	*shōriku;* or *yamagobō*	*Phytolacca esculenta* Van Houtte; pokeweed
26	人参	*ninjin*	ginseng
58	前胡	*zenkō; sengo*	*Peucedanum decursivum* Maximowicz; *Angelica decursiva* Franche et Sav.
42	半夏	*hosogumi; hange*	*Pinellia ternata* Breitenbach
55	升麻	*torinoashigusa* or *shōma*	*Cimicifuga simplex* Worusk; bugbane
9	升麻膏	*shōma-kō*	ointment of the foregoing
53	厚朴	*kōboku*	*Magnolia officinalis;* magnolia bark
45	吳茱萸	*kara-hajikami*	*Zingiber officinale;* ginger
3	吳茱萸丸	*kara-hajikami-gan*	compound of the foregoing
1	四味理中丸	*shimirichū-gan*	a compound
66	地楡	*jiyū; waremokō*	*Sanguisorba carnea* Fischery; lesser burnet
67	大戟	*daigeki*	*Euphorbia pekinensis* Ruprecht
25	大黃	*daiō; ōshi*	*Rheum officinale;* rhubarb
17	犀角	*saikaku*	rhinoceros horn
6	犀角丸	*saikaku-gan*	compound of the foregoing
13	屠蘇	*toso*	herbs for New Year's sake
15	巴豆	*hatō; hazu*	*Croton tiglium* L.; croton-oil seeds
38	干薑	*kanshō*	dried ginger-root
56	干藍	*kanran*	*Cymbidium kanran* Makino
12	度嶂散	*toshōsan*	compound of spices and herbs
54	支子	*kuchinashi*	*Gardenia jasminoides;* gardenia seeds
52	杏仁	*kyōnin*	apricot kernel
50	枳實	*kijitsu; karatachi*	*Citrus trifoliata;* 'thorny-lime fruits'
49	桃仁	*tōnin*	peach kernel
14	桂心	*keishin*	cinnamon; cassia bud.
43	桔梗	*kikyō*	*Platycodon glaucum* Nakai; campanula
5	温白丸	*ombyaku-gan*	a compound
33	漏蘆	*rōro; kurokusa*	*Echinops latifolius* Tausch; globethistle
41	烏頭	*torikabuto; uzu*	aconite; aconite root
65	牡丹	*fukamigusa; botan*	*Paeonia moutan;* Moutan tree; tree peony
39	猪膏	*chōkō*	fat of wild boar
68	玄参	*gomanohagusa; oshigusa; genjin*	*Scrofularia oldhami* Oliver
16	甘草	*kansō*	*Glycyrrhiza glabra* L.; licorice
60	當歸	*tōki; yamazeri*	*Ligustum acutilobum* Siebold et Zucc., or *Angelica acutiloba* Kitagawa
40	白朮	*byakujutsu; okera*	*Atractylodes japonica* Koidzumi

* Number in order of appearance in the list.
** *Kanji* in stroke order.

59	白芷	*byakushi ; yoroigusa*	*Angelica dahurica* Bentham et Hooker
35	白蘞	*byakuren ; hakushimu*	*Ampelopsis japonica* Makino; a vine; blue-berry climber
69	白頭	*okinagusa*	*Anemone pulsatilla ; Pulsatilla cernua* Sprengel; European pasque flower
31	皂莢	*saikachi ; sōkyō*	*Gleditschia horrida* Schneider; locust
23	石膏	*sekkō*	gypsum [CaSo$_4$.2H$_2$O]
11	神明白散	*shimmei-byakusan*	'Deity-bright spices and herbs'
7	神名膏	*shimmei-kō*	'Deity-bright ointment'
44	細辛	*saishin*	root of *Asarum* Sieb.
27	紫菀	*shion*	*Aster tartaricus* L.; aster or daisy
32	芍藥	*shakuyaku ; ebisugusuri*	*Paeonia albiflora ;* herbaceous peony
4	芍藥丸	*shakuyaku-gan*	compound of the foregoing
19	芒硝	*bōshō*	Epsom salts [MgSO$_4$]
24	芎藭	*onnakazura ; hajikami*	*Conioselinum univittatum ;* hemlock parsley
63	茵草	*insō ; minogome*	*Glyceria acutiflora* Torr.
47	茯苓	*matsuhodo ; bukuryō*	*Pinus densiflora* Sieb. et Zucc., or *Poria cocos* Wolf
28	茈胡	*ama-akana*	bupleurum
46	菖蒲	*ayamegusa ; shōbu*	*Iris japonica ;* sweet flag (root of)
71	蒪葵	*uguisu no sarugaki*	*Diospyros lotus ;* wild persimmon
8	萬病膏	*mambyōkō*	'panacea ointment'
51	葶藶子	*teirizu*	seeds of shadflower
61	蒴藋	*sakutaku ; sakuteki*	wild plant resembling the elder-tree, the dried sap used as diuretic
36	蘆茹	*azami*	thistle
22	蛇銜	*ōhebi-ichigo*	*Potentilla recta ;* wild strawberry
48	蜀椒	*saruhajikami*	*Polypodium vulgare*
18	蜜	*mitsu*	honey
57	豉	*kuki ; miso*	miso; fermented bean paste
10	賊風膏	*zokufukō*	an ointment
70	躑躅花	*tsutsujibana*	flower of azalea
34	連翹	*rengyō ; itachigusa*	*Rangium suspensum* Ohwi; or *Forsythia suspensa*
20	防風	*bōfū*	*Siler divericatum ;* one of the herbs in *byakusan*
37	附子	*bushi ; torikabuto*	aconite; aconite root; 'monkshood'
21	麻黄	*maō*	*Ephedra sinica* Stapf.
29	黄芩	*ōgon ; koganebana*	*Scutellaria baicalensis* George
64	黄耆	*ōki ; kibanaōgi*	*Astralagus membranaceus* Bunge
30	黄連	*ōren ; kakumagusa*	*Coptis japonica* Makino; golden thread

APPENDIX VIII
RECORD OF PRINCESSES
CONSECRATED TO SERVICE AT ISE
(*Saigū-ki* 齋宮記)

REIGN OF SOVEREIGN	NAME OF PRINCESS	DAUGHTER OF:	YEAR APPOINTED	NO. OF YEARS IN OFFICE
Sujin	1[1] *Toyosuki-iri-hime no Mikoto* 豐鋤入姫命	Sujin		
Suinin	2 *Yamato-hime no Mikoto* 倭姫命	Suinin		
Keikō	3 *Ionu* 五百野 (*Kusuhime no Mikoto* 久須姫命)	Keikō		
Chūai	4 *Iwashima* 伊和志眞	Chūai (granddaughter of Oojin)		
Yūryaku	5 *Wakatarashi-hime* 稚足姫 *or Shirakami* 白髪 *or Takuhata-hime* 栲幡姫	Yūryaku		
Keitai	6 *Sasage-hime* 荳角姫	Keitai		
Kimmei	7 *Iwakuma* 盤隈	Kimmei		
	8 *Miyako* 宮子	Dai-kannushi Ogoto		29
Bitatsu	9 *Uji* 菟道	Bitatsu		
Yōmei	10 *Sugate-hime* 酢香手姫	Yōmei		37
Temmu	11 *O'oku* 大來	Tenchi		
Mommu	12 *Takiko*[2] 多基子	Temmu		
Mommu	13 *Abe* 阿閇	Temmu		
Mommu	14 *Taki* 當耆	Temmu		
Mommu	15 *Izumi* 泉	Tenchi	701	
Mommu	16 *Tagata* 田形	Mommu	706	
Mommu	17 *Taki* 多紀	Mommu	703	
Gemmyō	*Chinu* 智努	Temmu		
Gemmyō	*Madokata* 圓方	Prince Nagaya		
Genshō	18 *Kuse* 久勢	Empress Genshō	717	6
Shōmu	19 *Inoe* 井上	Shōmu	727	21
Shōmu	20 *Agata* 縣	Shōmu	746	18
Kōken	21 *Koyake* 小宅	Empress Kōken (or Prince Miharu)	750	7
Junnin	22 *Abe* 安陪	Junnin	761	
Kōnin	23 *Sakahito* 酒人	Empress Shōtoku (Kōken)	774	2
Kōnin	24 *Gosen* 御遷 (*or Kiyoniwa* 淨庭)	Kōnin	775	8
Kammu	25 *Asahara* 朝原	Kammu	782	12
Kammu	26 *Fuse* 布勢	Kōnin	797	7
Heijō	27 *Oohara* 大原	Heijō	808	2

[1] The numbered list is taken from *Gunsho ruijū*, Tokyo, 1904, III, pp. 1–3. Other information is supplied from *Shintō daijiten*, II, article on 'Saigū', and Itsue Takamure, *Dainihon josei jimmei jisho*.

[2] As there are three princesses by the name of Taki during Mommu's reign, it seems possible there is some confusion due to inaccurate records.

REIGN OF SOVEREIGN	NAME OF PRINCESS	DAUGHTER OF:	YEAR APPOINTED	NO. OF YEARS IN OFFICE
Saga	28 *Uchi* 有智 (*or Jinshi* 仁子)	Saga	810	13
Junna	29 *Ujiko* 氏子	Junna	824	2
Junna	30 *Gishi* 宜子	Prince Nakano (granddaughter of Kammu)	829	4
Nimmyō	31 *Hisako* 久子	Nimmyō	834	14
Montoku	32 *Yasuko* 晏子	Montoku	851	6
Seiwa	33 *Tenshi* 恬子	Montoku	859	15
Yōzei	34 *Shokushi* 識子	Seiwa	877	2
Yōzei	35 *Keishi* 掲子	Montoku	(retired from No-no-miya)	
Kōkō	36 *Shigeko* 繁子	Kōkō	886	2
Uda	37 *Genshi* 元子	Prince Motoyasu	889	6
Daigo	38 *Jūshi* 柔子	Uda	897	34
Sujaku	39 *Masako* 雅子 (*called Rokujō Saigū*)*	Engi (Daigo)	933	3
Sujaku	40 *Nariko* 齊子	Engi (Daigo)		
Sujaku	41 *Kishi* 徽子	Prince Shigeakira (granddaughter of Daigo)	946	8
Murakami	42 *Hideko* 英子	Engi (Daigo)		
Murakami	43 *Tabiko* 旅子 (*earlier name: Etsushi* 悦子)	Prince Shigeakira	949	7
Murakami	44 *Rakushi* 樂子	Murakami	956	10
Reizei	45 *Hoshi* 輔子	Murakami	969 (did not progress to Ise)	
En'yū	46 *Takako* 隆子	Prince Shōmei (granddaughter of Daigo)	971	3
En'yū	47 *Noriko* 規子	Murakami	974	7
Hanayama	48 *Seishi* 濟子	Prince Shōmei	986 (did not progress)	
Ichijō	49 *Kyōshi* 恭子	Prince Tamehira	986	23
Sanjō	50 *Masako* 當子	Sanjō-in	1012	2
Go-Ichijō	51 *Senshi* 婥子	Prince Tomohira (granddaughter of Murakami)	1018	18
Go-Sujaku	52 *Yoshiko* 良子	Go-Sujaku	1036	7
Go-Reizei	53 *Yoshiko* 嘉子	Go-Ichijo-hō	1047	3
Go-Reizei	54 *Keishi* 敬子	Prince Atsuhira	1049	15
Go-Sanjō	55 *Toshiko* 俊子 (*called Higuchi Saigū* 樋口齋宮)	Go-Sanjō	1070	2
Shirakawa	56 *Junshi* 淳子	Prince Atsuyori	1076	3
Shirakawa	57 *Teishi* 媞子 (*called Ikuhōmon'in* 郁芳門院)	Shirakawa	1079	5
Horikawa	58 *Yoshiko* 善子	Shirakawa	1089	19
Toba	59 *Junshi* 佃子 (*called Higuchi* 樋口)	Shirakawa	1111	14
Sutoku	60 *Moriko* 守子 (*called Fushimi* 伏見)	Prince Sukehito	1125	17
Konoe	61 *Yoshiko* 姙子	Toba	1143	7
Konoe	62 *Kishi* 喜子	Horikawa-In	1152	3
Go-Shirakawa	63 *Ryōshi* 亮子 (*called Impumon'in* 殷富門院)	Go-Shirakawa	(did not progress)	

* The canonical or posthumous names of princesses are sometimes given.

REIGN OF SOVEREIGN	NAME OF PRINCESS	DAUGHTER OF:	YEAR APPOINTED	NO. OF YEARS IN OFFICE
Nijō	64 *Yoshiko* 好子	Go-Shirakawa	1160	6
Rokujō	65 *Yasuko* 休子	Go-Shirakawa	1166	3
Takakura	66 *Atsuko* 惇子	Go-Shirakawa	1170	3
Takakura	67 *Kotoko* 功子	Takakura	(withdrew)	
Go-Toba	68 *Kiyoko* 潔子	Takakura	1187	12
Tsuchimikado	69 *Shukushi* 粛子	Go-Toba-In	1200	12
Juntoku	70 *Hiroko* 熈子	Go-Toba-In	1214	5
Go-Horikawa	71 *Rishi* 利子	Go-Takakura-In	1226	5
Shijō	72 *Akiko* 昱子	Go-Horikawa-In	1234	4
Go-Saga	73 *Gishi* 曦子 (*called Senka-mon'in* 宣華門院)	Tsuchimikado-In	1244 (did not progress)	
Kameyama	74 *Yasuko* 愷子	Go-Saga Hōō	1262	9
Go-Nijō	75 *Sōshi* 奨子 (*withdrew from No-no-miya*)	Daikakuji Hōō (Go-Uda)		
Go-Daigo	*Kanshi* 懽子	Go-Daigo	1330	
Go-Daigo	*Shōshi* 祥子	Go-Daigo	1333	

BIBLIOGRAPHY

A EDITIONS OF THE *Engi-shiki*
(All published in Tokyo, unless otherwise stated.)

Keizai-zasshi-sha 經濟雜誌社. *Kokushi-taikei* 國史大系, XIII, *Engi-shiki*, 1904.

Kōten-kōkyūsho 皇典講究所. *Kōtei Engi-shiki* 校訂延喜式, 3 vols., 1929.

Kuroita Katsumi 黑板勝美, ed. *Shintei-zōho kokushi-taikei* (2) 新訂增補國史大系, VIII, IX, X, *Engi-shiki,* 1955.

Mozume Takami 物集高見, ed. *Kōgaku-sōsho* 皇學叢書, III, *Engi-shiki,* 1927.

Ookura Kunihiko 大倉邦彥, ed. *Shinten* 神典, Yokohama, 1936.

B REFERENCE WORKS
(All published in Tokyo, unless otherwise stated.)

Dai-genkai 大言海. Ootsuki Fumihiko 大槻文彥, comp., 4 vols. and index, 1937.

Daikanwa jiten 大漢和辭典. Morohashi Tetsuji 諸橋轍次, comp., 13 vols., 1955-60.

Dai Nihon chimei jisho 大日本地名辭書. Yoshida Tōgo 吉田東伍, comp., 6 vols. and index, 1938-40.

Dai Nihon jimmei jisho 大日本神名辭書. Dai-Nihon jimmei jisho kankōkai 大日本神名辭書刊行會, comp., 1937.

Dai Nihon josei jimmei jisho 大日本女性人名辭書. Takamure Itsue 高群逸枝, 1939.

Dai Nihon kokugo jiten 大日本國語辭典. Ueda Kazutoshi 上田萬年 and Matsui Kanji 松井簡治, comp., 4 vols. and index, 1915-28.

Fūzoku-jiten 風俗辭典. Sakamoto Tarō 坂本太郎, comp., 3rd ed., 1958.

Jingi-jiten 神祇辭典. Yamakawa Keiichi 山川鵜市, comp., 1924.

Jimmei jisho 神名辭書. Meiji-jinja shiryō henshūjo 明治神社資料編集所, 1921.

(Meikai) Kogo jiten (明解) 古語辭典. Kindaichi Kyōsuke 金田一京助 and Kindaichi Haruhiko 金田一春彥, comp., 1963.

Kokushi jiten 國史辭典. Tsuji Zennosuke 辻善之助, 4 vols. only, 1940-3.

Kotoba no izumi 言泉. Ochiai Naobumi 落合直文, ed., 5 vols. and index, 1921-9.

Nihon kenchiku jii 日本建築辭彙. Nakamura Tatsutarō 中村達太郎, comp., 1937.

Nihon kodai jimmei jiten 日本古代人名辭典. Takeuchi Rizō 竹內理三, Yamada Hideo 山田英雄, and Hirano Kunio 平野邦雄, 4 vols. only, 1963.

Nihon rekishi daijiten 日本歷史人辭典, 24 vols., Kawade shobō, 1931-61.

Nihon shakai minzoku jiten 日本社會民俗辭典. Nihon shakai minzoku-gaku kyōkai 日本社會民俗學協會, comp., 4 vols., 1952-60.

Nihon shokubutsu zukan 日本植物圖鑑. Makino Tomitarō 牧野富太郎, 1929.

Norito jiten 祝詞辭典. *Uda Toshihiko* 菟田俊彥, 1963.

Shikimei daijiten 色名大辭典. Wada Mitsuzō 和田三造, comp., 1954.

Shinten sakuin 神典索引. Yokohama, 1937.

Shintō daijiten 神道大辭典. Shimonaka Misaburō 下中彌三郎, comp., 3 vols., 1937-40.

Shintō shoseki mokuroku 神道書籍目錄 (A Bibliography of Shinto, 1868-1940). Katō Genchi 加藤玄智, comp., 2nd ed. 1943.

Shōsōin hōmotsu 正倉院寶物. *Senshoku* 染織. Shōsōin Office, 1963-4.

Shōsōin yakubutsu 正倉院藥物. Asahina Hirohiko 朝比奈泰彥, comp., Osaka, 1955.

Tokusen jimmyōchō 特選神名牒. Naimushō 內務省, 1925.

Wamyō ruijūshō 倭名類聚鈔. Minamoto Shitagau 源順, comp., during Enchō (923-30). '*Wamyōshō*'

C BOOKS AND ARTICLES IN JAPANESE

Abe Takehiko 阿部武彥. 'Engi-shiki jimmyōchō no jinkakujin' 延喜式神名帳の人格神, *The Annual Reports on Cultural Science*, Faculty of Literature, Hokkaido University, 4 (March 1955), pp. 77–94.

Aida Hanji 會田範治. *Chūkai yōrōryō* 註解養老令, Tokyo, 1964.

Akiba Takashi 秋葉隆. *Chōsen fuzoku no genchi kenkyū* 朝鮮巫俗の現地研究, Tambaichi, 1950.

Aoki Norimoto 青木紀本. 'Norito-shiki no seikaku' 祝詞式の性格, *Geirin* 藝林, III, 4 (August 1952), pp. 19–35.

Ema Tsutomu 江馬務. *Nihon fukushoku-shi yō* 日本服飾史要, Kyoto, 1936.

——. *Nihon fūzoku bunka-shi* 日本風俗文化史, Tokyo, 1957.

——. *Nihon fūzoku-shi zuroku* (1) 日本風俗史圖錄, Kyoto, 1945.

——. *Shinshū yūsoku kojitsu* 新修有職故實, Kyoto, 1942.

Fujino Iwatomo 藤野岩友. *Fukei bungakuron* 巫系文學論, Tokyo, 1951.

Fujitani Toshio 藤谷俊雄 and Naoki Kōjirō 直木孝次郎. *Ise jingū* 伊勢神宮, Tokyo, 1960.

Fujiwara Fuyutsugu 藤原冬嗣. *Kōnin-kyaku-shiki-jo* 弘仁格式序, in *Zoku-zoku gunsho ruijū* 續々群書類從, series 1:1, VI (1906), pp. 482–3, Tokyo.

Gotō Shūichi 後藤守一. *Nihon fukusō-shi* 日本服裝史, Tokyo, 1943.

Hanawa Hokiichi 塙保己一, comp. *Gunsho ruijū* 群書類從, III, Tokyo, 1903.

Harada Toshiaki 原田敏明. *Nihon shūkyō kōshō-shi ron* 日本宗教交涉史論, Tokyo, 1949.

Higo Kazuo 肥後和男. 'Nara jidai ni okeru shinjubutsu no kankei' 奈良時代における神儒物の關係, *Geirin*, III, 1 (January 1952), pp. 21–37.

——. *Nihon kodai-shi* 日本古代史, Tokyo, 1948.

Honda Masaji 本田正次. *Nihon shokubutsu meii* 日本植物名彙 (*Nomina plantarum japonicarum*), Tokyo, 1963.

Imaki Jinzō 今城甚造, Kuroba Kiyotaka 黑羽清隆, and Haga Noboru 芳賀登. *Nihon bunka-shi no shōten* 日本文化史の焦點, Tokyo, 1963.

Inokuma Kaneshige 猪熊兼繁. *Kodai no fukushoku* 古代の服飾, Tokyo, 1962.

Inoue Kaoru 井上薫. *Nihon kodai no seiji to shūkyō* 日本古代の政治と宗教, Tokyo, 1961.

Inoue Mitsusada 井上光貞. *Kodai shakai* 古代社會, Tokyo, 1952.

——. *Nihon kodaishi no shomondai* 日本古代史の諸問題, Tokyo, 1949.

——. *Nihon kokka no kigen* 日本國家の起源, Tokyo, 1960.

Ishii Ryōsuke 石井良助. *Taika kaishin to Kamakura bakufu no seiritsu* 大化改新と鎌倉幕府の成立, Tokyo, 1958.

Ishio Yoshihisa 石尾芳久. *Nihon kodai-hō no kenkyū* 日本古代法の研究, Tokyo, 1959.

Jingū Shichō 神宮司廳, ed. *Daijingū-gishikikai* 大神宮儀式解, 2 vols., Gifu, 1935.

——. *Ise no jingū*. 伊勢の神宮, Tokyo, 1956.

Jingū Shichō, Kyōdōbu 教導部, *Jingū saishi gaisetsu* 神宮祭祀概說, Ise, 1965.

Kamo Saiin-ki 賀茂齋院記, in *Gunsho ruijū*, 44. III, pp. 3–9.

Kaneko Takeo 金子武雄. *Engi-shiki norito-kō* 延喜式祝詞講, Tokyo, 1951.

Kawabata Sanehide 河鰭實英. *Yūsoku kojitsu* 有職故實, Tokyo, 1960.

Kida Sadayoshi 喜田貞吉. 'Engi-shiki no zusan' 延喜式の杜撰, *Rekishi-chiri* 歷史地理, XXXIII, 3 (1919), pp. 256–61.

Kimura Kōichi 木村康一. *Nihon no yakuyō-shokubutsu* 日本の藥用植物 (Japanese Medical Plants), 2 vols., Tokyo, 1958.

——, *et al. Wakan yakumeii* 和漢藥名彙, Tokyo, 1946.

Kiyohara no Natsuno 清原夏野. *Ryō no gige* 令義解, in *Kokushi taikei*, XII (1904), pp. 1–328, Tokyo.

Kobayashi Michio 小林嚴雄. 'Jingū no saishi' 神宮の祭祀, *Mizugaki* 瑞垣, 40 (October 1958), pp. 2–5.

Kojiruien 古事類苑, (articles) 'Saigū' 齋宮, IX, pp. 681–834; 'Sai-in' 齋院; IX, pp. 1169–1240; 'Jingi-kan' 神祇官, XIV, pp. 275–368, Tokyo, 1932.

Koremune no Naomoto 惟宗直本. *Ryō no shūge* 令集解, in Mozume Takami, *Kōgaku sōsho*, II, Tokyo, 1931.

Kōtai jingū gishiki-chō 皇太神宮儀式帳, in *Gunsho ruijū*, I (1904), pp. 1–51, Tokyo.

Matsumura Takeo 松村武雄. *Nihon shinwa no kenkyū* (1) 日本神話の研究, Tokyo, 1954.

Miyagi Eishō 宮城榮昌. *Engi-shiki no kenkyū* 延喜式の研究, 2 vols., Tokyo, 1955-7.

Miyoshi Kiyoyuki 三善清行. *Iken jūni-kajō* 意見十二箇條, in *Gunsho ruijū*, XVII (1904), pp. 115–28, Tokyo.

Morita Kimio 守田公夫. *Nihon no mon'yō* 日本の文様, Tokyo, 1957.

——. *Nihon no senshoku* 日本の染織, Tokyo, 1956.

Murao Jirō 村尾次郎. *Ritsuryō-sei no kichō* 律令制の基調, Tokyo, 1959.

Muraoka Tsunetsugu 村岡典嗣. *Zoku Nihon shisō-shi no kenkyū* 續日本思想史の研究, Tokyo, 1939.

Nagashima Nobuko 永島信子. *Nihon ifuku-shi* 日本衣服史, Kyoto, 1933.

Naitō Shumpo 內藤雋輔. *Chōsen-shi kenkyū* 朝鮮史研究, Kyoto, 1961.

Nakata Kaoru 中田薫. *Kodai Nikkan kōshō-shi dampen-kō* 古代日韓交渉史斷片考, Tokyo, 1956.

Nakayama Tarō 中山太郎. *Nihon fujo-shi* 日本巫女史, Tokyo, 1930.

Naoki Kōjirō 直木孝次郎. 'Amaterasu-ō-mikami to Ise-jingū no kigen' 天照大御神と伊勢神宮の起源, in Fuji Naomiki 藤直幹, *Kodai shakai to shūkyō* 古代社會と宗教, Osaka, 1941.

——. *Jinshin no ran* 壬申の亂, Tokyo, 1961.

Nihon bunka-shi taikei 日本文化史大系, III, *Nara jidai* 奈良時代, Tokyo, 1956.

Niida Noboru 仁井田陞. *Tō-Sō hōritsu bunsho no kenkyū* 唐宋法律文書の研究, Tokyo, 1937.

Ono Hikoroku 奧野彦六. *Ritsuryō-zen Nihon kodaihō* 律令前日本古代法, Tokyo, 1961.

Oota Akira 太田亮. *Nihon jōdai shakai soshiki no kenkyū* 日本上代社會組織の研究, Tokyo, 1955.

Oyama Tokujirō 尾山篤二郎. *Saigyō hōshi meika hyōshaku* 西行法師名歌評釋, Tokyo, 1935.

Saeki Ariyoshi 佐伯有義. 'Engi-shiki kōyō' 延喜式綱要, in *Nihon shūkyō kōza* 日本宗教講座, Tokyo, 1935.

——. *Shintō meimokuroku* 神道名目錄, Tokyo, 1944.

Saigū-ki 齋宮記, in *Gunsho ruijū*, III (1904), pp. 1–3, Tokyo.

Saitō Tadashi 齋藤忠. *Nihon zenshi, I, Genshi* 日本全史, I. 原始, Tokyo, 1958.

Sakamoto Tarō 坂本太郎. *Taika kaishin no kenkyū* 大化改新の研究, Tokyo, 1938.

——. 'Yōrō-ritsuryō no shikō ni tsuite' 養老律令の施行について, *Shigaku zasshi* 史學雜誌, 47 (1936), pp. 945–73.

Sakurai Hide 櫻井秀. *Nihon fukushoku-shi* 日本服飾史, Tokyo, 1924.

Sakurai Katsunoshin 桜井勝之進. *Ise jingū* 伊勢神宮, Tokyo, 1969.

Satō Jōjitsu 佐藤誠實. 'Jō-Engi-kyaku-shiki-hyō yakkai' 上延喜格式表約解, *Kokugakuin zasshi* 國學院雜誌, IX, 10 supp., pp. 1–8; IX, 11, pp. 9–10, Tokyo, 1903.

——. 'Engi-shiki-jo yakkai' 延喜式序約解, *Kokugakuin zasshi*, IX, 11 supp., (1903), pp. 1–6.

Satō Jumpei 佐藤潤平. *Kan'yaku no gen-shokubutsu* 漢藥の原植物 (On the Chinese Medical Plants), Tokyo, 1959.

Shimode Sekiya 下出積與. 'Sosenjin seiritsu no shakaiteki kiban' 祖先神成立の社會的基盤 (Social Foundations of the Establishment of the Worship of Ancestral *kami*), *Kanazawa daigaku hōbungaku-bu ronshū* 金澤大學法文學部論集, III (1955), pp. 51–74.

Shintō gobusho 神道五部書. (*Gochinza hongi* 御鎮座本記), *Kokushi taikei*, VII, Tokyo, 1904.

Shiratori Kurakichi 白鳥庫吉. *Jindaishi no shin-kenkyū* 神代史の新研究, Tokyo, 1955.

Sogabe Shizuo 曾我部靜雄. *Nitchū ritsuryō-ron* 日中律令論, Tokyo, 1963.

Takahashi Kenji 高橋建自. *Nihon fukushoku-shi ron* 日本服飾史論, Tokyo, 1927.

Takamure Itsue 高群逸枝. *Bokeisei no kenkyū* 母系制の研究, Tokyo, 1954.

Takeuchi Rizō 竹內理三. *Ritsuryō-sei to kizoku seiken* 律令制と貴族政權, I, Tokyo, 1957.

Takikawa Masajirō 滝川政次郎. *Ritsuryō no kenkyū* 律令の研究, Tokyo, 1931, 1966.

——. *Shina hōsei-shi kenkyū* 支那法制史研究, Tokyo, 1940.

Tanaka Takashi 田中卓. *Jingū no sōki to hatten* 神宮の創祀と發展. (Jingū kyōyō sōsho, 5. 神宮教養叢書第五集) Ise Shi, 1959.

Torao Toshiya 虎尾俊哉. 'Engi-shiki no shikō ni tsuite' 延喜式の施行について, *Geirin*, III, 2 (April 1952), pp. 29–45.

——. *Engi-shiki* 延喜式, Tokyo, 1964.

Toshimitsu Mitsuo 利光三津夫. *Ritsuryō oyobi ryōsei no kenkyū* 律令及び令制の研究, Tokyo, 1959.

——. *Saiban no rekishi* 裁判の歴史, Tokyo, 1964.

Tsuda Sōkichi 津田左右吉. *Jindai-shi no kenkyū* 神代史の研究, Tokyo, 1924.

——. *Jōdai Nihon no shakai oyobi shisō* 上代日本の社會及び思想, Tokyo, 1933.

Umemoto Kan'ichi 梅本寛一. 'Engi-shiki no ihon oyobi hampon ni tsuite' 延喜式の異本及び版本について, *Kokugakuin zasshi*, XXXIV, 9 (1928), pp. 26–53.

Umezawa Isezō 梅澤伊勢三. *Kiki hihan* 記紀批判, Tokyo, 1963.

——. *Kojiki-Nihonshoki* 古事記-日本書紀, Tokyo, Kyoto, 1957.

Wakamori Tarō 和歌森太郎. *Nihon minzoku-shi* 日本民族史, Tokyo, 1963.

Yamagishi Tokuhei 山岸徳平, ed. *Ookagami* 大鏡, 2 vols., Tokyo, 1947.

Yamanobe Tomoyuki 山辺知行. *Senshoku* 染織, Tokyo, 1956.

D BOOKS AND ARTICLES IN WESTERN LANGUAGES

Abbreviations:

BSOAS	*Bulletin of the School of Oriental and African Studies*
JA	*Journal Asiatique*
JAOS	*Journal of the American Oriental Society*
JOS	*Journal of Oriental Studies*
MDGNVO	*Mitteilungen der Deutschen Gesellschaft für Natur- und Völkerkunde Ostasiens*
MN	*Monumenta Nipponica*
MS	*Monumenta Serica*
TASJ	*Transactions of the Asiatic Society of Japan*

Asakawa, Kan'ichi. *The Early Institutional Life of Japan. A Study in the Reform of 645 A.D.*, Tokyo, 1903.

Aston, William G. *Nihongi, Chronicles of Japan. From the Earliest Times to A.D. 697*, I, II, London, 1896.

Bünger, Karl. *Quellen zur Rechtsgeschichte der T'ang Zeit, MS* Monograph IX, Peiping, 1946.

Bretschneider, Emilii. *Botanicon Sinicum*, London, 1882–95.

Brinkley, Frank. *An Unabridged Japanese-English Dictionary*, Tokyo, 1896.

Bohner, Hermann. *Tamuramaro denki* (Notes and Translation of Short Biography of Sakanoue Tamuramaro), *MN*, II, 2 (1939), pp. 241–53.

Casal, U.A. *The Five Sacred Festivals of Ancient Japan, MN* Monograph, Tokyo, 1967.

Chamberlain, Basil Hall. *Kojiki, or Records of Ancient Matters*, 2nd ed., Tokyo, 1932.

Crump, James I., Jr. 'Borrowed T'ang Titles and Offices in the Yōrō Code', Michigan State University Center for Japanese Studies, Occasional Papers, No. 2, (1952), pp. 25–38, Ann Arbor.

——. 'T'ang Penal Law in Early Japan', Occasional Papers, No. 4 (1953), pp. 91–102, Ann Arbor.

Czaplicka, Marie A. *Aboriginal Siberia*, Oxford, 1914.

Daifuku, Hiroshi. 'The Early Cultures of the Island of Kyushu, Japan', *SW Journal of Anthropology*, V, 3 (1949), pp. 253–71, U. of New Mexico Albuquerque.

Dumoulin, Heinrich, tr. 'Kamo Mabuchi's Erklärung des Norito zum Toshigoi-no-matsuri', *MN*, XII (1956), pp. 101–30.

Ecke, Gustave. *Chinese Domestic Furniture*, Tokyo, Rutland, 1963.

Fairchild, William P. 'Shamanism in Japan', *Folklore Studies, Journal of Far East Folklore*, XXI (1962), pp. 1–122, Tokyo.

Florenz, Karl. 'Ancient Japanese Rituals' (1), *TASJ*, XXVII, 1 (1900), pp. 1–112.

——. *Die historischen Quellen der Shinto-Religion*, Göttingen, 1919.

Guide to the Kansai Area, Nara and Kyoto. Japanese Organizing Committee, the Ninth International Congress for the History of Religious Science Council of Japan, Kyoto, 1958.

Gundert, Wilhelm. *Japanische Religionsgeschichte*, Tokyo, Stuttgart, 1935.

Haguenauer, Charles. *Origines de la civilisation Japonaise*, (1), Paris, 1956.

——. 'La Danse rituelle dans la cérémonic du Chinkonsai', *JA*, CCXVI, 2 (1930), pp. 300–50.

Haring, Douglas G. 'The Noro Cult of Amami Oshima; Divine Priestesses of the Ryukyu Islands', *Sociologus,* III, 2 (1953), pp. 108–21.

Henderson, Gregory and Hurvitz, Leon. 'The Buddha of Seiryōji; New Finds and a New Theory', *Artibus Asiae,* XIX, 1 (1956).

Hulsewé, A. F. P. *Remnants of Han Law,* Sinica Leidensia, IX, Leiden, 1955.

Holtom, Daniel C. *The Japanese Enthronement Ceremonies,* Tokyo, 1928.

——. *The National Faith of Japan,* New York, 1938.

——. 'The Storm God Theme in Japanese Mythology', *Sociologus,* VI, 1 (1956), pp. 44–56.

Jinja Honchō. *Basic Terms of Shintō,* Tokyo, 1958.

Johnes, Raymond. *Japanese Art,* London, 1961.

Kates, George N. *Chinese Household Furniture,* New York, 1948.

Katō, Genchi. *A Study of Shinto, the Religion of the Japanese Nation,* Tokyo, 1926.

——, and Hoshino, Hikoshirō, tr. *Kogoshūi : Gleanings from Ancient Stories,* 3rd ed., Tokyo, 1925.

Katoh, Lynn. See below, Yamanobe.

Kidder, Jonathan Edward, Jr. *Japan Before Buddhism,* New York, 1959.

Kluge, Inge-Lore. *Miyoshi Kiyoyuki,* Inst. für Orientforschung, No. 35, Berlin, 1958.

Kōno, Shōzō. 'The Hitachi-Fudoki, or Records and Customs and Land of Hitachi', tr., Sakai Atsuharu, *Cultural Nippon,* VIII, 2 (1940), pp. 145–81; 3, pp. 109–56; 4, pp. 137–86.

Lee, Jean Gordon. 'Chinese Furniture Collection', *Philadelphia Museum Bulletin* (Winter 1963).

Lewin, Bruno. *Aya und Hata : Bevölkerungsgruppen Altjapans Kontinentaler Herkunft,* Wiesbaden, 1962.

Martin, Ilse. Review of Karl Bünger, *Quellen zur Rechtsgeschichte* . . . *JAOS,* LXIX, 3 (July, September 1949), pp. 154–7.

Miller, Richard James. *An Historical Study of the Higher Administrative Officials of the Council of State in Japan in the 8th Century A.D.* (M.A. Thesis) Berkeley, 1946.

——. *A Study of the Development of a Centralized Japanese Government Prior to the Taika Reform (A.D. 645),* (Ph. D. Thesis), Berkeley, 1953.

Mills, Douglas E. *The Takahashi Uzibumi,* repr. fr. *BSOAS,* XVI, 1 (1954), pp. 113–33.

Nishizawa, Tekiho. 'Manual of Japanese Painting', *Cultural Nippon,* VIII, 3 (October 1940), pp. 51–82.

Ono, Sokyo. *Shintō : the Kami Way,* Rutland and Tokyo, 1962.

Paine, Robert Treat and Soper, Alexander. *The Art and Architecture of Japan,* London and Baltimore, 1960.

Philippi, Donald L. *Norito, a New Translation of the Ancient Japanese Ritual Prayers,* Tokyo, 1959.

——, *Kojiki, trans, with introduction and notes,* Tokyo, 1968.

Ponsonby-Fane, Richard A. B. *Divine Spirits of Shinto and Hirota Jinja,* Kyoto, 1934.

——. *Kamo Mioya Shrine,* Kyoto, London, 1934.

——. 'Nibukawakami Jinja', *TASJ,* x, 2nd series (1922), pp. 25–46.

——. 'Ohoyamato Jinja', *Bull. Meiji Japan. Soc.,* XL, n.d

Reischauer, Edwin O. *Ennin's Diary,* New York, 1955.

Reischauer, Robert Karl. *Early Japanese History,* A and B, Princeton, 1937.

Reitz, Karl. 'Heihaku—Mitegura—Gohei', *Folklore Studies,* I (1942), pp. 85–90, Peking.

Roth, H. Ling. *Studies in Primitive Looms,* Halifax, 1934.

Sadler, A. L. *A Short History of Japanese Architecture,* Tokyo, Rutland, 1963.

Saka, Jūbutsu. *The Ise daijingū sankeiki, or Diary of a Pilgrim to Ise,* tr., A. L. Sadler, Tokyo, 1940.

Sanjōnishi, Kinwosa. 'Notes on Dyeing and Weaving in Ancient Japan', *Cultural Nippon,* VIII, 1 (March 1940), pp. 101–26.

Sansom, George Bailey. 'Early Japanese Law and Administration', Pt. I, *TASJ* (2), IX (1932), pp. 67–109; Pt. II, XI (1934), pp. 117–49.

——. *A History of Japan to 1334,* Stanford, 1958.

Satow, Ernest. 'Ancient Japanese Rituals', Pt. I, *TASJ* (1), VII (19), pp. 97–132; Pt. II, *TASJ* (1), VII, pp. 393–434.

Schafer, Edward H. *The Golden Peaches of Samarkand,* Berkeley, Los Angeles and London, 1963.

——, and Wallacker, Benjamin E. *Local Tribute Products of the T'ang Dynasty,* reprint from *JOS,* IV, 1–2 (1957–8).

Snellen, J. B., tr. 'Shoku-Nihongi, Chronicles of Japan, Continued from 697–791 A.D.', Pt. I, *TASJ* (2), XI (1934), pp. 151–239; Pt. II, *TASJ* (2), XIV (1937), pp. 209–78.

Spencer, Robert Steward. 'The Noro, or Priestesses of Loo Choo', *TASJ* (2), VII, pp. 94–112.

Stuart, G. A. *Chinese Materia Medica : Vegetable Kingdom,* Shanghai, 1911.

Tange, Kenzō and Kawazoe, Noboru. *Ise, Prototype of Japanese Architecture,* Cambridge, Mass., 1965.

Thunberg, C. P. *Miscellaneous Papers Regarding Japanese Plants,* Tokyo, 1935.

Tsuchiya, Takao. 'An Economic History of Japan', *TASJ* (2), XV, 1937.

Tsunoda, R., DeBary, W. T. and Keene, D. *Sources of the Japanese Tradition,* I, Columbia University, New York, 1958.

Vannowsky, Alexander. *Volcanoes and the Sun—A New Concept of the Mythology of the Kojiki,* Tokyo, 1960.

Wedemeyer, André. *Japanische Frühgeschichte,* reprint, *MDGNVO,* 1930.

Yamanobe, Tomoyuki. *Textiles,* English adaptation by Lynn Katoh, Rutland, Vt. and Tokyo, 1957.

Yoshida, Tetsurō. *Japanische Architektur,* Tübingen and New York, 1952.

Zachert, Herbert. *Semmyō, die kaiserlichen Erlasse des Shoku-nihongi,* Berlin, 1950.

Ceremonial clay vessels for purifi-
cation at end of each month at Ise
Daijingū. Courtesy of Miss D.U.
Mizoguchi

'Kite-tail *koto*', Ise Shrine
Treasure. Courtesy of Miss
D.U. Mizoguchi

August mirror of Ise Grand
Shrine. Courtesy of Jingū Shichō, Ise Grand Shrine

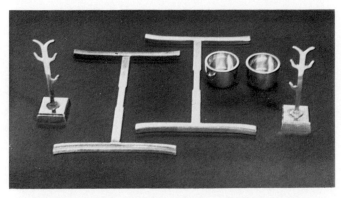

August spindles, shuttles, and reels; Shrine treasures.
Courtesy of Jingū Shichō, Ise Grand Shrine

Gilt-bronze brazier and charcoal utensils. Courtesy of Jingū
Shichō, Ise Grand Shrine

Canopy of silk damask for processions at Ise Grand Shrine.
Courtesy of Jingū Shichō, Ise Grand Shrine

GLOSSARY AND KEY

Items are listed under the form in which they appear most often in the translation; those occurring with great frequency are keyed according to the notes which explain them.

-A-

Abalone *(awabi)*, 42, n. 159; slices of, 162

Abstainers, child→*Mono-imi;* hereditary→ Imbe

Abstinence, 2, 6, 55, n. 262, 169; partial *(ara-imi)*, n. 174, 64; total *(ma-imi)*, 2, 62, n. 174

Ablution→Lustration

Achiki and Wani, n.358

Accountants *(kura-be)*, n.490, 180

Adzes, n.433

Aidono deities→Deities

Ainame (Aimube) festival, 'Together Tasting', 43, 88–94, n.290

Ainu→Emishi

Akabitsu (white boxes), n.188

Akawa (myōe)→Lustrous robes

Allotted lands (rice-fields, *handen)*, 21, n.353, 147

Allotments of rice, foodstuffs, etc. 120, 121, 156, 181

Ama (fisherman), 30; (nun), 54

Amadome (Haregoi), rain-stopping, 43, n.342

Amagashi, ordeal at, 5

Amagoi (Praying-for-rain Festival), 43, n.168, 107–8, n.341

Amaterasu-o-mikami, Sun Goddess, Great Deity of Ise, 3, 5, (18), 22, 25–36, 42, 47, 53, n.263, n.306, n.319, 123, n.393, n.397, n.415, n.490, n.495, 166, 167

Ambassador to T'ang, 43, 44, 112, n.344

Ame-no-uzume-no-mikoto, 5, 20, n.219, n.306

Ame-no-tajikara, enshrined at Ise, 47

Ame-no-ho-hi-mikoto, 44

Ame-no-koyane-no-mikoto, 6, 33, n.221

Ancestor-*kami* (ancestor-god), 32, 33, 36

Animal skins, 75, 106, 118, 157, 159, 165, 181

Anjō and *ange*, n.150

Aoi festival, n.295

Ara-imi→Abstinence

Arakida branch of Nakatomi, 34, 40, 48; Tadanari, n.100

Aramatsuri Shrine, 47, 49, 123, n.383

Arame (seaweed), n.161

Ara-mitama→Turbulent spirit

Architecture of Ise Shrines, 46, 49–50, 53; detailed, 133–40

Arrows (arrowshafts), 42, 50, 118, 119, 138, 166

Asuka-Kiyomihara codes, 8, 56

Asuka Shrine, 91

Atsuko, Princess, n.125, App. VIII

Atsuta Shrine, 119, 120

Auguring bamboo→Divination

August boat-shaped coffer *(mifunashiro)*, 134–5, n.432

August container *(mihishiro)*, 135, n.434

August districts *(mi-agata)*, 74, n.238

August food, n.404

Auxiliary Shrines of Shrine of the Great Deity, 124–5

Auxiliary Shrines of Watarai Shrine, 125

Avoidance→Defilements; Taboos

Azuki beans, same as red beans

Azuma, the East, n.208

-B-

Banquet of the Roads→*Michiae*

Bark-cloth *(yū)*, 42, 54, 60, n.155; ceremonial headdress *(yū-kazura)*, 54, 62

Bêche-de-mer *(iriko)*, n.419

Bitatsu Tennō, 30, 52

Bird-feathers, 138, 139

Bonito *(katsuo)*, 42, 61, n.159

Boundaries, festivals of, 104, 106, 113

Boundary of precinct of Ise Shrines, n.486

Bows (of catalpa and zelkova), 42, 118, 119, 138

Brewers, office of *(saka-be* of *saigū-ryō)*, n.490, 177

–C–

–G–

–H–

–Oo–

–P–

–Q–

–T–

(hakari), n.423; regular (shozei), n.222; rice-paddy (denso), 34, 35, n.195, n.400

Taxation→Bureau of Taxation

Temmu Tennō, 8, 31, 32, 34, 52, n.239, n.319, n.415

Temporary shrines on route to Ise, 167, 169

Tenchi Tennō, 7, 25, n.50, 31, 33, 34, 52

Thank offering→Miagamono

Three Great Ones (Royal persons), 61, n.163, 145

Three seasons, festivals of (sanjisai; miori-no-matsuri), 49, 132, n.475, n.548

Throne Hall, Shishin-den, n.271

Thunder Gods→Kantoki no kami; Naru-ikazuchi

Tie-dyeing (yuhata), n.216

Tokoronushi-no-kami (God of earth), n.517

Tomobe (tomokko), occupational groups, n.512

Toneri (system), 55, n.248, n.490, 153, 155, 156, 168, 180. See also Ryō-no-toneri; Udoneri

Tortoise-shell→Divination

Toshigoi festival, 13, 22, 26, 41, 42, 49, 54, 56, 59–65, n.149, n.174, 80, 118, 123, 146, 157, 170, 171; ritual for, n.182

Toso (spice for sake), n.567

Total abstinence→Abstinence

Toyosuki-irihime, Princess, 26, 30, 52

Toyouke Shrine→Watarai Shrine; -no-ōkami →Food Goddess

Treasure-house, 50, n.444

Treasures of the Great Shrine, 50, 135, 138–9, n.445

Treasury→Ministry of Treasury

Tree, cutting of, 131, n.133; spirits of, 43, 112

Tribute (chō), 21, 29, 35, 117, 118, 119, n.400, 147–150, n.512; cloth (chōfu; tsukinuno), 64, n.187, n.193; initial (mitsugi-nozaki), n.418

Tsubaha (ritual vessel), n.232, n.293

Tsukaibito (nobles), n.480

Tsukinami festival, 13, 22, 24, 41, 49, 56, 59, 64, 80–81, n.261, 97, 118, 123, 127–9, 146, 158, 159, 171

Tsukiyomi-no-mikoto (Moon God), Shrine to, 47, 49, n.304, 123–4, n.385, n.386

Tsumi→Offense

Tsumori chieftains, 32

Turbulent spirit (ara-mitama), 48, 123, n.305, 124, n.380, n.389

–U–

Uchindo, 42, 47, 48, 50, 51, n.381. See also Hinomi-uchindo

Udoneri, n.248, n.490, 155, 156, 161. See also Toneri

Uji (name-group)→Fujiwara; Hata, 32, n.524; →Hatori;→Isobe;→Imbe;→Nakatomi;→ Omi; Ooe, 76, Ooga, 121;→Soga; Usa, 121; Yamage-be, 131; Yamato, 76

Uji and kabane system, n.99

Ujigami (uji deities), 19, 32, 33, 34, 41, n.192, n.213, n.221

Ujiko (adherents), n.228

Unatari Shrine, 33, 90

Uneme, n.275, n.320, n.490; Yakako, 31

Upāsaka (ubasoku), n.499

Urabe→Diviner

–V–

Vajracchedikā (prajñā-pāramitā) Sūtra, 120

Various functionaries (zōshiki-no-hito; goshiki no hito, 72, n.224, n.356, n.489

Veils, n.466

Verbal response to ritual, 64, n.183

Vestal virgin, 53

–W–

Wakame (me), seaweed, 61, n.161

Watarai, District, 26–31 passim, 34, 47, 48, 123, 124, 170–2; Shrine (Toyouke-no-miya), 25, 29, 34, 40, 45–52, 62, 121, 124

Watarashi-hime (Takuhata-hime), 29

Watatsumi, deities of, 106, n.338, 122

Water-carriers (moitori-be), n.490, 162–3; deities of, 159, 175, 178, 180

Weavers→Hatori

Weaving Hall→Hatadono

Well, of birth, 102, n.325; festival of, 105, 154, 158, 159; sacred, 102, n.324. See also Deities of wells

Wetnurses (menoto), n.509

Willow box (yanagibako), n.459

Wind Gods, festival→Kaze-no-kami festival

Workers (workmen), 119, 135, n.370

–Y–